SPA ROYAL HALL
SATURDAY 16 July: 8.30 — 11.45 p.m.
PRESENTING
The SMALL FACES
WITH
THREE PLUS ONE THE SMALL FOUR
ADMISSION 7/6. OBTAINABLE AT THE DOORS ONLY.
SATURDAY 23 July: 8.30 — 11.45 p.m.
THE FANTASTIC SOUND OF
THE WHO
SUPPORTED BY
THE MANDRAKES 21st CENTURY
ADMISSION 7/6. OBTAINABLE AT THE DOORS ONLY.
SATURDAY 30 July:
THE SPENCER DAVIS GROUP
SPA ROYAL HALL
BRIDLINGTON
SAT. 23RD JULY
8.30 TO 11.45 P.M.
THE WHO
PLUS
THE MANDRAKES
21ST CENTURY
ADMISSION 7'6
CAR PARK • MODERN CAFE FACILITIES • LICENSED CATERING
TORQUAY
Town Hall
DREAMLAND
BALLROOM
MARGATE Tel - THANET 21212
THE WHO
also THE GAYLORDS
THURS. 25TH AUG. 8. P.M.
DOWNS BALLROOM
HASSOCKS (Nr. BRIGHTON)
SUNDAY, SEPT. 11
RAVE! RAVE! RAVE! SHATTERING!! THE
WHO
– PLUS –
THE DOMINATORS
– AND –
TONY SIMON DISC SHOW
ODEON DERBY
ON THE STAGE for One Night Only.
The Incredible
WHO
SPENCER DAVIS GROUP
SPECIAL GUEST STARS
THE FABULOUS NEW
MERSEYS
with their Fruit Eating Bears
BAND OF ANGELS
MIKE SARNE
THE WHO
the fantastic NEW merseys and their Fruit Eating Bears
MAX WALL
OSCAR
THE MAGIC LANTERNS
ODEON - DERBY
ODEON THEATRE : DERBY
STAGE SHOW
1st Performance at 6-15 p.m.
FRIDAY SEPTEMBER 16
FRONT STALLS 12/6
A26
No ticket exchanged nor money refunded
THIS PORTION TO BE RETAINED
Newcastle Students Rag Appeal
OCT 23-29-1966
MAJESTIC BALLROOM
THE WHO
THE ELCORTS
THE SECT
THE TRANSIT
OCT 26
10/6
NINE TILL ONE
REGAL
CAMBRIDGE
1st Performance 6-15
TUESDAY NOVEMBER 26
BACK STALLS 6/6
JJ29
No Tickets exchanged nor money refunded
TO BE RETAINED
ROYAL LINKS PAVILION, CROMER
Proudly presents
THE WHO
plus a really great group from the Midlands
THE MONEY SPIDERS
also our own
ALEX WILSON'S SECT
on
Saturday, February 11th
Notice to Members
WATERFRONT
TONIGHT
Britain's most exciting Group, just back from filming in France and No. 7 in the Charts this week
THE WHO
Tickets available at the door
Thursday, May 27:
SPENCER DAVIS
THE PAVILION — WORTHING
THURSDAY, NOVEMBER 24th
THE WHO
WE REGRET THE HIGH ADMISSION CHARGE BUT FABULOUS GROUPS COMMAND FABULOUS FEES
7.30 to 10.45 p.m.
Admission 7'6
GREAT GROUPS — GREAT ATMOSPHERE
CENTRAL PIER
MORECAMBE
IN THE MARINE BALLROOM
"Happy Jack"
THE WHO
THE DOODLEBUGS HAROLD GRAHAM
TICKETS 10/-
THE HEDGEHOPPERS ANONYMOUS
IN THE LOUNGE
THE WHO
TRAFFIC
THE HERD
The Marmalade
Compere RAY CAMERON
SPECIAL GUEST STARS
THE TREMELOES
TOWN HALL
TORQUAY
BY DEMAND THE RETURN OF
THE WHO
TRENDSETTERS LTD.
THE TELSTARS
FRIDAY 27TH AUGUST
TOWN HALL
TORQUAY
BY DEMAND THE RETURN OF
THE WHO
THE STACCERLEES
THE HUNTERS · THE EMPTY VESSELS
MOD FASHION PARADE
SATURDAY 20TH AUG.
FULLY LICENSED BAR
WHO
THE DICERS and THE HUNTERS
TORQUAY TOWN HALL
FULLY LICENSED
ADMIT ONE 7/6
Town Hall Torquay
RAVE ATTRACTION
THE WHO
PLUS TOP SUPPORTING GROUPS
Saturday 20th Aug. 1966
Admit ONE 10/-
THE WHO
OFFICIAL FAN CLUB
McGOOS
THE WHO
Sunday night on stage at 9.30.
As no tickets have been printed, doors will open at 7 p.m.
MEMBERS 7/6
GUESTS 10/-
BOWES LYON HOUSE YOUTH CENTRE, STEVENAGE
DISC-SPIN with guest D.J. 1/6
STEVENAGE DAY
BIG BEAT NIGHT
FOLK NIGHT at 2/6
THE FABULOUS
WHO
BIG BEAT RAVE at 5/-

THIS GUITAR HAS SECONDS TO LIVE

A PEOPLE'S HISTORY OF THE WHO

First published in Great Britain 2023
by Spenwood Books Ltd
2 College Street, Higham Ferrers, NN10 8DZ.

A CIP record for this book is available from the
British Library.

ISBN 978-1-915858-12-2 (hardback)
ISBN 978-1-915858-17-7 (paperback)

Hardback printed in the Czech Republic via Akcent Media Limited

Design by Bruce Graham, The Night Owl

Rear cover images: (clockwise from top left) Rod Blow, Sally Ramsay, Rod Blow, Daniel Smith, Patricia Fitzgerald

THIS GUITAR HAS SECONDS TO LIVE

A PEOPLE'S HISTORY OF THE WHO

Richard Houghton

Spenwood Books
Manchester, UK

ABOUT THE AUTHOR

Richard Houghton lives in Manchester, UK with his wife Kate and his pomapoo Sid. He is the author of more than 20 music books and has compiled authorised 'fan histories' of a number of acts including Jethro Tull, Simple Minds, Orchestral Manoeuvres in the Dark, the Stranglers, Fairport Convention, Shaun Ryder and The Wedding Present. He can be reached at iwasatthatgig@gmail.com.

ACKNOWLEDGEMENTS

I could not have completed this book without the contributions of the many Who fans who kindly got in touch with me when I first made an appeal for people to share their concert memories in 2016/17. I am also indebted to Joe McMichael and 'Irish' Jack Lyons' excellent *The Who Concert File* and Andy Neill and Matt Kent's equally excellent *The Complete Chronicle of The Who*, both of which are indispensable to anyone wanting to research the early history of The Who. But my labours six years ago unearthed a number of previously undocumented performances that did not appear in either book, and which are noted within the text of this one, including shows at the Locarno in Stevenage, the Corn Exchange in Rochester, Laurie Grove Baths at London's Goldsmiths College and Wem Town Hall in Shropshire, along with suggestions of at least two others – Whitchurch in Shropshire and Portrush in Northern Ireland – about which I'd love to hear more details. I can be reached at iwasatthatgig@gmail.com.

I am indebted to the staff of local newspapers up and down the land who enthusiastically helped in my appeal to find Who fans who wanted to tell their story. They did this by not only publishing my letter but often by an accompanying feature bringing back to life the night(s) that The 'Oo played their town or city. I could not have done it without them. In particular, I should like to thank: Steve Hill from the *Aberdeen Press & Journal*; Stewart Ross from the *Dundee Courier*; Mike Hill from the *Lancashire Evening Post*; Colette Wartbrook from the *Stoke Sentinel*; and Mattie Lacey-Davidson from the *Watford Observer*. I should also like to thank: Maureen Browning for the numerous images she supplied; vintagerock.com; Greg Brodsky at bestclassicbands.com; and Harvey Kubernik; Bruce Graham for his design skills and a great front cover; Bruce Koziarski for his web skills and Dan Newton at Invincible Brands for the same.

Finally, I should like to thank Kate Sullivan, without whose typing skills, infinite patience and domestic 'goddess-hood' this book would still be a work in progress. And my son, Bill Houghton, who at the age of four already knew the words to 'Sally Simpson'.

SPECIAL THANKS

Arthur Wyllie, Leigh Frankum, Jeremy Link, Michael Allen, Elaine & Dennis Marrison, Peter Dent, Bruce Woodward, Len Newman, William Havu, Roy Smith, Marc Starcke, Richard Dixon, David Sumners, Sheva Golkow, Peter Tidball, Alan Watters, Daniel Smith, Brian Brannan, Seth Davidson, Michael Watts, Emmet Burns, David Lee, Christian Suchatzki, Joe Murphy, Mauro Regis, David Swartz, Charles Balchin, Pat Thomas, Benjamin Dobie, James Phillips, Marc Librescu, Claus Stenhoj, Steven Rae, Steven Fell, Stuart Bray, Ira Knopf, Ian Capes, Michael Carr, Dan Smith, Bill Bruns, Kevin Murray, Jir Kroese, Richard Weiner, Brian Cady, Steven Burgess, Edmond John Starkey, David Barber, Paul Southeran, John Harris, Nigel Greenaway, Robin Phillips, Brian Jordan, Peter Smith, Jason Gifford, KC Loewen, Marc Starke, Vincent Jordan, Graeme Selkirk, James Bielecki, Gary Nicklin, Charles Balchin, Richard Harris, Hugh M Harrison III, Kathryn Harrison Siegel & Hugh M Harrison IV, Olivier Coiffard, Steve Cobham, Alan Butcher, Martin Reid, Christine Kettlety in memory of her son Thomas 'Tommy' Kettlety, Bert den Blaauwen, Wadge, Alan McKendree, Andy Crouch, David Brown, David Thomas, Ian Holmes, Janet Hepburn Tavendale, Lauren J Hammer, Kazuko I, Debbie Bruns, Mason Weinrich, David Hossack, Diane Corcoran, Laureen Claggett, Darren Hayward, Dan Smith, Peter Belt, Pamela Woodward.

INTRODUCTION

How many guitars have been smashed by Pete Townshend? How many people have had their hearing permanently affected by the volume that The Who played at? How many people were on the receiving end of a prank by Keith Moon?

These were the questions that I posed in the opening paragraph of the introduction to my 2017 book, *The Who – I Was There*. Sadly, that book has been out of print since 2018 and so, having acquired the rights, I've taken the opportunity to expand and update the book and publish it in a larger format.

Perhaps more than any other band that emerged in the 1960s, The Who is the group most associated with live performance. This is due to their memorable appearances, which often involved smashing up equipment on stage, hotel rooms off stage and – occasionally – each other, both on and off stage. It is also testament to the phenomenal number of shows the original line up – Pete Townshend, Roger Daltrey, John Entwistle and Keith Moon – undertook between 1963 and 1978. They performed well over 1,600 times, and when I first compiled this book I uncovered at least four previously undocumented performances by the group, so there may well be others.

Before The Who, Roger, Pete and John performed as The Detours. This book picks up the story of the band, renamed The Who, from May 1964, when Keith Moon joined the group. From the early days playing Motown covers, The Who were closely associated with the Mod movement, and there are several stories from Mods who saw them in that period. But the band transcended teenage rivalries and their reputation as a singles group to become one of the biggest rock acts in the world, playing the Monterey, Woodstock and Isle of Wight festivals, and going on to headline arena and stadium gigs around the world from the 1970s onwards.

This is a slightly lopsided and incomplete history of The Who, for which I make no apology. The eyewitness accounts from people who have provided memories of seeing the band have not been gathered on a systematic basis. But the book hopefully provides a new perspective on a familiar story.

Time and time again, the character that emerges most strongly from the stories is that of Keith Moon. Perhaps more than any other member, he was the heartbeat of The Who. For a lot of fans, The Who ceased to exist when Keith died on 7th September 1978, and it is clear from reading the accounts of the many people who saw him behind his kit that he brought something to the band that no other drummer – however, talented – could. Keith was a one off and, although the group has continued to exist in name, it isn't the same Who without Keith. Neither has it been the same Who since John Entwistle died in 2002.

That Roger and Pete carry on performing is to their credit, as The Who's songs continue to provide pleasure for thousands of people, and I've included memories of several post-1978 shows to reflect the longevity of their career. But to really understand The Who and the impact they had on the music scene you have to go back to the mid-1960s, to the time when postwar Britain was still waking up to what the possibilities were, to the time when someone smashing their guitar on stage was truly shocking. The Who were loud, explosive and in your face. The memory of seeing them live is seared into the consciousness of everyone who witnessed those early performances.

I hope, in reading this book, the reader is transported back to a time before Ticketmaster and the need for Access All Area passes, to a time when a band as big is The Who could turn up with barely any fanfare in a place as small as Cromer in Norfolk and give a show that would be burned into the memories of those that witnessed it. I would have loved have been at the Trade in Watford or the Station Hotel in Wealdstone in 1964 to see the early Who strut their stuff. Until someone invents a time machine, this may be the nearest we'll get to experiencing The Who in their early days and witnessing their evolution into rock legends. Unless, like more than 500 people whose stories are in this book, you can say 'I was there!'.

Richard Houghton
Manchester, UK
August 2023

THE 1950s
SHEPHERDS BUSH, LONDON, UK

KEITH ROWLEY

I grew up with Roger Daltrey and know him quite well. I was brought up by my grandparents at 22A Percy Road, Shepherds Bush. Roger lived four doors away, at number 16, until he was twelve years old, when he moved from the family rented house to a nice council house in Fielding Road, Acton. I remember our childhood vividly. Roger's father, Harry, owned an old taxi cab and he often used to take me, Roger and my brother John to Lancing on a Sunday. Roger in them days was known as Trog and he would well remember being one of the 'Percy Piddlers', which was the nickname for all the kids down our street.

My brother is Roger's age. I'm about four years younger. My brother knew him very well too. Roger went to Westfield and all three of us went to Victoria Junior School. We schooled together but not all in the same year. When I speak about Roger to people, I say what a really nice fella he was and he still comes across as a real nice fella now.

John remembers that Roger's nickname, Trog, came about because Roger could put his legs behind his head. John also says that Roger was kicked out of the school choir at Victoria Junior School as the music teacher said his singing was out of tune.

I know he supports Arsenal now, but in the early days he just wasn't interested in sport at all. You could play in the street in them days and you'd only have to stop every 15 minutes to let a car go past. He'd join in all the normal street games like Tin Tan Tommy with the can, and hide and seek. But if we stopped and put coats down and started playing football, then he wasn't interested. It always used to make me laugh. It'd be 'see you later, boys' and he'd just go in and sit on the wall and play on his mouth organ, so music was obviously in his blood. It wasn't in the family as far as I know. His mum or dad they weren't into entertainment at all. And he had a sister, Carol, and she certainly wasn't.

He always wanted a guitar and he decided he was going to make one. Roger made his first guitar from a block of wood. He and my brother John used to sit on his doorstep in Percy Road working on it, using just a knife and sandpaper. There was a music shop just around the corner, where Roger used to check his handiwork against a Stratocaster guitar which was in the window. He used to go and peer through the window of the music shop, get some ideas and then go home and gradually he'd finish making it. Any pocket money went to buying anything he could for it. It did play. He learnt on it.

My brother John remembers Roger took the guitar on a Boys' Club holiday to Plymouth and drove everyone crazy by continually playing 'All I Have to do is Dream' by the Everly Brothers, and changing 'dream' to Jean as that was his girlfriend's name. Roger could also play skiffle-type Lonnie Donegan music very well and his singing wasn't bad either. So it was a good guitar, and he was a very determined boy. I believe he still has this guitar at home.

John remembers Roger knocking on our door. They'd had a puncture and they wanted to borrow some money, which I think my brother lent them. I don't know whether he got it back or not. They were up and away then. They were smashing all their gear up at the time, and I

Clockwise from top left: a young Roger Daltrey (far right) (photo Keith Rowley); Keith Moon with The Beachcombers (photo John Schollar); Roger with his first car (photo Keith Rowley); Keith with The Beachcombers.

Clockwise from top left): Barbara Hicks saw The Detours at the Oldfield Hotel; Linda Sadler remembers Keith being very friendly with a girl from her Tottenham high school; Harold Mortimer helped run the Railway Hotel; Mick Shelton was dressed to kill in Derby.

don't think they made too much money in the early years.

Roger probably wouldn't recognise me now because I haven't seen him for years. The last time I saw him, me and my brother John went down to see him at his mansion in West Burwash. Rosie, his eldest daughter, had just been born.

In July 1962 Roger Daltrey, Pete Townshend and John Entwistle began performing as The Detours. Keith Moon had yet to join a band.

DECEMBER 1962
ROYAL BRITISH LEGION, HARROW, UK

JOHN SCHOLLAR

I was the rhythm guitarist in a band called The Beachcombers. Our drummer had left and we were using the drummer out of Cliff Bennett and the Rebel Rousers when they weren't working. So we put an advert in the *Harrow and Wembley Observer* looking for a new drummer. We held auditions at the British Legion in Harrow Central and we had four or five drummers turn up, including Keith. His dad brought him. We tried to put him off because we were 21, 22 and he was about 16. That's a big gap when you're that age. It was like a little kid coming in. We said 'you're too young, mate' because he was quite tiny. And he waited until everybody had had a go and then his dad came over and said 'come on, let him have a go. Even if he's no good, it'll give him a bit of experience.'

Within minutes, he'd got all his kit in. He'd set it all up outside knowing that he was going to have a go. With the other drummers, we were lined up across the rehearsal room and the guys came in and sat in front of us, facing the band. But Keith pushed all our gear aside and set up where the drummer should be sat. We said 'what do you want to do?' and he said 'well, give us a couple and I'll see if I know 'em.' And we did 'Roadrunner', which he later used to do with The Who, and which The Detours used to do as well, and then we did a Shadows number, which was real off beat called 'Foot Tapper'. He was absolutely superb and we all looked at one another in amazement. So we said to his dad 'well, it looks like he's in' and he said 'well, you'd better look after him because he's only a nipper.'

He was with us for about eighteen months. He completely changed the group. We used to do all the Elvis type ballads but Keith would rock 'em up. One time, Keith got hold of a duck call. We'd do 'Are You Lonesome Tonight?' and, when it got to a slow bit, Keith would get the duck call out and go 'quack quack.' Ron, our singer, used to go mad at him. One night Ron shouted out 'I've had enough of you' and Keith pulled a gun out and fired it at him. It was only a starting pistol but I thought Keith had shot him. When Keith left The Beachcombers, it was never the same. There was a big hole in the band. Not so much musically, but the fun side of it.

We did have some fun with Keith. We had red jackets, but we had gold ones before that. The suit that Keith inherited didn't fit him because the guy that left was bigger than Keith.

And Keith said 'I've got a gold lame jacket' so he used to wear that. We were based in West London but we did quite a few American air force bases. We played Mildenhall in Suffolk and we got told off there for going and kicking the tyres on a B-47 bomber. We saw this plane and it looked close but it wasn't, because it was bloody huge. The American military police were a bit heavy handed. They dumped us in the back of a jeep and took us back to the guard room. The policeman said 'how do we know you're not spies?' And we all had red band suits on so we said 'do you expect to see spies running around with bow ties and red suits?'

18 APRIL 1963
OLDFIELD HOTEL, GREENFORD, LONDON, UK

The Detours play the Oldfield pub on almost 60 occasions in 1963, and a further 12 times in 1964.

BARBARA HICKS

I used to go dancing at Greenford in the Sixties when the band were called something else. I can't recollect what it was. The place was always completely full and jumping, so I am not surprised they went places. I was about 20 and working at the BBC. I can't remember the price of admission but it was always packed. I was living in Denham in Buckinghamshire so went on the bus and underground from Uxbridge.

20 FEBRUARY 1964
OLDFIELD HOTEL, GREENFORD, LONDON, UK

The Detours change their name to The Who.

BARBARA HICKS

It took ages to get used to their new name.

2 MAY 1964
A PUB, NORTH CIRCULAR ROAD, LONDON, UK

Keith Moon joins The Who and appears with them for the first time.

10 MAY 1964
FLORIDA ROOMS, BRIGHTON, UK

JOHN RITCHIE

I'd seen The Who about three or four times at the Florida Rooms in Brighton, which was the old aquarium. I was a Mod, and the Florida Rooms was part of the Mod scene in Brighton. There was a lot going on there. The Montpelier Rooms was another venue that used to be open there. And the Tudor Bar, which was also on Montpelier Road, and which served Belgian lager, which was pretty strong old stuff in those days.

We all went off to Bournemouth one Easter weekend and then Torquay, all those sorts of places. We used to sleep in bus shelters and all sorts of things and my parents didn't have a clue where I was.

The Who started off as a Mod band. We used to go to the Marquee Club in Wardour Street and all those sorts of places, including a club in Brixton called the Ram Jam Club. We went every Sunday from '64 onwards until it shut in '68. I wouldn't dream of going there now, or anywhere like it. But they were different times.

HAZEL SMITH

I saw The Who in the Florida Rooms. It was next to the building that now houses the Sea Life Centre. My friend and I were packed in, standing very near the stage next to an enormous speaker. A very Mod Roger Daltrey had us drooling and Keith Moon's drumming and gurning had us mesmerised. I put my tinnitus down to that concert as I couldn't hear properly for a week afterwards after standing next to that enormous speaker!

24 MAY 1964
MAJESTIC BALLROOM, LUTON, UK

FRANK ABBOTT

I was very fortunate in the early Sixties to be a regular visitor to the Majestic Ballroom in Mills Street, Luton. In a period of just over twelve months saw The Beatles, the Stones and the High Numbers. I can't remember too much about their set list although Moonie really stood out as a character. I have always thought that they played 'I Can't Explain' but on investigation it wasn't released until later so now I'm not so sure, although I do remember 'Bald Headed Woman'. All the top bands came to the Majestic at that time for a cost of about five shillings (25p) entrance fee. Those I particularly remember were the Dave Clark 5, Gerry and the Pacemakers, Billy J Kramer, The Undertakers and The Big Three, although my particular favourites were The Kinks, who had just released 'You Really Got Me' in '64. It was an electrifying guitar riff.

29 MAY 1964
CORPORATION HOTEL, DERBY, UK

MICK SHELTON

I was a regular at the Corporation Hotel in Derby during the early Sixties. I like to think of myself as one of the small number of Mods who helped change the face of Derby's scene. The Corp, as it was known, was our Friday night mecca and Roger Groome, the landlord, had run a successful jazz club there for many years. He had the vision to cater for the new generation and set up the Friday R&B scene after most of the farming community had gone home. The hotel was situated opposite the Derby cattle market and Friday was a busy day in the town. The open spaces where the cattle pens had been was ideal for the scooter boys to show off their Vespas and Lambrettas. I remember well the night when The Who played under the name the High Numbers, something they often did in their early days, especially when manager Kit Lambert was not sure what sort of reaction they would get. He need not have worried – they went down a storm. The venue also hosted the Moody Blues, the Pretty Things, Steam Packet with Rod Stewart and Long John Baldry, Jimmy James and the Vagabonds, Zoot Money and his Big Roll band and many more. It was a great time to be a teenager.

Other sources suggest that they were called the High Numbers up until 20 February 1964, then The Who until 3 July 1964 when they reverted to the High Numbers. They settled on The Who in early November 1964.

20 JUNE 1964
REGENCY BALLROOM, BATH, UK

TONY CHURCHOUSE

They hadn't released any records. I was late arriving and my friends had said I'd just missed a great band who played so loud 'you could feel it in your stomach'. Luckily, they played a later set and so I can confirm this. During a break Roger Daltrey, Keith Moon and Pete Townshend were in the bar where we told them how we enjoyed what they played and had a drink with them. During the conversation Roger Daltrey stated he enjoyed fishing and asked if there was anywhere he could go. A friend said he fished too and, if Roger liked, they could meet up the next day to indulge in a spot of fishing together.

30 JUNE 1964
RAILWAY HOTEL, WEALDSTONE, UK

HAROLD MORTIMER

I was one of those who helped run the club at the Railway Hotel circa 1964. At the end of my teens in 1959 to 1961 I was a big fan of jazz, both trad and modern, as well as folk and blues. My lifestyle at the time led to me spending a few months 'on the road' in Europe and when I returned to London towards the end of that year things were really developing on the music scene. Bands were beginning to play old black American numbers in pubs and clubs. One of my earliest recollections is seeing Alexis Korner performing above the Roundhouse pub in Wardour Street with Charlie Watts on the drums. I was a regular visitor to Studio 51, aka Ken Colyer's Jazz Club in Great Newport Street, where they belted out their renderings of Chuck Berry, Bo Diddley and Coasters hits. Also at Colyer's were The Downliners Sect, who had a good guitarist. At the southern end of Wardour Street, I used to see Georgie Fame and the Blue Flames at the Flamingo Club, and The Animals played at the 100 Club in New Oxford Street. Then there were the Yardbirds at the Crawdaddy Club in Richmond Cricket Club, while Manfred Mann played at Eel Pie Island in Twickenham.

My enthusiasm for such music led me to start looking out for records, both new and used, of the original artists, and it was around then that one of my friends, Tony Brainsby, who went on to become a music impresario, introduced me to Guy Stevens who had an absolutely enormous collection of R&B records. Guy used to deejay his discs back-to-back once a week at the Piccadilly Jazz Club in Ham Yard, off Great Windmill Street, and I still remember the hypnotic effect the unfaltering rhythm of Chuck Berry's 'Run Rudolph Run' had on the dancers. Guy inspired me to seriously increase my own collection, to the point that I lived surrounded by shoeboxes full of 45s and cardboard boxes of LPs, fearful that they would all topple onto my bed and smother me one night. I still have a handful of them.

Another musician who played with Alexis Korner was Cyril Davies, and he formed a band that started doing a weekly gig at the Railway Hotel, Wealdstone. This was conveniently close to my home in South Harrow, so I became a regular there, going on almost any night a band was playing. The principal members were a pair of smartly dressed Jewish lads, one of whom I think was named Barney. I ended up with the job of playing records before the band started and again during the interval. On paper I was the 'Entertainment Manager', earning £2.50 a night. I developed a successful knack of mixing sounds ranging from authentic R&B such as Howling Wolf and John Lee Hooker, through mainstream Chuck Berry and Bo Diddley, to very early Motown. This was all put together before the night on a reel-to-reel tape recorder, then I would sweet talk the band into letting me switch on their PA and lean the microphone against the tape recorder's speaker – all very high tech!

Which leads me to The Who playing at the Railway once or twice before getting a regular weekly slot. This was about when they had just changed their name from the High Numbers. I particularly liked them because their covers of R&B material were well-played, they had dynamism and each member had charisma. But what made them really outstanding was that three quarters of the way through the evening they would go into an extended instrumental break, when Pete Townshend would turn round and fiddle with the controls on his amplifier before standing there rubbing his back against it while playing his guitar. This resulted in all sorts of weird and wonderful feedback noises which Pete attempted to control, while Keith Moon rattled away on his drums and John Entwistle thumped up and down the notes on his bass guitar. It is something that you hear perfected on 'Anyway Anyhow Anywhere'. Pete's windmill arm movement developed around this time. The one Who song I remember on the tape was a good cover of Marvin Gaye's 'Baby Don't You Do It', a number they later recorded.

I was in the club the night Pete famously made a hole in the ceiling above the stage, but the accounts of him smashing up his guitar afterwards are an exaggeration. What I recall is Pete's look of alarm quickly turning into a guilty grin, while gasps of surprise followed by laughter spread through the audience. Virtually my only other memories of The Who at the Railway are that for a small number of weeks, Roger Daltrey was in the company of the singer Millie (of My Boy Lollipop fame), and one night Chris Stamp, a tall and rather distinguished looking young man in a suit, came in with a stocky older and balding man; they stood near the entrance watching the band for about 30 minutes.

Many visitors to the club must remember 'Mad Mary', a lumpy and unattractive girl who always used to dance frantically on her own; no boy would be seen dead with her. There was occasional violence at the club, mercifully outside, one particular incident being when a group called the T-Bones turned up half an hour late. A large group of lads had their revenge afterwards, when the band were loading their equipment into their Transit van in the alley outside. On another occasion, I was accosted by three Mods, one of whom practically stuck a starting pistol up my nose on the landing of the stairs that led up from the club to the pub's bar. I persuaded a body-building friend to accompany me the next night (he was one of those people who could stand there rippling his biceps) and while I was buying him a drink at the bar, I quietly pointed out one of the Mods from the previous night. The face of the latter went white when he saw us looking, and without us saying anything he came over to grovel profusely. He blamed drugs, the use of which was commonplace at the club. You got the impression that nearly everyone was taking blue amphetamine tablets.

The sessions finished at 10.30 p.m. It would take half an hour to clear up, after which a small number of us (usually including Pete Townshend, Roger Daltrey and sometimes John Entwistle) made our way to a late-night coffee bar called the Kinkajou about three quarters of a mile away. Here we used to talk animatedly over Cokes and milkshakes 'til around midnight. One night a guy called John Altman was in a bit of a disagreeable mood and started an argument with Pete, which ended in a scuffle outside. John threw Pete onto the snow-covered pavement, at which I shouted 'cool it, man'. The shaken Pete misheard this and replied 'that wasn't cool!'.

A girl of 17 was in charge of the cloakroom, where people left their coats at the club; I often admired her leaning over the counter in her leather miniskirt. One night, I spent the last bit of money I had getting a taxi to the club with my tape recorder and other bits and pieces, only to be told by the Irish landlord Mick when I got there that the club had closed at short notice.

It had lost its license. What was I to do now? I would not be paid and I had no money to get home. In stepped the cloakroom girl, who bought me a drink and paid my fare. In response to her act of charity, I asked for a date. One thing led to another, and we have now been married for 47 years.

My wife is the youngest of three sisters, and her two siblings went to Ealing Art College where they got to know Pete Townshend. Consequently, all three of the girls visited the Railway, which is how my wife ended up with an evening job there. The extent of the friendship was that Pete and his then wife Karen later set up a housing charity, all tax deductible, and bough a flat in Ladbroke Grove which they rented out to one of my sisters-in-law. She still lives there today, although Pete sold out to a housing association some years ago.

If I have conjured up any vision of a musically hip and well-connected oldster, forget it. All that is long behind me. I've given up the long hair, I spent the last 28 years of my working life as a service engineer, and now I'm indistinguishable from any other old git of my age.

11 JULY 1964
TRADE UNION HALL, WATFORD, UK

JOHN ALBURY

I was one of the many Mods who frequently attended the Trade Union Hall in Woodford Road, Watford around 1963 and 1964 to see The Who and many other bands in those wonderful years of our youth. Just about every weekend we turned up on our scooters, parked outside, paid around 2/6 (13p) for a ticket and joined the usually large crowd to see the bands attending. The Who were regulars there, often alternating their appearances in Watford and the Railway Hotel a few miles away in Harrow and Wealdstone. They first appeared at the Trade on 11th July 1964 as The Who, with Keith, and I am pretty sure I was there as it was a day after my 18th birthday. They were back a week later and again I would have attended. They made nine or ten visits to Watford in 1964 as either The Who or the High Numbers and I must have seen them on four or five of those occasions. If we did not see them in Watford for a while, we would sometimes ride over to Harrow and see them at the Railway Hotel in Harrow and Wealdstone. But Watford Mods did not venture to Harrow for too long and vice versa. There was a bit of bad blood there.

At the Trade, I remember them playing as The Who and then changing their name to the High Numbers before changing back to The Who again, all in the space of a few weeks. Reputed to be the loudest band, they were responsible for my slight loss of hearing, but we loved every minute of it! I can vividly remember Pete Townshend smashing his Stratocaster into the corner of an amplifier and finishing off the guitar on the stage floor. We all cheered!

On one of their visits, Keith knocked over his drum kit at the end of the session. It could have happened more than once at Watford, but I definitely witnessed at least one instrument breaking session there with guitar and drums broken. It got very frantic there during that summer, as it was an energetic, crowded and 'must go' place. It was certainly the best venue in Watford for bands at that time until things got a little less raw, when the Top Rank opened in the town and we started to sell our scooters and progressed to cars. I sold my final scooter in late 1965. The Who had long departed small venues like the Trade.

The Trade Union Hall was a fascinating place for music in the 1960s. It was only really a basic village hall type of place with wooden walls and floor but the acoustics always seemed good with some of the greats of the time appearing at the weekends. It was nearly always 2/6 (13p) in old money for the entrance fee so five shillings (25p) if you went twice over the weekend. It was band nights on Saturday and Sunday.

Sometimes the boss, Joey Seabrook – who later became Keith Richards' bodyguard – gave a couple of us regulars a free entry. There was a painted backdrop to the stage, which may have been a Swiss scene with a door to the backstage area on the left facing the stage. There may have been another door on the right. It was hot and very noisy but fantastic. The girls were wonderful and the music superb.

There was no alcohol that I remember, but there were two pubs just down Woodford Road, two minutes away, which we frequented during half time. There were always rows of scooters up the left-hand side of the hall or out on Woodford Road and always the risk of bits being stolen off the bikes during the band performance as there was quite a market in the area for scooter accessories. It was a fantastic place where one grew up with music, atmosphere, great friends, the odd bit of Purple Heart taking, sometimes a little alcohol and a kiss or a little more on the way home!

LINDA WALKER

I was a Mod in the Sixties and went to the Trade Union Hall every week. The Who played at The Trade quite a few times in 1964 and 1965, before and after they changed their name from the High Numbers. We knew they were terrific but never thought they would be still going now. The Trade was always packed with Mods and there were some fights. There was no booze. You had to go to the nearby pub in the break. It was always packed for them, and you just knew how good they were. Some Rockers did attend but they didn't stay long - thank God – as it was not their kind of music. Keith Moon was my favourite. He was crazy, but so good. There were so many bands playing there – the Pretty Things, Rod Stewart Steampacket, Long John Baldry, George Fame. I have photos of The Who at the Trade, although I never photographed Keith Moon. Maybe he had nipped out for a pint!

LEN NEWMAN

This was my first time seeing The Who. It's the night that Chris Lambert heard them but couldn't get in because it was so crowded. He went to the Railway Hotel in Harrow the next week with Stamp and they signed up as the band's managers.

In 1968, I saw them at the Top Rank in Watford. I stood near Pete, and each time he talked about the next song, I said what was coming. In the end, he did the chat, said 'he'll tell you what it is,' and handed me the mic. I said the song title as he went into the opening chords. Keith Moon was on form playing the drums with rubber-handled Stanley hammers, with soapsuds coming out of one of the floor tom-toms and a pop up bar in the other. Very amusing. I recounted this about two years ago in an article about the show and Roger sent a message saying he liked my memory.

My last time seeing The Who was be at the Eden Project in July 2023. I was six rows back on Pete's side and they were on fire.

The Who play two shows at the Trade (on 11 and 18 July 1964) and then change their name to the High Numbers for six shows at that venue from July through to October 1964 before reverting to The Who by the time of their return on 7 November 1964.

12 JULY 1964
FLORIDA ROOMS, BRIGHTON, UK

DAVID GOODWIN

They were the High Numbers when I saw them. They were one of a number of groups who would turn up to be part of the Mod scene in Brighton on a Saturday night. That was more of a streetwise audience, whereas coming out into the sticks here you had the Teddy Boy, slightly Rockerish sort of people. Rockers were still the country bumpkins, if you like. I don't think they went to see The Who. They just went out because it was a Sunday night out. There wasn't much original material played at the Florida Rooms. It was 'Dancing in the Street' and things like that. It was always the same faces. There were no speculative people. It was always the same crowd who went to Saturday night at the Florida Rooms. They wouldn't have come up to the Ultra Club in Hassocks on a Sunday night. The main faces from Brighton wouldn't have come to Hassocks.

When I was at school, there was a guy called Phil Towner who used to dep for Moon when they played at the Florida Rooms.

Being a main face in Brighton in those days was quite a serious business and quite unlike awful film, which doesn't portray anything remotely like how it was. *Quadrophenia* doesn't portray Brighton in the right sense. In Brighton, if you were a few weeks out of the fashion you weren't cool. It was really sharp. You had to be correct. I remember taking a girl down to the Florida Rooms. She had a paisley miniskirt on and the girls were all pointing and laughing at her because it was six months late. You had to be just right to be accepted by the inner circle. Maybe it was only a hundred people.

The Who played the Florida Rooms 12 times in 1964 and, as the High Numbers, three times.

14 JULY 1964
RAILWAY HOTEL, WEALDSTONE, UK

VALERIE DUNN (NEE WATSON)

We used to see The Who, then known as the High Numbers, down the Railway Hotel, Wealdstone regularly on a Tuesday night. I probably saw them there four or five times. It was a great venue, a basement where we would also see Blues Incorporated with Rod (the Mod) amongst many others. The Railway Hotel in Wealdstone was a gig that they seemed to come along to quite regularly. It was down in the basement, down the steps. You could only get a drink upstairs in the pub. It had two entrances.

It was always a Tuesday evening that they had the various blues nights, when they had different bands playing. the High Numbers alternated with a few other bands. Another band who used to play regularly was called Garry Farr and the T-Bones. The singer was the son of the boxer whose name was also Gary Farr. And you'd have Alexis Korner and Blues Incorporated on other Tuesday nights.

I lived in Harrow and I'd go down with my friend and my sister. I went to Harrow School of Art and a lot of the art school lot, who were a little bit older than me and who I was a little bit in awe of, would go down. You'd see them all doing the amazing French jive.

It was probably Long John Baldry who instigated the blues nights. He had a friend who was on the door to take the money, but he would always be standing there chatting. I think it was Long John that actually ran the music events. I don't remember the landlord being particularly interested. Other than the Tuesday night blues, which was in the basement of the pub, the pub itself was quite rough. I just recall seeing people on the door at the basement of the pub on a Tuesday taking whatever it cost – a shilling – to get in.

When the High Numbers were on, it was slightly more the Moddy feel whereas on other Tuesday nights it would be more bluesy. You'd get more lads coming down when the High Numbers were on. They'd all do a dance called the Puppet, where they'd put their arms up and bob up and down. It was quite a small venue, and busy and packed. But standing at the front we'd watch Keith Moon because he would be such an entertainer. He was totally mad on the drums and completely gone. Pete Townshend would be swinging his arm around and getting feedback and John Entwistle was more in the background. He just got on and did his bit. And Roger Daltrey was up the front there singing. They probably did two sets. It was great because it was very intimate. We were right up the front, close, watching them. They were loud and of course you had all the feedback from Townshend's guitar. It was a great atmosphere. The Railway was great because it was so close for us living in Harrow so it wasn't far to get home. After that it went back to just being a rough old pub.

VAL MABBS

I was born and brought up in Harrow, so I lived in the area where The Who played a lot. I was a Mod and, particularly from 1964, was very involved in the Mod scene. There was an awful lot going on in the area at that time. The first time I saw The Who was when they were appearing at the Railway as the High Numbers. I may have seen them before that, but the earliest I had noted is 28th July 1964.

I remember us Mods gathering at the top of the hill in front of the pub, by the railway station, and there being a bit of chat about this band, the High Numbers, that were going to be on at the Railway that evening, and it being talked about them being The Who. Quite a number of Mods had gathered there with their scooters. Then we all queued up at the pub. The frontage was right on the hill, and then you went down the slope at the side which took you down to the basement area at the back of the pub, where you went in to see the band. There was quite a long queue waiting to get in to see them.

I saw a lot of bands at that time, but to see The Who at any time was an experience because they were quite different. They were extremely loud, particularly in that venue because it was very small for the volume they created. It was always very dark. They had one small bit of red lighting in there and it was very smoky, because a lot of guys smoked then. Smoking was quite trendy! It was a brilliant atmosphere. Some people might call it seedy but to me it wasn't. It was a good venue in that you were there with the band and the music was all around you. It was great – people danced and people just stood there and watched. It was very much part of the Mod scene.

That pub has gone. It was knocked down a while back and what's there now is called Moon House. I think it's quite nice that they've retained a little bit of the history there, although I'm not sure why it's specifically Moon as opposed to any of the others.

Girls didn't have scooters; only the guys had scooters. Sometimes they took you on their scooter, but having almost come off the back of someone's scooter once, it wasn't always a good idea. Not all the guys were good at riding them! The Railway was only a train stop away for me, or a short bus ride.

The group appeared at the Railway Hotel 16 times in 1964, appearing as The Who on 30 June 1964 and 2 November 1964, but as the High Numbers on the 14 occasions in between.

SUMMER 1964
HARROW WEALD MEMORIAL HALL
HARROW, UK

MIKE BISHOP

I saw The Who several times when they performed at Harrow Weald Memorial Hall. I believe that at this time they were still using the name the High Numbers when performing in Watford. I had several friends who saw them 'down the Trade' at Watford. I never did. The Memorial Hall was quite small and, compared to other venues in the area, would have had a fire certificate for 200-300 people. It was rarely full because it didn't have an alcohol licence. This put off most of my friends. The Railway Hotel was not far away and this was even smaller but had alcohol. Although I went there regularly, I don't remember seeing them there.

The audience at the Memorial Hall was almost entirely made up of Mods. As a Rocker, I was almost alone but contrary to most stories about that time we weren't constantly fighting and there was never any problem. Many of the Mods came, like myself, from Borehamwood.

Other bands performing regularly at the Memorial Hall were Cliff Bennett and the Rebel Rousers, The Pretty Things and later, The Moody Blues. The Who were by far the most professional. The other bands came on stage and tuned their instruments, checked their sound balances, discussed what they were going to play and started off. The Pretty Things didn't even balance their speakers which meant people moving around the hall to find a spot where the sound seemed okay. The Who, however, did all this unnoticed and unheard behind the curtains. The lights were dimmed and the curtains opened simultaneously with the opening number. They then continued with their set without stopping or chatting among themselves. The same with their second set. I can't remember the songs they performed (possible Benny Spellman's 'Fortune Teller?') but I was struck by Pete Townshend's astonishing ability to play with the distortion that he deliberately induced with his speakers. I've never seen him do it on film, or seen anyone else do it in such a controlled manner.

It has not been possible to verify that The Who appeared at the Memorial Hall.

31 JULY 1964
GOLDHAWK SOCIAL CLUB SHEPHERD'S BUSH, LONDON, UK

RICHARD WHITE

We were a small semi-pro band from south London called The Rivals playing the London circuit; a three guitars, drums, two-a-penny band. We all had daytime jobs and we used to get the odd gig here and there. One day we were offered a gig in west London at the Goldhawk Club. They weren't The Who then. I think they were called the High Numbers. They were absolutely amazing. I'd never heard such a dynamic band in my life and they seemed to have a cult following at the Goldhawk Club. As people they were very friendly and approachable. They were quite complimentary about us, although I don't think we were anywhere near their standard! We were just a bog standard band from the time, doing stuff like 'La Bamba' and rock classics that everyone did. They were in a different league altogether.

They were doing a lot of American material at that time. They used to do a really powerful version of 'Ooh Poo Pah Doo'. They were really into the American stuff – R&B and soul-type stuff. They used to give it the full Who treatment, with crashing guitar chords and Keith Moon thrashing around the drum kit.

The Goldhawk Club was larger than a big house. It was more like a large back room of a pub. I think it was licensed, because I'm sure we had a drink with Pete Townshend afterwards. Pete complimented me on my bass playing. He said he liked it. He was a nice guy and very complimentary about us. I think he was the brains behind the band. He told me they'd worked on Roger Daltrey's voice. It was too high pitched for them at one time and they wanted to bring it down a bit. They did it by getting him to sing into a tape recorder.

We used to bump into them later on. Roger Daltrey always had a crowd of girls round him. Keith was totally barmy. You'd be travelling somewhere by train and he'd be running through the railway carriages. He was very extrovert, but very likeable and very sociable. He loved talking to people and loved having a laugh.

We met them quite a few times at places like the Marquee Club. They would see us and they would approach us, and that was after they had had hits. They were still the same guys we met at the Goldhawk Club. They were good guys.

9 AUGUST 1964
HIPPODROME, BRIGHTON, UK

FRANK HINTON

They were called the High Numbers and were on the bottom of a bill headlined by Gerry and the Pacemakers. The other artistes were The Nashville Teens, Elkie Brooks – I remember both – and Valerie McCullam, who I don't remember and haven't heard of since! Daltrey was tossing his microphone high and expertly catching it and Townshend was striking his guitar in an aggressive windmill action. They are still doing it 50 years later. But the audience hadn't come to see them and did not appreciate the mic tossing. My friend says they often played at the Florida Rooms in Brighton as the High Numbers but the purple hearts he took then means he can't remember anything now. That isn't my excuse. I was a Mod by inclination. I followed fashion and wore the clothes, but I never took any drugs. I was never offered any and never even saw any.

16 AUGUST 1964
OPERA HOUSE, BLACKPOOL, UK

SYD BLOOM

They were still called the High Numbers. They were backing Adrienne Posta, The Beatles and the Kinks. They were doing all kinds of Beach Boys stuff at the time. They looked a bit like the Beach Boys, that surfing stuff, largely at the behest of Keith Moon, I suspect. When they came in the car park afterwards, I was talking to Pete Townshend and he was talking about Adrienne Posta and he said 'she started sniffing around The Beatles and got nowhere and then she started sniffing around the Kinks and got nowhere. And then,' he said, 'she tried to park herself on us.' And that's how I remember what the line-up was, because of Pete's anecdote.

STEVE GOMERSALL

John Entwistle was listening to The Beatles in his dressing room through the little PA speaker. The Fab Four were performing 'A Hard Day's Night' and Entwistle heard Lennon singing 'It's been a hard day's night and I've been wanking like a dog', because he knew the audience couldn't hear the words over the girls screaming.

WILLIAM WALTON, AGE 16

Myself and five boyhood friends embarked on a week's holiday in Blackpool. One of my friends' mums had managed to get us tickets to the Winter Gardens for a show featuring The Beatles. Unbeknownst to us, on this same bill were the Kinks, the Hearts, Adrienne Posta and the High Numbers. I can recollect being blown away by 'You Really Got Me' by the Kinks and by the on stage performances of Pete Townshend and Keith Moon. the High Numbers sang 'I Can't Explain' and some other songs and the raw rock and roll on show that night totally eclipsed The Beatles, who I was never a great fan of. Memories fade but a packed house, mostly of hysterical females throwing sweets and other items when The Beatles were on, is something never to be forgotten.

23 AUGUST 1964
HIPPODROME, BRIGHTON, UK

JEFF BYGRAVES, AGE 10

They were still called the High Numbers. It was like a variety show and they were first on the bill, supporting Dusty Springfield. Being Brighton in August, it was full of holidaymakers and they were so loud that everybody was walking out. I was ten years old and I loved it. Everyone came back in when they finished.

31 AUGUST 1964
CORN EXCHANGE, ROCHESTER, UK

KAY HUNT (NEE PETERS), AGE 15

Every Monday I went to the RSG club at Rochester Corn Exchange. They were called the High Numbers. I wrote in my diary that they were fabulous and that I had got their autographs and a bit of Pete Townshend's plectrum that had broken off. I got Pete, Keith and John's autographs but for some reason John signed his name 'John Brown'. I didn't know any different as I didn't know their names. I gave my book to Roger Daltrey but he just pushed it away.

I remember standing, with my hands on the stage, and enjoying the music with Pete

Townshend ramming his guitar into his amplifier and Keith Moon going crazy playing the drums. One of his drum sticks broke and I tried to get it but another girl was quicker than me. As they finished their gig, Keith pushed his drum kit over and kicked it around the stage. They were certainly different from any other band that had been there before.

4 SEPTEMBER 1964
KELVIN HALL, GLASGOW, UK

HENRY WRIGHT

I was a drummer and I was lucky enough to be asked to join Luly and the Luvvers that night. On the bill were the High Numbers (later to become The Who) and the Paramounts (later called Procul Harum). Top of the bill was Dave Berry. I thought The Who were exceptional and I had an argument with my mate that my wife remembers to this day. I thought The Who would be big and he didn't. I guess I won! After that, I would go and see The Who at the Marquee and once we played a TV date with them and Keith asked if he could use my drums, which he did. There was no damage to the drums but he broke my sticks. I also remember a night in London, UK with my brother, Tommy from the Luvvers, Leslie Harvie and Pete Townshend and going on a pub crawl in London, UK. We ended up at the Scotch of St James where we proceeded to take the mick out of Brian Jones. Good days.

8 SEPTEMBER 1964
RAILWAY HOTEL, WEALDSTONE, UK

BRIAN CHATTERS

I was a student at Bristol University but my home was in Eastcote, Middlesex. In the summer of that year, a pal and I used to go and see The Who regularly on a Thursday at the Railway Hotel, just outside of Harrow and Wealdstone station and when they called themselves the High Numbers. Some of the scenes in a documentary about the group that was screened in early 1966 were shot there. The Railway Hotel had a room in a separate building where bands performed. We went to chat up girls but also because they played a number of R&B songs. I particularly remember 'Heatwave' by Martha and the Vandellas and 'Spoonful' by Howlin' Wolf.

They were beginning to appeal to the Mods, although the audience was very mixed. My pal and I were neither Mods nor Rockers, but we did get some light-hearted banter from some of the Mods who called us Rockers. I don't recall any crowd problems, but the room in which they performed was always packed out.

The band did not smash up their equipment in those days. Pete Townshend played his guitar with his windmill action as he did in later times and Keith Moon was just as wild on the drums. There was one incident where he managed to cause his kit to fall apart and he asked if anyone had a screwdriver or knife. I carried a small penknife – there was nothing sinister about such things in those days and the blade was only about one inch long – so I offered it to Keith. He never returned it! They didn't wear obvious Mod clothes, although Roger Daltrey may have worn paisley shirts.

The band played from about 8pm to 10.30 pm with a short interval. Pubs closed at 10.30pm in those days. They always played the same EP during the interval. It was called *Singing the Blues* which featured 'It Will Stand' by the Showmen, 'Ooh Poo Pah Doo' by Jessie Hill, 'I Like It Like That' by Chris Kenner, and 'Mother-in-Law' by Ernie K-Doe. It gives you some idea of The Who's musical influences. They also featured 'Ooh Poo Pah Doo' in their act.

The Who performed as the High Numbers on fourteen Tuesdays at the Railway between July and October of 1964.

5 OCTOBER 1964
CORN EXCHANGE, ROCHESTER, UK

KEITH CRUST

I went with my mates Malcolm Burch, Bob Thomas and Billy Price. We all parked our Lambretta scooters inside the building, in front of the steps that went up to the ballroom. It was such a great night, Keith Moon smashing up his drums and Pete Townshend whacking his guitar on his amp. I had just bought a Vox guitar for £16, which was a lot of money then, and there was Pete Townshend smashing up a Fender Stratocaster!

KAY HUNT

After seeing them in August, the next time that I saw them was again at the Corn Exchange on 5th October. I wrote in my diary that they had changed their name to The Who. I can still remember after all this time how I felt watching them perform. They were truly unique.

SHEENA POPE, AGE 18

I was 18 and a Mod. I saw The Who at the Corn Exchange a couple of times in 1964 with my friends Fred McDonald, Brenda LePage and her boyfriend Roger. I believe it was on Monday nights. It was difficult to get there as I worked in London. They were a great group, not the usual good-looking boys, but quite dramatic and loved by Mods. I think they were called the High Numbers then. It was pre The Who and I loved them!

28 NOVEMBER 1964
CORN EXCHANGE, CHELMSFORD, UK

BARRY THOMPSON, AGE 20

They only sold soft drinks at the weekly Saturday night dance, so if you wanted to leave, you'd get a mark on the back of your hand that could only be seen under an ultra violet light which meant they'd let you back in. We'd pay to go in, nip out to the pub for a drink or two and nip back to the dance after. We didn't know from one week to the next who was coming. They said that this group was coming but we had never heard of them. When they were announced on stage, the compere said 'we don't know who they are but here are The Who!' And they were fantastic, very young and very talented. They did quite a wide range of songs, including 'Dancing in the Street'. I think we all knew that we were seeing something very rare and special as we all stopped dancing and stood and just watched in amazement. Pete whirled his arm like a windmill even in those days. They were absolutely amazing. They'd gone through the stuff that they'd got and were asking for requests and said they'd play anything.

They looked so young. I think that somebody had to drive them to the gig. But they were so good. You wouldn't believe how good they were for the age they were.

I paid something like half a crown (12.5p) to see them. You knew that they were going to be something special if they stuck together. They couldn't have got paid much for those gigs they were doing. They carried their own stuff in and carried their own stuff out and took it to bits.

When I told them I'd seen The Who before they'd made a record, my children were quite stunned. My grandchildren know who The Who are and they always say 'Grandad saw them before anybody'.

24 NOVEMBER & 1, 8, 15, 22 & 29 DECEMBER 1964
MARQUEE CLUB, LONDON, UK

IAN GARNER

I used to live in south London and every Tuesday I would go to the Marquee to see The Who. There was always a support group that usually received abuse from the audience, which was generally an 80/20 split between boys and girls. Most of the lads seemed to be noting the chords that Pete was playing. It cost 7/6 (37p) to get in. They were very loud as it was a small place and Roger often seemed to be out of it. They did lots of covers – Tamla stuff, 'Heatwave', 'Please, Please, Please' by James Brown – very well. I also saw them once at the Wimbledon Palais and for some reason Roger didn't show up. It didn't seem to make much difference!

The Who are recorded as having played the Marquee six times in 1964 and a further 22 times in 1965.

1965
TOTTENHAM HIGH SCHOOL, LONDON, UK

LINDA SADLER

I a small girls' grammar school where behavioural standards were very high. A girl (whose name I can't remember) had been absent from school for a few days and somehow the school got information that she was at Keith Moon's flat in Finsbury Park. Our headmistress drove there and knocked at the door. Keith answered and she asked for the girl, who came to the door dressed only in a pair of tights! The headmistress demanded the girl get dressed and drove her back to school. The Tottenham Royal ballroom was next door to our school, and the same headmistress confronted Dave Clark and asked him to change his rehearsal times to avoid hordes of schoolgirls hanging around the Royal waiting for him to come out.

15 JANUARY 1965

The Who's first single, 'I Can't Explain', is released.

JOHN SCHOLLAR

Keith rang me up one day and said 'I'm coming over.' And he came over on the bus from Wembley, because he never used to drive, and this was when he made his first record, which was 'I Can't Explain'. He came in and he'd got a pile of records under his arm. He was getting stuff in from the States at that time – Beach Boys, Jan and Dean – because we were both into all this surfing music. He put this record on an old Dansette record player and he said 'what do you reckon to this lot? Who do you think it is?' I said, 'I know it's you, you daft sod.' I knew straight away it was him because I could tell by his drumming.

I remember when my dad was seriously ill and they told him to move out of London because of all the fumes. I rang Keith's mum and said 'oh, my mum and dad are moving Friday' and I gave her the address and said they wanted to keep in touch. A couple of nights after, there was a knock at the door and there was a Rolls-Royce outside with a chauffeur in it and Keith came in with his wife. I said 'what are you doing?' He said 'I've come to say goodbye to your dad, mate.' He drove right across the other side of London to do that.

NIGEL SUTCLIFFE

Ever since I initially heard 'Carrot Springs' on Radio Luxembourg – that's what I first thought 'I Can't Explain' was called – I found the Brunswick singles. I played 'Pictures of Lily' over and over. When I got *A Quick One*, I played it on the school classical player the loudest I could in the assembly rooms. I was at St Bees School in Cumberland. It was a boarding school with forced haircuts and fagging. I'm 15 and starting to rebel…

16 JANUARY 1965
CHELSEA COLLEGE OF SCIENCE & TECHNOLOGY, LONDON, UK

ROGER KINSEY

I saw The Who on a Tuesday night at the Marquee Club in Wardour Street, London in October or November 1964. I was a fan from that night onwards. I was a student then at Chelsea College of Science and Technology and we eventually persuaded the Entertainments Chairman of our college to book them into a dance the following January 1965. The price they were paid was £75 and the Entertainments Chairman consistently moaned for the rest of his year that they were the most expensive support group he had booked, as he usually only paid £50.

17 JANUARY 1965
NEW THEATRE, OXFORD, UK

NIGEL MOLDEN

It was a Sunday concert. The band closed the first half of a show headlined by PJ Proby. All that was known about them was the little that had been written in the *NME* about 'I Can't Explain'. The equipment had been set up stage right, presumably to facilitate the other performers on the show. My clearest memory is that they played considerably louder than any of the other bands. I also remember Roger Daltrey deliberately dropping the microphone onto the stage in a destructive kind of way. By the end of the short set, Pete Townshend was also thrusting the end of his guitar neck into the speaker stack, presumably to create a feedback effect. The band certainly made an impact on the music scene. 18 months later, we had at school a young French assistant. It was very unusual for popular music to be discussed at school but young Pierre was very keen to tell us sixth formers that his favourite group was '*Ze Woo*'!

3 FEBRUARY 1965
LOCARNO BALLROOM, STEVENAGE, UK

MAUREEN BROWNING

My sister and I saw The Who on many occasions, especially in their earlier years. We were also very lucky to know them fairly well and met them on many occasions, usually going backstage.

My sister was three years older than me and we were very lucky that we had great parents who realised we loved music and bought us tickets for, and were our 'teenager taxis' to and from, many live shows at what was one of the very best times for music. I have many examples of their autographs in both my own and my late sister's autograph books, as well as signed photos. Some of the sets of autographs have John Entwistle signing as John Brown, a surname he used for a while. He also used the surname Alison for a time too, which was his girlfriend's name.

John and Keith also wrote their addresses in my book, and they would keep in touch, letting let us know if they were playing nearby. There is also a note from February 1965 that John's car reg was 459 VPP, but why that is in my autograph book I have no idea. I also have a small signature for John Daltrey, with a note I wrote saying he was their road manager.

CHRISTINE MACLEAN

I have searched my childhood diaries for references of when I went to see The Who. It seems like I was quite a fan! I lived near Stevenage New Town and most bands came to the Mecca, or Locarno Ballroom. I went to see The Who there in 1965 on Wednesday 3 February, Wednesday 14 July and Wednesday 3 November. I also saw them at the Bowes Lyon in Stevenage on Friday 18 June.

DAVID MACLEAN, AGE 15

'You going tonight?' 'Yeah, I'm going.' That's me and Snotty Glynn talking about seeing The Who at the Mecca Locarno Ballroom in, maybe, 1964? It was the first time they came to Stevenage New Town, the Mod capital of North Hertfordshire. Snotty had seen The Who at the 100 Club in Wardour Street a couple of weeks before. Snotty was a proper Loona. He had all the gear – a two tone tonik suit from Mr John on Carnaby Steet, Hush Puppies and bright red socks, but no scooter. He couldn't afford one, not like Jenks and the gang, all covered in Parkas and chrome.

Me and Snotty met outside the Mecca around 8pm along with Jenks, Smithy and Clivey Bogbrush (on account of his hair). We were underage, but no one seemed to care, least of all the bouncers. Once inside, it was really rocking with music blasting out from the Stones, Yardbirds, Kinks and Tamla Motown.

Squeezed right up front next to the stage, surrounded by blokes and just a few birds, the band was the only thing on my mind and when they exploded onto the stage with 'I Can't Explain', the place erupted. Me and Snotty went crazy. I was a spotty 15-year-old just teaching myself guitar and Townshend was God. I had never seen or heard anything like it. The Rickenbacker howled and roared into action, followed by great arching windmills from this guy from the streets. Totally original. He wore a brown-and cream-check jacket, or maybe it was the shirt, cream strides and brown alligator shoes. Smartly cut Mod with attitude – I couldn't take my eyes off him. What style!

The set was loud, brash and unforgettable, with the ritual demolition of drums, guitar and amplifier. What a night. I caught the 802 bus home to Bandley Hill with Snotty. That was the start of a Who love affair which continues to this day and includes *Live at Leeds* - and *Live at Leeds 2*!

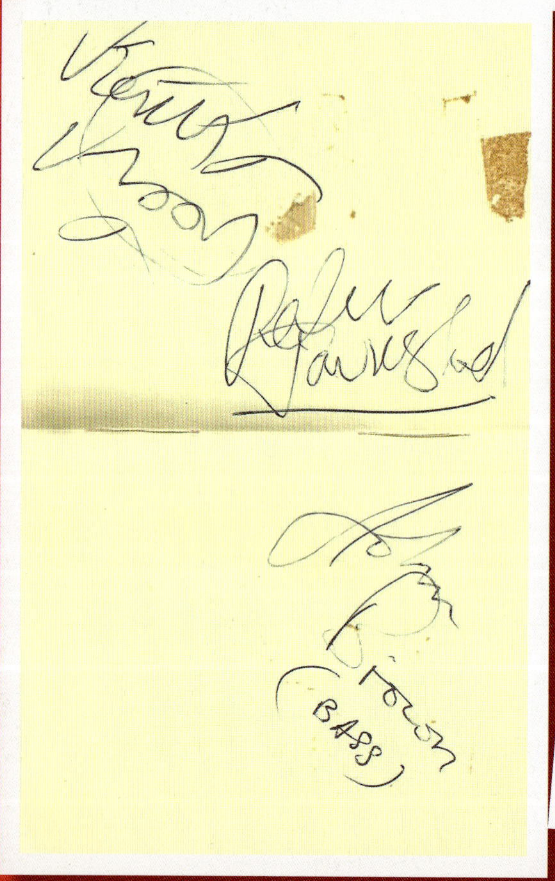

Clockwise from top left: Valerie Dunn on the Tube; Valerie's membership card for the Railway Hotel; Linda Walker's photos of The Who at the Trade in Watford; Kay Hunt's High Numbers autographs.

Saturday, 27th March

Mark Gold Promotions present

THE WHO & COPS 'N' ROBBERS

Tuesday, 30th March

GRAND FINALS

of the Herts & Essex Beat Contest

MORNING COFFEES - LUNCHES - AFTERNOON TEAS

OLD HOUSE CAFE

High Street, (Windhill) Bishop's Stortford

Telephone: 4673

Everything home made, including cakes to order
Also a range of gifts for every occasion

STAR ARTISTES, BANDS AND SHOWS FOR EVERY OCCASION
BEAT GROUPS, WEST END FLOOR SHOWS, GALA ACTS
CHILDREN'S ENTERTAINERS, ETC.

FOR ALL ENTERTAINMENT

Wheeler Entertainments Ltd.

MANAGEMENT — AGENCY — PRODUCTION

Sawbridgeworth 2302

SAWBRIDGWORTH HERTS.

For details of advertisement rates in this Programme telephone Bishop's Stortford 4735

Printed at R B W PRESS, Water Lane, Bishop's Stortford. Tel. 2976

Clockwise from top left: Gordon Heath was at the Trade in Watford; Chris Ferguson (left) met Keith Moon in Bournemouth (photo Chris Ferguson); Helen Kayes saw The Who at the Harrow Tech Ball; Mick Lynham remembers The Who trying to back out of their booking at Hemel; Barry Thompson was impressed by the youthful-looking Who; flyer for Bishops Stortford.

PETE WRIGHT

I was an apprentice toolmaker. I was outside working on my motorbike when my mum said, '*Ready Steady Go!* is about to start.' I said 'I must finish this off' and she went back indoors and then came out again and said 'come and look at this crap that's on here now'. It was The Who. I missed a bit of it, but they were doing 'Daddy Rolling Stone.' It was so so different from anything else I'd ever seen. I got back to work on the Monday morning, at the apprentice training school, and I said 'did you see that crap on Ready Steady Go! on Friday?' and someone said 'they're at the Locarno Wednesday night.' You could see the Locarno ballroom across the railway line, out of our factory window, so we went down.

I've still got my first wage packet. Three pounds three and a penny (£3.15) and there's no tax and no national insurance because I didn't make the threshold for those two things. I'm standing there on £3 a week. I stood on tiptoe at the bar to make 'em think I was 18, and I bought a light ale for 1/6 (7p), a big outlay, and he's smashing his bloody Rickenbacker to pieces and then he picks another up and carries on. Those Rickenbacker guitars were £199. And that was it. The seed was sown. I've seen them over 100 times since.

12 FEBRUARY 1965
YOUTH CENTRE, LOUGHTON, UK

PETER DENT

I first saw them at my secondary school, the Brook School on Roding Road in Loughton, Essex, around the time 'I Can't Explain' was released. I was on the committee of the youth centre and we thought they were just another group that played in halls, schools, etc. We couldn't sell tickets as no one had heard of them. On the night, I helped serve them coffees. The youth centre had booked them for a return gig at the same cost as the first visit. After the success of 'I Can't Explain', they wanted more money, but we held out as per the agreement. This time (2 April 1965) I had people knocking on my door at home asking for tickets. My future wife was at one of the shows and got one of Keith's drum sticks, although it's been lost over the years. After starting work, I became a scooter boy and began following them, seeing them at Walthamstow Odeon, Charlton, etc. – great times. At the Rhodes Centre in Bishop's Stortford, all four of them came down the steps to the side of the hall and Moonie had a ride around the car park on my Vespa GS160.

3 MARCH 1965
LE DISQUE A GO! GO! BOURNEMOUTH, UK

CHRIS FERGUSON

I had a band called Nite People who were based in Bournemouth around the period that The

Who played there. I met Keith at a party. He came to a friend's 21st birthday. The both of us being drummers, we started chatting. He had a girlfriend in Bournemouth – I think they eventually got married – and he kept coming down here. I went out on a couple of drinking sessions with him. He was a great guy and not as crazy as people made him out to be.

Keith's girlfriend was Kim Kerrigan and lived in Bournemouth when he met her on 3 March 1965. She was to become Mrs Keith Moon.

MARCH 1965
TRADE UNION HALL, WATFORD, UK

GORDON HEATH, AGE 17

I lived in Pinner during the Sixties and went to many gigs in the area to see mainly local groups. The term 'band' was only used if you were talking about one of the big bands, like Ted Heath's. My nickname at school was Ted because of the Ted Heath Band's widespread fame. I used to see The Who at the Trade. Many gigs were on a Sunday evening. I would go on the train from Hatch End station and meet my friend Derek, who travelled from Harrow and Wealdstone station. He'd stick his head out of the window as the train came into Hatch End and I would run to jump in the compartment. This was in the days of individual compartments. It was also before we had cars.

I had heard about The Who. I knew they were going to be good as soon as the curtains opened for their set. Groups playing at the Trade all used their own sound equipment, and the amount of amplifiers and speakers on the stage for The Who was more than I had ever seen before. They were stacked from floor to ceiling on both sides of the stage. When they played, the volume of sound was deafening. I'm sure I am suffering from some hearing loss now because of going to those gigs. The notes from John Entwistle's bass guitar were so low that you didn't so much hear them as feel them through your body. Your chest seemed to vibrate on the inside. Keith Moon was the most manic drummer around at the time, and probably ever. Roger Daltrey would often carry a bunch of steel rings, about the diameter of a tambourine, which he would thrash against the mic stand in time with the beat. This was part of the violent undertone that was part of The Who's act.

Then there was Pete Townshend and his guitar. At some stage in the act, he would stand in front of one the speakers, his back to the audience, take both hands off the guitar and push it against the speaker with his body. Somehow, he would make that guitar play itself. The sound energy from the speaker was somehow causing the guitar strings to vibrate. Sometimes he would thrust the guitar really hard and I'd be thinking about the cost of repairing or replacing the equipment, but Pete didn't seem to care. I never saw him smash up a guitar.

The sound The Who made live was never even close to being captured on any recording. You just had to have been there to know what it was like. It's hard to remember details of individual gigs from so long ago but I do remember seeing The Who at the Trade not long after 'I Can't Explain' was released. They ended their set and the evening with that song and it was so loud I walked back to the station with the sound of it ringing in my ears. I decided I had to go out and buy the single, partly to try to help the boys get into the charts, because we considered them to be one of 'our' groups. I used to write on my records the date when I bought them and my copy of that single shows 13 March 1965.

The Trade was always packed but it was well run, with plenty of doormen to make sure there was no trouble. But my friends and I did used to joke that if you got stabbed in there, it was so crowded that nobody would know until the end of the evening when you fell to the floor.

Gordon buying 'I Can't Explain' on 13 March 1965 after hearing it played live would suggest a previously undocumented appearance at the Trade.

20 MARCH 1965
GOLDHAWK SOCIAL CLUB SHEPHERD'S BUSH, LONDON, UK

KEITH ROWLEY

I would go whenever they were down the Goldhawk because it was just a ten-minute walk down the road. I remember seeing them there on a Saturday night shortly after 'I Can't Explain' became a hit. I was there with my fiancée. With them being a local band, it was absolutely jam packed. The Goldhawk Club was just a big terraced house along a string of houses. They used to play in a room that was probably not a lot bigger than somebody's large front room. And it was absolutely rammed. You couldn't move to dance. On this particular night, some nutter started swinging a baseball bat around his head and you could suddenly have got another 50 people in! The group were looking on in horror but they went into 'I Can't Explain'. It helped defuse the situation and prevent what would have been a riot.

21 MARCH 1965
TRADE UNION HALL, WATFORD, UK

VAL MABBS

The Trade was a working men's club which became known by us as 'the Trade' because it was a bit more trendy that way, I guess. My diary for Sunday 21 March 1965 says: 'Went to Trade. Queue right up past the station corner for The Who.' And then I've written: 'The Who were marvellous. Walls were running with water. So packed.' I remember this one very clearly. It was absolutely jam packed in there. Everybody was just watching them and the walls of the place were literally running with sweat. At that point, they were doing their smashing up thing, because Pete Townshend would be whirling his guitar around, bashing it into the stack of amps behind him. I think they were real amps but they might not have been, because I think they used dummy ones at times. They'd have the whole stack of Marshall amps and they certainly produced the sound that indicated that they had quite a bit of power behind them. Pete Townshend would bounce the guitar off the stage and it was just very different.

I also saw them there on a couple of other dates, 7 and 29 November 1964, where I noted seeing them but hadn't actually written a great deal about it. I saw them a number of times at the Trade. We would normally take the train because the Trade Union Hall was right next to Watford Junction station on the mainline down to Harrow & Wealdstone and Headstone Lane. There was a little pub almost opposite where people used to gather and have a drink or stand around, even though we were too young. Mods would congregate around the time gigs were due to start gigs before going in. The whole Mod thing was a lot about standing around and being seen, wearing the right clothes and being a part of that movement.

MICHAEL WILSON

My girlfriend, now my wife, followed all the live bands in those days. They were exciting times. Moonie was a complete nutter - in the nicest possible way! Townshend also had his moments. We first saw The Who at the Trade Hall. Then a few weeks later they were at the college in Hemel. We used to get the bus from Abbots Langley to Hemel Hempstead with our crazy clothes on and our weird haircuts. When we look around today, nothing much has changed. Great days!

22 MARCH 1965
PARR HALL, WARRINGTON, UK

JOHN HEWISON, AGE 17

Every Monday there were top groups at the Parr Hall, including the Kinks, the Moody Blues, the Hollies, Them with Van Morrison, the Nashville Teens and many more. I was fortunate to see them and especially The Who. I can still see Keith Moon completely trashing his drums very early in the set and borrowing the support act's drums. I recall Pete Townshend and Roger Daltrey destroying their guitars and amps and leaving the stage in tatters, smoking and nearly in flames, with the crowd standing open-mouthed in disbelief.

27 MARCH 1965
THE RHODES CENTRE BISHOP'S STORTFORD, UK

ADRIAN JAMES

They played with a supporting group, the Cops 'N' Robbers. They smashed their equipment. It seemed to start when Keith Moon broke a drum stick and threw it into the crowd. It was thrown back at him. Keith then kicked over his drum set, stood on the bass drum and put his stick through the drum skins. Pete was playing and getting reverb from the amps. He started to bounce his guitar off the floor of the stage and jammed his guitar into the amps and speakers until he broke it. I have the flyers advertising the forthcoming attraction from October 1964 through to February 1966, with The Who's autograph on the April 1965 one.

JULIE KITCHENER, AGE 16

I went to almost all the concerts held at Rhodes that year. The first 40 or 50 girls admitted on the door got in free, so if a fairly well-known group was coming we would queue from about 4pm, with rollers in our hair, get our hands stamped on admission at 8pm, disappear to my parents' house along the road and then turn up for the evening all dolled up. Often the groups would arrive early to set up so we got to see them and maybe get autographs. We were just lucky that this promoter, Alan Goldsmith, got these groups before they became really famous. We saw all the stars. When The Animals came it was five shillings (25p). It was a lot of money so we were allowed to pay it in two instalments. With The Who, we were frightened that they were going to smash up their guitars.

ANDY PEEBLES

I saw The Who at the Rhodes Centre in 1965. It might explain why I spent 46 years in broadcasting.

1 APRIL 1965
TOWN HALL, WEMBLEY, UK

HELEN KAYES, AGE 18

I and my now husband Peter saw them at the Harrow Tech College Rag Ball. They had probably been booked as an up-and-coming-but-not-yet-made-it band, but 'I Can't Explain' had just entered the charts so it was very exciting to see them. Donovan played at the same event.

7 APRIL 1965
DACORUM COLLEGE, HEMEL HEMPSTEAD, UK

JOHN DEALEY

I was a big Who fan from the beginning. At school one of my friends had a copy of the High Numbers' 'I'm The Face'. I bought all the early singles and albums on Brunswick and then came the opportunity to see them live at the Dacorum College. I snapped up a ticket and was at the front, shoulders on the stage. What a performance! The entire place was going mad as Townshend smashed his speaker with his guitar for the ultimate feedback and there was Moon going mad on the drums and a young Daltrey and Entwistle both doing their own thing. Acts such as Them, the Undertakers, the Naturals and the Bo Street Runners all played the Dacorum College, and all of them were kicked into touch by the electric performance of The Who.

MICK LYNHAM, AGE 16

Hemel's split into different areas and every area had a youth club. My mum ran Gadebridge youth club and she did the bookings at Dacorum College to raise money for the youth clubs, because the clubs had to be subsidised. Once a month or so they'd have a live act and it was my mother's job to book them, through a booking agent. In the Sixties, groups were coming out here, there and everywhere. Some lasted, some didn't. They'd have a local group and a main act come out of London. We had Screaming Lord Sutch there. He was rubbish.

When my mum said 'we've got the Who booked' the first thing we said was 'who? Oh yeah, that's a new group that's out.' The Who were booked prior to them becoming famous. They were under contract and were trying to get out of it because they'd got a hit record with 'I Can't Explain'. It was a very small venue with a little stage and we didn't get thousands of people. You're probably talking hundreds. But there were loads of people there that night.

They didn't smash up their equipment. As they finished, Keith Moon kicked the drums over a bit and a few of the amps went over, but not all of them. And they didn't stick any guitars through amps. But my mum thought 'oh my God. What's happening here?' Because she hadn't seen anything like it.

My sister actually went out with Keith Moon for a while. She was a little bit younger than me, a bit of a groupie. She went to a few more of their gigs. I don't remember going backstage but my sister probably did with my mother. My mother would have been backstage while they were on. We were out the front.

It didn't have a bar or anything. There was no drink. I certainly wouldn't have been allowed to drink even if there had been a bar. My mother would have been on top of me like a ton of bricks!

SUE STOW, AGE 14

My first favourite record was 'I Can't Explain'. I played it over and over and would dance in my bedroom. When I got The Who's first album and joined the fan club, I was at odds with most of my friends who were into the Stones or The Beatles. I was No 201 in the fan club. Going to Dacorum College was brilliant. My Dad helped out in a local youth club and volunteered to help out that evening so I begged him to take me. We were first in the venue so I stood right at the stage. I could touch Roger Daltrey's feet but I only had eyes for Keith Moon – he was brilliant! They were loud and so exciting to watch, ending with the usual smashing of items on stage. My Dad wasn't impressed.

8 APRIL 1965
OLYMPIA BALLROOM, READING, UK

NEIL CLARKE, AGE 18

I was in the top group in Reading in the Sixties. We were the Falcons and then we became the Dark Ages. We supported all the top groups at the Olympia; Manfred Mann, the Animals, the Searchers, the Rolling Stones – and the Kinks, when 'You Really Got Me' was number one. When The Who arrived at the venue, 'I Can't Explain' was at number 10 in the charts. I spoke to their manager, Kit Lambert, and suggested they plug in to our Vox AC50 amplifiers. Kit rejected this out of hand. I thought this was a bit big-headed and was because they were in the charts. We played the first half and then on came The Who. Needless to say, Keith Moon's drums were flying everywhere and Pete Townshend broke his Rickenbacker in half, so I was glad they didn't use our amplifiers. Pete was around 20 at the time and I said to Pete 'how can you smash a Rickenbacker in half?' He said, 'We get the guitars on HP, pay the deposit and then we disappear.' I remember I bought my American 1964 Stratocaster for 100 guineas (£110) and sold it for £50. That guitar is worth £10,000 today.

STEPHEN REID

My dad put The Who on at the Olympia. He had 672 people in through the door and had takings of £217 and eight shillings. Their fee was £97 and ten shillings and he banked a profit of just over £100. He put them on again at the Blue Moon in Cheltenham on 11 August 1965 where 481 people came to see them. Their fee had increased to £126 but he still made just over £63.

9 APRIL 1965
STAMFORD HALL, ALTRINCHAM, UK

JOHN BILLINGTON, AGE 14

I used to enjoy asking the old ladies who worked behind the record counter in the Co-op in George Street 'can I have the latest by The Who?' 'The Who?' 'Yeah, The Who.' Or, 'Have you got Them?' Who's Them? They had no idea. My friend had turned 15 in the April. He got me a job at Stamford Hall. 'The job' involved whatever Frank Bell, who was the promoter of the concerts, wanted. Frank was an ex-professional boxer and a PE teacher at Wellington Road school. A massive bloke, he used to stand on the door in a dinner suit with white shirt and black bow tie. Basically, it was a youth club organisation. The turns they had on were nothing great, no recording artists or anything, but round about that time things started happening. The Who was the second gig I worked. I only worked about five or six, because we never got paid, which was fair enough. Because at our age we shouldn't have been working, but we got a bottle of Coke and we had to do anything that Frank Bell asked us to do. We had to work the door and take the money. Frank would stand blocking the entrance so there was never any mither or people diddling us.

The Who concert was originally advertised in the *Altrincham Guardian* the week before they came and it said members 2/6 (13p), membership free, new members three shillings (15p). They'd just been on *Top of the Pops* singing 'I Can't Explain', and the following week's *Guardian* came out on the day of the concert advertising a 100 per cent increase in the admission price to six shillings (30p), or 6/6 (33p) on the door. Some people would not pay that entrance fee to see The Who. People were saying 'you must be joking. It was advertised as such and such.' We just looked at Frank Bell and he would say 'do you want to come in or not?' and people turned away, so the place was only half full because he'd whacked the price up.

The Who were on at 9 o'clock. The support group had to do a slot first and another slot afterwards, and another part of our job was opening and closing the curtains after each act finished. They were on ropes which you had to climb up, like the big ropes at the school gym. I was about six foot two and thought I was pretty strong, but these bloody things only moved about two inches every time I hung on them. I never worked so hard as I did trying to close the curtains after The Who were finished.

I'd never heard feedback. If I'd have got feedback at home, it was a mistake. The time Townshend spent creating the most ridiculous noises, standing right next to his amp and rubbing his guitar up and down the speakers and what have you, was just phenomenal. How long he'd had his amps I don't know. They were Marshall double stack 200-watt amps, one on top of the other. They'd draped a Union Jack over them because the mesh covering the speakers had been ripped by him sticking his guitar into it.

Keith Moon finished the whole set by kicking his drums off his little platform onto the stage and Roger Daltrey was stamping on some of it. The audience were just stood there with their mouths open. I don't believe anybody clapped as they went off – they just stood there in shock. I couldn't concentrate on trying to close the curtains, seeing the chaos that was going on. It's not whether you think it was entertainment. It was just so totally different from anything that had been before, and when he started wrecking stuff you'd be thinking, 'I'm saving up to buy this and he's just destroying what he's got.'

He nearly had the thing on fire at one time. There was smoke coming out of it and he got the feedback going again and he'd lean back on it so that it almost fell over. Then he'd walk away from it and it would be rocking backwards and forwards. His windmill bloody action and the fact that he could hit chords and hit the actual strings when he was doing it – we'd never seen anything like it before.

He had four input jack slots on his amp and, about a quarter of the way through their performance, he just turned around and punched down on the actual jack and snapped it off into the amp. Then he pulled his lead out and whacked another in the next available slot. He continued doing this during this show to keep doing it after every few songs. After he'd done three, he walked straight to the side of the stage where the support group were all stood watching, pulled the jack plug in lead off the support band's bass guitar, walked back to the stage and rammed that one in. And his final, final, final act of the concert was that he smashed that one.

His arm was coming down and I could see the face of the bass guitarist from the support band. The lad was going 'no!' but Townshend bashed it up and walked off. The lad was nearly in tears, going 'what am I going to do?'. They were due on next and he probably got another one off somebody else, but it was just total disregard by Townshend for absolutely anything.

The other thing that we'd never seen before was some guy singing and swinging a microphone out around his head and over the crowd and being able to catch it, and knocking the microphone stand so it would fall flat beside him and then standing on it so that it'd shoot straight back in front of him.

Keith Moon never stopped absolutely knocking seven shades out of his drum kit the whole night, while John Entwistle never batted an eyelid the whole way through. He stood completely still on the complete opposite side of the stage to me and played his bass. He walked off amid the chaos when they finished as if nothing had happened. They did no more than 45 minutes and there was no encore, because they'd kick everything over and walked off, leaving the roadie to pick it all up.

I couldn't class it as enjoyable music but as a spectacle it was just something else. I remember they played 'I Can't Explain' twice and Bo Diddley's 'I'm A Man'. I recognised some of the tracks when my friend bought the first album when it came out.

Townshend stormed straight off the stage so I didn't speak to him. But Keith Moon was a dead genuine and friendly sort of a lad. He clambered over his kit and I asked him how Pete could justify smashing stuff up like that. Keith said, 'Oh, he's only bought that guitar today. He bought it in Altrincham. He buys one every time we go in a music shop.' I said, 'How the bloody hell can he afford that?' Keith said, 'It's on HP. They'll never get the money off him.'

Keith wore a white t-shirt and a pair of jeans. John Entwistle had on a really good shirt with tab collars, a black leather waistcoat and Cuban heel boots. The Who were promoting themselves as being a Mod band but John was dressed like a Rocker, with big sideboards, but it didn't matter what he wore or anything. Roger Daltrey had a pair of loafers, like slip on shoes, that I really, really wanted.

When The Who played in Manchester in 2000, I went with a mate. It was the best live concert I've ever seen, and I've seen a lot. On the tram into Manchester, my mate said, 'I've actually seen these in Altrincham, you know.' We've been mates for something like 40 years and we'd never discussed it. I said 'I was working on the bloody stage that night.'

15 APRIL 1965
VICTORIA BALLROOM, CHESTERFIELD, UK

JOAN ROWLAND, AGE 23

I was working for Top Rank in the same building as the Victoria Hall and went into our changing room to be confronted by these four scruffy lads crashed out and asleep on our settees. I was told they were an upcoming group. I had never heard of them. As staff, we were allowed to attend performances if we chose to so I rang a friend and she came down to join me. Later, these 'boys' went out to their old van to get out their instruments. They seemed to have been sleeping on straw in the back of the van. I went to the ballroom and they began playing. One of them was playing a guitar and made exaggerated circles with his arm as he plucked the guitar strings. Then they started smashing up their instruments, at which point I left, because it looked quite dangerous. My husband has been to see The Who recently and thought they were great. To which I replied, 'They've come a long way since Chesterfield then!'

23 APRIL 1965
OASIS CLUB, MANCHESTER, UK

ADELE KAIN

My husband Pete and his cousin Sue were regular customers at the Oasis Club on Lloyd Street, which was alcohol free and therefore open to teenagers. Pete remembers that he and Sue were aged 16. He said, 'We were standing at the back and the manager of the club was next to me. He didn't think much of the band that was on stage. 'I wouldn't pay that lot in washers!'. The band he was talking about was The Who.'

26 APRIL 1965
TOWN HALL, BRIDGWATER, UK

ROGER BOWERMAN

I'd read in *Record Mirror* about the radical way The Who approached their music, with amp abuse, use of feedback and other innovative sonic techniques. It was a pretty vivid exposition of what they were like live. The impression given was that they were an important west London group following in the footsteps of the Stones and The Yardbirds. This was an opportunity to see and hear them close up. My friend Les had a car and we went over with our girlfriends. I'd never been to Bridgwater Town Hall before. There wasn't a large crowd of interested people in front of the stage so we were able to watch them unimpeded. Their performance more than lived up to the hype in the article. When we went in, 'I Can't Explain' was playing over the PA system and they came out and gave an amazing show. The sheer physicality and controlled aggression of their performance set them apart from any other bands I'd seen.

During 'I'm A Man', the singer walked off stage and didn't come back for some time. There seemed to be some tension between Pete and Roger. Pete shouted to Entwistle 'Where the fuck is Roger?' He had to keep going with all his antics to cover the singer's long absence, with his repertoire of wind milling, blipping out morse with guitar's pick up selector switch and shoving the guitar into the amp covers. He controlled the large amount of feedback he was coaxing through his Rickenbacker guitar to great effect. He also introduced 'Anyway, Anyhow, Anywhere' as their next single before performing it.

When they were packing up their equipment, I stood on a chair in front of the stage and got Pete's attention. I asked if we could have autographs for our girlfriends, which he kindly collected from the other members of the band. He seemed a very nice bloke.

MIKE TUCKER, AGE 15

My diary entry for Monday 26 April 1965 reads:

Meeting ----- at Town Hall, The Who up Town Hall (going). Back to school, rotten day. Walked ----- home from Town Hall.

Not a lot of insight, but what do you expect from a 15-year-old? The Town Hall in Bridgwater had live music pretty much every Monday and many of the people playing there went onto to greater and long lasting things, so we were kind of spoilt for a small town in Somerset. It was the time of my early Mod days and The Who fuelled that along with the Small Faces who played there the following September. Like most 15-year-olds, the interest was girls and music – in that order!

3 MAY 1965
MAJESTIC, NEWCASTLE-UPON-TYNE, UK

EDDIE HOGAN

I saw The Who at the Majestic for five shillings (25p). It's now the O2 Academy. I especially remember Townshend's unusual overhead circular windmill arm movements as he played his guitar.

6 MAY 1965
TWO RED SHOES, ELGIN, UK

NEIL MUNRO

It all started for me by going to see The Beatles, because they were number one! Getting big names to Elgin and the north of Scotland was the work of one Albert Bonici. Later we moved to the Town Hall to see the Searchers, the Swinging Blue Jeans and Brian Poole and the Tremeloes. The Two Red Shoes ballroom, or the 'Boots' as it was known locally, was owned by the Williamson family, big recycling merchants whose business is still on the go. I had heard of The Who. I remember they were quite loud.

TOM FORSYTH

I was the bass player in an Aberdeen-based band called The Delinquents. We played rock 'n' roll standards and Motown and we covered chart songs. Occasionally, we would rehearse at The Lads Club in Hutcheon Street for a couple of hours in the evening and then throw open the doors and play a few numbers for the kids in lieu of payment for use of the hall. On the night in question, we had been rehearsing 'I Can't Explain', by a new band called The Who, which had charted recently.

At the end of the evening, Delinquents drummer Stewart Kemp and I went for a burger and Coke at the ABC Bowling Alley's café in George Street. Stewart stopped in his tracks and said 'that's Roger Daltrey of The Who!' Right enough, there were Roger Daltrey sitting at the counter with John Entwistle. We went across to say 'hi' and started chatting, telling them of the coincidence that we had been rehearsing their son. I asked where the rest of the band were and Roger said that Keith was bowling. Keith throwing the bowls energetically, once on to the lane next to his, and having a great time. He finished his game and joined us.

Roger bought me and Stewart a Coke. He said they were playing The Two Red Shoes in Elgin in a couple of days and that they had hired His Majesty's Theatre, the biggest and most prestigious theatre in Aberdeen, the next day to rehearse for a TV appearance the following weekend. I told him that The Delinquents were playing Elgin on the same night as they were, at the New Elgin Hall. Roger invited us to come along to His Majesty's Theatre the next day to watch the rehearsal.

Next day, I met up with Stewart and we headed for the theatre. The girl at the box office directed us down to the stalls. When we entered the auditorium, we were met by the fantastic sound of the band in full flow doing a song we didn't know. It turned out to be 'Anyway, Anyhow, Anywhere', which was to be their next single. We made our way down near to the front of the stalls and sat down. The band were sounding great, but a guy we took to be their manager and who I later assumed to be Kit Lambert was directing proceedings from the stalls. He would shout up directions, sometimes stopping the band to make a point. He was particularly keen to give Pete Townshend directions as to how to handle his guitar when rubbing it on his amp and controlling the feedback. When the rehearsal ended, Stewart and I went on to the stage for a chat and John offered to sell me one of his bass amps. I declined the offer as I had just bought a new Vox AC50 amp.

Keith and Stewart discussed drumsticks. Keith reckoned that it was better to buy packs of cheap practice ones than expensive high-end sticks. The poorer-quality wood meant they broke more easily, meaning more sticks he could throw into the crowd as souvenirs. As we parted, Roger told us to look them up at the Two Red Shoes in Elgin after our respective gigs.

Next day, The Delinquents headed north and we played our set at the New Elgin Hall, after which we loaded our gear into the van and headed over to the Two Red Shoes. The doorman wouldn't let us in, but he sent someone to tell the band that we were there. Roger, Keith and John came out to see us. We chatted for a while and then we said we had to head off home to Aberdeen. As we were about to leave, Keith said: 'Hold on!' He came over and said 'see ya' as he threw a stink bomb into our van. What a hoot! What a stink! We laughed all the 70 miles back to Aberdeen with the windows in the van wide open as we tried to clear the air. It was a hilarious end to a brilliant close encounter with a great band.

9 MAY 1965
DE MONTFORT HALL, LEICESTER, UK

MITCH IRVING

I was in the audience when they appeared on a package tour. The warm up group was The Naturals, then Marianne Faithful, The Who and top of the bill Tom Jones and The Squires – a really diverse collection.

20 MAY 1965
TOWN HALL, KIDDERMINSTER, UK

PETER STUBBS

During the last couple of numbers, Keith ended up with only his cymbals!

21 MAY 1965

The Who release their second UK single,* 'Anyway Anyhow Anywhere'*. It was released in the US on 5 June 1965.

22 MAY 1965
ASTORIA, RAWTENSTALL, UK

MICHAEL SMITH GUTTRIDGE

I played with The Avalons at a packed Astoria Ballroom, supporting The Who. Everyone was eagerly anticipating the headliners. We played our set, as did the other supporting group The Imps. We had to do another set as Keith Moon had gone walkabout in Rawtenstall, borrowing our drummer's jacket. We'd been sharing a backstage area with The Who and they were a friendly lot. Keith was probably the friendliest whereas Pete Townshend kept himself apart a little bit. He was drinking red wine from the bottle, unaware that Keith had urinated in it!

Our drummer, Roy, got to play Keith's Ludwig kit as they stripped down his own and took it off stage to make room for The Who's. Afterwards, Roy commented on the solid sound of Keith's bass drum, which Moon put down to the beater. He gave it to Roy. He also gave Roy a handful of drumsticks, which he still has.

The Who were using an old ice-cream van – the ones with the elevated roof. One of their road crew offered to sell us a Vox 100-watt amplifier. This was something beyond our wildest dreams as we were using Vox AC30s. I think he wanted £100 for it. Apart from the fact we didn't have that kind of money, the amp was stencilled all over with the name of the TV show from which it had been 'liberated.'

27 MAY 1965
PAVILION BALLROOM, WORTHING, UK

WENDY GREENE

I saw The Who on two occasions. Both times they were supported by my ex-husband Dave's band, Mo'Henry. Dave was lead guitarist. At the second gig, he bought a Vox AC30 amp from the Who's roadie, Cyrano, nicknamed because of his large nose. At the Worthing gig, a girl stole Keith's target t-shirt. I was able to tell him which school she went to, but not a name.

DAVE GREENE

We supported The Who that night. When we were packing away our gear at the end of the night, Keith and John and the roadie, Cyrano, came and chatted with us. We were particularly impressed that they had some Vox AC100 amps, the most powerful you could get in them days, which I'd only ever seen The Beatles use. One of the three aforementioned said, 'You can buy one from us if you like.' We thought they were pulling our legs, but when the price was mentioned – £15 – we quickly handed over the cash and the deal was done! I think Keith said they had ordered them in for a *Ready, Steady, Go!* appearance a night or so previously and had 'accidentally' forgotten to leave them in the studio. They got themselves quite a reputation for borrowing gear, mainly from Sound City, and then 'forgetting' to return it. I don't know if they just took a shine to us that night or if they had a regular sideline going.

I had the pleasure of meeting Mr Moon again in 1970. I had just joined a prog rock band called Raw Material and we were playing in a private late night drinking club somewhere in Kensington. We had just gone into our tiny 'dressing room' to take a break when who should walk in but Moonie. He said, 'Just come to say well done lads, and keep up the good work,' and handed over the bottle of Scotch he had been swigging from before disappearing into the night. I always thought that was a great gesture. How many other people of his stature would have taken the trouble to say hello to a bunch of unknowns?

JANE MELHUISH

Growing up in Worthing, West Sussex as a teenager in the Sixties meant going to the Pier or the Assembly Hall on a Thursday night. Apart from The Beatles and the Stones, all the top groups played there. We'd take the 106 bus, buy ten No.6 ciggies and pay five shillings (25p) admission for a lesser-known group, 7/6 (37p) for a famous one. We were friends with local group The Total, who supported many bands, so we were allowed access backstage. I was there for The Who's performance in 1965 when Pete Townshend smashed his guitar up. Afterwards, we were backstage and, trying to be helpful, I carried some of the drums down to their van. Roger Daltrey said, 'Don't drop any of that!' Nice, eh?

DATE UNKNOWN
LAURIE GROVE BATHS, LONDON, UK

JOHN STARKEY

Laurie Grove Baths were Victorian public swimming pool and slipper baths in a narrow street located behind Deptford Town Hall. The main pool was surrounded by individual changing booths. The building had a gabled roof with partially glazed sections and was supported by metal rods across, from side-to-side and with vertical rods from these up to the roof apex. All this generated quite an echo chamber effect. The pool area was boarded over for social events and I don't think the pool underneath was drained out. I used to go swimming there during the day time on occasions. Detailed recollections of The Who are sadly sparse, but I went to one of their live 'gigs' – we called them dances or hops in those days. This must have been in autumn 1964 or 1965. The event was organised by the Art School social secretary, who organised some very good events with live bands at Goldsmiths College.

The Art School social events were even then what today would be called a bit edgy. The Bonzo Dog Doo-Dah Band played at a number of events while I was at Goldsmiths. I think the lead singer Vivian Stanshall was in the Art School at some time. The only other celeb alumni I was aware of then making their way in the world was Mary Quant. One of the Art School's early Balls led for a while to a ban on such events, as three summons were allegedly issued after one I attended – too much noise, selling more tickets than licensed for and no license for a stripper!

I remember the poster advertising The Who dance with the iconic O with its arrow pointing to two o'clock – an abbreviation for the male gender. Regrettably, I cannot remember any of the songs played during this gig, but I do remember that they smashed up all their kit at the end! The venue for this dance was comparatively small and it was standing only, but I don't remember it being particularly packed out. There was still room to walk about and dance nearer the stage. Somewhere in my head I have a figure of £30 as the cost to hire The Who.

I remember listening to 'My Generation' on pirate radio. The stuttered 'f's in 'why don't you all fffff away' was chanted by us students in karaoke fashion and considered very daring. I don't think Kenneth Tynan had yet said the 'f' word live on television.

10 JUNE 1965
BOWES LYON HOUSE YOUTH CENTRE STEVENAGE, UK

MARY ABRA

I went to see them with my sister Margaret. Margaret has an entry in her diary on Thursday 10th June 1965: 'Went to see The Who. Cost me 5/-. Alan chucked me, almost lost my coat, nearly suffocated & crushed to death and my foot started to hurt.'

Poor Margaret. It doesn't sound as though she had a very nice time! I just remember Keith Moon threw his drum sticks out to the crowd at the end of the performance.

This appearance by The Who at Bowes Lyon House is not recorded elsewhere.

13 JUNE 1965
MANOR LOUNGE, STOCKPORT, UK

COLIN JOY

The Manor Lounge was a former café set in the basement of the Wellington Picture House. Unlicensed, it could hold up to 1,000 people and the roof was covered with egg boxes as soundproofing to avoid annoying the picture-goers above. Bands like The Who, Cream, The Yardbirds, Long John Baldry, the Small Faces and Pink Floyd would turn up and play unannounced, and you might find Pete Townshend or Freddie of Freddie and the Dreamers having a pint in the pub across the road. As a music venue it was Stockport's version of the Cavern Club in Liverpool. The Who should have played the venue in May 1965 but their van had broken down on the motorway. We had heard of the band through pirate radio. They were classed as Mods – the equivalent of northern Rockers who were drenched in the Mersey Beat sound – so there was a lot of interest in going and seeing them. There were about 400 to 450 people there that night.

The band were dressed in typical plain shirts and trousers-not the late 1960s coloured types of the Carnaby era – and played a very sombre set of covers. They were not loud as they are today, but easy on the ears. The basic set-up was amplifiers and drums but no PA. Townshend had yet to master his trademark clock swinging guitar playing and the low roof meant Daltrey could not throw microphones around. Entwistle was, er, just John Entwistle – he stood there looking bored and never moved. But the highlight of the set was Keith Moon's enthusiastic drumming, emphasising all the words in the songs. Most of what they played was cover versions except for 'I Can't Explain' and 'Anyway, Anyhow, Anywhere'. My brother remembers they started playing some of the same songs again later just to space out the set.

The set was only short – approximately 45 minutes - but after they had finished the band stayed on stage shaking hands and signing autographs in appreciation for the reception they got from the audience. Most bands scarper out of the back entrance quick, but not The Who. They stuck around with the crowd and even joined them in the pub just across the road.

17 JUNE 1965
BOWES LYON HOUSE YOUTH CENTRE STEVENAGE, UK

PETE WRIGHT

The Locarno at Stevenage was a stronghold for Mods and they played there at least four times. But over the road there was a brand-new facility built called Bowes Lyon House. Bowes Lyon was a cousin of the Queen who lived locally. And The Who were appearing there as well. It was a Thursday night.

The Who were on *Top of the Pops* that night, probably for 'Anyway Anyhow Anywhere', and they were going to be flown down from Manchester to Luton Airport after the show and then from Luton airport to the gig. You could cut the atmosphere with a knife. The curtains were drawn. They had four TVs on the stage so we could watch *Top of the Pops*. The Who came on first because they wanted to get away, and they were using somebody else's instruments because, unbeknown to us, their gear was set up on the stage at the Locarno, behind the curtains. The girls in the audience went absolutely berserk when The Who came on *Top of the Pops*. When they finished, a couple of these tellies were dragged out and just thrown over the balcony.

The heat was unbearable. It was about nine o'clock at night and this bloke comes on and he says 'I've had a phone call from the manager. The Who are with him. They're in his car and they're on their way.'

In the end the curtains opened and the audience went berserk again. I was looking at the group and they honestly looked terrified. That was probably the first time they had that Beatles-type adulation. Being on the telly, and the delay in them appearing which allowed the atmosphere to build, was what caused it.

18 JUNE 1965
FLORAL HALL BALLROOM, MORECAMBE, UK

SYD BLOOM

I used to go to the Oasis in Manchester and all over the north to see them, which was relatively infrequently. I remember Morecambe Floral Hall because the place was totally deserted. I was able to park right outside on the promenade. After quite some time, the ticket kiosk suddenly opened up and the old lady there clearly hadn't a clue who or what was happening, but she relieved me of the entrance fee and in I went. I walked in the bar and there was nobody else in the place apart from Roger Daltrey. He was clearly freaking out at the lack of interest in the band. He said 'I can't believe this. We were down at Eel Pie Island and they were queuing for two days to get in.' He bought me a drink and said 'come backstage with us' and took me into the dressing room for a chat and to meet the others. John Entwistle was really nice and extremely friendly. He was musing at length about his surname and whether his family's roots were in the north. Townshend was in another place, completely supercilious and aloof. And while I bet there weren't 60 people there that night, Keith Moon still managed to pick a fight with somebody.

CHRISTINE BOWLES

My friend Anne and I saw The Who the first time they played in Morecambe. We'd seen them on *Ready, Steady, Go!* and thought they were amazing. But the audience only consisted of about 50 or 60 people, as the much better-known Searchers were on at the Central Pier that night and everyone else we knew was going there. Some boys we knew told us they'd sat with The Who in the bar before the show. We stood in front of the stage and it was as if they were playing just for us, although they played as if they were playing to 5,000. I remember Pete Townshend's fingers were bleeding at the end. They had just released 'Anyway, Anyhow, Anywhere', which soon went up the charts, so the next time they came was to a packed Central Pier. They played at the Central Pier at least three times more and I went to see them every time. Keith Moon often threw his drumsticks into the audience at the end and I once caught one. I no longer have it. My brother 'borrowed' it and I never saw it again.

TREVOR OWEN

I was in a band called the Milestones and we supported The Who. Me and the drummer, Paul Wilkinson, set up our equipment in the afternoon and then went to the fairground with Roger and Keith. There was a big dipper ride called the Cyclone, which our friend Bish worked on, and he let us go on for free. Bish never used to come to take money off anybody he knew. We had about four goes round on the Cyclone. That always sticks in my mind, going on the fairground with Keith and Roger.

I play keyboards and guitar. I went down to London for three months. The manager of The Who was going to get me work in Germany playing these air force bases but a lot of them had closed down. He had offices on Edgware Road and he said, 'I've got you a job in London for three or four months at a little place called the Plughole Club.' It was five dinner times and five nights. We ended up down there for three months. But I didn't like London. The worst three months of my life. I haven't been back to London since.

DAVID LONGHURST-PIERCE & DEN MARRISON

Phil & Den and the Flowerpot Men had formed in September 1964 as part of the first intake of students at the new Lancaster University. After intensive practice, a budding impresario organised a list of gigs for us, including booking us to open for The Who at the Floral Hall in Morecambe in June 1965. In those days, tour itineraries were driven by percentages and money, with arrangements made by lunatics who had no idea where places were located. When The Who reached Morecambe, they'd played Stevenage the night before and were due to play Uxbridge the day after. And there was no motorway network to ease the burden.

The Floral Hall stage was big as it had a revolving centrepiece like at the London Palladium. But nobody used it anymore; the gears had worn and it only moved in jerks. The Who's roadie had set up by the time we arrived. Keith Moon's drum kit was enormous. As we stood at the front of the stage, we wondered how one drummer could possibly play all that kit.

Keith turned up at around 3.30pm and spent the next two hours practising. We set up around all the other kit amidst the deafening sound of Moon's drumming and then left him to it. At 6.00pm, we returned for our sound check. The Who were already doing theirs. Roger Daltrey apologised and reckoned they would be 20 minutes more. They finished and while Moon made more noise and Townshend played around with a few adjustments, Roger came to chat. 'You guys are a bit cramped for space up there. I'll shift a few things around to make it a bit easier for you.' He did. 'Don't worry about that huge drum kit making yours look like a toy set. We have a cover for it so you can't see it when you're playing. I'll get it put on when he's finished.' He did. 'I'm not too happy with the PA. What do you think? It's got too much treble for me. Yeah? I'll get them to take a bit off. Yeah?' I nodded. He did. 'You played here before? Bit rough, isn't it! There's only one bloody dressing room and that's the size of a khazi. Pete's had to perch in the corridor. What are you lot doing?'

It was clear that Roger Daltrey was the leader of The Who. He was off towards the stage, shouting at Keith to stop so we could do our soundcheck. Keith took no notice. He yelled again from the edge of the stage. No response. Then Keith paused, put down his sticks and leaned forward to adjust a hi-hat. Roger didn't need a second chance. He jumped onto the stage, yelling a stream of expletives, explaining there was work to be done and telling Keith to get his butt into the dressing room – else! Pulling a funny face, Keith Moon ran off backstage. Roger jumped back onto the dance floor. 'Prat,' he said, as he walked past. 'See you later.' We got on with our sound check.

That night the Floral Hall was full to bursting. The dance floor was full, the atmosphere electric and we played our best set yet. We finished, and for the next 20 minutes, you could feel the tension build. With The Who positioned on the stage, the lights came up on just as Keith Moon and Pete Townshend hit drums and guitar chords simultaneously. It was so loud people were holding their ears. There was no tune for a couple of minutes and then John Entwistle's spotlight was raised as he joined in with a bass run to add to the decibels. Roger Daltrey emerged from the back of the stage and the noise evolved into a Motown song that was at last recognisable. They played for over an hour to rapturous applause that was akin to worship. We had never experienced anything like it. Townshend wasn't so much playing his guitar as waging war on it. He'd broken strings before halfway and simply played another instrument. There were no notes, just chords! Nor had we seen anything quite like Keith Moon. Rhythm? Hard to tell! Beat? Lots of it! Noise? It was nuclear! This wasn't a drummer. This was a demented, double-jointed windmill battling against a hurricane!

John Entwistle was playing his bass like a lead guitar; the runs were picking out melodies, playing so loud that everything in the building was vibrating. Did we like this cacophony? Not much! It was noise. What we did like was the new, improved Roger Daltrey! Sometime between The Detours, when Den had first seen him perform, and The Who, his voice had acquired a range, a power and a tonal quality that were all of a new dimension. They finished. The audience slowly drifted away. We moved our kit from the stage and gathered in the corridor where Pete Townshend had re-perched. He was sat on an amp, messing with a guitar and wearing a vacant expression. He ignored us. Moon and Entwistle had gone. Roger Daltrey came out of the dressing room. 'Hey! Thanks, lads. Keep at it. You never know in this game!'. The two of them were off to the stage door for the signing and screaming.

27 JUNE 1965
STARLITE BALLROOM, GREENFORD, UK

CHRISTINE MACLEAN

My three friends and I had the opportunity of a lift to the venue and back, so I am not sure exactly where it was but it was so exciting to be in a London venue. The room was filled with Mods in the latest fashions and all dancing the latest dance craze. We got fairly near to the band, although we were not allowed to stay until the end. We were overawed by the experience and took that dance back to Stevenage and proudly showed off our new moves at the next opportunity. Luckily my boyfriend, later my husband, was also a Who fanatic.

28 JUNE 1965
MANOR HOUSE BALLROOM, IPSWICH, UK

JOHN MOORE

It was the shortest set that I can recall there, lasting no more than 30 minutes, but it was long enough to see what an amazing drummer Keith was. Promoter Ron Lesley had booked them before 'I Can't Explain' hit the charts, so they only received a fee of £400 and they were doing the minimum possible to fulfil their contract. Ron booked them in Ipswich again on 1 November 1965 at St Matthews Baths, no doubt at a much higher fee. My friends and I didn't go, in protest at the abbreviated nature of the earlier event.

DAVID GOODWIN

By the end of 1964, middle of 1965, the whole Mod scene was done. It wasn't cool anymore. But 18 months later, there were still these people zipping around on chrome-plated scooters with aerials on them. The genuine Mods were '64, not '66. Although it got a lot of publicity, it was not a large circle of people. The Teddy Boys, the Rockers, were a little bit older than the Mods. To me it was just an excuse for people to turn up and have a barney.

7 JULY 1965
MANOR HOUSE, LONDON, UK

WENDY GREENE

After seeing them in Worthing, Dave and I also went to the Manor House in north London to see them but I was taken ill. As we were leaving, Keith Moon recognised me and waved and came to the dressing room door. A fan had cut a lump out of his and John's hair at the Worthing gig and I'd neatened it up for them. I kept the off-cuts until recently, when I sold them along with their autographs and a picture.

9 JULY 1965
LOCARNO BALLROOM, BASILDON, UK

ROY KEBBELL, AGE 18

I travelled from Southend with my two brothers on an Eastern National 151 bus. It was a very exciting performance with animated performances from Townshend, Daltrey and Moon.

Entwistle was quite impassive. When the band were not playing, they wandered around the ballroom. Townshend was just as surly then as he appears to be today.

CHRIS STEVENS

I was the drummer in one of the support groups, The Premiers. The other band on the bill was a more accomplished local outfit called The Monotones. Our band was Canvey Island-based and a bit of a youth club band, all very young at 15-16ish, so supporting The Who was a big deal for us. The previous year we won a local 'battle of the bands' competition, beating an embryonic Dr Feelgood, then known as The Heap and featuring Wilko Johnson. Wilko later went on to make the *Going Back Home* album with Roger.

11 JULY 1965 ST GEORGE'S BALLROOM, HINCKLEY, UK

MERVIN WALLACE

Of all the groups that appeared at 'The George', most eagerly awaited were The Who and the Small Faces. This night will always be remembered by the 300 or so teenagers that were there. The stage at The George was minute by today's standards, about a metre high from the ballroom floor and dropping away about a foot on the band's side. There was even less space on their return visit on 26 March 1966 as three bands played that night. Both Keith and Pete were, we suspected, drug-fuelled for the performances we saw, but the mayhem was kept on the small stage, out of harm's way.

14 JULY 1965 LOCARNO BALLROOM, STEVENAGE, UK

LYNNE WALTERS

Stevenage was very much a Mod town. The Mecca was a traditional old-fashioned dance hall and Saturdays were over 21s night. Wednesdays, however, were for us teenagers and was the best night of the week. Every other week there was a live band. In just over a year we saw the Rolling Stones, the Swinging Blue Jeans, the Hollies, the Dave Clark 5, Them – and The Who. The Who were very much a Mod band then. They appeared several times and were at their most anarchic and raw, with Pete Townshend smashing up his guitar and amplifier at the end of each night. Their following tended to be Mod boys who liked to dance quite manically in a crowd, usually having taken a few pills to give them energy. But my most vivid memory of those concerts is of two classmates getting in the back of the van with The Who after the show, an activity the girls referred to as 'Who rolling'!

PETE WRIGHT

Pete had these Vox Beatle amps, one of which had a Union Jack over the front. They hadn't gone over to the Marshalls at that time. Back at the Locarno, they had the big Marshall 8x12 cabinets. Everybody else had tiny Vox AC50 amps. They had a big band there every Wednesday. Keith had this double bass drum kit which no one had ever seen before. And Pete was switching guitars. When it got to 'My Generation', he did swap from a decent guitar to a cheapie, which he then smashed up. I always remember that transition.

One time they were at the Locarno, Heinz had been there. They had scaffolding in front of the stage for him to hold the women back. And they left the scaffolding there for The Who the following Wednesday. We had got chatting to these two girls at the Bowes Lyon. One of them was a blonde and she'd made the acquaintance of Keith. When they were at the Locarno next time, she was right at the front, leaning against this scaffolding and she had an overnight bag with her. And we saw the other girl and she said, 'Yeah, she's going back to London with Keith afterwards.' I'm sure he was married to Kim at that time, and this girl was the spitting image of her. The other girl subsequently went off with Reg Presley of the Troggs.

From then on. I used to buy *New Musical Express* and see them whenever I could. I'd go to work as an apprentice and I had a motorbike and it'd get to 3pm in the afternoon and you'd think, 'How can I get home, have a bath, have my dinner, get changed and get to Reading (or Aylesbury or somewhere) on my motorbike?', with a 1950s motorbike in 1966. If I hadn't have done that, and if I'd paid a bit better attention to my job, I might have done better than I did at work. At this point, you could go and see The Who twice a week for five bob (25p) if you could get there.

16 JULY 1965
ATHLETIC GROUND, CHELTENHAM, UK

MIKE CRAWSHAW

I was walking through town to the gig with a few friends when a Transit van pulled up alongside us. Pete Townshend, who we recognised immediately, stuck his head out of the door and said, 'Oi mate, where's this Athletic Ground we're playing then?' We all joined in supplying instructions, the door slid shut and off they went. If I'd been a bit sharper I could have said 'give me a lift and I'll show you'. When we reached Albion Street, where the venue was situated, there was a mass of state-of-the-art scooters parked up, as far as the eye could see. Many of these belonged to the London Mods, who had come down to support their band. We were in awe! I have seen The Who many times since over the years, through their great and not-so-great times, and reminisced over this gig when I bumped into John Entwistle in a bar in Cheltenham not long before he died. He remembered the gig fondly.

ALAN CONDY

My girlfiend Mary, now my wife, and myself attended both the Cheltenham gigs they played in 1965. The support band on this occasion was The Yardbirds, featuring Jimmy Page on guitar. I still remember wondering why he was playing his guitar with a cello bow. The Who were the most exciting best live band we have ever seen. We also got see them at the O2 a few years ago, with Keith and John playing along on the big screens, and that was amazing too.

JIM DILLON, AGE 18

It was a warm July evening and the Kinks and the Yardbirds were also on the bill. I was just exhilarated to be at a rugby club gig, I remember drugs being bandied around, although I didn't participate. We had a couple of drinks and I had a great evening. We were mesmerised by the way Keith could juggle his drumsticks and play simultaneously. The Who were so iconoclastic that they were worshipped for the sheer audacity of their performance.

KEN DOUEL

It was an outside concert organised by Cheltenham Rugby Club, hence myself and friends who were rugby players at various Gloucester clubs went. I would have been the main guy wanting to go as I was music mad, especially the blues aspect that both groups were playing at the time. The price was ten shillings (50p) but being tight buggers, we found a way in without paying. My memory of the whole event would have not been aided by plenty of drink, which was the norm for a weekend. The band members were in one of the marquees having a drink. They were just a bunch of Sixties lads.

MAURICE RUSSELL, AGE 20

There wasn't a very large crowd. I went to the concert to see the Yardbirds, who were headlining. I stood near the front. I remember Roger Daltrey was wearing pin-striped trousers and a girl said to him 'I like your trousers'. He shouted back, 'They are pyjamas!'. The Yardbirds were good – but The Who stole the show!

BRIDGET WARD, AGE 16

I have kept my ticket all these years, which still shows the little rip on the left which they did when you entered. I wasn't quite 17 and it was probably the first concert where we did not sit down but danced in awe of the loud music. They were dressed strange and that the music was loud. It was wonderful!

CHRIS WATSON

It was an evening rock concert, run by the rugby club with a makeshift stage outdoors. We were stood out on the field. It started at about half seven and went on until nearly midnight, three

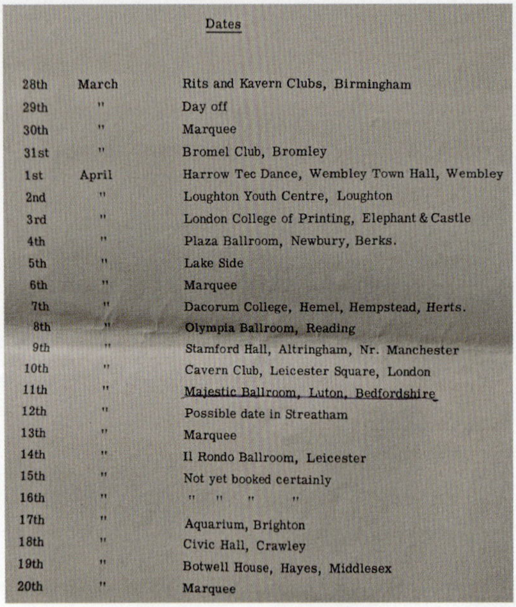

Dates

28th	March	Rits and Kavern Clubs, Birmingham
29th	"	Day off
30th	"	Marquee
31st	"	Bromel Club, Bromley
1st	April	Harrow Tec Dance, Wembley Town Hall, Wembley
2nd	"	Loughton Youth Centre, Loughton
3rd	"	London College of Printing, Elephant & Castle
4th	"	Plaza Ballroom, Newbury, Berks.
5th	"	Lake Side
6th	"	Marquee
7th	"	Dacorum College, Hemel, Hempstead, Herts.
8th	"	Olympia Ballroom, Reading
9th	"	Stamford Hall, Altringham, Nr. Manchester
10th	"	Cavern Club, Leicester Square, London
11th	"	Majestic Ballroom, Luton, Bedfordshire
12th	"	Possible date in Streatham
13th	"	Marquee
14th	"	Il Rondo Ballroom, Leicester
15th	"	Not yet booked certainly
16th	"	" " " "
17th	"	Aquarium, Brighton
18th	"	Civic Hall, Crawley
19th	"	Botwell House, Hayes, Middlesex
20th	"	Marquee

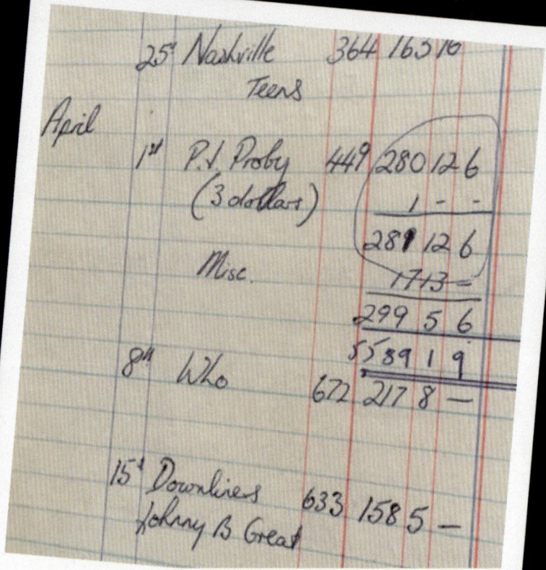

25th Nashville Teens 364 163 10
April
1st P.J. Proby (3 dollars) 449 280 12 6
1 - -
281 12 6
Misc. 17 13 -
299 5 6
589 1 9
8th Who 672 217 8 -
15th Downliners Johnny B Great 633 158 5 -

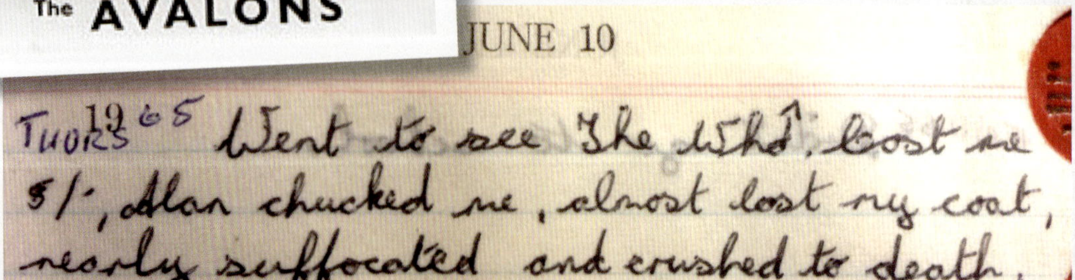

JUNE 10

1965 THURS Went to see The Who, lost me 5/-, Alan chucked me, almost lost my coat, nearly suffocated and crushed to death, and my foot started to hurt.

Clockwise from top left: Maureen Browning's 1965 tour schedule from the fan club newsletter; Stephen Reid's dad put The Who on at Reading Olympia; Wendy Greene first saw The Who in Worthing; Margaret Abra's diary entry on seeing The Who complete with arrowhead; Michael Smith Guttridge's band The Avalons supported The Who at the Rawtenstall Astoria.

FESTIVAL FRINGE EVENTS

ATHLETIC GROUND
FRIDAY, 16th JULY. Dancing 8-1 a.m.

BIG BEAT

THE YARDBIRDS THE WHO

Shades of Blue PARLOPHONE the HELLIONS PYE

Tickets 8/6 in advance from Town Hall, 10/6 on the day. Full Bar and Catering.

Clockwise from top left: Christine Bowles opted for The Who over the Searchers; Cheltenham ad from Mike Williams; Chris Stevens' band The Premiers were support for The Who in Basildon; Ken Douel found a way to get into the Cheltenham gig without paying; Maurice Russell was at the Cheltenham Athletic Ground.

bands with The Who in the middle. The Ravens were a local girl band. They weren't very good but I suppose you have a local band to open. They were followed by The Who, who created more interest than The Yardbirds, whose lead guitarist then was Jeff Beck. If that had been on tour round the country, The Who would have ended up headlining.

Their gig was brilliant. They had a Mod following which was a new wave, a bit of a social phenomenon, a new way of dressing. They were doing the Motown thing, performing 'Dancing in the Street'. Some of the Mods got up on stage and were doing the Mod dance. I suppose I was a Mod, although I didn't get up on the stage.

The Who smashed most of their stuff up at the end. It was a very visual thing. I hadn't seen anything quite like that. I was fascinated by them and I loved the music.

A whole fashion industry came up with The Who, with the hairstyles and the different things, and everyone was dressing like that. The Who were the band that everybody followed if you were Mod. It was all very fascinating at the time. They're iconic now. But back then it was new; the beginning of something different.

MIKE WILLIAMS, AGE 18

The gig was in the open air and The Who were the main support band. One of the other support bands was the Hellions, who had Jim Capaldi and Dave Mason in their ranks, both of whom went on to play with Steve Winwood in Traffic. So there I was, going into the Athletic Ground, and I saw Keith Moon and Roger Daltrey stood together by the gate and chatting about how big the crowd was. I was struck by how short in stature they were.

When they came on stage, a few of the crowd shinned up the rugby posts to get a better view. We had never seen anything like this before and what followed was explosive. The Who wore all this coloured Carnaby Street gear, including bullseye logos, pop art, Union Jack – the lot! They had this amazing strobe light show, which is common now but wasn't back then, and they brought their own travelling fans and dancers from Shepherds Bush. We even saw them share the stage with the band at times which, again, wasn't the done thing then. Then there was boys dancing together and we thought that was odd. It was also strange to see dancers on their own. The whole experience was a ground breaker.

The Yardbirds followed and, although they were good musically, it was such an anti climax.

After the gig, my friends and I hung around and followed the band as they made their way to the railway station. We saw Pete Townshend and Roger Daltrey on the platform, waiting for their train to London. I'm not sure where Moon and Entwistle were.

OLD GEEZER

The Who and the Yardbirds were playing a 'Battle of the Bands' at the Cheltenham rugby ground. We already had a flimsy friendship with The Who, originating with my girlfriend's acquaintance with John Entwistle, and I had made contact with Keith Moon in The Ship in Wardour Street, Soho, across the road from the Intrepid Fox, the two pubs favoured by most of the beat groups, including Rod the Mod. For a few short months, we were staying in Cheltenham and The Who were about to play in our new home town. As usual, we couldn't afford the ticket price for two. Leaving my girlfriend at the front gate, I made my way round the back streets, following a couple of adventurers bent on finding a way of bunking in. We came upon a street of small terraced houses butting up against the back of the grandstand. Up a drainpipe, on to the roof and along to the front end. There we had to slide down onto another lower roof and then onto the ground.

There I went, bumping and sliding downwards, to end up with a bang in the open-air gents' urinal and who should be standing facing the wall but Entwistle and Moonie? 'Oi, oi, what's up?' 'Well,' I said, 'the girl is outside by the gate and we can't afford to get a ticket.' 'Okay,' said Moon, 'we'll sort that,' and he immediately started climbing the wall to the street outside, as I was watching his brown trousers split right up the bum seam. But a few moments later he was back inside the gate with her alongside. God knows how he explained himself to the gate keeper. I don't remember much of The Who's set, but I do recall watching the Yardbirds with Keith Relf up front. Whether it was Jeff Beck or Eric Clapton on lead guitar I could not be sure.

That night, a couple of the band turned up at our rented flat in Lansdowne Crescent as we'd promised a party. Roger Daltrey was in his brand new top-of-the-range black Austin Westminster and three of us went for a little spin down the A4 to look for a mate who had hitched to Bristol to score some smoke. The old two land road was slow and we were looking into passing vehicles when we spotted him in the cab of a lorry. It was near a roundabout and Roger turned the car around to catch up with them. We flagged the driver down and brought our mate back to the party. It was a great night.

17 JULY 1965
TOWN HALL, TORQUAY, UK

LEE BROWN

I was in a band called The Hunters and we supported them. There was some sort of tension between Roger Daltrey and the rest of the band and they said 'we're not staying over there with him', and so came and shared our dressing room while the other bands were on. Keith Moon gave my then girlfriend, and now my wife, one of his drumsticks; she might still have it. I remember the huge blisters on Keith's hands and the cuts on Pete Townshend's hands from where the guitar strings had cut into them. A few years ago, I was in Kew and walked past a street café. Pete Townshend was sat outside having a coffee. He looked up so I said 'hello Pete'. I didn't want to bother him but he seemed quite friendly so I said 'we played with you as a support band down in Torquay' and he said 'oh, I remember Torquay – sit down and have a coffee'. I sat down and had a half hour chat about his career and life in general. He remembered Lionel and he remembered Torquay, because they played there a few times. He's a very nice man.

LIONEL DIGBY

As a promoter working in Devon and Cornwall, I booked The Who several times, beginning in 1965. I put them on in Torquay more than once, but also at the Flamingo Ballroom in Redruth. I remember Keith Moon was up on a four-foot-high drum riser that was six foot six by six foot six. They had great big speaker cabinets, four on the bottom and four on the top, and Townshend always put his guitar through the same top right-hand speaker every time, so he was only damaging the one speaker each time. He never used his best guitar to do it with. He'd change it just before they did their final number.

I paid The Who £300. That was the top rate for a band that had had two or three hits. I only paid Cream £150 for the warm up dates they played for me. But The Who got so big they outgrew the venues that could hold 1,500, and when they started doing stadiums, they didn't do the ballroom circuit any more. Their charisma grew, their popularity grew, their hits grew. The place was packed even the first time for The Who.

Of course, they still played places like the Marquee Club in London, which wasn't very big. You never got paid very much playing there. I'd go up with some of my bands and do a support there and it would cost you more to get there than what you got paid. It was a grotty place, in a basement, with a big high stage. But playing the Marquee was a prestige thing. The Marquee was always in the papers. I called Torquay Town Hall the Marquay Club for a while.

1, 8, 15 & 22 AUGUST 1965
BRITANNIA PIER, GREAT YARMOUTH, UK

STEVE DUNN

I was the lead singer with a Yarmouth band called The Mi££ionaires and we appeared on several of the Sunday shows including three shows with The Who on the pier. We also played with Donovan, Tom Jones, David Bowie and Dana in 1965 to packed houses on both of the evening shows throughout the season. Robert Stigwood's agent originally employed us to do the 'soundings' at the Yarmouth Hippodrome for the upcoming Swinging Blue Jeans show. We were considered clones of the Hollies and Herman's Hermits, and Stigwood contracted us to play for the summer season.

I still remember Keith Moon wrecking his drums and Pete Townshend demolishing one of the many guitars he destroyed on stage. The group members tended to be aloof with the rest of the artists, probably because they were so far ahead of us all both musically and culturally. They gave the impression that they couldn't care less what people thought of them, which in many ways explains why many of the youth of today have exactly the same attitude. The difference was The Who's incredible talent, which left us as musicians in awe of what they were capable of both musically and in the way they presented themselves on stage. Townshend had that something that Jagger has, that draws their audience towards them and, guru-like, convinces fans that they are unequivocally the best and to be loyally followed, leaving no doubt that the show they have just witnessed is a one and only life experience which no one outside the theatre can be privy to.

REG GARROD

I worked at the Britannia Pier for ten years from 1965, as House Manager and then as Accountant and Deputy General Manager. The Who appeared in a number of Sunday night concerts during this period, doing two shows a night to an audience of 1,511 per show. My main memory is of the night the audience started to leave the auditorium because stink bombs were being let off in the theatre. We asked our security man to go and investigate the source. Much to our surprise, he came back to tell me the culprit was the drummer Keith Moon. He was throwing them into audience from the stage; our general manager, John Powles, had to have a word with their manager. The dressing rooms often contained broken equipment after the shows.

MICHAEL LADBROOKE

To get an opportunity to see a band like The Who on a fairly regular basis was almost too good to be true. My friends and I saw them every time they appeared in the town. We didn't have to queue to get tickets. They were still a bit of an acquired taste even then, and there were more middle of the road acts in Yarmouth on Sunday nights to attract people. The Who didn't have their future repertoire of hits, so a few covers were included, mainly Motown and Beach Boys. There were always plenty of holes in Pete Townshend's amps but this was prior to arriving in Yarmouth. Much to our disappointment, we never saw them smash any equipment.

PAULINE CATTON, AGE 16

I remember going for a day out with my family to Yarmouth in the Sixties. We got tickets to see Donovan and were devastated when he didn't turn up but saw the support act, The Who. They were great, but I remember my dad saying they were too loud. The audience demanded their money back and went to the box office after the show to receive it, so we saw The Who for free and a great show it was.

DON WALKER

I was an apprentice at Rolls-Royce Derby when I heard 'I Can't Explain'. This turned the light on for me. A group of friends from Derbyshire went to Great Yarmouth on holiday and we saw that The Who were playing at the Britannia Pier. Donovan was headlining, although he failed to turn up, along with Dana whose best attributes were her breasts and not her singing. A local group also featured but I seem to remember they were not very good. When The Who came on, the place erupted with the audience yelling 'smash your guitar, Pete.' He did not. When Donovan failed to show, we all expected The Who to come on again but no luck, as the crap local band finished the night. After their first song, the place was empty. Leaving the show, we came across a Ford Thames van that would not start. My mate Stu, being a motor mechanic, dived in to help fix the problem. It was The Who's transport. What a night - and what memories!

The Who are booked to play for four successive Sundays, performing two shows each time, and were co-billed with Donovan. When Donovan failed to appear, The Who refused to play for longer than contracted and the second show was cancelled.

6 AUGUST 1965
5TH NATIONAL JAZZ & BLUES FESTIVAL RICHMOND-UPON-THAMES, UK

KEITH SHURVILLE, AGE 16

My mate John Fensome and I were at the Richmond Jazz and Blues Festival. It was an unbelievable experience. The John Cotton Sound were followed on stage by the Moody Blues and then The Who. Keith Moon lived up to his reputation with some abrasive drumming and Pete Townshend smashed up his guitar. Roger Daltrey never stopped strutting his stuff while John Entwistle strummed his bass as if nothing else was happening around him. The Who were not top of the bill; the final act that dragged the night past midnight were The Yardbirds, with Keith Relf ending the set with 'Heart Full of Soul'. The Tube station was informed the gig was running late and so they held the Tube until everyone got on.

11 AUGUST 1965
BLUE MOON CLUB, CHELTENHAM, UK

ALAN CONDY

The Blue Moon was our local Mod club. It was just a small club with a capacity of not more than 100. The stage was about twelve feet by ten and rather crowded with Keith's drum set and amps, but he was thumping and manic just as we liked it. My claim to fame is that Roger powered his way to the stage past where I was at the bar and trod on my foot. As I turned to see who'd done this, he snarled at me and stormed onto the stage. Best gig ever!

NELSON HAWKES

My late wife and I and our friends saw many groups at the Blue Moon. We had heard of The Who but they were not a huge band at that time and we were used to some relatively big names. We thought they 'dressed funny'. They appeared on the small corner stage, and when Entwistle raised his guitar up, it sometimes hit the low ceiling polystyrene tiles, which he then played up. It was a hot night and so when Daltrey and Moon started to spray the dancers with water from plastic lemon-shaped Jiffy containers, we all rushed to the front – only to find Moon's still contained lemon juice!

CHRIS WATSON

The Who's second Cheltenham gig was a few weeks after the rugby club show. I was a member at the Blue Moon Club. It was only small but a very good venue if you liked live music. It was housed in a big building, with Burtons the Tailors on the ground floor, then a snooker club and the Blue Moon at the top. I don't remember a supporting act for The Who, who were completely defeated by the low roof and the small stage. They went through the repertoire again and smashed the stuff up. Keith Moon was slinging the drums around but it was such a small stage that he was worried about the drums rolling off the stage. I can remember him shouting 'move back, move back'. Townshend couldn't do the windmill stuff because the roof was too low.

MIKE WILLIAMS

The club was the sister club to The Blue Moon in Hayes, Middlesex, which was owned by the Norman brothers, Eddie and John, and Bill Reid. It was on the top floor of a building, up two flights of stairs. The first floor was a snooker hall and the ground floor was Burton's Tailoring, where we used to go to get measured up for our Mod suits. The club was very small and the condensation, low lighting and smoky atmosphere were far removed from today's modern venues. The sound was deafening. The story goes that they were unhappy at their appearance fee and decided to end their set half an hour early.

19 AUGUST 1965
ASSEMBLY HALL, WORTHING, UK

JOHN FEEST

Keith had a small kit and they had small amps. The support band was a local group called The Zabres. Looking back, they were magic days – as we only paid 6/6 (33p) to see them.

20 AUGUST 1965
PAVILION BALLROOM, BOURNEMOUTH, UK

DICK IRISH

It was a ballroom and standing only, so quite a crush if you wanted to see the group up close. The audience was somewhat surprised when Pete and Keith didn't destroy their equipment. I think Pete only destroyed his guitar when he would get maximum publicity for the band.

SUSAN PAVITT (NEE DEVEREUX)

I went with my then boyfriend Tony Reeve. Having only previously seen local bands play, it was something special. We were able to dance as the gig was held in the ballroom. There were a lot of people there.

PHIL PROWLES

When I went to see The Who I was amazed that there were only 30 people there. I thought to myself, 'How can a band of this calibre play to this amount of people? It's going to be different one day.' I wish I'd kept the tickets, but I was only a young lad. You don't realise, do you, that you are sitting on history?

29 AUGUST 1965
KING MOJO CLUB, SHEFFIELD, UK

DENNIS LAWSON

I can't remember ever seeing Pete Townshend smile, despite seeing the group on numerous occasions in the Sixties. I watched them many, many times in Sheffield, particularly at Peter Stringfellow's King Mojo Club, I remember being there when Pete got an electric shock from his Rickenbacker guitar and went backstage in some discomfort. The group continued as a threesome for a couple of songs and it was still a brilliant sound. Pete only came back when Stringfellow appealed for some rubber-soled shoes for him. He continued with a 12-string. Incredible!

The Who's van is stolen from outside Battersea Dogs' Home whilst members of the road crew are inside making enquiries about getting an Alsatian guard dog. The van is recovered in Clapham, minus the group's gear.

4 SEPTEMBER 1965
SPA ROYAL HALL, BRIDLINGTON, UK

GRAHAM PRICE

I played bass guitar in a group called Three Plus One. We supported The Animals, The Hollies, Gerry and the Pacemakers and The Who. The Who were always popular in Bridlington and Scarborough, attracting 2,500 each visit. We supported them twice. On one of these gigs, The Who had just had a full lorry load of equipment stolen and the road crew arrived with brand new Vox gear, a new Stratocaster in sunburst for Pete and a new set of Premier drums for Keith. They proceeded to set up and then test it to make sure it all worked, mainly at full volume! We were in awe at the sight of 500-watt Vox amps and speaker cabs and that unforgettable smell of new electrical gear warming up. When their manager arrived, he said we had to use their gear to avoid moving stuff around but we were not used to this volume. We managed to use our PA system, a 100-watt Marshall, which was quite a rare sight and which attracted interest from their roadies and crew.

Moonie appeared and proceeded to voice his displeasure at the replacement Premier drum kit he was expected to play. He went on to trash it and asked our drummer, Derek, if he could use his Ludwig set. Derek agreed, but pointed out that we would like it back in one piece as we had other commitments and couldn't afford the £1,000 it would cost to replace it. Keith gave it a good work out but there was no damage.

The bass guitar that John Entwistle was playing was a new type, based on a lyre shape with quite large horns, and a big change from the Precision he (and I) usually played. It had a long neck and four extra frets and long headstock that required longer, hand-wound not available off the shelf. He told me he liked it so much he bought two more guitars as he didn't want to be stuck if he broke a string. His guitars travelled with him, hence not being stolen with the rest of the band's equipment. He asked if I wanted to borrow his gear but I had a 1961 Fender Precision bass (number F000137) in Fiesta Red which I loved so declined his offer. Following his death, it appeared John kept every guitar he'd ever owned, 300 plus. That's probably a few more than Pete Townshend has. At the end of the show, Pete broke the neck on the brand new sunburst Strat putting it through the speaker cabinet. I could have cried.

We later talked backstage with the group and the crew and laughed about how busy they were kept with gaffer tape and screws, etc. repairing 'wear and tear' to the kit.

JOHN HALL

I was the drummer in a band called The Roadrunners that, along with Three Plus One, supported The Who at the Spa. We played a kind of blues, a lot of the Stones, a lot of The Beatles and some of the Mersey chart sound. We had a bass, a rhythm, a lead, drums and a singer who used to do tambourine and maracas. I'd harmonise with the singer, with a microphone held between my legs. We were based in Driffield. I'm mentioned in Woody

Woodmansey's recent book. That's my only claim to fame!

Supporting The Who was a massive event for us as a small group. I was 18 or 19 and from a country town, so I was massively excited but a bit awestruck and a bit dumbstruck by the way they performed and by the damage they did to their instruments. I can remember arguments amongst the members of The Who, in the dressing rooms and backstage, about how smashing their instruments was costing more than they were earning.

Moonie always used Ludwigs, the top ones. He'd smashed some drums and looked at my Premier kit but passed on it and went to the other group, who had Ludwigs. My drums weren't the massive make that the others were.

DAVE WESTAWAY

I was a singer in a band that supported The Who. We got £25 for it. We got the gig because we were one of the groups that were on the list and used as residents at the Brid Spa. There would be top line bands on every week. You were gobsmacked by the time The Who had finished. As a band they were brilliant. But I remember them smashing everything up. All our gear was all paid for on hire purchase, and we were paying quite a bit of our wages out to make the repayments, so you can imagine how we felt.

PAT RAMSHAW, AGE 11

My best friend and I would stand outside the stage door and collect band autographs. On one such evening we were there, autograph book in hand, when our attention was diverted to the top of the slope where an open-topped Mini was emblazoned with a Union Jack. Standing to attention in it were four people singing 'God Save the Queen' as it descended the slope towards us. What an entrance! The autograph book has long been lost, but that image of The Who in that Mini will stay forever.

GORDON SYKES

Brid Spa could hold quite a few folks in those days, all standing on the dance floor. It could be quite a crush, but great nights. I have two memories of The Who's two visits. One is of going for a drink beforehand in a nearby bar and finding Moonie 'entertaining' several local girls. The other is of standing in front of the stage alongside a mate who was screaming at Townshend 'don't break it – give me the bloody guitar!' as he repeatedly smashed it into the speakers.

11 SEPTEMBER 1965
IMPERIAL BALLROOM, NELSON, UK

GEORGE GRIMSHAW

I was fortunate to see The Who three times at The Imp, as the venue was affectionately known. You knew there was going to be a wall of sound as the roadies set up the stage with an array of speaker cabinets, far more than their contemporaries used. I counted 40 twelve-inch or 15-inch speakers at the first gig.

During one number, Moon was hitting the drums so hard that one drumstick splintered and flew into the watching throng. At the end of another show, he kicked the entire drum kit off the stage and into the audience. Bass drum, snares, cymbals all went rolling across the stage and ended up in the laps of the seated, screaming girls.

JOE NICHOLSON

They didn't play for long in those days. No back catalogue, so normally a few covers. I remember them knocking their equipment over. But it was the sheer size and amount of speakers that stood out. I'd never seen a band with so much volume. They were loud but good.

STEVE PUGH

I saw them twice at the Imp in Nelson. Aged 16 or 17, I was in a fledgling rock band and we just loved their music. I remember how loud they were, how huge their amps looked, how extensive Keith Moon's drum kit was and how he used every last little bit of it – just how 'together' they seemed, like giants. I felt like they almost didn't see the crowd, that they played for themselves not for an audience; as though it wouldn't have mattered if the place was empty, and as if this is what they did, this is who (sorry!) they were. The Imp was a pretty nasty building with a corrugated metal roof. We used to go to see a lot of acts there (and try to work out what chords they were using). The Who were the only band that got the roof to vibrate in sympathy with their music. Our ears would pop and crackle for hours - into the next day - after a Who gig. They seemed like supermen to us and, me being an aspiring guitarist, this was especially true of Pete Townshend. His technique was so dynamic, essentially rhythm guitar but used as both the foundation for as well as the 'decoration' on every song. He was like a shaman or mystic, a literal whirling dervish... building up to the destruction of guitar ('that's a genuine Strat the mad bugger is wrecking') and speaker cabinet ('bloody hell, that's a 4x12 Marshall cab he's just rammed his guitar into, he is totally off his head!'). His and Moon's acts of violence on their instruments ('omigod, he's just disintegrated a top-of-the-line Ludwig kit') seemed inexplicable shocking, thrilling, sacrilegious and yet satisfying to hard up school kid band wannabes. I saw them again years later, minus Keith Moon, and the fire had gone out. I was glad they didn't do any more kit smashing as it would have been totally phony.

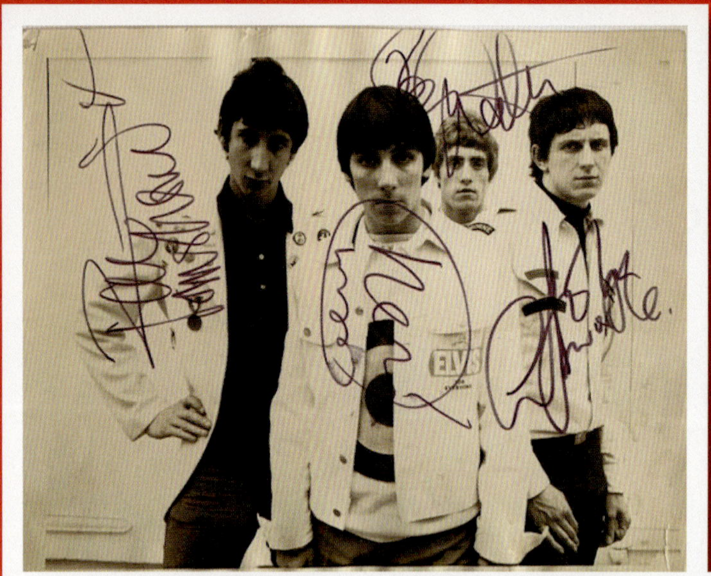

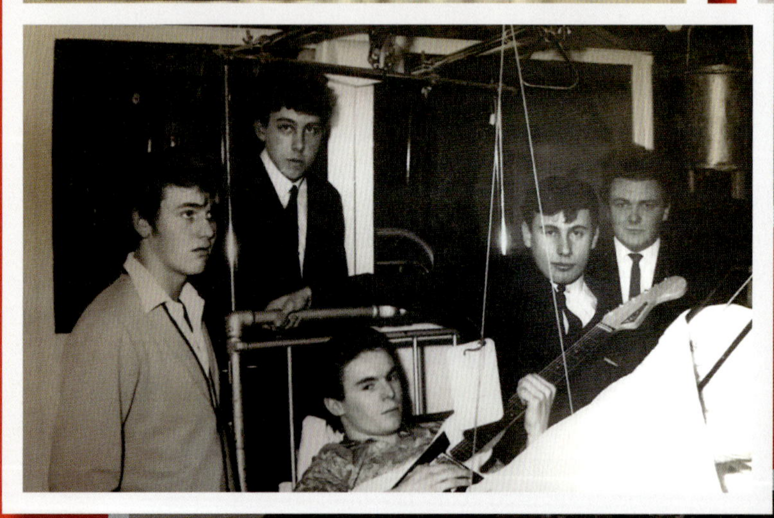

Clockwise from top left: Lionel Digby got a signed photo of The Who, Pauline Catton was at the Great Yarmouth gig and got to see The Who for free after Donovan cancelled; John Feest remembers seeing The Who in Worthing for just 6/6; Steve Dunn was in The Mi££ionaires when they were support in Great Yarmouth; Phil Prowles and his band The Caymen went to see The Who in Bournemouth.

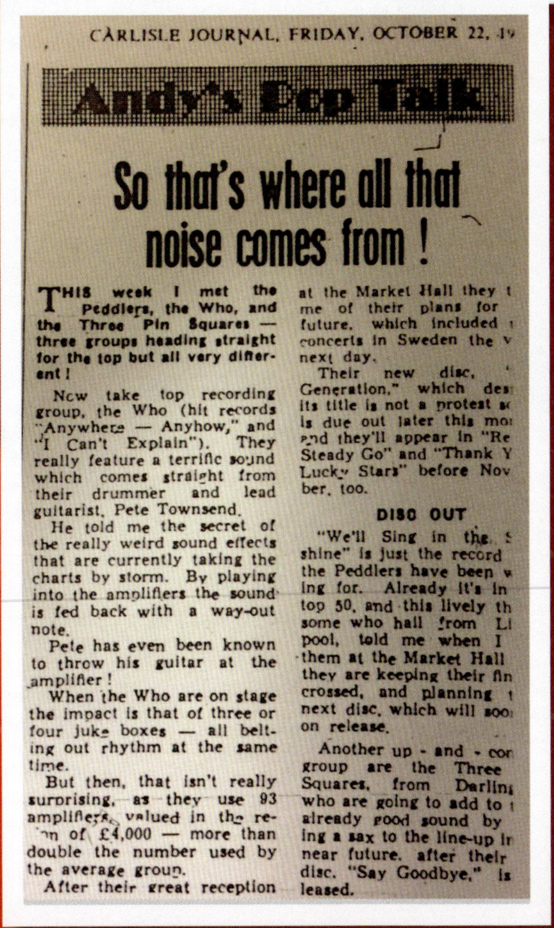

CARLISLE JOURNAL, FRIDAY, OCTOBER 22, 19

Andy's Pop Talk

So that's where all that noise comes from !

THIS week I met the Peddlers, the Who, and the Three Pin Squares — three groups heading straight for the top but all very different !

Now take top recording group, the Who (hit records "Anywhere — Anyhow," and "I Can't Explain"). They really feature a terrific sound which comes straight from their drummer and lead guitarist, Pete Townsend.

He told me the secret of the really weird sound effects that are currently taking the charts by storm. By playing into the amplifiers the sound is fed back with a way-out note.

Pete has even been known to throw his guitar at the amplifier !

When the Who are on stage the impact is that of three or four juke boxes — all belting out rhythm at the same time.

But then, that isn't really surprising, as they use 93 amplifiers, valued in the re-[illegible]n of £4,000 — more than double the number used by the average group.

After their great reception at the Market Hall they t[illegible] me of their plans for [illegible] future, which included [illegible] concerts in Sweden the v[illegible] next day.

Their new disc, [illegible] Generation," which des[illegible] its title is not a protest s[illegible] is due out later this mo[illegible] and they'll appear in "Re[illegible] Steady Go" and "Thank Y[illegible] Lucky Stars" before Nov[illegible]ber, too.

DISC OUT

"We'll Sing in the S[illegible]shine" is just the record the Peddlers have been w[illegible]ing for. Already it's in [illegible] top 50, and this lively th[illegible]some who hail from Li[illegible]pool, told me when I [illegible] them at the Market Hall they are keeping their fin[illegible] crossed, and planning t[illegible] next disc, which will soo[illegible] on release.

Another up - and - com[illegible] group are the Three [illegible] Squares, from Darling[illegible] who are going to add to t[illegible] already good sound by [illegible]ing a sax to the line-up in [illegible] near future, after their [illegible] disc, "Say Goodbye," is [illegible]leased.

Clockwise from top left: Reg Garrod worked at Great Yarmouth's Britannia Pier and remembers Keith Moon letting off stink bombs in the auditorium; Billy Lester's band the Corvettes supported The Who in Bridlington; Andy Park had a pop column in the paper in Carlisle; Raymond Doney saw The Who at The Pill in Milford Haven; Pete Grear's band The Beathovens supported The Who at Nelson's Imperial Ballroom.

9 OCTOBER 1965
MARKET HALL, CARLISLE, UK

ANDY PARK

A guy called Duncan McKinnon ran a company called Border Dances. He used to bring bands up and run them in Scotland Wednesday, Thursday and Friday. But Saturday was always Carlisle, at the Market Hall. It was like a big barn. It held about 1,500 people and the sound was awful. When I was 18 or 19, I had an accident and ended up in hospital for ten months. I went into hospital sport mad and came out pop music mad, because I used to listen to Luxembourg and Caroline in hospital. I started doing a column for the local paper called *Andy's Pop Talk*. I interviewed Pete Townshend after the Market Hall gig and he talked about how he got his guitar sound and the group's plans to tour in Sweden.

A band like Brian Poole and the Tremeloes would have a couple of speakers and couple of amps. When The Who arrived, it took about three hours to set the equipment up. I've never seen as much equipment in my life. They had 93 amplifiers. In them days, lads in bands were interested in the music but also in girls. The Who weren't interested in girls. They were more interested in what sound they could get. It took them a good two hours to get the sound right before they were happy. And instead of standing at the front playing out to the audience, Pete was more sideways, playing into his amplifier so that he could hear what it sounded like.

14 OCTOBER 1965
SKATING RINK, CAMBORNE, UK

OLD GEEZER

We got there early and sat around with Roger in particular as he chatted with a promoter lady called Mrs Smith, who also put on shows at St Austell. Their definitive single, 'My Generation', had recently been released and the PA was not working properly, if at all. I remember standing in front of the stage shouting at Roger 'we can't hear you!' while the others thrashed their way through an instrumental set full of feedback and histrionics, minus vocals. I don't think there were too many people in the audience that night.

22 OCTOBER 1965
PILL SOCIAL CENTRE, MILFORD HAVEN, UK

KEVIN CROTTY

I and three other lads from Pembroke Dock would catch the 7pm Hobs Point to Neyland ferry and drive to Milford Pill every Friday, usually returning home in the early hours on Saturday morning. I remember Keith's drumsticks flying out of his hands. He had a quiver full of replacements which had all virtually gone by the end of the gig. And I remember Roger changing a few words when he sang 'My Generation', singing 'why don't you all fuck off?' instead of 'why don't you all fade away?', much to the amazement of the Sunday school girls!

RAYMOND DONY

Whenever a big name came to the Pill, a friend would hire a bus to take us there from Pembroke Dock. A load of us went to see The Who. I was learning the guitar so was really looking forward to seeing Pete Townshend. The Who came on stage and boy were they loud! Pete Townshend windmilled almost every song and Keith Moon hammered his drums, throwing his broken drumsticks into the audience. I wasn't impressed with the musical content. The only thing I came away with was a headache.

PHILIP GOODRIDGE, AGE 16

I've seen The Who seven or eight times, three times with Keith. This was the first time. I had to beg my mum to be allowed to go. I was a young, little 16-year-old boy and the Pill Social Centre was a rough hole. You could guarantee a fight every time. I'd imagine 200 people would have been the capacity, max, and I thought it was going to be bouncing there but, honestly, I counted the people and there were genuinely only 16 people there. No one danced all night. People looked really bored and I was the only one in there that was interested. They'd had all these stars there like the Hollies, Lulu, Freddie and the Dreamers, the Searchers, and people liked to dance to pop music. No one at all danced to The Who. But I had my elbows on the stage and I watched them play their whole set. They seemed to be going hell for leather. When they finished, I stayed and watched them take all their kit down themselves and I talked to them, mostly to Roger Daltrey. He was my hero and he talked to me for ages. He was really, really nice. I was a Mod then. Well, I thought I was a Mod, anyway. Keith Moon was bouncing off the wall. John Entwistle didn't say anything. Pete Townshend? Well, there he was. I had a drumstick and I had their autographs. I haven't got the autographs anymore because I gave them to a girl I was going out with – or thought I was going out with!

LESLIE GUTCH, AGE 20

Despite being in the sticks, the Pill Social Centre attracted more than its fair share of big name acts in the Sixties. I remember going to see the likes of Tony Rivers and The Castaways, Freddie and the Dreamers, Dave Dee & Co, The Pretty Things and The Hollies. I was there that Friday night when The Who performed. Needless to say, the joint was packed. I was positioned up against the stage, caught in an excited forward press when the band appeared. I was unable to move back and found myself stuck right next to Pete's large Marshall amp. When he struck his first chord I was literally deafened. I could see the veins standing out on Daltrey's neck as he sang and I could see Keith Moon hitting his kit, but all I could hear was a wall of noise coming from Townshend's amp. They were without doubt the loudest band to appear at the Pill in those heady days. I also remember Keith Moon chucking several sticks into the crowd and kicking his kit all over the stage when they finished their set, but no guitar smashing took place on that particular night. I was left partially deaf in my right ear ever after. Many thanks, Mr Townshend!

RUTH WALTERS, AGE 16

I only lived five minutes from the Pill Social Centre so me and my friends managed to see quite a few 'hit parade' bands at that time. It wasn't a big venue. You didn't get big crowds to the events so there was no worry about getting in. You just turned up and me and my friends were always amongst the first. It was a small stage inside and there was a small refreshments area – nothing fancy. I remember Roger Daltrey as being very well groomed and dressed. He looked beautiful in fact. I always remember his hair as being perfect in the then Mod style. Townshend was also immaculate, in a long dress coat. I don't recall Entwistle as he wasn't my favourite, but Keith Moon was, as always, mad on the drums. They were all fabulous. They were all young and they were like gods to us girls. I didn't have anything to wear that night so my mother lent me one of my father's shirts. It was a gold brocade shirt with a collar and with buttons down the front. I wore it with brown trousers. I always was a bit different to everybody else dress-wise, so this suited me on that occasion. As us girls crowded around the front of the stage gawping at the band – there were no bouncers in those days – Keith Moon threw a drumstick into the small crowd at the front. I grappled with another girl and I managed to get the drumstick. What a trophy! I was definitely 'over the Moon' with that. But I tore my father's brand-new shirt in the process, which didn't go down too well with my mother. I didn't care. I had my prize and was the envy of all my friends. That is why I always remember seeing The Who. They were a fabulous band, and my dad's shirt got torn!

23 OCTOBER 1965 THE RHODES CENTRE BISHOP'S STORTFORD, UK

RAY GREENALL

I remember buying the first album at a music shop in Strutton Ground Market in Westminster, where I was at college. I must have lent it to someone because I've not got it any more. We used to go to the Rhodes Centre every Saturday night, regardless of who was on. The Who were obviously a big attraction. I was fairly near the front, on the right-hand side. I remember the drummer of the support band, because they were from Sheering, as I was, and I knew he'd invested every penny he'd got in his set of drums.

When The Who started to smash everything up, the roadies were bringing on spare kit, including drums for Keith Moon. I remember seeing this bright red snare drum with a sparkly finish being brought on. It wasn't Keith's snare, and he knew it. He didn't attempt to play it. He twirled his drumstick around his finger, grabbed it like a dagger and very deliberately stabbed straight through the snare.

The show ended and we were parked round the back, so we came out of the Rhodes and turned left to go around the building, where there was a dustbin area. Keith Moon was lying there in a heap, having been given a bit of a pasting. One of the roadies had asked to borrow the snare from the support band. They'd told the drummer, 'Don't worry, if there's any damage done we'll pay for it in full.' It was his drum that got damaged and when he asked for his money, they told him to eff off. So he took it out on Keith Moon.

The town council banned them from ever appearing in Bishop's Stortford again. It didn't harm their career.

29 OCTOBER 1965

The Who release their third UK single, 'My Generation'.

29 OCTOBER 1965 STARLITE BALLROOM, GREENFORD, UK

VAL MABBS

I have a diary note that says we queued for ages for this gig and paid 9/- (45p). We would get the bus up to Sudbury and then walk along the Allendale Road to the Starlite. They were there a few times, but there was a big queue waiting to see them this time. We were in the foyer and I remember Roger walking up and down the queue, talking to people and spreading the word a bit. I had a conversation with him in later years, when I was working in the music business, and said ow I remembered that he was strutting up and down beside the queue when were there. I think he took it in slightly the wrong way. I wasn't inferring that he was being arrogant. As the lead singer, Roger had to push himself out there, having characters like Moonie and Townshend behind him.

6 NOVEMBER 1965
ST GEORGE'S BALLROOM, HINCKLEY, UK

GRAHAM AUCOTT

I saw them twice at the George Ballroom in Hinckley, once at Granby Halls in Leicester, once at the Lanchester Polytechnic and once at The Belfry golf club. When we saw them at Granby Halls, that was the first time I'd seen Daltrey swinging the microphone out and pulling it back on the cord. They were on a raised stage. That was a good performance. The Belfry was a good performance. The second performance at the George Ballroom that wasn't so hot.

You went upstairs to get in the George Ballroom. You could probably get 500 in there. There was an upstairs bar, and if you could get upstairs to the balcony, you could see out all over the other revellers and the bands. But it was a poor stage and acts had to squeeze through a single doorway. Arthur Brown nearly set the place on fire with his horns.

I can't remember any trouble. You didn't argue with the bouncers up in the George Ballroom. Being local lads, we could get tickets. It felt good. I was a Mod at the time. I had an original American Parka that had jungle instructions on the inside. It used to stink when it got wet. You'd go and park your scooter up in what we used to call the Scoot Cave, which was the back of some shops where there was a lot of robbery going on in those days. If you had wing mirrors, chrome racks and stuff on your scooter, somebody would come round and pinch 'em. But then we'd come marching down and go straight in, hand the tickets in and we were in. The Mods who were coming from Coventry and Leicester were taking a chance and had to queue to get in. It was a good time to be alive. There were lots of things going on and there was full employment, so everybody had a bit of money.

18 NOVEMBER 1965
TOP OF THE POPS, MANCHESTER, UK

DAVE HOUGH

My sister Linda met The Who at one of the very early *Top of the Pops* television programmes and she and her friend got to know them well, to the extent that Linda babysat for Keith Moon for a long time. And Roger Daltrey brought her back home to London a few times.

The Who appeared on the BBC's* Top of the Pops *eight times in 1965.

19 NOVEMBER 1965
GLAD RAG BALL, EMPIRE POOL, WEMBLEY, UK

BRYAN BENNION

I had an Instamatic camera and regularly took photos. The first time I saw The Who was at the Dungeon in Nottingham in October 1965 but later that month I went down to London to see The Who at The Glad Rag Ball at Wembley. I saw them again in 1966 at the Odeon in Derby.

23 NOVEMBER 1965
DOROTHY BALLROOM, CAMBRIDGE, UK

BOB SIMPSON

I was the drummer in the support band the Tykes. The Who were very loud, although not as loud as Jimi Hendrix whom we also supported there, and put on a great performance. I even had Keith Moon wander over to me at the end of the evening and offer to help me pack up my drum kit! He was stoned, with eyeballs the size of saucers. It was not long before Roger Daltrey and a roadie came over and collected him. I have a copy of the ad from the *Cambridge News* advertising the gig. My girlfriend at the time added in 'The Tykes' because we only got the support gig the day before and had missed the newspaper's print deadline.

28 NOVEMBER 1965
OASIS CLUB, MANCHESTER, UK

DAVE BROWN, AGE 17

I saw The Who live on a Sunday night, the day before my 18th birthday. I'd missed them when they'd played the Oasis Club before. 'My Generation' was at No. 2 in the charts, so they had suddenly become big. We queued up outside on the pavement for what seemed like an eternity

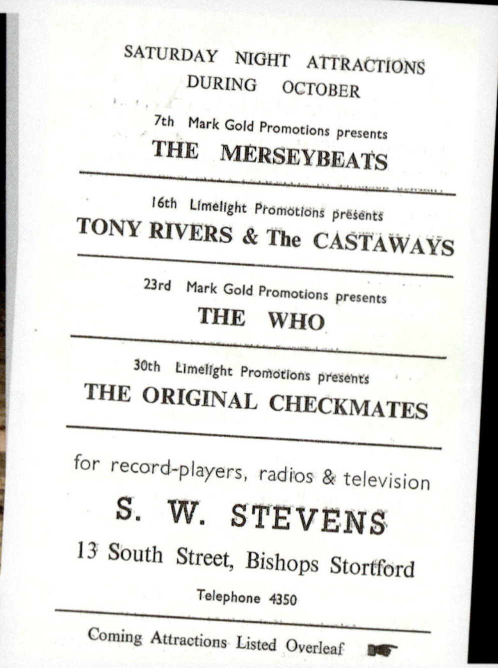

SATURDAY NIGHT ATTRACTIONS
DURING OCTOBER

7th Mark Gold Promotions presents
THE MERSEYBEATS

16th Limelight Promotions presents
TONY RIVERS & The CASTAWAYS

23rd Mark Gold Promotions presents
THE WHO

30th Limelight Promotions presents
THE ORIGINAL CHECKMATES

for record-players, radios & television
S. W. STEVENS
13 South Street, Bishops Stortford
Telephone 4350

Coming Attractions Listed Overleaf ☛

Clockwise from top left: Ruth Walters (second left) got a Moon drumstick but tore the shirt she was wearing; Bishop's Stortford flyer; two photos of The Who in action at the Glad Rag Ball at Wembley's Empire Pool in November 1965 – photos Bryan Bennion; Graham Aucott saw The Who five times.

COME DANCING AT THE

HOBSON ST. Dorothy CAMBRIDGE

TONIGHT

ADMISSION 7/6

THE WHO

WITH THE TYKES

"The Group that cause a sensation everywhere they play"

TOMORROW

IN THE BALLROOM—

PARTY NIGHT for the OVER 20's BALLROOM DANCING to

Bob Kidman & the Dorothy Orchestra

9 p.m. - 1 a.m. Admission 5/-

Entrance - Hobson Street

IN THE 'BEAT' ROOM—

The Dawnbreakers

The Zodiacs

8 - 11.45 p.m. Admission 3/-

Entrance - Sidney Street

SATURDAY

8 p.m. - 11.45 p.m.

Ladies 7/6, Gents. 8/6

BALLROOM DANCING TO—

BOB KIDMAN & THE DOROTHY ORCHESTRA

featuring PETER DEAN at the HAMMOND ORGAN

'BEAT' DANCING TO—

E GLASSMATES (with Angela Dean) - THE TYKE

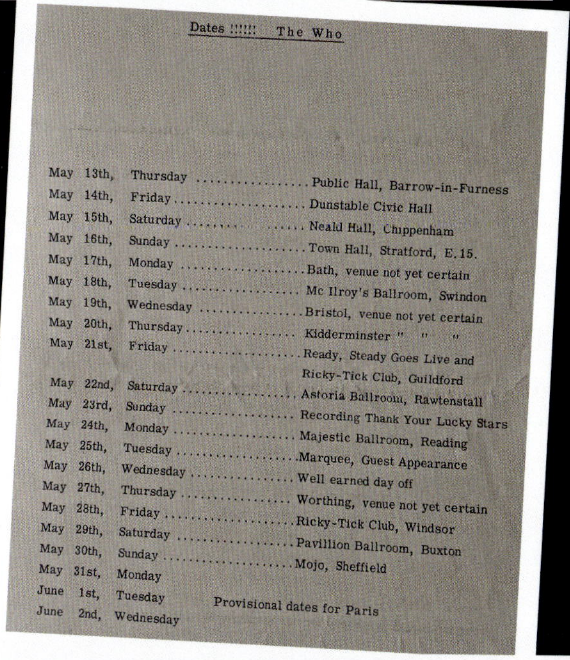
Dates !!!!!! The Who

May 13th, Thursday .... Public Hall, Barrow-in-Furness
May 14th, Friday .... Dunstable Civic Hall
May 15th, Saturday .... Neald Hall, Chippenham
May 16th, Sunday .... Town Hall, Stratford, E.15.
May 17th, Monday .... Bath, venue not yet certain
May 18th, Tuesday .... Mc Ilroy's Ballroom, Swindon
May 19th, Wednesday .... Bristol, venue not yet certain
May 20th, Thursday .... Kidderminster " " "
May 21st, Friday .... Ready, Steady Goes Live and Ricky-Tick Club, Guildford
May 22nd, Saturday .... Astoria Ballroom, Rawtenstall
May 23rd, Sunday .... Recording Thank Your Lucky Stars
May 24th, Monday .... Majestic Ballroom, Reading
May 25th, Tuesday .... Marquee, Guest Appearance
May 26th, Wednesday .... Well earned day off
May 27th, Thursday .... Worthing, venue not yet certain
May 28th, Friday .... Ricky-Tick Club, Windsor
May 29th, Saturday .... Pavillion Ballroom, Buxton
May 30th, Sunday .... Mojo, Sheffield
May 31st, Monday
June 1st, Tuesday Provisional dates for Paris
June 2nd, Wednesday

Clockwise from top left: ad for Cambridge's Dorothy Ballroom with The Tykes; Tony deMarco saw Roger Daltrey deal with a stage invader in Hastings; May 1965 fan club tour schedule from Maureen Browning; The Flowerpot Men opening for The Who at The Floral Hall in Morecambe (left to right) Dave Pierce, Phil Howard, Den Marrison, John Charters & Paddy O'Sullivan - photo Richard Fagence; Maureen Browning's autographed Who photo.

on Lloyd Street and the queue eventually stretched back into Albert Square. While we were queuing, all four of the group arrived and quickly disappeared inside. Not long after, Keith Moon emerged on his own, jumped into a taxi and sped off.

Eventually, we all managed to cram into the club. I can't remember if anyone else was on that night but I do know that the club was on the verge of being wrecked. Keith Moon had not returned and the crowd were getting restless. The compere kept coming on the stage trying to calm everyone down. I remember him saying that they had four of The Who backstage and were waiting for the fifth member to arrive. He obviously didn't realise that there were only four in the group…

Eventually, Keith returned before things turned nasty and away they went. They didn't have a very big repertoire in those days, as they were just starting out. I remember them singing 'My Generation', 'Anyway, Anywhere, Anyhow' and 'I Can't Explain' but I can't remember what else. On 'My Generation', instead of 'why don't you all just fffffade away?' became 'why don't you all just ffffuck off?'! In timely fashion, they smashed up one of their amps.

My mates and I saw a number of groups at the Oasis, including Wayne Fontana, The Hollies, The Move, The Rockin' Vickers, The Moody Blues, The Pretty Things, Manfred Mann, Jeff Beck, Keith Relf, Dave Berry, The Big Three and Pinkerton's Assorted Colours. We went to some of the other clubs around but none were like the Oasis. They were great times.

3 DECEMBER 1965

The Who's first album,* My Generation, *is released, produced by Shel Talmy.

HARVEY KUBERNIK

Shel's tenure with The Who was very brief. In those days, producers and engineers were very involved in the mix. Often the bands would go home and would not even stick around for the mix. Shel is not the guy that some of The Who and some of the Kinks have portrayed him as for decades. I think it has to do with an entry level production deal or production contract. These things happen to people when they are 20, 21, 22 or 23. I think the band has been very cruel to Shel Talmy's brief but potent involvement with them on that first album.

As a producer and engineer, he brought very important technical aspects to the recording of that first album because he'd worked with some surf groups. And he really knew about a louder sound or mic position and stuff like that that I think influenced things like *My Generation*. I don't think he's been given enough credit. Shel Talmy went over there initially for a six week visit in about 1963. He was an engineer out here in Los Angeles. He had experience working at a place called Conway Studios where the guy was an engineer was called Bill Parr. The studios were very advanced out on the West Coast while some English studio engineers were still wearing white lab coats.

Shel was a whizz kid. He either found The Who or he was assigned them – I was never quite sure how it worked. And he probably had a very good solicitor, with very good paperwork on

The Who and the Kinks and a production agreement kind of situation. No bands are ever happy with their first record. That being said 'the producer as star' was a pretty new concept in England. Mostly they were staff or they were record label people doing the supervision. I think Shel had a little bit more to do with it than just supervising the session. He did know a lot about mic placement and tape.

4 DECEMBER 1965
CORN EXCHANGE, CHELMSFORD, UK

WHIZZ BATES

I saw The Who play twice at the Chelmsford Corn Exchange. I lived in Romford which, back in the Sixties, was an hour away. Ten of us would drive right up the door on our scooters. The Corn Exchange was a lovely building – pampas grass each side of the stage and full to capacity with local Mods – who chased us out of Chelmsford, I think because our fashion was more up-to-date! Unless you saw The Who live in those days, you have lost out. They were a very visual act – brilliant guitars and fantastic drumming from Keith Moon, and fantastic singing from Roger. The added bonus, although it might sound mad these days, was the smashing up of the equipment at the end. Great days, and I wouldn't change it for anything.

6 DECEMBER 1965
ELTHAM BATHS, LONDON, UK

COLIN BUSSEY

It was rather disappointing as Roger Daltrey had lost his voice for some reason so was not present. But the rest of the band still sounded good and loud, and made up for him not being there.

8 DECEMBER 1965
CORN EXCHANGE, BRISTOL, UK

ANDY MUNDY, AGE 15

We didn't have purpose-built venues then. Most bands played the market halls in small market towns if they could. The Corn Exchange belonged to the city council and only held 300 – 500 people. It was Bristol's equivalent of Liverpool's Cavern Club. Bands would play the Marquee Club in London, the Corn Exchange in Bristol and then a club in Birmingham, in a triangle.

Even the Stones played the Corn Exchange. A lot of the bands already had a top 20 hit, and it was a dance venue – the bands would play and the girls would throw down their handbags.

I saw The Who play there twice. The stage was built around four palladium-type stone pillars, two of which were the front of the stage. There were these enormous speakers at floor level all over the stage. I was stood no more than ten yards away and I remember Pete Townshend finding these pillars very handy for smashing his guitar. And Keith Moon would obviously smash up his equipment. It wasn't long after the war and most people were careful about looking after their bicycle or the tools in their workshop or whatever. But The Who used to smash up their equipment and you would stand there thinking, 'You're never going to make it if you don't look after your equipment.'

The people who used to turn up were the Mods. It was more-or-less the same old faces that turned up. And it was all smart dress code, long leather coats and smart shirts and ties. All that was on sale was Coke and fizzy drinks so there was no problem getting in. Anadin and Coke was quite popular with people in those days to get their buzz. Then things like bombers came on the market, not that I took these things at all (but I knew people who did). They would be bought, sold and exchanged outside. There were always a couple of police on duty but they never had a clue what was going on!

It all ended at the Corn Exchange in 1967 when the Locarno and bigger venues opened, where the bands could make more money. The Corn Exchange is an indoor market now.

13 DECEMBER 1965
FEDERATION CLUB, NORWICH, UK

TIM CLAXTON

I was there right at the front and could have touched Roger Daltrey's feet! As a Mod born in 1950, they were 'my band.' They were everything I had hoped for, and more. I was shocked when Daltrey sang the 'F' word in 'why don't you all fade away?' But at the end, when I was expecting Townshend to break up another guitar, there was a bonus as Moon wrecked his drum kit as well. The Who left the stage in turmoil with drums, cymbals and broken guitars strewn about. I loved it so much that even today I can still recall those magic moments. I shared them with John Entwistle many years later in a Cotswold Hotel, and what a lovely man he was.

PAUL TAYLOR

I lived in North Walsham at the time and styled myself as a Mod, acquiring a Vespa Sportique – complete with fish-tailed Parka, chrome crash bars, etc. – on my 16th birthday in May of 1965. A few fellow local Mod friends and I went to see the group at the Federation Club. The stage was only two feet high and the crowd gathered on the dance floor immediately in front. This was prior to their guitar and drum smashing exploits. They performed very professionally and did not disappoint.

JOHN WARD

They were due to appear at St Andrew's Hall, a much larger venue, about two weeks before but cancelled through illness. The warm up act was a local group called Lucas and the Emperors, a favourite of ours who played for an hour and a half. The Who came on and played for an hour. The most memorable thing was the sound – it really made your body vibrate. We had not heard any groups as loud. The music was unbelievable, such energy. It was a great time for us. We were about to leave school and we had a real sense of freedom, all down to the music of the time. We were so fortunate to have lived through it. I remember the casual clothes – the shirts, trousers and winkle-picker and chisel-toed shoes. We carried our transistor radios around with us all the time, listening to the pirate radio stations!

SALLY RAMSAY

My friend and I stood near the front. Press reports of the evening were not very complimentary, but as a teenager I was less concerned about the quality of their musicianship than seeing them in person. The venue was crowded and sadly the years have faded my memories in any detail. However, I do remember my friend and I going upstairs to the Green Room after the concert. How this came about, I have no idea. We were certainly not groupies in either behaviour or appearance. I remember Pete and Roger were in the room along with several other people. I had a conversation with Pete who told me he could not read music. He also let me touch his nose! The encounter was short and interesting and, for teenage girls, very exciting. I have a photo of Roger, Keith and John taken with a polaroid camera. It shows them on a balcony. Keith was not in Norwich for the 1965 concert and the Industrial Club did not have a balcony. I must have taken the photo the following year on the Britannia Pier in Great Yarmouth, where they played on 24 June 1966. I didn't go to the concert but the photo is a treasured possession. It's just a shame there was no opportunity for a selfie!

23 DECEMBER 1965
PAVILION BALLROOM, WORTHING, UK

MALCOLM BALDWIN, AGE 21

I went with my friend Steve. My seat was in the gallery which shook quite violently. I seem to remember it was very hot. The music was so loud that I thought the gallery would collapse. It was quite an experience – it was uncanny knowing that the music scene had changed so radically.

PETE SMITH

Loads of acts appeared in Worthing, either at the Pier Pavilion in winter or the Assembly Hall in summer and I saw many of them, including the Small Faces, Jimi Hendrix and Pink

Back to the news -

As you will probably have read in the Musical papers last week, The Who gave up their residency at the Marquee last Tuesday - Kit Lambert gave a party for all who had helped them whilst at the Marquee - everybody seemed to turn up, including Eric Burdon of the Animals, Lulu the Mojos, Cathy McGowan, Lionel Bart, Terry Stamp and Jean Shrimpton, television producers, journalists, disc jockeys - it was a great evening although I'm not sure how everybody managed to get in! There were also quite a few London fans and the whole thing went off very well. The reason for giving up this residency is that the pressure of work all over the country is making it increasingly difficult for the boys to get back to London every Tuesday - however they are going to make a guest appearance once a month, the first being on 25th of this month.

There is a possibility that the group will be going to Paris for about three days at the beginning of next month, this rather depends on when the E.P. is brought out over there. By the way, the French are not doing better than you and the E.P. is to include both sides of the two singles!

There have been so many questions sent in about Roger, Keith, John and Pete that I'd better get on and answer them on the next page or you will never get this letter.

Remember

The Name : ANYWAY, ANYHOW, ANYWHERE,
The Date : 21st May
The Aim : No.1.

Clockwise from top left: Maureen Browning's programme from the Who & Spencer Davis Group tour; Ian Dalgleish's ticket for The Who at Newcastle's Club A Go Go; Jill Carman-Stewart got Roger's autograph on her arm but her mum made her wash it off; fan club newsletter extract from Maureen Browning; Colin Stanley was at Great Yarmouth's Tower Ballroom.

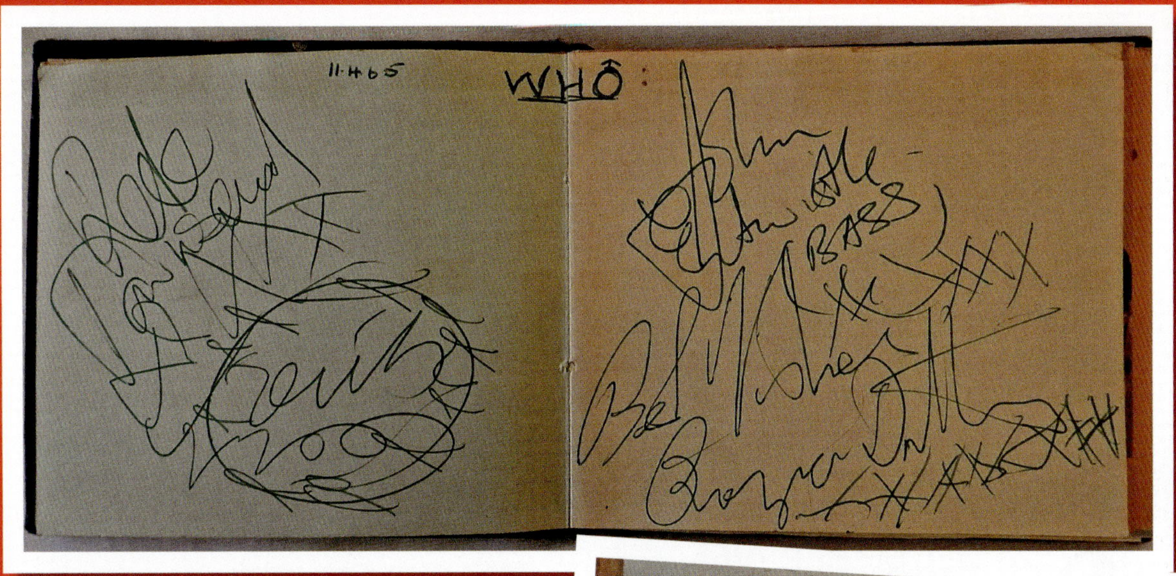

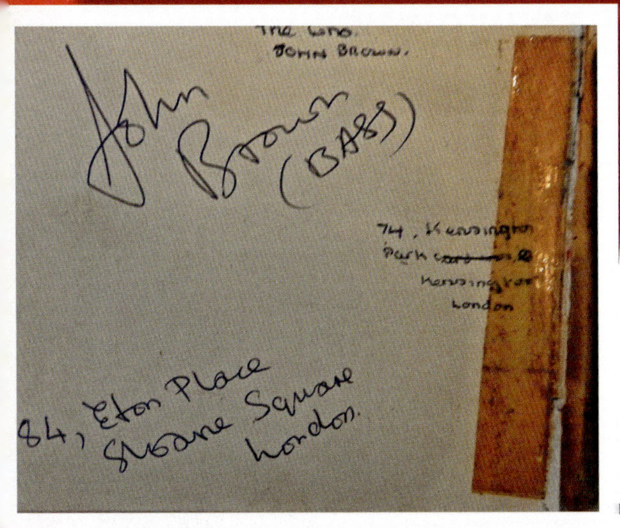

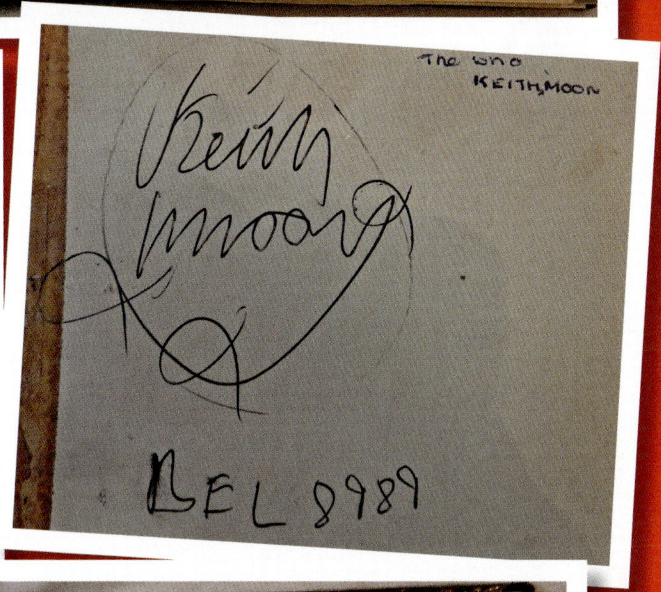

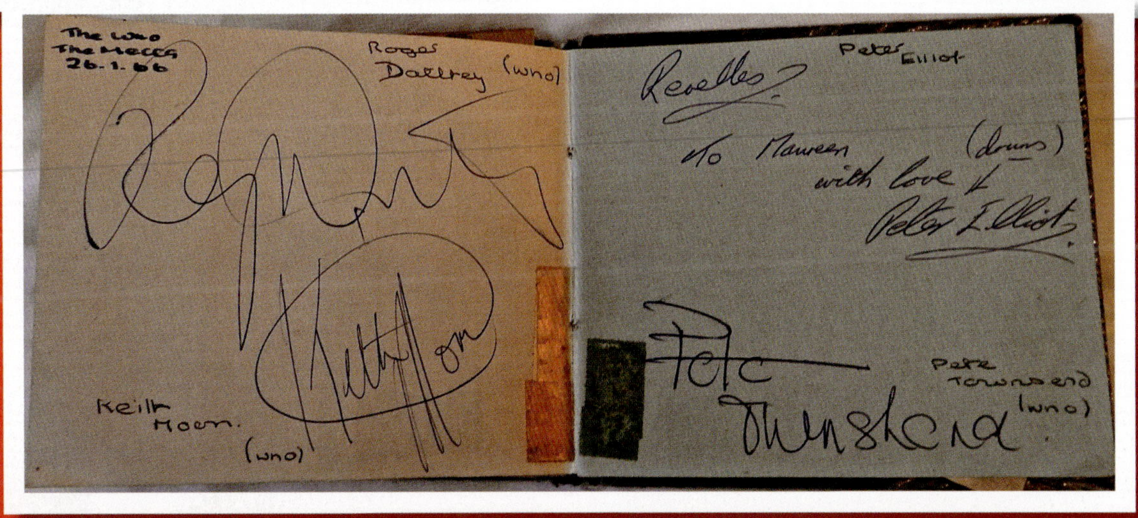

Autographs from Maureen Browning's collection

Floyd. The best was The Who. I first saw them at the Assembly Hall when they had just released 'I Can't Explain' and the last time was also at the Assembly Hall, when they basically performed *Tommy*. On one occasion, we were waiting outside when their van, driven by Keith Moon, drove along the promenade and he called out 'they're not coming' at which some people, not realising who he was, started to walk away, much to Moon's amusement. We also saw Pete Townshend driving himself along the sea front in an old black Morgan hard top. They did perform, and I remember them starting with 'Heatwave' and ending with 'My Generation', at which point Moon threw both his drumsticks and his drums over the top of his head and into the crowd.

24 DECEMBER 1965
PIER BALLROOM, HASTINGS, UK

TONY DEMARCO

My enduring memory of the evening is of some idiot, no doubt the worse for drink, attempting to climb on the stage to accompany Roger Daltrey on 'My Generation'. Roger's riposte was to thump him over the head with the mic, whereupon he collapsed back into the audience.

ANDRÉ PALFREY-MARTIN

Christmas Eve 1965 was the first time that The Who visited the 'Happy Ballroom' as it was known. This tour was in support of their first album. However, despite the 7/6 (37p) ticket price for the first 200 patrons, and 10/- (50p) after that, the hall was only half full. They were playing 'My Generation', which was always the last number. Everyone knew what would happen next and was very hyped up for it. Even Bob Knights, who was the general manager of the pier and who wanted nothing and nobody to cause problems – in his words it was 'my pier' and his word was law – sensed that Pete Townshend was just about to go into his guitar and amp-wrecking routine. The song finished and, in a flash, Bob was on stage. He grabbed the microphone from Roger Daltrey and said, 'Oh, look at the time. It's almost midnight and we have to be out by then. Can I have the curtains closed please, and many thanks to tonight's group, The Who, and to all you boys and girls out there in the ballroom. Go quietly, and take care as the deck is a little slippery with the frost.'

The band were dumbstruck, but even they did as they were told. Truly we all knew who was in control, but that was his way of ensuring a peaceful end to what had been a successful evening.

2 JANUARY 1966
DOWNS HOTEL, HASSOCKS, UK

DAVID GOODWIN

I attended both Who gigs at the Downs Hotel, aka The Ultra Club. I probably saw most of the Sunday night shows there over a period, starting with Georgie Fame and The Blue Flames, the Small Faces, Nashville Teens, The Birds, The Artwoods, The Yardbirds (who failed to turn up), The Hollies, Sounds Incorporated and others I have forgotten.

KAREN TYRRELL

The Who played at the Downs Hotel twice as far as I know. I kept a diary throughout 1965 and 1966 and a note of who I saw there, and also who I saw at a pub called The Pilgrim in Haywards Heath. The dances at the Downs on Sundays and at the Pilgrim on Thursdays and every other Saturday were organised by two guys, Mick and Jim (Mick once played in Johnny Kidd and the Pirates). The Who's support act on this night was a great band from Lingfield in Surrey called Johnny Fine and the Ramblers. I remember being disgusted at the way The Who were famous for smashing up their instruments and made sure I disappeared into the bar towards the end so I didn't have to witness such unnecessary vandalism. The Downs was demolished. The Pilgrim was still there the last time I looked but had been turned into a supermarket. I couldn't even think about shopping there…

KEITH BRAINE

I saw them at the Downs and three times at the Florida Rooms in Brighton, right by the seafront. When I saw them at the Downs there was a bit of an altercation. The two people who ran the Downs were Pete Tree and Pete Shorland. They used to organise the groups and take the money on the door. (Captain Brown owned the place.) The Downs had a bar upstairs where all of the drinkers and the older kiddies sometimes were, and then you went to the side down a big wide hallway and into a big room downstairs. It had a bar down there. Nobody ever asked your age. Most Mods would drink Merrydown and black.

It wasn't that big a place, but it would be heaving. Pete Shorland used to organise everything and one of their mates who was built like a shithouse was on the door and there was never any trouble. We never used to pay to go in, because we knew Pete. They had a lot of groups down there, and it's quite surprising because it's in the middle of nowhere, Hassocks, even in this day and age let alone in that day and age. But it got the groups.

I'm afraid The Who weren't very good that night. Keith Moon impressed, but it was a very small venue compared to what they went on to do. And there was the altercation. Johnny Fine and the Ramblers were on one stage and The Who went on and Pete Townshend said something like 'get that load of shite off' and Johnny Fine did a hand gesture with his thumb above his lip and the other long forefinger up to his head, indicating 'large nose', and Townshend was a little bit upset to say the least.

At the end, Townshend broke his Rickenbacker and the bass guitarist of our group got a bit of the head of the Rickenbacker and put it on his guitar. People used to think his bass guitar was a Rickenbacker, but it wasn't. It was Pete Townshend's head stock.

I was a Mod. I had a Lambretta. My mate was the flash one, with the Vespa SS which had just come out. We used to go down to Brighton, to the Mods and Rockers, and didn't get up to much trouble. Just a bit of sugar in the petrol tanks of the motorbikes and things like that! I used to have a drink and then get on my scooter home. You wouldn't do it now but there was hardly any traffic then. I was stopped once and was told to walk down the middle of the road, on the line, and that was it really. 'Off you go.' Different times. Some of them good, some of them bad.

ANDRE WELLS, AGE 18

I was an apprentice bricklayer and sort of a Mod. I had a scooter. You made sure you didn't go to coastal towns on bank holidays, otherwise you might have got caught up in trouble. Where I was brought up was only 15 minutes from Brighton over the downs, so you had to be a bit aware of what was going on at bank holidays. The first time I saw them was at the Downs Hotel, about six miles north of Brighton. It was a basement part of the hotel and a bit scruffy. I saw them smash up their equipment. I didn't realise that was what they did. They broke it all up.

9 JANUARY 1966
COSMOPOLITAN CLUB, CARLISLE, UK

ALAN SEWELL, AGE 19

I played lead guitar in and arranged some of the music for a six-piece band from Annan. We played at the Cosmo most Sunday nights, supporting many well-known groups. We were originally called The Aztecs until Les Leighton – the owner of the Cosmo – suggested we changed our name to The Sad Eyes, as he reckoned we looked sad on our promotional photos. On the night of The Who's performance, the venue was packed and the audience noisy. Myself and other band members watched The Who's performance from both the 'sky top' bar and the bar behind the stage. My main memory is of Keith Moon's drums and cymbals crashing down from the upper tier of the stage onto all the equipment, and Pete Townshend smashing his guitar onto one of his amplifiers.

23 JANUARY 1966
CO-OP HALL, WARRINGTON, UK

MIKE KELLY

Groups of us lads used to get the bus in from the village of Burtonwood to the Co-op Hall 'dance' in Warrington. It was a place of innocence and a good place for us village lads to meet savvy town girls. It was our Las Vegas. There was no alcohol served at the show and certainly no drugs around so, as under-age drinkers, we'd have a pint in the British Tar or the Three Pigeons on Tanners Lane. Most weeks it was just records being played. The DJ was called Dave Warwick. I never heard of him for 40 years and then he popped up on local TV as the agent for Paul Burrell, Princess Diana's infamous butler. There were no more than 150 teenagers at the Who show. I went on to see them again at the original Isle of Wight festival.

29 JANUARY 1966
IMPERIAL BALLROOM, NELSON, UK

IAN GASKELL

I was a regular attendee at the Imp and in January of 1966 I was eager to see my heroes, The Who. My abiding memory was the incredible volume of their performance; I had ringing in my ears for two days afterwards. I had managed to secure a place near the front and, for anyone who knows the venue, I was just behind the unforgettable sofas, so right at the front! The Who dutifully arrived via the revolving stage and I was struck by Pete Townshend's brown suit, which seemed out of character with the Pop Art reputation. Their set got louder and louder and the climax of the show was 'My Generation', Townshend windmilling his arms with predictable gusto. As Moon launched into his drum solo, I observed Pete disappear from stage only to return armed with what looked like his normal guitar. On a closer examination, and being a guitar player myself, it became obvious that his expensive guitar had been replaced by a cheap copy! He then proceeded to destroy it against a fake Marshall amplifier which had been on stage throughout the performance but not switched on. The frantic drumming of Moon ended in a crescendo of smoke and sparks as the kit was finally dispatched to drum heaven.

30 JANUARY 1966
BEACHCOMBER CLUB, LEIGH, UK

ROB DEE

In the late Sixties, I was the DJ at the Beachcomber in Leigh and Bolton along with being the all-night deejay at the Twisted Wheel in Manchester. The Beachcomber was three clubs in Bolton, Leigh and Preston. If they booked somebody in and they had a van, with a bit of luck they could use them at all three venues. The owner, Eddie, asked me to suggest some bookings and I gave him a list which included The Who. He booked them all. We did three gigs with The Who – gigs at Leigh, Bolton and Preston Beachcombers all in one night.

It was the height of the Mods versus Rockers thing and Keith was patently a Mod. At Leigh, someone threw a bottle at Keith Moon. He promptly stood up from his kit and lobbed it back. He carried on with blood streaming from his head for the last few numbers, but it was getting a bit out of hand and they all piled into van as fast as possible to go to Bolton. In Bolton, the town centre was absolutely jam-packed with people who didn't know what was going on. It delayed them getting to Preston.

The first time I'd met The Who was when they were the High Numbers. There was also a band called The Action, who were the best white soul band in the country. They had a massive following in London and The Who were doing the same kind of numbers – a bit of Motown, 'Dancing in the Street', all that kind of stuff – and The Action were a big problem for The Who's management, because they were better. Reg, their singer, told me before his death that The Action were paid off with a lot of money – about half a million quid – by the record label to disappear, so that they could promote The Who. The Action were a red-hot band at the time. A lot of kids like us followed them around.

The Who take part in a three-night trial package tour with a number of other acts. The dates are organised by The Who's management, Kit Lambert and Chris Stamp, and promoted by Robert Stigwood with a view to a future four or five week tour if they're a success.

5 FEBRUARY 1966
ODEON CINEMA, SOUTHEND-ON-SEA, UK

DAVE BRABBING, AGE 16

I had just started work as an apprentice engraver in Westcliff-on-Sea, when I bumped into an old school friend who asked me if I wanted to go to see Screaming Lord Sutch at the Southend Odeon as he had got a couple of free tickets and back stage passes. These had been obtained by my friend's brother, who knew the then Odeon manager, Arthur Levenson. My friend and I were both big fans, mainly because Sutch ran a pirate radio station which we always listened to just off the Essex coast at Shivering Sands called Radio Sutch!

We met Lord Sutch backstage and he seemed quite a nice bloke, although a little bizarre. We also saw some of the other acts backstage who were just hanging around. They included The Merseybeats, The Fortunes and Graham Bond. Keith Moon seemed quite mad. He was playing practical jokes on just about everyone who was around. We then went to watch the concert, which was both exciting and mad, with all the girls screaming. It was difficult to hear anything.

17 FEBRUARY 1966
CLUB A GO GO
NEWCASTLE-UPON-TYNE, UK

IAN DALGLEISH

The club was packed out, with the condensation dripping off the walls. The Who put on an energetic performance and, as they finished their set, Moonie kicked his drums over and hit Pete Townshend on the leg with his cymbal. This resulted with a fierce glare aimed at the drummer. I enjoyed the set but most of the audience was not impressed, many preferring a more soul-based act. You could say they did not go down very well. I still have the original handbill from that night.

18 FEBRUARY 1966
VOLUNTEER HALL, GALASHIELS, UK

KATH SYMONS

It was a wonderful time for us teenagers in this very quiet rural area of Scotland, because there was a local promoter called Duncan MacKinnon who brought lots of top bands to our local venues. I saw the Kinks, Jeff Beck and Rod Stewart before they became world famous. With lots of local good bands, there was live music every weekend. I remember them playing and how exciting it was to see them in the flesh, with Keith Moon and Roger Daltrey standing out. Keith was wild on the drums!

19 FEBRUARY 1966
MEMORIAL HALL, NORTHWICH, UK

PETER SCOTT

The Memorial Hall, Northwich was called the Morgue, where my father ran the Saturday night dances – that is what we called them back then in 1966. I was still a schoolboy but, due to the family connection, was the MC. My dad used to book his acts via Arthur Kimbrell who ran the Midland Variety Agency. Arthur begged my dad to book a band called The Who for a 45-minute spot for, I think, £30, promising they would be in the charts when they appeared. Like many others, I was able to see acts like The Beatles, Stones, Walker Brothers, Original Drifters, Hollies, John Lee Hooker, Marianne Faithful, Donovan, Dave Berry and The Who for between 7/6d (37p) and 10/- (50p). The Morgue was meant to be licensed to hold 850 people but the highest attendance was 2,350 for the Walker Brothers.

On the night The Who were on, we arrived at about 6pm as normal. When I walked into the main hall the first thing to hit me was the amount of equipment on stage. The stage was about five feet higher than the dancefloor and on each side of the stage was a stack of speakers about 15 feet high. Most bands of the time used to have one speaker sat on a chair each side. The band's amplifiers were set across the stage with the drum kit on the elevated platform. The roadies had arrived early and set up. The problem with this was that every week there were two local bands appearing, on this occasion from Crewe and Liverpool. When this was explained to The Who's road crew, they were quite happy for the support groups to use the equipment. Before the doors opened at 6.45pm, the roadies had a sound check. The whole place shook and vibrated while this took place, causing the hall manager Mr Lewis to threaten to not allow the show to take place. The roadies lowered the volume to his satisfaction, but I could see it was just a way of appeasing him and that full volume would be on again later. The support groups had now turned up and were very happy to be able to use the equipment provided.

The crowd built up steadily through the evening. The doors closed at 9.30pm. Quite a number of the lads used to come in and then get a pass out and go to the Penryhn Arms opposite, returning just before the doors closed. The main act always went on at 10pm. I would go and see the act about 15 minutes before this to chat about what was going to happen eg. how they wished to be introduced, their finishing number, if they would be doing an encore and other odds and sods. 'Don't let the girls grab you!' was my final bit of advice.

At about 9.58pm, we were stood behind the curtain. I asked the guys if they were ready, and then went out front and announced 'ladies and gentlemen, Harry Scott presents for your entertainment – sensational chart band, The WHOooo.' The curtains went back and The Who struck up their opening number. The sound was incredible. The crowd were in raptures. I have never heard that level of noise before or since. One of my tasks, with the help of a lad called Keith Robinson, was to stand at the side of the stage and gently push back into the crowd any girls that tried to get up. And if people fainted, then between us we would get them out of the milling throng. The audience used to be very good in those days and gave us great assistance. The problem on this night was that it was impossible for Keith and I to take up our normal position owing to the noise. Neither of us wanted to end up deaf. The Who were very good, never allowing themselves to be grabbed by the audience and we managed to stop any stage invasion.

When I signalled for the boys to play their last number, everything seemed hunky dory. They finished with 'I Can't Explain' and the crowd loved it, but within seconds chaos erupted as Pete Townshend and Keith Moon went on a wrecking spree. Guitars were being used as sledgehammers on the amps and the drum kit was all over the stage. Needless to say, the crowd loved it. The curtains closed and I went on stage to wrap the spot up, absolutely gobsmacked. Composing myself, I thanked the band for the performance and was stunned when they appeared from behind the curtain to take a bow. Obviously, no encore could take place as the stage was in chaos. A record was put on and we all left the stage. As we walked to the dressing room, I was astonished to be asked by the band if I thought the crowd had enjoyed it and if I thought it a good show!

The lads went to change but sought me out before they left to say thanks for having them. Off they went into the night, leaving a very happy audience who had witnessed a fabulous gig. The chaos on the stage meant the final act had to rush to get their own equipment on stage for the last spot which probably lasted 10 to 15 minutes. The hall had to be cleared before midnight to comply with the law; you could not be open on a Sunday.

20 FEBRUARY 1966
OASIS CLUB, MANCHESTER, UK

CHRIS PHILLIPS

The Oasis was a cellar club and everyone from The Beatles to the Stones played there. Going into see them one night we saw Moon, Enty and Townshend pull up in a car outside. Artists and punters used the same door. Daltrey was in the Nag's Head pub across the road with his Mod bird. I saw him there but didn't speak to him. We proceeded to go down the stairs and were halfway down when I got charged in the back and tumbled to the bottom. There was a body on top of me, clutching a bottle of Courvoisier brandy. It was Moonie. He had his finger in the top of the bottle. It hadn't broken and he hadn't spilt a drop. He had a big smile on his face. 'Alright, mate - want a drink?' I had a swig while he was still half on top of me!

JOHN SANDERSON

They were late in coming on because no one could find Moonie. He was eventually found in a bar near Piccadilly. He was brought to the club and, because there was only one way in and one way out of the club and it was packed to the rafters, we had to pass him over our heads to the stage. He hit the stage and he didn't miss a beat. The stage looked like a scrap yard when they had finished – broken amps and the odd Rickenbacker with no neck. Fantastic!

25 FEBRUARY 1966
MAJESTIC BALLROOM, WELLINGTON, UK

DAVID BAGNALL, AGE 16

I have seen The Who live on five occasions and this was the first time. Roger Daltrey didn't turn up and we were told he was ill. They still put on a great show, with Pete Townshend taking over on vocals. In those days bands didn't do particularly long gigs. But 20 minutes was still quite short. I was a trainee photographer for the local paper. The owner of the venue, Dennis Boyle, would often let me in for nothing if I took a picture of the group in the dressing room, and I photographed the Small Faces and the Alan Price Set that way. But it didn't happen on this occasion, possibly because Roger wasn't there and they just didn't want their photo taken. I suppose I was easily satisfied in those days, but it was great to see a band I was already into so close up. The Beatles weren't as good as The Who. It was a waste of time going to see The Beatles, because all you could hear was people screaming. I don't think anyone screaming could drown out The Who. You could be outside the venue and still hear it, which is why they're all deaf.

ADE FELTON, AGE 15

Roger Daltrey was not singing that night because he had a bad throat. They tried to perform without him and they just did 20 minutes, and then there was another band, probably The Big Three from Liverpool or someone like that. The Who were the top billing so they must have been quite well known. That's why it was very disappointing that they only did 20 minutes. The support act was better. To be fair to them, they wanted to fulfil the engagement but didn't have enough stuff to do more than 20 minutes without the lead vocalist. It was all of them singing, and it was obvious that it wasn't working. It wasn't 'right we've done our set and we're off'. It's like 'we're trying, we're trying. No, this isn't going to work.'

BRYAN JOHNSON, AGE 20

I was with my younger brother and a friend. Roger Daltrey was ill and Pete Townshend did vocals. They were brilliant. But my best memory of the night was a drum solo by Keith Moon. It's a long time ago but I will never forget that drum solo.

26 FEBRUARY 1966
STARLIGHT ROOM, GLIDERDROME BOSTON, UK

NICK BASFORD

I was brought up in the Lincolnshire market town of Spalding. Between 1965 and 1967, the place to be on a Saturday night was the Gliderdome in Boston, 16 miles north of Spalding. Boston Gliderdrome started as a dance hall in the 1930s, hosting swing and dance bands, and by the early '60s it was into rock 'n' roll and the likes of Joe Brown, Billy Fury and Marty Wilde. Tales are legendary about performers having to make their way to the stage through a sometimes hostile audience and dodging punches from local yobs and jealous boyfriends!

In November 1964, the 'new' Gliderdrome was unveiled. The old ballroom was now a huge bar with a counter at each end and a stage for local acts on the side. On the other side of the foyer was the custom-built Starlight Room, with several hundred lights in the ceiling. During slow smoochy dances the 'stars' would come out, and there was a revolving stage so that as one group disappeared the next one came round. This was a dance hall capable of holding 3,000 people which hosted all the big names in popular music.

The Who appeared as a trio. Roger Daltrey was absent (suffering from laryngitis – at least, that was the official excuse!) so Townshend, Entwistle and Moon performed as a threesome, with Townshend doing all the lead singing. They wore Mod-style parkas just like hundreds in the audience, many of whom had travelled some distance. The *Lincolnshire Free Press* carried a piece on the concert and the reporter desceibed the audience as 'a sea of centre-parked heads.' They did all their big numbers like 'I Can't Explain' and 'My Generation' and seemed to go down well with the crowd, unlike the Small Faces, who got pelted off with Coke bottles!

23 MARCH 1966
TOWER BALLROOM, GREAT YARMOUTH, UK

HELEN PLANE

Keith Moon cut himself and I had a hanky with his blood on it. I didn't realise at the time it was that important, so have no idea where it is. My cousin Wendy might have it.

COLIN STANLEY, AGE 16

Roger Daltrey banged the cymbal and cut his hand on the side and all the girls threw handkerchiefs up on the stage. He picked some up, wiped his hand on them and threw them back into the audience, who began fighting over them. They were good. They were really good.

They went on before Peter Jay and the Jaywalkers and they absolutely blasted the place. And Peter Jay said 'Fucking hell. How do we follow that?'

24 MARCH 1966
STARLIGHT BALLROOM, CRAWLEY, UK

JULIAN DUNCALFE

I paid 7/6 (37p) to see The Who. They put a row of chairs in a semi-circle around the stage to prevent people getting on it and I was asked to sit on one of them, just a few feet away from the speakers. Keith Moon was drumming with his flies open and occasionally tossing sticks into the crowd. The set ended with Townshend bashing his guitar into the speakers just in front of me and Moon kicking his drums all over the stage. All that teenage angst was expressed so brilliantly in their songs.

DAVID GOODWIN

Keith Moon stood on my toe when walking past and brought us a drink and had a chat. He was utterly bonkers! I might also have seen them at Chislehurst Caves in Kent.

25 MARCH 1966
ARCADE RECORD SHOP, HERTFORD, UK

CHRISTINE SMITH, AGE 14

I persuaded a friend to go to the Arcade Record Shop in Hertford town centre to meet The Who after school. They were either opening the record shop or promoting one of their records. My friend and I were the only people to turn up and I was given their autograph on a picture of the group. I didn't understand the significance of all this, even though I loved their record in the charts, and I discarded it in later years, going on to love Motown and Rock Steady. How foolish was I? The arcade in Hertford is no more, which is a shame as it was a nice little cut through from the bus station.

MAUREEN BROWNING

One of the most memorable gigs we saw was at Hertford Corn Exchange in 1965. Until a few years ago I wouldn't have been able to tell you the date, but just before my sister fell ill, we were in Hertford and saw the door to the Corn Exchange open, so we sneaked in and asked if we could have a look around. We got chatting to a chap there and told him why we were taking a nostalgic sneaky-peak, and he showed us a framed handbill, showing the date, that it started at 7.30pm and that it cost 10/6d (52p) to get in! The support act was the Modern Blues Six.

It was a very memorable gig, with them playing all their early music, plus the classic covers they always did in those days – 'Barbara Ann', 'Heatwave', 'Daddy Rolling Stone', 'Shout and Shimmy', 'Runaround Sue', 'See See Rider' and 'Dancing in the Street'. The band asked how we were getting home. We told them our parents were picking us up. They called our parents, who they had met before, and said they would drop us off as they were going past Stevenage. Could you imagine that happening today with even a B-list one-hit wonder?

They were also on *Saturday Club* on BBC radio once, when Brian Matthew was still presenting it, and my sister and I had a request read out! Our dad was a grocery shop manager and we wrote the request on a paper till roll, which ended up a few feet long. That probably got it noticed.

When my sister died, I found some items which we collected back then – a broken drum stick from Keith, a guitar string from Pete, an old penny coin and plectrum from John and a button off Roger's shirt. I still have the High Numbers 45 of 'Zoot Suit' and 'I'm The Face', but in the mid-70s I donated a copy of 'I Can't Explain', signed by all four members of The Who, to a charity auction. I wonder what that would be worth today?

ALAN GOLDSMITH, AGE 25

Some so-called 'expert' said The Who never played in Hertford but they did. I put them on there, and I've got the press cutting about them visiting the local record shop. I paid them £50 plus a percentage. There was a huge queue and the young guy with the clicker was sitting on the stairs, counting the attendance. I was going way over the percentage so I had him thrown out. I just paid them £50 cash. It was licensed for 400 but I wasn't very good at counting and I got 600-700 in there. I had 900 for Stevie Wonder.

I used the name Mark Gold. We used to flypost everywhere in those days, and because it said Mark Gold Promotions Present, everyone from the Council was looking for this Mark Gold to prosecute him but he didn't exist, because it was really me. We never put our names on the posters. The only people who put their names at the top were the people on a sort of ego trip. I was more focussed on the money side so I didn't go bankrupt. No one was interested in who Alan Goldsmith was, or Joe Bloggs. They were interested in the act.

When The Who broke things up, and smashed bit of amplifiers and all the guitars, we just swept it up and put it all in the bin. It would be worth a bloody fortune now.

I got on very well with Keith Moon, although he was as mad as a hatter. They were all ok. Pete Townshend was a bit distant but we didn't getting chatting to any of them. You'd go to the hall, the band would turn up, you'd go up and say 'hi, you're on at 7.30', or 8.30, or whatever it was. We were too busy working, with the big queue outside and the bouncers, making sure there were no fights and so on. And the band would be getting on with their stuff, setting up and tuning up.

Before the Sixties and The Who, everything was very drab and then suddenly all the girls were in high heels and stockings and suspenders, Mary Quant and Mr Freedom, all the latest fashion and the hairstyles. Everyone throughout the world wanted to have the fashion that the London girls had. All the guys had Prince of Wales suits and clothes from Take 6, Cecil Gee, etc.

I think it will go down as one of the biggest social revolutions this country has ever seen, because it was a very suppressed and class-conscious society. Rock 'n' roll changed all that. We broke that mould. Suddenly girls were opening dress shops and coffee bars and people like me were promoting shows. I was managing The Diamonds and it went on from there. We broke the mould and money poured in. I was earning £10 a week in an office and 40 or 50 quid on the side. I was going to the south of France with my girlfriend for holiday. Everything was exploding and they couldn't control people like me. And we were flash at the time, you know, young like you are.

My daughter talks about sex and rock and roll and orgies and all that. That didn't happen. We were all too busy making money. The girls weren't on the pill. That had just started to come in. They just went to a gig, got in the van and went home. Obviously, if you got a girl, you had a grope round the back of the hall and all the rest of it. But there was none of this wild orgy thing. If there was, I bloody missed it!

On 4 April 1966, the High Court in London, UK granted Shel Talmy an interim injunction preventing the group from continuing to record pending his claim to have an exclusive recording contract with them.

9 APRIL 1966
PAVILION GARDENS BALLROOM, BUXTON, UK

MICK SHELTON

The Derby Mods were en-route to Manchester for a night at their beloved Twisted Wheel. It was obvious that we should stop off at Buxton to watch our heroes. With the band in full swing and the Derby boys showing off their dancing skills to the delight of the local beauties, it became apparent that the local boys, mainly Rockers, were not happy. A fight ensued, which was not unusual in those days. But what amazed me was when Roger Daltrey leapt from the stage, kicked one of our assailants and jumped back on stage, almost without missing a beat. Magic! Sadly, we were removed from the premises but we went on to have a great night at the Wheel.

14 APRIL 1966
GAUMONT CINEMA, SOUTHAMPTON, UK

ALAN BURDEN

The whole balcony was moving and my ears were whistling for a week after the concert!

22 APRIL 1966
GAUMONT CINEMA, DERBY, UK

MARGARET ADAMS, AGE 15

My father would send his apprentice to the box office at 7.30am the day it opened to get my friend and I front row seats. That accomplished, our next task was to get the afternoon off school. We both had dental appointments, ie. we forged letters to our teachers. Then it was down on the bus to join the other fans around the Gaumont to wait for the groups to arrive. We had written to the fan club, of which we were members, to get a letter to go backstage. The previous week we went to the manager of the Gaumont with said letter, but he was having none of it. Disappointed? Yes. Deterred? No. On the afternoon of the gig, we showed the letter to the assistant manager who organised for us to go backstage after the first show and meet our idols. We could not believe our luck. We got personalised autographs, which I still have. Backstage, I remember Keith drinking something, Pete eating something and Roger being really kind and making sure we had everybody's autographs. I can't remember a lot about the show apart from 'My Generation' and not really believing we were there.

TRICIE DELAHAY

I had gone on a coach group so we were all excited teenage girls. I will never forget the evening. When they sang 'Substitute', the roof virtually lifted off!

PHIL DOXEY, AGE 14

I was two months short of my 15th birthday. We sat in cinema seats, a few girls screamed and tried to run to the front, but were immediately ushered back to their seats. The Who smashed some equipment. I didn't see The Who again until my 65th birthday in 2017.

23 APRIL 1966
ODEON CINEMA, ROCHESTER, UK

DERMOT BASSETT

One evening in early 1965, on a long-forgotten TV programme, I saw The Who for the first time. Saw? Fell in love with more like. I didn't know it at the time, but it was the start of a lifelong obsession. I'd never seen or heard anything like it before and who was that drummer? At school the next day, the big discussion seemed to be 'did you see that drummer on TV last night?'. It was just over a year later that I got to experience Keith Moon and them live, at Rochester Odeon. Both houses, of course.

Other highlights came and went. Seeing what people call the 'Pictures of Lily' drum kit but what I remember Keith calling 'the engine' live for the first time is one, shining in the lights as the curtains came back at Maidstone ABC in 1967. Especially as Keith had beaten The Tremeloes' drum kit into submission in the first house!

28 APRIL 1966
WITCHDOCTOR, CATFORD, LONDON, UK

BILL CHEWTER, AGE 15

I went with schoolfriends. The place was packed. It couldn't have cost much to get in. They used to smash up their guitars and drums at the end of their act. My brother Robert saw them at Charlton.

30 APRIL 1966
CORN EXCHANGE, CHELMSFORD, UK

JILL CARMAN-STEWART, AGE 15

I ended up backstage and Roger asked me which was the best pub in Chelmsford. I walked with them to show them all. Roger wrote his autograph in red biro on my arm and I was so excited but when I returned home my mother was horrified. She scrubbed it off as she said I would get blood poisoning. I was so upset as I couldn't show it off to my friends!

MARION PARKHURST, AGE 15

My friend Linda and myself saw The Who in Chelmsford. I would have been there against my parents' knowledge - my dad is now 94 and still none the wiser! The hall was packed but we had a great view. Roger had trouble keeping his words in sync with the guitars when he sang 'My Generation'. They were so full of energy and not very big. Keith was breaking drumsticks and throwing them into the crowd. After being jumped on and shoved about, I managed to catch one. Unfortunately, I've since lost it during one of many house moves. They went on to smash their equipment, which I found a bit frightening. We hung around for a while after and stood staring at Keith as he sat all on his own, wearing a huge brown fur coat, on the front of the stage. We didn't have the nerve to speak to him. We went home on the backs of scooters.

1 MAY 1966
NME POLL WINNERS CONCERT EMPIRE POOL, WEMBLEY, LONDON, UK

JOHN WALLACE

The *New Musical Express* used to do an annual awards event – best single, best newcomer and so on. The Who were there with people like Herman's Hermits and Wayne Fontana and the Mindbenders. We saw them on television in black and white. The stage was set up with the plinths all set up for the drum kits because there were so many musicians coming on and doing their bit. They'd come on and do one, maybe two numbers and then disappear. God knows how they managed the PA in those days because they were so technical about stage set up. I remember there was a bank of guitars on these stands, running along the side of the drum platform. And Moon decided to trash the kit and he damaged other people's guitars, which was spectacular. Everybody was outraged!

DERMOT BASSETT

It was eight days later that I saw them again, this time at the Empire Pool Wembley for the *NME* Poll Winners Concert, where Keith was on a very high drum riser and finished their two song set by kicking his drums off the front of the riser. With just the Stones and The Beatles to follow, Keith wasn't going to be upstaged by anyone!

8 MAY 1966
ARCADIA BALLROOM, CORK, IRELAND

JEAN KEARNEY

Me and my pals were a group of very giggly schoolgirls who stalked them around various hotels in the city. We phoned various hotels asking if The Who were staying there with the predictable responses: 'The Who?' 'Yes, The Who.' 'Who do you want to speak to?' 'The Who.' And round and round it went. We never did find out where they were staying.

11 MAY 1966
CORN EXCHANGE, BRISTOL, UK

JOHN HARRIS

I'd been gripped by the picture of Pete Townshend with a row of smashed Rickenbackers hanging on his bedroom wall, and fired up by the energy, power, mayhem and freedom in the TV footage of 'Anyway, Anyhow, Anywhere' and 'My Generation'. We licensed them to break all the rules and we loved it. But nothing prepared me for the sheer impact of seeing The Who live for the first time.

The Corn Exchange was the premier Bristol venue for blues-based and emerging music, run by the enterprising Uncle Bonnie each Tuesday under the unlikely title of the Bristol Chinese R&B Jazz Club. It was a superb place to really listen to a band – not too large, with a small projecting stage surrounding a couple of pillars, so you could get very close to the action. We learned about the forthcoming acts from posters at the Corn Exchange itself, and through word of mouth. There were no tickets in advance, so to be sure of getting in you needed someone to bag a place for you near the front of the queue, which often stretched right round the block.

A hundred or more of us pressed ourselves tight against the stage to watch The Who setting up two or three yards in front of us. This was the first time I'd seen double-cabinet Marshall stacks – a far cry from the standard Vox AC30s used by other bands. When Pete Townshend tested the system with a power chord, it was so very loud that all one hundred of us found we had thrown ourselves back several feet in shock, as if we were a single being.

I'd listened to every track on the first LP again and again, dissecting each one to try to understand what made this strangely different music so exciting. What The Who played that night I can't now recall. Still vividly with me are the sheer energy, the driving forcefulness – and the volume. The set was so loud in that small venue that my ears physically hurt, and to be able to bear it I had to move to the side and stand on a table. I clearly remember my ears ringing continuously for five days afterwards.

Would they smash all their gear at the end? In the event, for the final number Pete swapped his Rickenbacker for an old solid-body guitar, which he aimed repeatedly at the nearest pillar on the stage, glancing it off – the marks were still visible months later – before finally bouncing it robustly against the floor. Keith kicked his drums over and Roger did his trademark microphone swirling. But it was enough. We'd glimpsed The Who in destructive mode and we were happy.

Their drive, imperiousness, rebelliousness and intensity blew me away. Their stage show became even more commanding and powerful later in the Sixties but, for me, the rawness, the edge, the unbridled power of this first experience of The Who live was just extraordinary.

JOHN RUDGE, AGE 15

It was my first experience of the might of The Who. We joined the queue at the back of the Corn Exchange and didn't think we'd get in. I seem to remember it was expensive – ten bob

(50p)? It was announced that Keith Moon was ill and could not play that night, and his place was taken by Viv Prince of the Pretty Things. David Grimshaw, bass player for a local band called The Pentagons who had recently broken up, was there as was The Pentagons' former manager, Brian K Jones. Brian said John Entwistle had disappeared and asked if David could help out. David went backstage to offer his services to Pete and Roger, who were now running late and being pressurised to go on. Daltrey, mindful that they were already one down with the Pretty Things' drummer sitting in, said, 'No offence mate, but those people out there have paid to see The Who, not the two of us.' David apparently suggested that their music was basically twelve bar blues, only to be told by Townshend 'it's a little bit more complicated than that!'.

David's next memory is being stood behind the stage holding a Fender bass and Daltrey pleading to him to wait. With seconds to go, John Entwistle appeared through the curtains at the side of the stage. He'd been out enjoying the local market bars behind the Corn Exchange. This ended David's claim to fame… and the band went on! All I remember is that it was amazing. I vividly remember Pete saying 'now this is song from our new album – our only album' and they played 'A Legal Matter'.

12 MAY 1966
PAVILION BALLROOM, WORTHING, UK

SONIA JOHNSON

My friend and I worked in a shop for low pay. Dancing and fashion were our lives, and seeing groups was the highlight of our week. I remember seeing The Who in the early days, when they had recorded 'I Can't Explain'. My main memory of them is from a later date. I was typical of a lot of girls then, with long blonde hair and very short skirt. It was getting near the end of the evening when one of the girls who always hung around the front of the stage hoping to be noticed came up to me and said that I had been invited back to the band's hotel room. I declined the offer and went to get my bus.

14 MAY 1966
PALAIS DE DANSE, BURY, UK

CHRIS (CJ) SMITH

I went with my mates hoping for a great and explosive set! On this occasion they didn't trash their equipment. Pete Townshend settled for ramming his Rickenbacker back into the big Marshall stacks behind him throughout the set. I can only remember them playing 'Substitute', 'A Legal Matter' and a couple of other tracks off their first Brunswick album, although they may also have done 'Barbara Ann' and the 'Batman Theme' off the *Ready Steady Who* EP. Roger Daltrey was absent, leaving Townshend to handle vocals. I found out years later that Daltrey had been sacked around this time – from his own band! I remember talking to John Entwistle just before they went on, asking him for plectrums, to which he replied, 'I don't use them lads,' so we asked to look at his fingers, which were as hard as nails. I also got his autograph on a picture I took with me from a magazine like *Jackie*. I still have it.

PHIL SPENCER, AGE 17

I recall it being 7/6 (37p). Townshend was smashing the equipment and finally his guitar. Can you imagine seeing that live in such a small, packed venue? I am informed that they were a trio as Roger Daltrey couldn't appear. I don't remember that, but I do remember where I stood! I loved The Who since first hearing 'The Kids Are Alright', 'Anyway, Anyhow, Anywhere' and 'I Can't Explain'. The Rocking Vicars were active locally and recorded a version of the Who song but called it, 'It's Alright'. I don't know why.

TED TUKSA

Roger never turned up. I have heard different reasons as to why. Pete had to do all the singing. I don't know if he was annoyed that Roger wasn't there, but the equipment was completely destroyed.

21 MAY 1966
FLORAL HALL, SOUTHPORT, UK

SUE MCGOWAN (NEE GREEN)

I was present at two of the three concerts The Who played at the Floral Hall. On the first occasion I went with a group of school friends and on the second with a boyfriend. There was no advance booking in those days; most people were older school children and young working adults who could not afford to pay in advance. Very few people were older than about 19. You paid on the door from the wages you received. Advertising was by posters which appeared around the town perhaps a month before the performance, which gave us time to save up. Prices for bands like The Who were 8/6 (43p) compared with perhaps two shillings (10p) for a less well-known band like Pink Floyd! Very few people had their own transport and so most people were dependent on the last bus or train. There was never any trouble, and no alcohol. Soft drinks were available. The first half of the evening was devoted to dancing to records played over the sound system followed by a break, followed by The Who. Most people gathered around the stage. There was no seating. They always finished by smashing up their instruments whilst Keith Moon drummed insanely! Many people found the smashing up quite scary. I know that I did. The band looked so much older than us. Some of the 'big' acts, like Long John Baldry and Chris Farlowe, ended by coming off stage and dancing with the audience but The Who never did.

The Who also played the Floral Hall on 18 February 1967 and 3 June 1967.

DAVID MELLING, AGE 19

I went with my girlfriend at the time, her friend and the friend's boyfriend. They were the only band on. There were between 100 and 200 people there. Some people were sat on bleacher seating towards the rear but we were stood on the dance floor twelve feet from the stage listening to them. They didn't smash their instruments. The only song I can remember them playing is 'I Can't Explain'. I was more of a Mod than a Rocker, but I wasn't really a Mod. It wasn't really a Mod audience. Keith was a real character. Each member of the group was memorable but he was particularly good, and very energetic.

On Friday 20 May 1966, Keith and John arrived two hours late for a gig at the Corn Exchange in Newbury to find that Roger and Pete had gone on stage without them, appropriating the bass player and drummer from support group the Jimmie Brown Sound. A fight ensued, in which Keith received a black eye and a broken ankle.

Moon told a journalist at the gig that he and John were quitting. Keith missed the next few shows, only returning to the drummer's stool on Wednesday 25 May 1966.

23 MAY 1966
LOCARNO BALLROOM, BLACKBURN, UK

DAVID ALMOND

One of them had broken his arm and someone stood in for him. I remember, because they only played for about half an hour and it was only a little cellar club.

ADRIENNE JENKINSON, AGE 15

It was an under 18s night at the Locarno. Roger Daltrey and Peter Townshend were on stage. Keith Moon was absent so another guy was drumming. They played a good tight set of their earlier hits including 'My Generation'. No guitars were smashed! They were very gracious towards their appreciative audience. Afterwards Roger was modestly collecting cables from the stage. I remember a girl shouting, 'Hey, Roger! Have you any fags?'. He had not got any cigarettes but smiled through those blue eyes as he willingly signed my autograph book. Ten minutes later, we discovered that Pete Townshend was going to leave via the back door. We dashed around and managed to obtain his autograph as well. Pete was quite shy, very obliging and polite. The Who were without airs and graces, a hard-working and talented band who put on a fantastic show. I could not wait to tell my school friends the following day.

JIM PITTS, AGE 16

The thing that sticks in my mind is that Keith Moon didn't turn up that night. It was the day after they played Rawtenstall. I was looking forward to seeing Keith Moon throwing himself around on the drums. In Blackburn there was a coffee bar where all the buses gathered and set off from and it was called the KJ Coffee Bar. It was known as the Mod place in the 1960s. Everybody tended to meet up there and then get into the pubs that you could at that age. You had to be very careful: 'Don't go in no rough pubs and keep your nose clean.' And then we'd go off to the Mecca. It was just the start of us going out drinking at 16 years old.

There were definitely Mods in Blackburn. I remember seeing all them there, jumping around doing the Mod dance. They were all grouped together, all cliquey. I was looking down from the balcony and they were over to the left-hand side of the stage. I remember thinking 'oh, that's such-a-body and such-a-body' who were the main Mod people. They were a little bit older, 18, and two years was a big difference at that age. There were a lot of people there but it wasn't that packed that you couldn't walk around. I remember walking down and standing in front of them as well, squeezing my way through to the front. It was a good show. They were quite exciting.

Keith didn't turn up and they apologised. I can't remember what they said. They didn't say much about it, but there were rumours about a fall out between the band members. but I don't remember them announcing that on stage. I remember Pete waving his arms around, the windmilling that he did. I remember Roger Daltrey jumping around like he did on *Top of the Pops*. He had a semi-dance kind of thing, throwing the mic around a little bit. I remember him jumping around a little bit. I don't remember it being a particularly long show.

28 MAY 1966
SOUTH PIER, BLACKPOOL, UK

TONY BEADEN

I was at the South Pier in Blackpool at the same show as my friend Neville Lee, collecting autographs, and I met the group. I helped to carry some of Keith Moon's drums to the theatre and also got their signatures in my autograph book. They were very nice lads and very pleasant to talk to. I think Cliff Bennett and the Rebel Rousers were on the same bill.

NEVILLE LEE

The Who played a concert at the South Pier, Blackpool and support was from the Pretty Things. I didn't see the concert. I was an autograph collector so I was outside, and obtained a number of fully signed pictures of the band from magazines such as *Fabulous*. None of these pictures seem to have survived the years and I have only one set. They were all happy to sign all my pictures and those of the two or three others who were there, and I particularly remember how pleasant Keith Moon was. After signing everything that was requested of him, Keith chatted on to us for a while before heading with the other wild man drummer, Viv Prince, to the bar.

SYD BLOOM

I used to roadie for a few bands. I was the only one who could drive at our age. One of the bands was the Rockin' Vickers, who were quite big in the north. They supported The Who at South Pier. Because I used to bang on and on and on and on about The Who, they actually recorded a version of a Who song. Pete Townshend actually slightly rewrote 'The Kids Are Alright' for them to do it as 'It's Alright', in a very plodding, pedantic way. They released that as a single largely, I suspect, at my behest because I just used to annoy everybody about The Who.

Because it was the season – because it was Blackpool – they had to do two houses, 6.20 and 8.45, which was anathema to most bands. A mate of mine came out to see them and said, 'I thought you said they were good?' He said 'The Rockin' Vicars blew them off stage.' I said, 'You're kidding me?' The Who just blew the place apart for the second half. They just weren't trying for the first house.

Support acts that evening are recorded elsewhere as the Rockin' Vickers (featuring a pre-Motörhead Lemmy), the Birds (whose line up included Ronnie Wood) and Oscar (featuring Paul Nicholas, who would play Cousin Kevin in the film* Tommy*).

7 JUNE 1966
HIT HOUSE, COPENHAGEN AND FYN'S FORUM, ODENSE, DENMARK

HARRY KERSHAW

I was the bass player and main vocalist in a Danish band called the Exchekers during the '60s, and we made a few records. We were scheduled to play two gigs with The Who in 1966. The gig in Fyn's Forum went terribly wrong and the place was wrecked whilst The Who were on stage. After the gig had finished, Roger Daltrey had pulled a chick and because girls were not allowed in his hotel, and maybe to avoid getting ribbed by the other members of the band, I said he could come to my apartment in Copenhagen with her. He stayed the night and we chatted in the morning – he was a nice guy.

17 JUNE 1966
CITY HALLS, PERTH, UK

SANDRA BOYLE

We lived in Dundee but often travelled through to Perth to see bands. If we missed the milk train home we had to hitchhike. We were Mods, they were heroes of ours and they were absolutely fantastic. After the show, me and my friends Evelyn and Betty met Roger Daltrey and John Entwistle and got chatting to them. Keith Moon was up on the balcony and obviously away with it, as he was playing imaginary drums! I do not know where Pete Townshend was.

Roger and John asked if we would like to go to a party in Edinburgh, where they were staying. Only being 17 or 18, and quite innocent, we said we couldn't as we had to get the milk train home as we were working the next day. I did not have anything for an autograph, but Roger Daltrey wrote on my arm with a little drawing and his name. I did not wash it off for a week, until it was starting to be too faded to read. My then boyfriend (now husband) was jealous and wouldn't speak to me. He remembers a girl called Diane Low running onto the stage and launching herself at Pete Townshend to land a kiss on his cheek. It was funny as he is about six foot and she was only about five foot two. He took it well.

18 JUNE 1966
MARKET HALL, CARLISLE, UK

GORDON RAE

They arrived in a black limousine and they took Roger Daltrey to the infirmary after he strained his voice and vocal cords. No wonder they put up a great performance both times.

19 JUNE 1966
MCGOOs CLUB, EDINBURGH, UK

BRIAN BRANNON, AGE 17

This booking must have been made at very short notice as the only publicity was in the local newspaper the night before. There were no tickets on sale in advance. It was just a case of paying seven shillings and sixpence on the door. Word went round very fast. I was in the fifth form of a local grammar school and six of my school friends and I got there very early, in our best Mod clothes, before the doors opened to ensure we had a good position in this standing room only club. I played rugby with the McGoos owner, Lawrence De Marco, and when he saw me in the queue, he let me in without paying, which was great for a permanently broke schoolboy.

It was a hot summer's night and there was no air conditioning. Within an hour the place was packed with Who fans and condensation was running down the walls. The place was sold out. Whilst we had all bought their records and seen them on *Top of the Pops* and *Ready Steady Go!*, we could hardly believe they were playing live here in a little club in our home town. The support act was one of Edinburgh's best local bands, The Hipple People, but no one was taking much notice of them as everyone was desperate for them to finish and get off so we could get our first sight of The Who. There was a really long delay after The Hipple People left the stage while Moon's drum kit was hammered into position, but eventually all four members of The Who ran on stage and went straight into a really fast version of Martha and the Vandellas' 'Heatwave'. The audience was open-mouthed at the energy and power with which they played. We had never seen a band play with so much aggression.

There was no talking to the audience between songs. They went straight into the Beach Boys' 'Barbara Ann' followed by 'CC Rider', then a current American hit for Mitch Ryder and the Detroit Wheels, played much faster than the original versions. It surprised me that they were not playing only Pete Townsend's songs but soon the audience erupted as they played their hits – 'I Can't Explain', 'Substitute', 'I'm a Boy' and 'Anyway, Anyhow, Anywhere' – and then finished with an incredibly powerful and violent 'My Generation'. Pete Townshend added more holes to his stack of amps by ramming the neck of his Fender Telecaster into them again and again. The song closed with him throwing the guitar high into the air, and walking off stage before it landed. It crashed onto the stage floor and the neck broke as Keith Moon hit his cymbals for the last time. Keith struggled to kick his drums down from his elevated position as the roadies seemed to have nailed them firmly into position. But they too soon crashed onto the stage before he, Roger Daltrey and John Entwistle ran off stage to join Pete. With the stage littered with drums and a broken guitar, there was no chance of any encore.

I subsequently found out that the broken Fender guitar had been borrowed from the lead guitarist of The Hipple People, as Pete's Rickenbacker guitar had fallen apart before they went onstage as a result of damage inflicted the night before. (He was reimbursed by The Who's managers.) My friends and I still talk about that night.

25 JUNE 1966
COLLEGE OF FURTHER EDUCATION CHICHESTER, UK

ZIGGI JANIEC, AGE 19

The college had been in existence for a year or so, and had formed the basis of a student union, with each department offering a student to sit on the fledgling committee. I had some

Clockwise from top left: Kath Symons was at the Volunteer Hall in Galashiels; John Harris was at Bristol's Corn Exchange where the 'Chinese R&B Jazz Club' was held; Sonia Johnson was invited back to the band's hotel room but declined; John Rudge recalls that Keith Moon was absent; Chris Smith got his *Jackie* poster signed at Bury's Palais de Danse.

Clockwise from top left: Tony Beaden got the band's autographs in Blackpool; three members of The Who photographed in Great Yarmouth - photo Sally Ramsay; Sue Riley's first ever gig was The Who at Barnsley Civic; Julia Janiec is tired of her husband talking about The Who's appearance at Chichester FE College; Jim Pitts remembers the Mods dancing to The Who in Blackburn.

previous experience in running dances and in managing a local R&B group called The Nightmares so was asked to run as social secretary. We'd have a dance each term and book three bands for each event. We used some local schoolboy bands and also booked acts via The Beat Ballad and Blues Agency in Worthing. Dances were always a sell-out and live music was still the preferred choice. Our nearest competition was the Guildhall in Portsmouth and venues in Brighton. I booked The Who from a London-based agency called Mayfair three months before the event for the magnificent price of £400. They were contracted to do two 45-minute spots.

By the time they came to play our college dance, 'Anyway, Anyhow, Anywhere' was climbing up the charts. Tickets were so in demand that every time it was 'I couldn't get tickets, I couldn't get tickets'. A guy on the committee said 'I know a printer.' I don't want to imply that the fire safety rules were broken, but in those days things weren't that serious, and Health and Safety hadn't even been invented. Basically, we had a hall that could hold 400, stretching to 500 if no one was looking, and The Who were not too interested in doing such a small gig because they could have been somewhere else playing for a larger fee and to a larger audience. But they turned up and they honoured the contract.

All those that came to dance had a great time and the organising committee were pleased with the feedback. We raffled about six of their LPs which were signed. Keith Moon was very entertaining and the most animated of the band. The language was blue during the setup and performance, which was something not encountered before on previous dance gigs here. Sometimes I dine out on this thin claim to fame but my dear wife, who was there at the time, does get bored with it.

CHRIS WEBB, AGE 17

I was studying at the college and remember seeing the posters advertising the concert. Many of the students did not believe The Who would come to do a show there but I bought a ticket which I think cost ten shillings (50p). Well, The Who did turn up and they did a brilliant show. Some bullies gatecrashed the show and started picking on some of the audience, including me and the friends I was with. They probably thought that guys dancing and enjoying the band without girlfriends in tow was not right. What a mistake to make! Not only did they get a rebuff from some of the people they were trying to intimidate, but Roger and Pete stopped the group playing and warned these thugs that if they did not stop and leave, then they and the band's helpers would come and sort them out. Needless to say, when the penny dropped, the bullies' bravery vanished and they left with their tails between their legs.

Many years later, I managed to get tickets for The Who's concert at a music festival at Beaulieu in the New Forest, sadly without John Entwistle or Keith Moon. Those tickets cost £30 but they were well worth it as the show that Roger and Pete put on was still fantastic.

26 JUNE 1966
BRITTANIA THEATRE, GREAT YARMOUTH, UK

JOHN BULLOCK

I only saw them on stage once at Great Yarmouth's Britannia Pier. It was a Sunday evening concert. All four members of The Who were by then at the top of their game and the music was very loud and vibrant. The one outstanding memory of that night is Keith Moon aiming one of his drumsticks at the first few rows of the stalls at the finish of 'My Generation'. The stick flew pass many ears – we were sitting in row C! If only I had picked up the stick it would have been worth a couple of shillings. My wife-to-be, Mary, was a fully blown Mod so The Who was the group to be associated with. She still loves them today and enjoyed watching Pete and Roger perform 'Baba O'Riley' at Glastonbury in 2015.

16 JULY 1966
CIVIC HALL, BARNSLEY, UK

LESLIE SIMMONS

My Dad was manager of the Civic and had the budget to book big bands. He'd had a lot of trouble with the fire brigade over the size of audiences they were attracting, and for The Who the fire officer said he was going to put two firemen on the front door and use a clicker to limit the number of people coming in that night. Now, my Dad had gone top dollar for The Who and had worked out that, however many people were allowed in, it wasn't going to cover the bills. His office overlooked the front of the Civic so he left the doors shut for as long as he dared. A massive queue built up and people were banging on the doors, asking to be let in. He opened the doors at the last minute. People were just piling in past the fireman to where they had to pay to be admitted. The fireman wasn't able to keep count and click everyone in.

JAMES BRADBURY, AGE 15

We were very young and didn't have any money, hence I didn't attend the Civic Hall. We'd spend our evenings walking around the town drinking coffee and pretending to smoke cigarettes at the Aloha coffee bar, so named after the recent popularity of Elvis's *Blue Hawaii* film (we were supposed to be doing homework). I even used to take out my father's Ronson Variflame lighter which, when turned up to full, gave a very impressive display! Mind you, it used quite a bit of gas and I had to secretly refill it when I got home.

Whilst I was not at the Civic Hall when The Who played, I followed them to the Broadway Bowl, around a mile or so outside Barnsley town centre, where I got my copy of *My Generation* signed by John Entwistle and Keith Moon. They were having an after-gig drink in the bar. I still have the record and sleeve. My friends and I constantly played 'I Can't Explain' and the other early singles until our parents could take no more. And we were drinking cider back then – very trendy.

GLENN FEARONS, AGE 15

The parents of my girlfriend at the time owned a shop and so she'd get tickets for groups like The Who, the Small Faces and the Kinks. It was a great concert but I particularly remember watching Keith Moon, because I've always been a fan of drummers. He seemed to finish every number, have a rub down with a towel, reach for a bottle of beer from a crate, open it, drink it down and off he'd go again. That's all I remember, apart from at the end when everything went ballistic and everything went all over the stage.

DENNIS LAWSON, AGE 18

I was the bass player in a local group, and we were sixth form students at the local grammar school. Originally, we played Shadows stuff before we got hit by the sound of The Who. We won a best bands competition and were invited to be the warm up band at the Civic Hall for our idols. We couldn't believe it.

We had the de rigueur Vox AC30 amps and were set up in front of the curtains with about two feet of stage, almost falling into the orchestra pit. The Outer Limits were set up behind us and The Who were set up behind them. When The Who came on, and you saw these 100 watt Marshall amps, it was like the Berlin Wall. We were totally taken aback.

We came on at 7.30pm. People were trickling in as we were playing, and we played to an audience of about a dozen, which grew to about 50 people by the end of our set. Because they were our idols – as they still are now – we finished with three Who songs: 'Substitute', 'The Kids Are Alright' and 'My Generation'. Our drummer, Paul White, even scattered his drums at the end. Can you imagine the reaction of the small number in the audience?

We didn't think for one moment that any of The Who would be there, because the Outer Limits were coming on after us (they went on to become Christie and had a hit with 'Yellow River'). We didn't think The Who would be there until about 9pm. So we went backstage and there was Pete Townshend there and we were like, 'My God, what have we done?' Can you imagine our reaction? Pete Townshend was standing there. 'Cheeky bastards' was his opening gambit. I think – I hope - I detected a twinkle in his eye.

And then Roger Daltrey came in, with his long golden locks, his curly hair and a woman on each of his arms. 'Guess what these bastards have been doing?' said Townshend. And then Moonie came in.

The Civic Hall is really old-fashioned and they've got these massive curtains that are about 20 foot long. And, Moonie being Moonie, he just shot straight up 'em and was 20 feet in the air. Fortunately, this was behind the scenes and the audience couldn't see it, but we were thinking 'what the hell's happening here?'. The rest of the band were acting like it was completely normal. 'Not unusual for him,' said Roger Daltrey. Keith then leapt – actually leapt – 20 feet back down onto the floor and landed on all fours. His eyes were like saucers. I think he'd probably had a glass of Pepsi or something.

We were lucky enough to meet the group properly that night. Pete Townshend gave Rod Senior, our lead guitarist, a master class on how to get maximum effect and reverb by using open strings wherever possible in his chords. He said to him 'don't play the chords. Don't play a D there. Play both strings.' And just the slightly different sound that it made, you began to appreciate some of the sounds that that guy was hearing even in '66. This was very effective on the intro to 'Substitute'.

Pete even allowed us to stand in the wings by the curtain, two or three yards away, and watch them perform. What an experience! I was just totally mesmerised. I remember what Moonie was like when he was going. He was the only guy I saw at the time who had two bass drums. How he got this beat going with two bass drums, God only knows. It was absolutely fantastic. We'd said to Pete Townshend beforehand, 'Will you be smashing your guitar up?', and he replied 'it all depends what mood I'm in'. And he did. He smashed his guitar on stage and handed it to Rod as he left. Afterwards, we said, 'That Rickenbacker is £333 in our local shop. How much do you get paid for this?' They got paid £400 for the gig. (We got paid £20.) He said, 'Oh, I don't make any money. This is just stuff for the fans.' In those days they didn't make anything from playing live. All the money was made on the records.

There was a guy there called Chris Stamp. I thought he was a roadie. He was moving all this stuff. I was talking to him and said 'do you want a hand?' but he said 'no, I can manage'. I later found out he was their co-manager. He was talking about this girl he was after called Chrissie Shrimpton. She'd been going out with Jagger and he was after her. It was like we were looking into a goldfish bowl filled with mid-Sixties pop stars. You had to pinch yourself. 'Are we here?'

SUE RILEY, AGE 14

I remember going with a friend from school, and maybe her older sister. We were up on the balcony and had a really good view. It was my first concert by someone famous. I had pin ups of them, Keith being my favourite as I thought he was the best drummer ever. I still have a scrapbook with clippings in from *NME*, *Jackie*, etc. I still have a collection of their records.

MIKE TONRA

I was on stage at the Civic to witness The Who's only appearance in Barnsley. I was doing DJ work and local radio broadcasts and I was part of a team of six compering shows at Barnsley Civic Hall. This gave each of us access backstage to any of the concerts. I got paid between 2/6 (13p) and 5/- (25p) depending on the size of the audience. The manager of the Civic was a John Simmons who had come up from London. He had big ideas about booking artists at the Civic Hall and I think the only three bands that we didn't have, and it was only because we couldn't get bums on seats to make it a viable proposition because of the seating capacity, were the Rolling Stones, The Beatles and The Hollies. The fee was dictated by where an act was in the charts. If the group didn't have a hit in the Top Tenor Top 20, the agent could negotiate a better deal to get them.

The auditorium was packed with screaming teenage girls and their lads, with an atmosphere of excitement and anticipation on the back of The Who's recent chart and LP success with *My Generation*. Prior to the concert, I took my copy of *My Generation* to their dressing room and asked them to sign it. I was half expecting them to decline to do so, but, amazingly, each signed as I took it round them. I later sold their autographs, something I now regret.

Their performance consisted of all their well-known hits up to that time, R&B standards and a self-penned instrumental – 'The Ox'. It was a sensational night, and I was standing just a few feet away from Pete Townshend when he started smashing his amplifiers. When the manager said, 'Quick, he's going to push the speakers over,' the crew, manager, agent, compere and team were all standing behind the speakers because they were going to fall. Townshend was going at them like he had an axe. He just swung the guitar and smashed it into the front, right at the end, and the amplifiers were all down. Keith Moon was smashing his drum kit up in a frenzy. It was mayhem. This is what the kids had come to see. That's what there was excitement about – the destruction they were witnessing. Keith, wet through from his exertions, was the last to exit the stage, walking off through his kit and the debris from the mayhem. It was a typical night for a Who concert, or so I was told.

There were two girl Who followers backstage with us as the set finished. They were from Wythenshawe in Manchester. We had chatted with them throughout the concert. One was called Sue. A little later, we were all in the dressing room and Keith enquired about late night action in Barnsley. There was none at this time, other than Barnsley Bowl which was a bowling alley off Dodworth Road, behind what is now the main Ford Polar Garage. I told Keith this and it was agreed he would follow me in my Mini, with me taking the two girls. He did, and we had a couple of frames of bowling together, with my main attention moving from Keith to Sue. I think she was a groupie. She told me she was John Entwistle's girlfriend, which was the carrot which got me to take her back home over the Pennines. We went back to Wythenshawe with the promise of meeting up with some of the members of the group.

She was really attractive and we started with a friendship, and her mum and dad asked me to come over. I kept going over to Manchester hoping for – ahem, well you can imagine what I was hoping for – but her parents were really friendly but good Catholic, so every time I went over to visit, we got separate rooms. It was the Swinging Sixties but not everyone was swinging. Eventually the miles and the driving back in the early hours of the morning got to me and I thought, 'Sod it. I've had enough of trailing over to Manchester.'

23 JULY 1966
SPA ROYAL HALL, BRIDLINGTON, UK

PAUL JENKINSON, AGE 14

Bridlington Spa was the largest dance hall on the east coast of England. You could get 5,000 people in there at any one time, and everyone played there – Little Richard, Roy Orbison, Ike and Tina Turner, Three Dog Night. Free played here twice. For a 14-year-old, it was just crazy. I was the drummer with 21st Century who supported The Who. We were on first, The Who were the main band and then there was a band on afterwards called the Mandrakes, whose singer was Robert Palmer. He was from Scarborough originally. The rest of 21st Century were a lot older than me, in their late teens and early twenties. Their drummer broke his leg one Saturday afternoon and I got a bang on my door saying, 'We understand that you've got a drum kit – do you want to join a band?' I said I did and they said 'oh good, because we're playing tonight'. We did two gigs that night and they never asked the other guy back.

You'd heard rumours about The Who wrecking gear and seen little bits on TV, but when you saw it first-hand it's like 'wow!'. I can remember the roadies ripping all the cellophane off the amps and everything, including the Premier kit. I had a red glitter Premier kit myself at the time, as did Moonie.

They finished their act with 'My Generation' and they destroyed everything on stage. There was nothing left. It was all mashed. John Entwistle smacked his guitar right on the top of the amp and, as he walked downstairs into the changing rooms, chucked the two halves of his guitar – it was all held together by the strings – and said 'here, fix that if you can'.

I think Moonie was in a Bentley and they were staying at the Windsor Hotel in Bridlington. I never saw it myself but somebody said that he smashed it into the back wall of the car park. Townshend got in an Austin 1800 and just revved it until it seized up. It was absolute carnage.

BILLY LESTER

My group The 21st Century had already appeared with The Who in a previous line up the year before, as The Corvettes. After meeting them for a sound check in the afternoon, they allowed us to use their PA system and invited us back to their hotel for drinks and a game of darts.

The evening concert was a sell-out, with The Who living up to their reputation as a visual rock concept, and the audience were treated to a brilliant performance as they tirelessly and powerfully went through their hit songs – 'Substitute', 'I'm a Boy', 'My Generation', etc. During the afternoon soundcheck, I had noticed a roadie taping up a red Rickenbacker guitar that was all smashed up and wondered why. I decided to stand in the wings of the stage to watch them perform. Towards the end of their show, dry ice was blown across the stage and a roadie appeared next to me and then squatted behind Pete Townshend's Marshall stack. When Pete started to attack his speaker with his regular guitar, the roadie began to rock the stack to and fro. Amidst the dry ice, this seemed like Pete was hitting the Marshall with his guitar. However, a second roadie then appeared next to me and swapped the regular guitar for the taped-up version with Pete. The audience could not see this because of the amount of dry ice onstage.

Pete then proceeded to smash this guitar on the stage floor and the guitar fell apart, whereupon Pete threw it into the frenzied crowd quickly followed by the two roadies diving in to retrieve it. Roger Daltrey twirled his microphone above his head before hurling it into the audience, Keith Moon kicked his drum kit all over the stage, threw his drum sticks into the crowd and fell backwards off his drum stool, not realising that there was a six-foot drop from his drum platform to the stage floor. Fortunately, he was uninjured and walked off the stage looking a bit dazed.

SUE ROBERTS (NEE SCOTT)

I was a massive fan. I was right at the front of the stage and waiting to catch one of Keith Moon's drumsticks when he threw them in the audience at the end of the concert. However, the drumsticks didn't make it that far this time. After a manic drum finale, Keith kicked the drums over and promptly fell off his stool, knocking himself out. He was carried off the stage by his roadies. Just a day in the life of Keith Moon I suppose!

JOHN LESSENTIN, AGE 17

I was on lead guitar and vocals with a band called Three Plus One and we supported The Who on their second visit to Bridlington Spa during 1966. The Spa manager, John Stephenson, was also our manager, hence we got to support all the top bands at the Spa. Tickets were 7/6 (37p). Two twin wheelbase Transit vans arrived with all the gear. First in on the stage was the drum roadie. He was about to hammer blocks of wood with six-inch nails into the stage to secure the bass drums when John, the Spa's manager, said 'you are not hammering nails into my stage'. The roadie replied, 'Either I do, or The Who won't play tonight.' He nailed the blocks to the stage.

A crowd of around 5,000 were standing in the hall by 8pm. I knocked on The Who's dressing room door with three guitars. Pete opened the door, grabbed the guitars and pretended to smash them. They were autographed by all the band who also autographed a piece of paper for me. Our roadie then grabbed a pack of Izal toilet paper and copied The Who's signatures, selling them to the crowd for a shilling each.

The Who allowed my band to play 'I Can't Explain' and 'Anyway, Anyhow, Anywhere'. They took to the stage at 9pm, finishing around 10.30pm. They were very loud and a roadie held Pete's speaker stacks to stop them moving across the stage due to the volume. The drums were smashed, fireworks let off and Pete smashed his Telecaster to bits against a concrete pillar. We stood at the side of the stage and I grabbed the headstock and the first three frets with the strings hanging off. It was a hell of a night.

Bridlington Spa is now limited to 3,300 people after a health and safety risk assessment. There was none of that in 1966.

PETER BELT, AGE 18

I was in a band called Three Plus One who played regularly at the Spa Royal Hall, Bridlington on Saturday evenings supporting famous groups. Usually, two local groups did a stint on stage before and after the main attraction but we had to be finished for 11.45pm to pack up and be out for midnight under the terms of the entertainment licence. We were lucky enough to support other bands like The Searchers, Swinging Blue Jeans, Animals, Small Faces, The Foremost, Four Pennies and several more that I can't remember now. As a new band member, I was learning all the group songs during the 1966 World Cup tournament.

When we were setting up our gear on stage, The Who roadies had already set up their gear on stage with the usual large amplifier and speaker combinations and our small Vox AC30 amplifiers were very diminutive compared to theirs. I remember Pete Townshend coming on to the stage while we were setting up and offered me the opportunity of using his big amp and speakers. I politely refused, explaining I had only just got used to the settings on my own amp for the different songs that we played.

During The Who's performance, we stood in the audience at the front of the stage where we got an ear bashing from their speakers and some members of our band were able to pick up splinters of wood from Pete Townsend's Fender Telecaster, which he drove through his speaker cabinets and smashed to bits on the floor.

BILLY LESTER

The Who said we could call and see them off from their hotel the next day. The first car out of the hotel car park was a white Aston Martin driven by Roger, then Pete in a bottle green E-Type Jaguar and, lastly, a Rolls-Royce Silver Shadow containing a grinning Keith Moon and John Entwistle with their own chauffeur, as neither had a driving licence at the time. We waved them off down the road. Even though they would soon forget us, we knew we would always remember them.

28 JULY 1966
QUEEN'S HALL, BARNSTAPLE, UK

PETER GLEAVE, AGE 16

A gang of us would go to the Queens Hall every week to see a chart act. The Who were head and shoulders above the other acts. They were that good, the fighting in the audience stopped. But at the end of the show, a bare-chested Roger Daltrey came out from behind the curtain and offered to take a heckler outside!

PETER REVELEY, AGE 18

I was at that concert, or 'dance' as we thought of them in those days, with a mate from Appledore and a number of school friends from Bideford Grammar School – Richard Ashley, John Blackmore, Neil Cooper, Martin Petherbridge and Richard Mendham. I remember the event well, not least because after the interval, Mendham came back to the dance floor rather dishevelled. When asked what had happened, he commented 'just had a fight with that daft drummer in the bar'. He'd had a fight with Keith Moon, probably over a girl.

MARILYN SMYTH, AGE 18

I saw them before I left home, aged 18, when they were fairly unknown. It was more of a dance hall than a theatre. Incidentally, my brother has researched the family tree and it seems we are related to Roger Daltrey. My maternal grandmother was a Daltrey before her marriage.

20 AUGUST 1966
TOWN HALL, TORQUAY, UK

DAVY JONES

I was in a band called The Sixth Sense. Lionel Digby booked us twice as support for The Who at Torquay Town Hall. It was at a time when The Who were being fractious with each other and the others weren't talking to Roger Daltrey, so he shared our dressing room while the rest of The Who used the other one. We'd been on stage and had gone to the bar when Jeff Ramsell, our road manager, went up the stairs to our dressing room to look for us, just as Roger was coming out. Jeff said to him, 'Roger, have you seen the Sixth Sense?' and Roger said, 'Yeah, they're a fucking good band!' When Lionel heard that story he said, 'We'll put it on the publicity posters!'

We supported them again the following year. There was a servery in the backstage area, where they did teas and coffees and where Ma Digby used to do sandwiches and Cokes. She had moved a big chrome tea urn into the backstage area. Keith Moon came into the backstage area, bought a Coke from Ma Digby and left it, half finished, on the top of the tea urn. The show was a total sell out. The Town Hall was supposed to hold 1,200 and Lionel had got 1,500 in there. The place was sweating, with so many people in there the condensation was running down the walls. It was absolutely bouncing. Jeff came into the backstage area, saw the half-finished Coke up on the top of the tea urn and necked it. Keith Moon then came down the stairs from his dressing room and said 'who had my fucking Coke?'. Jeff said, 'It was me, Keith. I'll get you another one.' And Keith Moon said, 'You couldn't fucking afford it.' For the rest of the evening, Jeff was flying high as a kite. We could hardly keep him on the ground. It was the first and last time he ever took drugs.

All the groupies used to try and push through the stage door, and I was at the top of the stairs letting small groups of girls into the dressing room to see The Who and get their autographs. All these Moddy girls were coming up the stairs, and I'd let three or four in at a time, and another three or four in after they left. One girl had a very fashionable keyhole dress on, with holes down each side. When she came into the dressing room, Keith Moon launched himself at her like a chimpanzee, trying to get his feet around her waist. His feet went in through the holes in the side and almost pulled the dress off her.

In 1969, The Who were headlining on the second day at Plumpton Racecourse. Roger had a new Stingray sports car and during the afternoon he came out around the back of the showground where people were collecting around this car and talking to him. Jeff and I wandered over. He said, 'Oh hello, you guys. You're the guys from Torquay, aren't you?' He didn't remember our names, but he remembered where we'd played with him. He's a really, really good guy. He changed in our changing room and there was no side to him at all.

23 AUGUST 1966
SHERWOOD ROOMS, NOTTINGHAM, UK

TINA SEARCY, AGE 16

My friend and I were at the front of the queue to go in very early when we found a stray dog. We took him to the police station on Canal Street and when we got back, the queue was 15 people deep. They were brilliant, even though the instruments got broken.

24 AUGUST 1966
ORCHID BALLROOM, PURLEY, UK

BEV ROWLAND

I discovered their music back in the early '60s when I was a Mod. We used to go to a place called the Orchid Ballroom where you just queued up, paid to get in and ran to the front. I saw The Who there twice and was absolutely smitten. They were exciting, risqué, loud and there were loads of Mods. The sight of Keith Moon kicking his drumkit over and Pete Townsend smashing his guitar was just magic. I managed to catch Keith's broken drumsticks which, alas, I have lost over the years. I'd have looked after them more carefully had I realised they would go on to be one of the best rock bands in the world. I've seen them since at the Albert Hall, for a Teenage Cancer Trust gig, not knowing that it would be John Entwistle's last ever London gig. I still love their music and have carried that over to my sons, who have both seen The Who live.

25 AUGUST 1966
DREAMLAND BALLROOM, MARGATE, UK

JOHN SANDERS

The Dreamland had a weekly dance on Sunday nights with a top line (or soon to be) act. But on 25 August 1966 there was something special, so special that it was held not on a Sunday but a Thursday night. We had heard about The Who, but we were not prepared for what happened. The music was so loud and so powerful that we were all entranced. Nobody was dancing – apart from on the spot as we slowly but surely pushed forward to be nearer the stage and nearer certain deafness.

At least one of the strings on Pete Townshend's guitar broke mid-number and Pete snapped. He smashed his guitar over the top of one of the amplifiers, snapping off the headstock. Picking up another guitar, he seemed to get lost attempting to slot back in with the others and then he totally lost it, kicking and pulling over parts of Keith Moon's drum kit. Despite this, Roger Daltrey continued playing which seemed to provoke Pete even more, resulting in him thrusting his guitar into amplifier after amplifier, trying to stop the music. By the time they left the stage, it was just piles of rubbish. The atmosphere in the ballroom was one of shock, with everyone slowly and quietly leaving to go home, none of us stopping to collect souvenirs from amongst the mess!

PETER TIDBALL

Keith was amazing. At times he would throw a drumstick into the air and catch it. Sometimes he would drop it, but he had a row of spares on his kit. Eventually he ran out, so he got a torch and went round the stage looking for any that might be there. This was all the time that the band was playing. He kicked his drums off the stage at the end. Other recollections are of Roger twirling the mic by its long lead around his head, barely missing Pete. And as the mic passed the speakers, each one gave out feed back in succession. It was an amazing sound. Great vocals as well. And there was John, one of the most talented bass players of all time, working his understanding with Keith, and Pete's brilliant guitar playing and showmanship, which finished with him smacking his guitar to the floor many times. It all added up to a phenomenal night. They finished off with smoke bombs! Afterwards, we were walking home and all I could hear was a ringing in my ears. Thankfully, it only lasted for about half an hour!

2 SEPTEMBER 1966
LOCARNO, BASILDON, UK

BARBARA WEBBER

My friend Chrissie had asked me to make up a foursome. I had only left school the previous summer. I worked in a bank in London and my pay was £510 per annum, so with the train fares and paying Mum for my keep, there wasn't much left for me. I had only a few 'going out' clothes so I wore a dress from the summer I left school. It was yellow, silky and sleeveless with black stripes round it. I must have looked like a demented wasp but I thought I looked 'the bee's knees'!

The Mecca was packed. To be honest, The Who had never floated my boat. I was more into Motown and soul. We started at the back where the boys could prop up the bar, but when the concert began, I was soon itching to get down the front. Chrissie wouldn't leave her man, so off I went. Hanging on the front of the stage, I saw the guitars being smashed, the drum kit falling over and, with the incredible music, the crowd going wild. It was quite an eye opener for this country girl. I don't think I saw my date again, as I spent all the gig down at the front.

10 SEPTEMBER 1966
CORN EXCHANGE, BEDFORD, UK

STEVE COBHAM, AGE 14

A local coach firm used to offer combined coach and gig deals and I booked a ticket to see The Who, along with some friends from school. I was 14, and I'm amazed I was allowed to go. It was the first proper gig I'd been to with a name band, and I was a massive Who fan. The Corn Exchange was a Victorian pile in the town centre and quite grand. I'd actually been there a few years before to play recorder in a schools music competition – so I played a gig there before The Who! 'I'm a Boy' was in the charts. To be frank, it was all a bit overwhelming and very, very loud indeed. Of course, what everyone was waiting for was a guitar to be smashed. Pete didn't disappoint. Just before their last number, a roadie hopped up onstage and handed him a Rickenbacker to replace the one he'd been using for the set. He flipped the doomed guitar over and you could see that the hollow body was held together with green Meccano strips. This was obviously a recycled instrument. He poked inside and a very loud buzz came out of his Marshall stacks. Whatever he did that for, he seemed happy to use the guitar and the band launched into 'My Generation' and the Rick got well and truly totalled while Moon was kicking over his drums. And that was it. I was absolutely buzzing and the gig set me off going to see more bands, although I never saw The Who again.

11 SEPTEMBER 1966
DOWNS HOTEL, HASSOCKS, UK

MICK BLACKBURN

I first saw the Who at the Florida Rooms in Brighton, where they played regularly as the High Numbers. I only remember them playing the Ultra Club in Hassocks once. I helped set up

Clockwise from top left: John Lessentin's band supported The Who at Bridlington; Billy Lester's poster advertising the Bridlington gig; Marilyn Smith is a distant cousin of Roger Daltrey; John Sanders was at Margate and saw The Who destroy their kit; Bridlington saw The 21st Century support The Who.

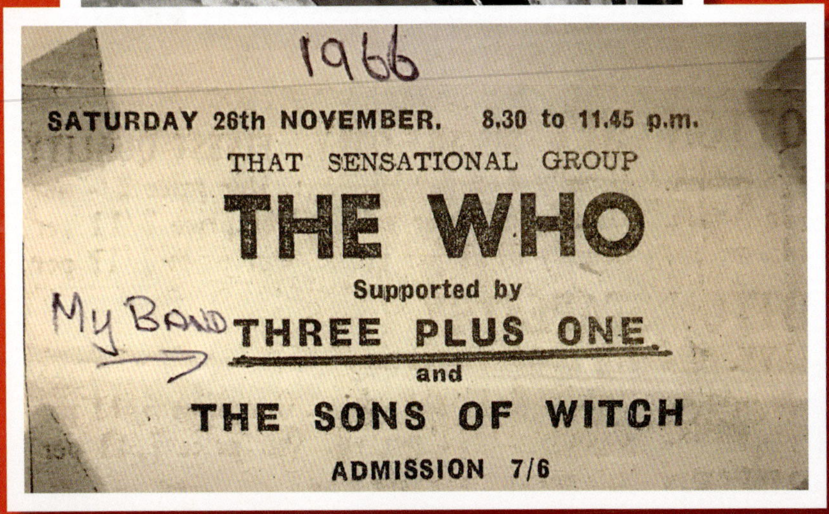
1966

SATURDAY 26th NOVEMBER. 8.30 to 11.45 p.m.

THAT SENSATIONAL GROUP

THE WHO

Supported by

My Band → THREE PLUS ONE

and

THE SONS OF WITCH

ADMISSION 7/6

Clockwise from top left: Mick Blackburn set up the equipment for support band The Dominators at the Downs Hotel in Hassocks; Phil Bower fell asleep after a few pints but was woken by The Who; Dave Carmichael got a tuning peg from the remains of Townshend's guitar; John Lessentin's Bridlington ticket; Janet Hepburn Tavendale (left) was at Perth City Halls.

equipment for local band The Dominators, who were playing that night as support band. We commented on the state of their amplifiers, especially Pete Townshend's, which was covered with a Union Flag to disguise the many attacks it had received from his guitar. Pete managed to break the neck off his guitar that night and, as it was of no further use, he left it behind. Rescued at the end of the show by The Dominators' lead guitarist, it was subsequently repaired and used for many gigs afterwards.

RICK DIVALL

I was playing in a local band and we supported The Who at one of their gigs that year. We started off as Rob and the Dominators, but Rob left so we became a harmony band as none of us would admit to being a singer. The Who turned up very late, which meant we had to play much longer than expected, which was annoying, especially as they got paid massively more than us. As expected, they smashed up their gear and one of Pete Townshend's pickups flew off the stage, where one of my friends managed to retrieve it. It has been on one of his guitars ever since.

MARIANNE HOBBY

My husband Mick was in The Dominators when they played on the same bill as The Who in 1966. I was not there that evening; my husband and I hadn't yet met. Sadly, he died in 2011. Graham, who was also in the band, collected a pick up from one of the smashed Who guitars.

GRAHAM GORING

I played in The Dominators with Rick Divall and Mick Hobby at the Downs Hotel with The Who. I didn't know we would be backing them until I turned up at the gig and saw the poster. I remember Keith Moon arriving in his white Roller and parking it haphazardly. On The Who's last number, Pete Townshend changed his guitar from behind his equipment and brought out a Rickenbacker. He smashed it against his Marshall stack, a bit went flying, there was a scrabble and I managed to grab a pickup. I've still got it.

The Downs Hotel had a basement which accommodated up to two hundred people. It was our local Sunday night place, where we could see some big name bands. I cried for years when they knocked it down.

DAVID GOODWIN

When they came back a few months after their first appearance at the Downs, they did a very powerful top notch performance. The difference in the two performances was astonishing. This time we got a more professional performance, like they would give at a theatre rather than a 250 capacity dance hall. The difference between the two performances was chalk and cheese.

JOHN RITCHIE

I lived six or seven miles away. Hassocks is such a small, sleepy little town, but it all happened in those two or three years. When I think back about it now and tell my children, it's almost unbelievable how good it used to be there. It was a hotel run by a gay ex-RAF captain called Pete Shawland, who had connections with show business. He and two other guys used to get all the people there. Because he was also gay and was a friend of this guy, Long John Baldry used to serve behind the bar.

It was downstairs and the bar was at the top of the place. The stage was probably eighteen inches high and the people on the dance floor were all right there. That's how close everybody was to everything that was going on.

Everybody apart from The Beatles and the Stones appeared there. People used to come from miles around. It was 2/6 – just half a crown (13p) – to get in. If you had a pound, you could get extremely drunk. It was the highlight of the weekend, to be honest. The Who were really good. That's when they used to smash up their gear and it was all going into the crowd and all sorts. People had never seen anything like it.

MIKE ROBSON, AGE 13

I saw them with Keith several times. The first time was The Downs Hotel in Hassocks. I lived in Burgess Hill, a couple of miles down the road. it was a rescheduled gig from a cancellation the month before and there were handbills on every lamppost in the area advertising it. 'I'm a Boy' was the latest single at the time. I went there on my bike and sneaked in through the toilet window so my view was very restricted. It was wild. They still did a lot of Motown covers then. I only went the once though. At 13, it was a forbidden place! They were always the best show in town. The next time was April 1967 at the Dome in Brighton; the undercard was Cream, Crispian St Peters and The Merseys. It was an excellent show – everything got smashed and I saw a bloke run off with Keith's snare drum, which had fallen off the stage. The last time I saw them with Keith was Charlton in '76. It was a great show but there were no smash ups and Keith was off the boil. He wasn't as innovative and I think he was knackered after the first ten minutes!

15 SEPTEMBER 1966
GAUMONT CINEMA, HANLEY, UK

PHIL BOWER, AGE 16

I went with two friends to watch The Who, although I remember there were good supporting acts, including John Walker of the Walker Brothers. We caught a bus to Hanley and called into the now-demolished Vine for a few pre-show drinks, despite being under age! Not being used to the beer, I fell asleep during the first part of the show, but was woken up when The Who came on – they were so loud I would have woken up anyway! They were brilliant and we enjoyed the performance, climaxing in Keith Moon kicking over his drums and Pete Townshend smashing his guitar on the bits of drum kit left. In truth, having seen The Who on TV, the destruction was one of the main reasons why we went to watch them.

SANDRA BROWNSWORD, AGE 16

I saw The Who at the Kings Hall in Stoke-on-Trent on 19 March 1966 when I got all four autographs, and later the same year at the Gaumont Theatre in Hanley, when they were on the same bill as the Walker Brothers. I again obtained Keith Moon and John Entwistle's autographs. They arrived in a Bentley registration number LLF 905! My main memory is the sheer volume of their performance.

MIKE JONES, AGE 16

My first 45 was 'I Can't Explain' and my first album was *My Generation*. I heard from my cousin, Tim, who lived in Wellington at the time, that they had appeared at the Majestic but I didn't go to see them. I'd also heard that they'd played at Wem Town Hall as well but that it hadn't been good value for money as they had only performed three songs. Acts would sometimes have two bookings in one night and the archives might show that they appeared at, say, Wellington but earlier in the evening had played a short set somewhere else, not too far away.

I first saw The Who in Hanley at the Gaumont Theatre just as 'I'm a Boy' was released. The support act was Cream! I went on to see them a number of times between 1967 and 1969 at the Civic Hall in Nantwich. The hits had pretty well dried up and they were on comparatively hard times but still amazing. I saw them both before and after the hall was extended, and I remember Pete Townshend commenting on how much better the venue was.

I went with a mate, Bill, who managed to get thrown out just as the curtains opened for the opening chords to 'I'm a Boy'. So, Bill and I were 65 in 2017 and what do you buy a guy who has everything? I managed to buy a mint copy of the Reaction label single of 'I'm a Boy' and framed it and gave it to him as a reminder of what he missed all those years ago! I'd forgotten the lyric 'my name is Bill and I'm a headcase'. He drew this to my attention and asked if it was a comment on his mental state. I guess it was.

TERRY VICKERS

My mother worked at the Hanley Gaumont cinema, now the Regent. Loads of artists played this venue when they were on tour. I was in my early teens but my mum managed to wangle a job for me on the stage for most of the concerts. I had to stand in the wings and then walk across the stage with the tabs before and after each act, pulling back the microphones, etc. to move them out of the way. It was an unpaid job but I was at an age when I would have willingly paid for the privilege of being there.

The management of the Gaumont were very concerned that Keith Moon would do something crazy after their final stint. To their relief, apart from sending his drums flying over the stage he only managed to burst a bag of sugar (or possibly flour) onto the stage. Towards the end of their act, he also donned a motorbike crash helmet he'd had borrowed from a guy working backstage.

I was alongside Pete Townshend during the concert and I noticed that there was a pre-prepared cut in his speaker cabinet into which he inserted his guitar at the end of their act. The audience thought this was part of the 'smashing up of the equipment' at the end of each gig which had become their trademark!

During an interval, I asked Keith Moon for his autograph and whether he could give me a spare drumstick as a memento. He led me backstage where he had a sports bag crammed with new drumsticks and invited me to pick one!

After the show, I was outside the Gaumont with my mother and a few other employees, waiting for our lift home, when Keith and John Entwistle, dressed in their garish stage attire of satin trousers and shirts etc., appeared from the stage door and headed down the street towards us. The walk soon changed to a gallop as they began to be chased by a couple of girl fans. A Bentley then drove past and a short time later, the car headed back up the street and sped out of sight with Keith, John and the two girls all inside!

16 SEPTEMBER 1966
ODEON CINEMA, DERBY, UK

CARL CHESWORTH

Between 1965 and 1967 I was on the projection staff at the Odeon before transferring to the Superama/Odeon Pennine in Colyear Street. We would often present 'one night only' stage shows. The Who were supported by the famous variety theatre artiste Max Wall, and I was working on the stage. I usually helped operate the two follow-spots up in the projection room and I remember Max Wall being booed off the stage during his famous Professor Walloski routine and the tour's manager asking me to bring the curtain down on him as the audience were becoming threatening.

The show's compere was pushed back on stage to quell the restless audience and the following act had to make a quick entry! I remember taking my autograph book that evening and being able to talk with Max Wall. There were tears in his eyes as he signed my book for me and said that television had ruined him. In his variety days he could tour the halls for weeks on end with his various sketches but, once on television, everyone had seen him. He cut a very sad and dejected figure as he shook my hand and walked out of the theatre stage door.

The Who lived up to the audience's expectations and, as expected, smashed all their instruments up at the end of the show. I was sent on stage during this mayhem, on both sides of the footlights, to retrieve the Odeon's microphones and stands. What a night that was!

BARBARA ZOPPI, AGE 16

I think The Who are the best group we've ever had in this country. I was on the front row. I met Pet e Townshend afterwards. I managed to get front row tickets by going early. I lived on a farm but I'd go to my friend's on my bike, getting the workman's bus and going and sitting on the very cold steps. If we didn't get the front row, we didn't want to go. We were first in the queue as usual when it opened at 9am. We paid very little for tickets. It was no more than five bob (25p), possibly less. I wish I'd kept the ticket. They were loud, loud, loud – the loudest thing I'd ever heard, and it probably still is.

Roger had just been driven off by an attractive brunette in a low blue sports car when Pete came down the steps in the dark looking like a flasher, wearing a flasher mac and carrying an old battered brown suitcase. He very quietly and politely asked us the way to the Midland Hotel, a few streets away. He admired my friend's little fur jacket and the gold star on her face. Pete Townshend is my number one joint best writer, with Neil Innes. I just love everything about The Who. I always have and always will.

I think Roger Daltrey had the best voice. I saw him doing *Tommy* in Nottingham a few years ago and it's one of the best concerts I've ever seen. He stopped a few bars into the first song and spoke to the band a bit and started again and then waved his arms. Then they stopped again. They couldn't get it right. A bloke shouted out 'get on with it!' and Daltrey turned around and said 'you wanna come up here and say that?'. Dead silence! He's little, but would you argue with him?

14 OCTOBER 1966
QUEENS HALL, LEEDS, UK

BARRY LEONARD

I and my mates saw this all-night do they did. Jimmy Savile was the man in charge on stage. Yes, loony Moon did smash up the set when they had done, but what a night to remember.

CHRIS SMITH

The Queen's Hall was a huge tin can and the sound would echo but that didn't worry them. They played one hit after another and I can't remember any introductions at all. They looked exactly like they did on telly in their Mod gear. Did Townshend wear his Union Jack jacket? I'm not sure. Anyway, they were totally impressive and put on a professional performance despite the sound problems.

The third time I saw The Who it must have been 1973 or 1974. I was sitting on the second to front row at the Marquee Club in London. At the end they smashed up a lot of equipment. Keith totalled the drum kit and Pete broke his black Gibson 335 into splinters. A piece landed at my feet and picking it up I found it was the piece with the yellow Gibson guarantee. It was like viewing a war zone up close and personal. I gave the guarantee splinter to a painter friend who is a big Who fan so he could do a Peter Blake-type Who collage.

18 NOVEMBER 1966
CITY HALLS, PERTH, UK

JANET HEPBURN TAVENDALE

That Friday night my friends and I had been at our usual Girl Guide meeting followed by a visit to the village chip shop. Hanging about on the shop doorstep, someone mentioned that The Who were playing at the dance at Perth City Halls. We decided we should go. One of the boys agreed to drive us in his baby Austin car – I don't think we gave him much choice. We all ran home to change out of our Guide uniforms and gather again a few minutes later at the car. I still remember my dear father welcoming me in, thinking that was me home for bed earlier than usual, only to hear that I was going straight out again and to a dance 15 miles away. I still remember his caution (well, his quiet word 'no') as I quickly ran upstairs to my bedroom to get changed into my mini-kilt and my mother's pre-war shirt, made from black-market silk bought by her in Germany just before war broke out. When I came back downstairs, my beloved dad quietly handed me a ten shilling (50p) note and told me to have a good time. And we did!

Entry at the door was seven shillings and six pennies (37p) – no advance booking, no waiting months for the exciting event, no sitting in numbered seats! My memory is that we danced. It wasn't a concert. We watched Keith Moon knocking his drums around and we danced – not just like the dancing in the aisles you can see at a concert today. The way I remember it was that they were just the band at the dance that night, albeit a particularly exciting band that we already knew about.

In 2016, my husband bought two tickets to see The Who playing in Glasgow on my birthday, so it was a celebration of the actual day and a reminder of my youth! It was slightly more expensive than the 37.5p spur of the moment that I (or rather, my dad) paid in 1966 and required slightly more advanced planning!

19 NOVEMBER 1966
MARKET HALL, CARLISLE, UK

IAN REED

As a penniless art student, and with only money for beer, I was in the bar of The Crown and Mitre Hotel in Carlisle with friends, the plushest hotel in town. We knew The Who were performing in the Market Hall but we had no tickets. The four lads standing next to us asked if we were going to gig and were we art students. It was The Who! We explained our situation and Roger said he always wanted to be an art student and was sympathetic to our plight. 'Come with us and you can get in if you pretend to be part of our team to set up on stage!' We spent the entire performance standing in the wings and must have had the best 'seats'.

24 NOVEMBER 1966
PAVILION BALLROOM, WORTHING, UK

JOHN FEEST

The next time I saw The Who, Keith was surrounded by drums and they had progressed to Marshall stacks. I remember being at the foot of the stage when Keith demolished his kit and a cymbal and stand landed right in front of me. It could have done me a lot of damage.

26 NOVEMBER 1966
SPA ROYAL HALL, BRIDLINGTON, UK

DAVE CARMICHAEL, AGE 17

I was playing lead guitar in a band called That Feeling. We played soul music – Wilson Pickett, James Brown, Sam and Dave, etc. – recent chart stuff. There was a big dance floor in the Spa. It's quite a high stage and we were stood right near the front at one side on the right-hand side, where Pete Townshend was stood. I can't remember what he was using, probably a Rickenbacker, but for the last number Pete changed his guitar for a Fender Telecaster. At the end of the song, they got all the feedback going and he took his guitar off, got it in his hand and was banging the neck against his big amplifier stack. Bits came flying off the guitar and some of it landed on the floor. One of the metal ferrules that's part of the tuning peg at the end of the guitar neck came off and landed near me on the floor. I've still got it.

3 DECEMBER 1966,
MIDNIGHT CITY, BIRMINGHAM, UK

JOHN BILLINGHAM

The Who came to my attention through my friend's eldest sister. She was also a Mod but a couple of years older than we were. She'd been going down to London with her boyfriend and got a copy of 'I Can't Explain'. This single really opened our eyes. I bought the single myself and every single after up to 'Pinball Wizard'.

The Midnight was a real Mod club underneath the famous Ye Old Moat House Club in Bradford Street. It couldn't sell alcohol and customers 'liked' drugs, especially purple hearts. It was raided and basically didn't last after that. I was bought the ticket to see The Who for my 17th birthday, which was on the 15th of the month. I went with Rob South, a friend from school who was same age as me. I wore a Neville Reed three-button, waisted herringbone suit with a twelve-inch centre vent, a smart white shirt with plain black tie and black basketweave shoes.

It was a Saturday night and all I can really remember is that – it was great! The Midnight City was a small club and we were right there with my heroes. They opened with 'Heat Wave' and did stuff off the first and second LPs, finishing with 'My Generation'. The atmosphere was sweaty and electric. Roger put his soul into the vocal, Pete was really animated, Moon was Moon and John was as enigmatic as ever. It was a great performance, and the best I ever saw after Otis Redding at the Birmingham Hippodrome. Someone has written on the web that Keith Moon collapsed and was taken to hospital. I have no recollection of this.

10 DECEMBER 1966
EMPIRE THEATRE, SUNDERLAND, UK

KEVIN GREEN

I was in the front row with my friend David Hunter. I'd never seen anything like it. I saw The Beatles at the end of '63, topping the bill at the Empire, and I saw the Stones at the Odeon in Newcastle in '65. But The Who were great. No screaming girls so you could hear them play – and they could play!

17 DECEMBER 1966
IMPERIAL BALLROOM, NELSON, UK

DAVID ALMOND

We played with them twice at the Imp, in December 1966 and again in November 1967. We got the gig through an agency. The first time we played with them there was a band called the Rockin' Vickers. And the Rockin' Vickers reckoned The Who nicked the song 'The Kids Are Alright' off them. We were in the downstairs dressing room when The Who all came in. On the wall the Rockin' Vickers had written 'who are The Who anyway?'. And Pete Townshend borrowed a pen and wrote underneath 'if you don't know now you never will.'

Moon didn't have a driving licence and neither did John Entwistle so they used to turn up in a chauffeur-driven Bentley. We saw it outside. There were three dressing rooms at Nelson. I went to the upstairs dressing room looking for my mates who I was playing with, and Keith Moon was drinking vodka and lime juice. He poured me a drink and we talked for about 20 minutes about drums, Premier and sponsorship. I think he was sponsored by Zildjan cymbals. It was a good conversation. His kit was the one with 'Pictures of Lily' on. He was just relaxed. He wasn't drunk or owt like that. I think Daltrey and Townshend

L.M.D. ENTERTAINMENTS LTD.

Telephone 22383
24 HOUR TEL-STOR
TELEPHONE ANSWERING SERVICE

The oldest established entertainment agency in the westcountry

DIRECTORS: T. M. R. DIGBY · R. E. DIGBY · L. H. DIGBY
PRODUCTION HOUSE: 19 HIGHER UNION LANE · TORQUAY · DEVON

VARIETY ACTS ★ DANCE BANDS ★ STAR ATTRACTIONS ★ BEAT GROUPS

1047. THE WHO.

This Agency is not responsible for any non-fulfilment of Contracts by Proprietors, Managers or Artistes, but every reasonable safeguard is assured

An Agreement made the 25th day of July, 1966.
between Bay Rose & Management, Flamingo Ballroom, Redruth,
hereinafter called the Management of the one part and L.M.D. ENTERTAINMENTS Ltd, TORQUAY,
hereinafter called the Artiste of the other part

Witnesseth that the Management hereby engages the Artiste and the Artiste accepts an engagement to present THE WHO. appear as XXXXX. or in his usual entertainment) at the Dance Hall/Theatre and from the dates for the periods and at the salaries stated in the Schedule hereto.

The Artiste agrees to appear at ONE Evening / XXXXXX Matinee performances at a salary of £300.

SCHEDULE

ONE Day(s) at Flamingo Ballroom, Redruth. on Wednesday 27th July, 1966.
XXXXXXX Day(s) at on
XXXXXXX Day(s) at on
XXXXXXX Day(s) at on

ADDITIONAL CLAUSES

a. The terms are inclusive of all expenses for the above band.
b. ~~It is agreed that the Management will provide and pay for microphone equipment and grand piano.~~
c. It is agreed that the above band will appear in person throughout the performance of his Orchestra/Band Act.
d. Playing times to be decided by the management but it is agreed that the above band. will not be required to play for more than a total of One 40 minutes XX hours, in one evening.
e. The Artiste shall not, without the written consent of the Management, appear at any public place of entertainment within a radius of 25 miles of the venue during a period of 4 weeks immediately prior to and 2 weeks immediately following the engagement.
f. The artiste to arrive not later than 7.0 p.m. and be set up for playing by 8.0 p.m.
g. All financial settlement to take place with Artiste on the Evening.
h. The management agrees that any other bands performing the engagement shall be composed of members of the Musicians Union.
i. The Management/Artiste agrees that any future bookings arising from this engagement, either directly or indirectly shall be handled by the Agents L.M.D. Entertainments Limited.
j. The Management/Artiste agrees to pay commission on any return bookings at the above venue.
k. The Management shall not be held responsible for any cancellation of any performance due to circumstances beyond its control.

Remuneration to L.M.D. ENTERTAINMENTS LTD. At Band Houses' Discretion.

Signature
Address

Please Sign and Return

NAME OF ACT THE WHO No.

THE ROBERT STIGWOOD ORGANISATION LIMITED

Cables: Stigwood London

5 de WALDEN COURT
85 NEW CAVENDISH STREET
LONDON, W.1

MUSeum 2216-8

This Agency is not responsible for any breach of Contract by Proprietors, Managers or Artistes, but every reasonable safeguard is assured.

This agreement is subject to the terms and conditions of the standard form of contract approved by the Variety & Allied Entertainments Council of Great Britain on 13th August, 1963.

AN AGREEMENT made the 5TH day of MAY 1966
BETWEEN Lionel Digby
(hereinafter called "the Management") of the one part
AND New Action Ltd.
(hereinafter called "the Artiste") of the other part. WITNESSETH that the Management hereby engages the Artiste and the Artiste agrees to present/~~appear as~~ THE WHO
(or in his usual entertainment) at the venue/s on the date/s and at the salary stated in the Schedule hereto.

SCHEDULE

One ~~day~~/evening performance at The Town Hall, Torquay, DEVON.
on Friday 29th July 1966
for a salary of (a) £ 300.
or (b) £ or of the gross door and advance receipts whichever is the greater.
Minimum admission prices (members) (guests)

SPECIAL CLAUSES:

1. The Management agrees that any other Band performing the engagement described in this Agreement shall be composed of members of the Musicians' Union.
2. The Act shall not appear at any public place of entertainment within a radius of 10 miles of the venue mentioned above for weeks prior to and during and 2 weeks after this engagement.
3. Performing times 1 session/s of 40 mins. between 8.p.m.-11.30.p.m.
4. Band to arrive at venue not later than: 6.30.p.m. Equipment by 7.00.p.m.
5. Cash/~~cheque~~ payment On Night to Band.

IMPORTANT
PLEASE NOTE CLAUSE 5.
PAYMENT MUST BE MADE AS STIPULATED.

6. In the case of percentage engagements, the Management must provide the Artiste or his representative with a written statement of the full details of ticket numbers, admission prices and number of patrons and provide full facilities for the checking of the same.
7. The Management to check details of venue, fee and performing times upon initial receipt of contract/s and notify The Robert Stigwood Organisation Ltd. immediately of any alterations.

Signature L. Stamp Permanent Address

The Who

DATES FOR JANUARY/FEBRUARY

JANUARY 13th. EMBASSY SWANSEA AND SKEWEN RITZ.
14th. MUNICIPAL HALL PONTYPRIDD.
15th. HACKNEY BIG BEAT AND THE TWO PUDDINGS STRATFORD.
21st. GLENLYN BALLROOM FOREST HILL.
22nd. SMETHWICK BATHS AND THE ADELPHI WEST BROMWICH.
23rd. THE CO-OP WARRINGTON.
24th. THE LOCARNO STEVENAGE.
28th. THE UNIVERSITY EDGBASTON BIRMINGHAM.
29th. IMPERIAL NELSON.
31st. THE YOUTH CENTRE NEWPORT.
FEBRUARY 4th. THE ASTORIA FINSBURY PARK.
5th. THE ODEON SOUTHEND.
6th. THE EMPIRE LIVERPOOL.
7th. CHATHAM TOWN HALL.
11th. WIMBLEDON PALAIS.
12th. DREAMLAND MARGATE.
13th. THE COMMUNITY CENTRE SOUTHALL.
14th. THE TOWER BALLROOM NEW BRIGHTON.
17th. CLUB A GO GO NEWCASTLE.
18th. THE DRILL HALL DUMFRIES.
19th. THE MEMORIAL HALL NORWICH.
20th. MANCHESTER.
26th. BOSTON GLIDERDROME.

P.S.

SOME OF THE ABOVE DATES MAY BE ALTERED SO PLEASE CHECK ON THEM BEFORE YOU ARE DISAPPOINTED.

Clockwise from top left: Sue Roberts (in green) was at the November 1966 Bridlington show; two Who contracts signed with West Country promoter Lionel Digby; tour schedule for early 1966 from Maureen Browning

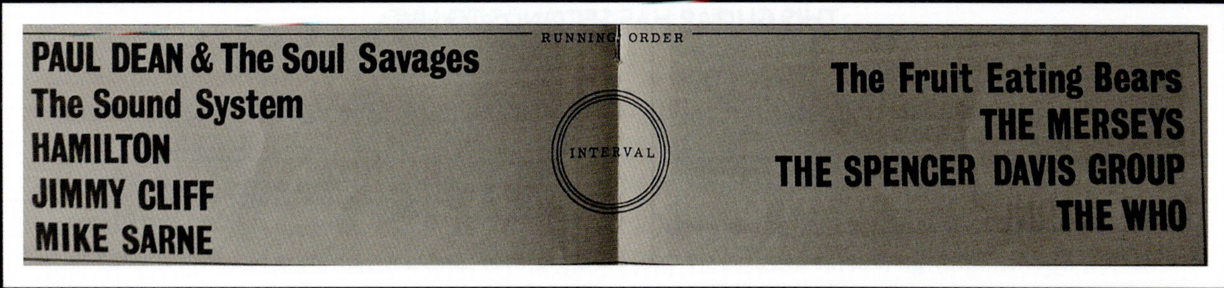

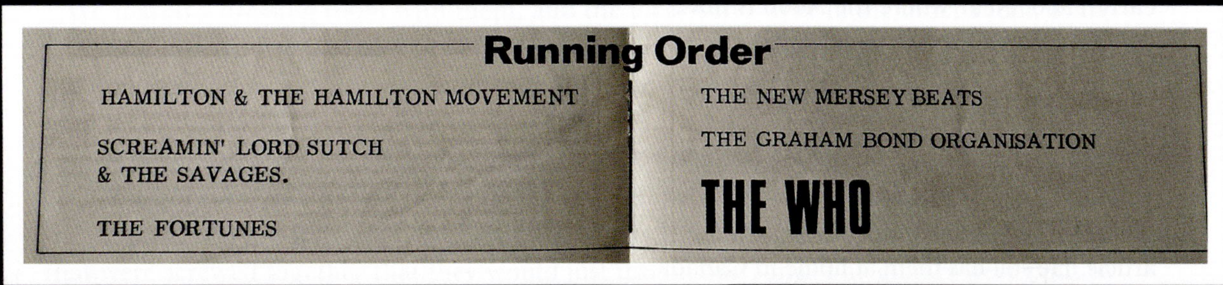

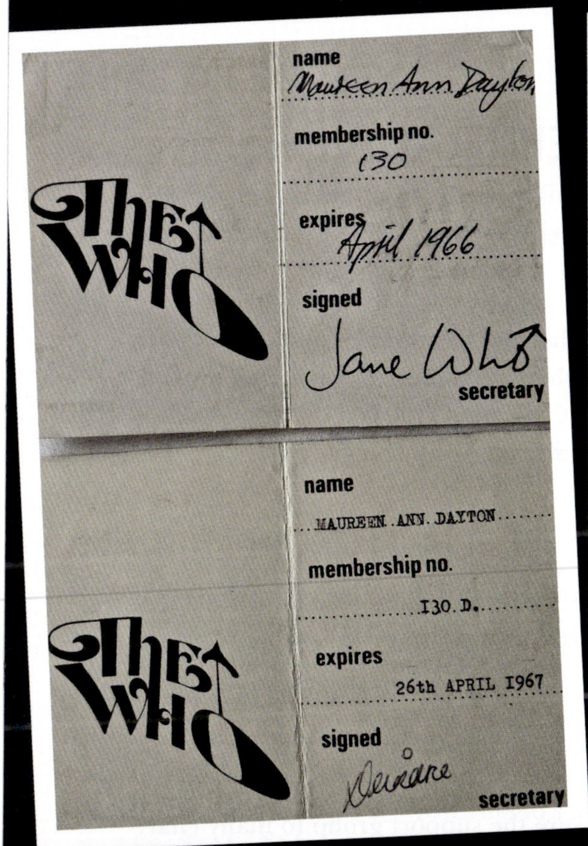

More items from Maureen Browning's memorabilia collection.

BARRY ANCILL

Before the gig they went around Kirkby town centre in a convertible American limo.

25 JANUARY 1967
KINGSWAY THEATRE, HADLEIGH, UK

JENNY RAWLINGS

One of the supporting groups was Sounds Around. I was going out with the chap who drove their van. I seem to remember all the girls connected to Sounds Around were only interested in The Who. I didn't get to meet them.

26 JANUARY 1967
LOCARNO BALLROOM, BRISTOL, UK

MIKE PARRY

I was a Bristol Mod. It was packed that night. I found my way upstairs and climbed on a table with my head touching the ceiling. The Locarno had a revolving stage and, as soon as they started warming up with their double stack Marshalls, they drowned the records being played out to the dance floor. At one point, Daltrey was dragged off stage and into the audience and the remainder of the group carried on as if nothing had happened. They played for about 45 minutes. Midway through 'My Generation' all broke loose! Townshend had already got through two guitars. The third went into one of the amps at the end, the drum kit came off the stage in bits and, after all this mayhem, they coolly walked off the stage with the broadcast message to the crowd 'that was The Who!'.

29 JANUARY 1967
SAVILLE THEATRE, LONDON, UK

ALAN BUTCHER, AGE 13

I asked my parents to take me to see my favourite band, The Who, a band I loved seeing on TV's *Ready Steady Go*. The Jimi Hendrix Experience were supporting and so I would be seeing my two favourite drummers, Keith Moon of The Who and Mitch Mitchell of the Experience. After exciting sets by The Koobas and Jimi Hendrix, the Shepherds Bush band had to be good – and they were! I remember Roger Daltrey sitting on the edge of the stage as the girls tried grabbing his legs whilst the rest of the band played on. I loved them so much that I saw them more than other band after that night, and I have seen a lot of bands over the years.

11 FEBRUARY 1967
ROYAL LINKS PAVILION, CROMER, UK

PAUL TAYLOR

After seeing them at the Federation Club in Norwich, I next saw them with my then girlfriend (now wife) in Cromer. 'Happy Jack' was part of their set and this time they did smash guitars and drums and they finished by clearing the premises by letting off a smoke bomb or flare.

CHARLES THIRTLE

I was employed by the *Eastern Daily Press* in their advisement department at Cromer, handling weekly display copy for the Links, which was then under the co-ownership of brothers Nigel and Rod Blow. The Who advert had a bold type face set across the entire two column width. The text declared: 'The greatest show staged in Norfolk: the most fantastic night in the history of pop: the night you will remember for the rest of your lives.' It ticked all of those boxes.

The Pavilion on Overstrand Road was the ballroom of the former Royal Links Hotel and lent itself admirably as North Norfolk's venue for top notch bands of the 1960s and '70s. I was often asked to help out as part of the crowd control team, the night of the Who gig being no exception. Two balconies situated either side of the dance floor had stairs leading directly onto the stage. My station for the night was at the top of one of the flights, to prevent over enthusiastic fans gaining access to the stage below. So I had the best view of the action, near to and directly above the band, and I was being paid to do it!

The atmosphere was electric and when The Who shaped up to play the crowd went wild. The band gave their all to every number played, notably 'My Generation' and their latest release, 'Happy Jack'. During the final number, a roadie fixed flares to the backs of the amps. When they were lit, all hell broke loose. The band kicked and threw their equipment around and smashed their guitars. It was seriously unbelievable to watch. I believe this larger-than-life quartet stayed the night at the Danish House Hotel in nearby Overstrand with a quiet drink or three.

Sadly, the Royal Links Pavilion is no more. It was destroyed by fire on 5 April 1978. The last high-profile band to perform there was the Sex Pistols on Christmas Eve 1977. The night The Who rocked at Cromer Links was the best gig staged there – ever.

ROD BLOW

My father bought a caravan site in 1964 and it came with the ballroom of the adjoining hotel. We started doing some dances in the ballroom with a local trio on a Saturday night and before

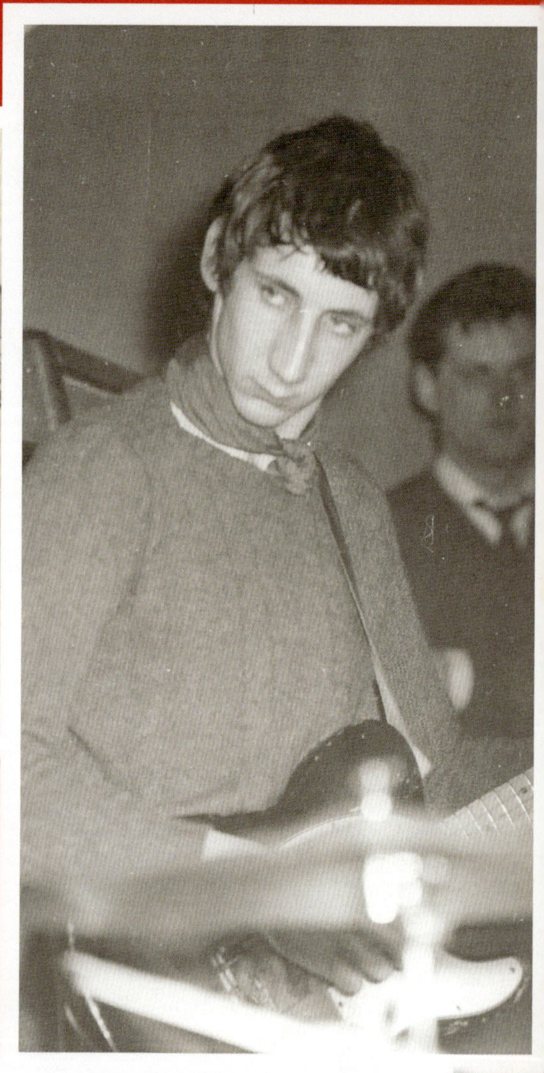

Clockwise from top left: Annette Flynn remembers wearing a gold lurex halter neck mini-dress when she saw The Who; David Scott decided admission to the Who gig in Morecambe was too expensive; The Who in action in Cromer - photos Rod Blow.

Clockwise from top left: Roger on stage in Cromer, Norfolk - photo Rod Blow; Carole Naylor was at Southport and chatted to Roger; the swimming pool where Leslie Ladd met The 'Oo; Arthur Wyllie remembers The Who's 1967 Aberdeen gig as the best gig ever; life changed forever after Patricia Marx saw The Who.

very long the first group came in and that was it. It just rocketed from there. In a very short space of time, we went from having a trio on a Saturday night to having three groups, one of which was The Who, who were the biggest. We had to put on the biggest back up, in terms of facilities and people and all the rest of it, that we'd ever done. We booked all our groups in through Robert Stigwood and had to pay £600 for 40 minutes for The Who, the most we'd ever paid for a group. We had two other groups on that night, so with all the add-ons it cost us about £1,000 to open the doors, which seems quite an insignificant amount now but it was massive at the time, and it frightened the life out of us to do it. But we have never regretted it.

You almost didn't have to advertise it. We only advertised the gig in the normal way. We did 100 posters every week. I would set off on a Monday morning putting them in shop windows and coffee bars, and in the evening my wife came with me and we went round the pubs and clubs. It would be a whole day and a whole evening of putting up posters. And we had the usual adverts running in the *EDP* and the *North Norfolk News*. But that was all we had to do, because everybody knew what was going on and who we'd got coming. The kids were all our friends and we used to talk with them and they'd say 'what about that group? What about this group?'. It was very much a family affair. And the kids were fantastic.

And we paid for coaches to come in from various areas, meaning the kids travelled for free. You'd get 40 or 50 kids coming in and the only condition we made was that the coaches had to arrive at eight o'clock, so we had that number of people in at the door and paying the money right from the start of the night, instead of waiting for people to drift in. We'd have up to ten coaches coming in from all over Norfolk and we'd go out at night time and pay the drivers off in cash. It was a brilliant system. It meant we were fully operational right from the word 'go'.

The ticket price at the door was five shillings (25p) every Saturday night and always included at least two groups – a local one and a nationally known one. When we put The Who on, we did our sums and estimated we'd have to charge 12/6 (62p), which was a huge amount of money bearing in mind your average teenager was probably earning £3 or £4 a week. It was quite a large percentage of their wage to come to us. But we did it and we got about the best part of 2,000 kids through the door that night. Health and safety would have a nightmare today.

It was just absolutely steaming. We would laughingly say that we shoved the kids out the back door to get some more in at the front. And, at 2,000 in the door, we made a small profit. It was only a small profit, but it was a brilliant, brilliant event.

Roger Daltrey turned up on his own in the late afternoon. He was just so natural and normal and pleasant and asked if we could set up a television which he'd brought with him. He was fascinated with the Monkees, who were major on television then at teatime, so we set a TV up in the changing room, and he and I sat in there on our own for the best part of a couple of hours talking about how things were going and then watching *The Monkees*. He wanted a bottle of vodka so I got him a bottle of vodka. And there he sat. He didn't get plastered, but he had a drink. And it was just so natural and normal, two people talking, which was extremely pleasant.

I then went over to where one or two of the crowd were arriving. The rest of the guys turned up, one by one, in various classy cars. I remember one was a Bentley Continental and one was a Lincoln Continental. I went over to pick up my fiancée (she became my wife) because she used to do the door. Doors were at eight, and when we drove up the road to the Links at seven o'clock, the queue stretched for several hundred yards down the road. We thought, 'Oh my God. How are we going to cope?'. It absolutely terrified us.

We got two or three bouncers to stand on the door and let ten or a dozen people in at a time, where my wife sat taking the money. We'd never had to do that before. There was so much money being handed over she was having to funnel the notes into cardboard boxes because there wasn't room for both the notes and the change in the till.

God knows what the temperature was in the hall with that number of people in. It must have been quite frighteningly high. But when you're young you don't notice that sort of thing. You just get on with it, with the excitement of the night. We had no trouble. You didn't have the fights that you'd have today; you probably couldn't stage it today. I stood on the corner of the stage whilst The Who did their performance and some of the photographs of the event show how close the kids were. They were literally just touching Roger Daltrey's feet.

The noise was absolutely phenomenal and it was a wonderful, wonderful night. We breathed a sigh of relief when it was all over, because the tension was quite immense when you saw that number of people and realised that we'd got to control it and make it work.

Afterwards, The Who's minders said to us, 'Look, the boys will want something to eat and drink afterwards. Where can they go?' This was North Norfolk. Everything had shut up and gone. We rang up North Repps Country Club and spoke to a guy called George Hoy. We said, 'George, any chance of you staying open so the boys can come down?' and he said 'yeah, no problem'. George rang us up the next day and said, 'Don't bloody do that again. All they had was a glass of milk!'.

11 MARCH 1967
TOWN HALL, WEM, UK

RON PUGH

I was in Wem Town Hall when The Who came to town. They arrived quite late with instruments already on stage. Their turn lasted about 30 minutes. At the end they trashed the instruments. We were told that they had also performed at Whitchurch, ten miles north of Wem, earlier that evening.

TERRY CONNOLLY

I lived in the market town of Wem, some ten miles north of Shrewsbury. A popular venue in those days was the Saturday dance at the Town Hall. Some household names of the day were regular visitors, which was quite a coup for such a small town. At one of these nights The Who were the headline act.

I remember my mates and I were riveted to the spot as they blasted out all their hits of the day.

For their finale, the smoke and fireworks started in earnest, culminating with Townshend smashing his guitar and Keith Moon hurling his drums into the audience. This was a first for me and my mates and we gleefully threw them back at Moon, much to the hilarity of the rest of the band.

DES CLORLEY, AGE 22

I remember them coming to Wem in what I think was 1968. I was home on leave from the RAF. The day of the event, which was a Saturday, myself and a couple of pals were in a café in the town playing on a pintable. This was lunchtime, the café was called Obertellis and my mother worked in there.

We had just had our lunch when six guys walked in. It was The Who! They ordered food and sat in an adjoining room. We didn't have tickets for the event as I only arrived on home from leave earlier in the day. The guys had their food and then, as they were paying Mrs Obertelli, a lovely lady who was known as Ma was asked by Roger Daltrey which was the nearest garage to the town as they were returning to London after the event. By this time, it was 2.30pm. She didn't know as she didn't drive and was in her seventies. I said, 'Mr Daltrey, there are no garages open in the town as they all closed at 1pm on a Saturday afternoon.' There were only three garages in town that served petrol in the town at that time. My pal Jack Minshall had garages but several of those also closed at 1pm.

I knew of a garage I used regularly when at home which was only four miles from Wem, on the main A49 London to Liverpool trunk road, so I gave them instructions on how to reach it as it was six miles nearer than Whitchurch or Shrewsbury. As they left, they said 'thank you' and went to their vehicles. A few minutes later, Keith Moon came back and said, 'We have forgotten the route and would one of you go in the first vehicle and show us the way?' Myself and Jack said we would both go, one in the first vehicle and one in the second.

When we got to the Town Hall rear, where they were playing that night, parked there were two Rolls-Royce cars and a beaten up large white Ford van. I agreed to sit in the first Rolls-Royce, the first time I had ever sat in a Roller in my life, and Jack sat in the second. The van also came along for petrol.

We got the fuel and they signed autographs for about ten minutes for other people who were there and then we returned to Wem. I must say I was glad to get back as Keith was driving and he wasted no time with his foot on the pedal. We got out of the cars and Roger and Keith plus the other four guys said 'thank you' and that they would see us that night. But we had no tickets as they were all sold out.

Roger said 'wait a minute', went inside the town hall and came out again with four tickets, two for me and two for Jack. He also said that if we went back at 6pm, security would let us watch the sound checks and the lighting people getting ready for the event at 8pm, which we did.

They also bought myself and Jack a drink at the bar and gave us a mention when they appeared on stage at 8.45pm, after the supporting group came off stage. They were a fantastic group of lads, as were the roadies, and they played a brilliant set.

17 MARCH 1967
UNIVERSITY, EXETER, UK

PAUL WALTERS, AGE 17

The Who played at the university and our band The Velvet Touch backed them. We were all about 17. We were quite in with the university because Neil, our bass guitarist, worked there as a lab technician. We played there with Tina Turner, the Bee Gees, loads of them. We were playing in the refectory, a long rectangular hall with two stages facing each other. We were on the same level as The Who, and only about 20 feet apart. Their roadies set their gear up while we were setting up ours. They were showing us how they put the smoke bombs in the fake speakers so that when everybody starts smashing stuff up, the smoke goes up everywhere. It was one of the roadies' jobs to go up and light the smoke bombs. It looked like part of the PA but it wasn't. It was quite funny, watching the road managers set the stuff up, putting these little fireworks everywhere and telling us their little tricks; how they changed most of the guitars they smashed up so there wasn't as much damage going on as you thought.

The Who were late and looked like they'd had a few drinks. We finished, pulled our stuff back from our side and The Who got up and started doing their thing. At the end of their set, they started smashing their gear up. Entwistle looked like he was totally disinterested. Moon just pushed the drum kit over, which wasn't really that spectacular, while Townshend smashed his guitar on the floor. But these smoke bombs were going off with sparks and stuff everywhere, making it look more spectacular than it actually was.

Because of how the hall was set up, and because there was 2,000 people in a room that really only held 1,000, people couldn't see. They started climbing onto our stage, where we'd stayed to watch the show, and the drunken students started to smash our gear up as well. Our drum kit got smashed up. Our new Orange PA, which we were very proud of, weighed a ton and that got pushed over.

Afterwards, we packed up what was left of our gear and were talking to the university guy who was in charge of the gig. We said, 'This isn't good enough. We're playing in a band, semi-professional, and we've now got no gear to speak of.' And The Who said 'we'll go down to the local store in the morning and we'll sign the stuff off.'

Our drummer's father was a solicitor, and he was really mad that his son's drum kit was wrecked. He turned up at Bill Greenhalgh's, which was our local supplier of equipment, and The Who's stage manager and Roger Daltrey and Entwistle turned up. While they were playing around with different instruments that Bill had, they signed up to let us have this equipment, so we got an upgraded Orange PA system and a much better Premier drum kit than we'd actually had, all written down to The Who's record label. And the university signed it off as well, so if there were problems with the label, the university would pay for it. We weren't held liable in any way.

About ten years ago, I met a couple in the centre of Exeter and they said 'we recognise you. You used to be in a band. You won't believe this but we met you at The Who concert.' And it turned out they had been at that gig. They remembered the audience getting a bit fraught and throwing our drum kit around. They met at that gig, got married and went to have a kid called Roger and a kid called Pete!

24 APRIL 1967
PAVILION, BATH, UK

NORMAN WHITEHALL

The Who gave an amazing show in front of a packed audience of 500 plus at a standing only show. After the last encore, John and I scouted around the outside to find a likely entry point to the dressing room area. WE scrambled through an open window and to our surprise landed right in amongst The Who. Roger, Pete and John were in the room on their own and found our entry quite amusing. They were not at all fazed and chatted away to us about the gig and where we had travelled from. Finally, Keith Moon arrived in the room and he was just as crazy as everyone wrote about him. It was a once in a lifetime experience for a couple of music fanatics from Bristol. I am so glad they didn't all die 'before they got old...'.

3 JUNE 1967
FLORAL HALL, SOUTHPORT, UK

EDWINA SWADEN

I was well underage to be going to Southport on a night out, and especially thumbing a lift from some random stranger. I lied to my mother about where I was going; she thought I was going to my friend Barbara's house. Barbara was allowed to go anywhere she wanted as she was two years older than me. We got ourselves ready in the shortest of mini-skirts with our near-as-dammit Mary Quant hairstyles. I remember dancing a lot, as we did in those days. Not much drinking went on until later, all we were interested in was the music.

I remember vividly Keith Moon going ballistic and kicking the drums over, with sparks flying everywhere. I'm not sure if Pete Townshend joined in with his usual smashing of his guitar, because I got really frightened and thought, 'If my mum finds out about this, I'm in big trouble,' so we just ran outside. I may even have been crying. Guilt… that's what a catholic mother does to you. I do remember it was just great or, as we would say in those times – gear!

I've seen them since at the Liverpool Echo Arena and things were a lot different, with more instruments and the technology, but Roger Daltrey's voice was still amazing. In 2020, we were thinking of going to see them again but when we saw the price of the tickets…? No way. I think I paid 3/6d (18.5p) to get into the Floral Hall. My friend remembers it as 7/6d. I can't think I'd have had that amount of money, but maybe that's why I had to thumb a lift?

CAROLE NAYLOR, AGE 15

I chatted to Roger Daltrey outside who told me that Keith Moon was ill and couldn't appear that night. As he was my favourite, I was devastated! Keith was my crush. That night he was replaced by a someone from a group called John's Children and for years I was convinced it was Marc Bolan!

9 JUNE 1967
GOLDEN SLIPPER BALLROOM MAGILLIGAN, UK

CIARAN TONER

It took place seven years before I was born, and it's remarkable that any band came to this part of Ireland, when the Civil Rights movement was starting and conflict was not far away (the first major battle between Unionist forces and the Civil Rights marchers was to occur very close to the venue, along Magilligan Strand). Magilligan is an isolated rural farming community in County Derry, 60 miles from Belfast, 20 from Derry city and over 150 miles from Dublin. The Golden Slipper was a typical Irish dance hall that featured local popular dance bands, and people would travel by bus from surrounding towns to the Slipper. I believe The Who appeared as part of a whistle stop tour of venues, possibly having come from a previous appearance in Portrush in County Antrim, 40 minutes away. Their appearance in Magilligan was short, possibly less than 20 minutes and some locals remember them as being very loud. The audience punch up afterwards seems to be remembered here more than the band's appearance.

BERNARD MCNICHOLL, AGE 21

The Golden Slipper held about 300 and it was packed. I was there with my sister, Rose Dorrans, and the music was brilliant. The sound was so much different from what we usually heard from the Irish show bands. Rose thought the music was very loud! Some of the songs I recall are 'Happy Jack', 'My Generation', 'The Kids Are Alright' and 'La-La-La-Lies'.

BOBBY BRADLEY

The dancehall probably held about 2,500 people. That's what the average kind of crowds would have been. It was a big thing The Who coming to Magilligan. I was a keen follower of them. My brother's band the Bankers Showband was the back-up band for The Who that night. The chairs were all over the place when The Who came on. They'd asked if they could use his band's equipment and they wrecked it all. He got compensated but they went ballistic on the stage, smashing the drums and the keyboards and amplification. They were fantastic.

GERARD O' BRIEN, AGE 17

I went with two of my friends. We were very excited. They came on stage around 10pm and played for about an hour. They had a stand-in drummer as Keith Moon was ill. I was disappointed about that but the music was brilliant. At the end they did their stage act. Pete Townshend bashed his guitar up and down on the stage floor and smashed it against the amplifier. The drum kit was knocked over and smoke appeared. I thought this was fantastic. I had never seen anything like it. Afterwards, Roger Daltrey came down amongst the audience. He was wearing a bright pink shawl and was chatting and asking questions.

JOHN SOMERS, AGE 17

I was playing guitar in a wee local showband. They would bring groups who were in the charts over from London and employ a showband as support. We played with The Move, Herman's Hermits, Marmalade, Freddie and the Dreamers and Slim Whitman. We'd be playing to an audience of a couple of thousand people who would dance the night away. There no bars in the dance halls. The local bars closed at ten o'clock and the dances were always billed as being from 9pm to 1am or from 10pm to 2am, so we'd be playing for three, three and a half hours, and you weren't getting very much money for it. The Who were very nice guys. I had this picture in my head that they were horrible gits, nasty people who wrecked hotels and such. But they were nice to us.

They brought their own gear. I can remember Pete Townshend coming in with a red Stratocaster and my friend Kenny said 'don't be breaking that guitar – give it to me!' and Pete said something like 'don't worry, it's not a real one'. It took them ages to set it up. They were using Watkins WEM stuff. You wouldn't have seen the back wall of the stage because of the big stack of amplifiers they were using. When they played, they were putting things through the cabs and you could hardly see them for dry ice. The place was dense with ice. And there was all this mayhem on stage, and an awful lot of noise from the drums. The thing I remember most is how loud they were. I've never heard anything as loud. It was scary how loud it was.

STEVEN MCCRACKEN

I'm too young for it, but my granny used to talk about how The Who stayed in a wee caravan at the bottom of our low yard. She'd turned the farm into a big guest house, but it was still a farm. At the very bottom of our second yard, the lower yard, we had a wee caravan down there for guests. Just a few extra beds. When they played in Magilligan, The Who stayed in the yard. The Slipper was at the top of our lane, so it was handy. I didn't know anything about it until the neighbours told me. I said to my gran, 'What's this about The Who?' and then she told me.

The Who travel to the United States in June 1967 to perform a group of shows, including appearing on the closing day of the Monterey Festival. Their 30-minute set features exploding coloured smoke bombs and Daltrey, Townshend and Moon all destroying their equipment, Townshend reducing his Stratocaster to splinters. Next on the bill,

Jimi Hendrix manages a feat few could accomplish, upstaging The Who by setting fire to his guitar on stage.

18 JUNE 1967
FIRST MONTEREY INTERNATIONAL POP FESTIVAL, MONTEREY, CALIFORNIA

PAUL BODY

If you read UK music paper the *NME* in the early part of '67, you knew who Jimi Hendrix was. They compared him to an African Bushman as he was so wild on stage. When we heard he was playing the Monterey Pop Festival we had to see him. We didn't know anything about how to get tickets. That wasn't going to stop us, and neither was my having a job, which I quit to go to Monterey. Originally Jimi and The Who were playing on different days. As much as we wanted to see Hendrix, we bought tickets for Sunday. I think we voted on it. We saw Otis Redding, Janis Joplin, the Electric Flag, Buffalo Springfield and The Byrds with David Crosby and that STP sticker on his guitar. Eric Burdon introduced The Who and they opened with my favourite Who song, 'Substitute'. Then they saluted rock 'n' roll's past with a scorching version of 'Summertime Blues' and destroyed the stage during 'My Generation'. Some people were shocked but I had seen them do it on TV, so I knew what was coming. As the smoke cleared, I had visions of 'Pictures of Lily' in my mind.

JOHN A GREENWALD

Call it an almost-all-access pass. In effect that's what I had at the Monterey Pop Festival, allowing me to go almost anywhere I wanted except backstage. The perks of being an usher. An awesome perk at that, all because my history teacher was in charge of the ushers. By the time The Who stepped on stage on the Sunday, rumours had been rife that The Beatles were going to be appearing and the audience was throbbing with excitement, helped along by an encore performance by Janis Joplin. The the lads managed to crank up the adrenaline levels even more. When they got to the 'My Generation' finale with Townshend's windmills, Moon's smoke bombs and the big guitar smash up at the end, they had audience members' eyes, mine included, popping out of their sockets. How do you top this? What I didn't know was that after his soundcheck, Jimi Hendrix had raced around the Monterey Peninsula looking for lighter fluid…

JIM WILLIAMS

I saw Jimi Hendrix at Monterey and I said, 'I've gotta try and meet that guy in my lifetime if I can.' And one time it happened. Me and a group of guys drove to Sacramento in my hot rod to see him, see him burn his guitar and everything. I sat right up in the front balcony. Whoever played there, the only way out was one door at the back, up a couple of steps and then about 30 yards across the street to get to the limo. So as soon as the show finished, I ran out the side door and around the back and waited. The doors opened and it's Jimi Hendrix, dressed just like you think, and you gotta think fast because he's on his way and his bodyguards are trying to get him to his limo. I said, 'I saw you at Monterey.' He goes, 'Oh really? What did you think of the gig?' I said, 'Man, that was outta sight but I was wondering about the guitar, you know? Did you plan it, or how'd you figure it?' He said, 'Well, I knew Townshend and The Who were going to do some off-the-wall thing so I had to do something for 'em to remember me by. The Who destroyed the stage and everything they owned, and as Pete walked past me, he mumbles 'follow that if you can' or something weird. Luckily, I had something in my bag that I could pull out.'

HARVEY KUBERNIK

I'm an LA native and I first heard music in the late Fifties around town on the AM radio. I was really at the centre of the surf music world. There were some hit records from England. England was not considered a strange place to us. We saw acts on *The Ed Sullivan Show* from England. Disc jockeys like B Mitchel Reed started playing music from England that we've never heard before. He played 'My Generation' and I'd never heard anything like this in my life. It blew my mind. And then The Who played things like 'Bucket T' and Reed would say things like 'and that drummer with that group, he really digs the surf music of LA.'

Now we didn't really know the name Keith Moon or anything, but he would play a Jan and Dean record and then 'Bucket T' or something like that. He started playing The Who. He really leaned on The Who. He'd say 'they may be coming to town'. And on radio station KFWB there was a British disc jockey called Lord Tim, Tim Hudson. The Who got their airplay here initially through B Mitchel Reed and Lord Tim. So we were primed. This guy says, 'I have a test pressing, I'm playing you an acetate of a great new tune you're going to hear next year called 'Pictures of Lily'.' I never heard anything so monumental in my fucking life. Well, where's the band already?

There was some kind of promotional situation where if you went to a white front record store, one of our big department stores, and bought an album of The Who or Jimi Hendrix or the Association, you got tickets to see them play at the Hollywood Bowl. This is maybe November of '67. The vibes and the reverberations and the impact of The Who and Jimi Hendrix playing Monterey were that more airplay happened, and then they were on *Shindig!* doing 'Can't Explain'. It vaulted them right up there with The Beatles and the Stones. LA went mad in '67 for these groups.

Pete Townshend is the best interview subject ever invented. That's another reason LA supported The Who. Pete Townshend knew how to talk. For a guy that keeps thinking 'I'm frustrated and angry at the world' and smashing his guitar in 'My Generation' and 'Can't Explain', when he talked to *I* magazine or the *KRLA Beat* magazine out here, or even occasionally when he did AM radio interviews and later FM radio out here, he was talking for all of us as teenagers. To our frustrations, to world view, to wardrobe, to alienation. For Pete, playing and talking would get him laid, make him money and, most importantly, give him control in the recording studio. The media liked Pete Townshend and they like him even today because they just ask the question and he goes.

29 JULY 1967
BOUTWELL MEMORIAL AUDITORIUM BIRMINGHAM, ALABAMA

BILL HENDERSON

I went to the show with a college friend from Birmingham and our girlfriends. This was the summer between our sophomore and junior years in college. I travelled from a small Mississippi town 200 miles away and this was my first trip to Birmingham. It was quite an adventure. I remember the smog hanging over the city from all the steel plants. A local radio station put these shows on several times a year. Usually they were called the 'Shower of Stars' but they may have used other names too. The show would have six to eight acts with each doing two or three songs. In the 1950s, the performers were country music stars, but they had shifted to pop and rock by 1967. Herman's Hermits were the headliners at the show I went to, and I remember Lou Christie singing 'Lightning Strikes'. Lou had a very distinctive voice and singing style. I had not heard of The Who and was surprised by their performance. I don't remember what songs they did but I do remember them smashing their instruments at the end. I didn't 'get' this and it made no sense to me. You can imagine the contrast between the soft, smooth sound of Herman's Hermits and the raw style of The Who.

In 1967 it was rare to get to see the stars in person or even on TV. For the most part, all we knew about the bands was how they sounded on the radio and records and how they looked on album covers. When you heard that one of your friends had been to a concert, you wanted to know all about the show. I remember telling my friends about the show in Birmingham, including The Who smashing their instruments. I had to start leaving this part out of my description of the show, because I couldn't answer the inevitable question: 'why did they do that?'

7 – 11 AUGUST 1967
AMBASSADOR THEATER, WASHINGTON DC

BILL HAVU

The Who's manager (and our ex-manager) Tom Wright brought Pete Townshend to see Jimi Hendrix on his five-night run at the Ambassador after he quit the Monkees tour. My band was supporting Hendrix. And Pete came to our apartment on Corcoran Street near Dupont Circle to visit Cam Bruce, our lead singer. Pete, Cam and Tom had gone to school together in London and hadn't seen each other for three years after Cam and Tom were asked to leave England because of drug possession. Pete strummed out chord changes he'd been working on for *Tommy* on an old acoustic, Cam began playing along on another acoustic and I played a tabla or bongos. We jammed for about an hour. And before he left, we had Pete sign his name under the light switch, right under Jimi's. I wonder what the next renter thought. I can hear them now... 'Yeah, right! Sure that's their signatures!' Or 'Who?'

11 AUGUST 1967
CIVIC CENTER, BALTIMORE, MARYLAND

BILL KNIPP, AGE 11

My brother took me to Baltimore Civic Center for what was labelled *The British Invasion*. The opening act was the Moody Blues, then The Who and the headliner was Herman's Hermits! Two years later, Herman's Hermits was playing Holiday Inns and The Who were huge! The biggest thing I remember is The Who breaking up their equipment.

13 AUGUST 1967
CONSTITUTION HALL, WASHINGTON DC

PATRICIA MARX, AGE 15

The first time I saw The Who – by accident, when they played as one of the supporting bands on the Herman's Hermits tour of the USA in the summer of 1967 – I was hooked. Their second album, *A Quick One*, which was called *Happy Jack* here in the States, had just come out but I hadn't heard it. I hadn't heard 'My Generation' either. I was completely wowed by the music and the lyrics, by the crazy drummer who drummed so fast he was a blur and by the rock singer who could sing beautifully. The carefully controlled chaos, the strong individuality of each member, their colourful costumes and each one competing for full attention of audience members. As they swung into 'My Generation' for the finale, I finally realised I had heard that song at least on the radio but I did not know Pete would smash his guitar at the end, which I thoroughly enjoyed. I loved the entire set but especially remember 'Boris the Spider', 'Pictures of Lily' and the mini-opera. I thought at the time, as I am sure every Who fan has, 'God made this band for me.' Hermann who? I was 15 and my life had changed forever.

17 AUGUST 1967
MEMORIAL AUDITORIUM CHATTANOOGA, TENNESSEE

LESLIE LADD, AGE 12

They came to Chattanooga, Tennessee for the local radio station show, *The Jet-FLI Spectacular*. I went with my older sister, Glenda, and our neighbour and her mom. I was thrilled to see Herman's Hermits but when The Who came on stage and smashed their instruments at the end of 'I Can See For Miles' I was mesmerised! I still get a thrill when I hear that song. After the show, my neighbour's mom took us to meet them where they were staying at the Downtowner Motel. They were all sunning themselves by the pool. I was so shy about meeting these older and famous guys, but Keith broke the ice when he told me he had a sister also named Lesley. I thought Roger was the cutest and he gave us a sweet smile. Pete didn't say much. They asked my neighbour's mom if she would go buy them some Bourbon, since they were underaged to buy in Tennessee, and she did. I had them all sign my autograph book.

23 AUGUST 1967
ATWOOD STADIUM, FLINT, MICHIGAN

ROGER WHITE

They were opening for Herman's Hermits and played on a high school football field in Flint, Michigan. I'd just gotten my driver license and took five girls from the Herman's Hermits Fan Club – but I wanted to see The Who! They played in the afternoon and we sat on the school bleachers. The girls found out what motel the bands were staying at and we went there after the show. The girls were so excited to actually meet the Hermits, and it was Keith Moon's birthday. This was the same party where Keith drove a Lincoln into the pool. I didn't see this but I was hanging around the pool and met Pete Townshend. He was kicking the lounge chairs into the pool and was really pissed off, ranting about the stupid girls adoring the Hermits and not paying any attention to real musicians like him. I agreed, we sat and talked a while, then I had to gather up the Fan Club and drive back to Detroit.

17 SEPTEMBER 1967
THE SMOTHERS BROTHERS COMEDY HOUR LOS ANGELES, CALIFORNIA

HARVEY KUBERNIK

There's another key moment in Who history when they have a TV booking on the *Smothers Brothers Comedy Hour*. They destroy their instruments on stage and Keith destroys his drum kit with a cherry bomb. That thing was filmed eight blocks from where I live and down the street from my high school, Fairfax, where Shel Talmy also went to high school. That show on TV was the talk of the town. That was like The Beatles on *Ed Sullivan*, when The Who destroyed their equipment. Why are you destroying your equipment? There's smoke bombs. There's craziness. What a way to make an impact on people. I don't know if it was about Gustav Metzger and all that art stuff that Pete Townshend talked about, the art of the destruction of the instruments. It was hard enough to find money for petrol out here.

6 OCTOBER 1967
BALLERINA BALLROOM, NAIRN, UK

ANNELLA FLYNN, AGE 15

It was a Friday night and there was a special bus running from Tain to the gig in Nairn, picking up in towns and villages along the way. My friend and I got on the bus in Invergordon. We were both 15 years old and I was wearing a gold lurex halter neck mini-dress. It wasn't actually my dress – it belonged to my friend and she was wearing something of mine. Still at school, we didn't have much money and used to swap clothes. We were just on a night out to see a chart group. They weren't called 'bands' in those days. When we got to the Ballerina, the dancehall was heaving. The group had already had about ten chart hits so they were a big draw. I remember the ladies toilets were up some steps and, because of the massive crowd and all the pushing and shoving, the door to the toilets came off the hinges!

ROB MILNE, AGE 17

The Ballerina in Nairn was my favourite music venue when I was growing up in the North of Scotland. I saw lots of great bands there including Cream, Juicy Lucy, Status Quo and the Herd. It was a converted church with an artificially lowered roof, making it a very intimate venue. With a capacity of maybe 200-300 a tiny stage, it was great for getting up close to the band. The Who were no exception. There was no bar, only a small place for soft drinks. Just after the support act finished, which was a local band, I remember standing next to Roger Daltrey and a gorgeous blonde.

When The Who came on I was about two rows back from the stage and I remember Pete Townshend coming on, plugging in and windmilling his Rickenbacker. The volume was incredible! He wore a gold Regency-style jacket with a frilly shirt. Daltrey was in a fringed leather jacket and wearing bright orange trousers. I couldn't work out if he had a bit of hose pipe down his inside leg or if he was particularly well blessed in that department! John Entwistle was wearing a denim-style dark green leather jacket and Keith Moon was in a t-shirt.

The band had just returned from their first American tour and went through their normal repertoire of songs. I recall Pete telling us he had written a rock opera and the band would play some tracks from it, which they duly did. This was not *Tommy* but *Rael.*

This was the first time I had ever seen a double-necked Gibson SG. It was black but the thing I remember is that it was split in two and held together by two bolted stainless steel plates on the front, having obviously been smashed up by Pete at an earlier gig and then patched up by the guitar roadie. They played really loudly. I also remember Keith Moon breaking loads of sticks, but some he just sent spinning, unbroken into the crowd where they were fought over as souvenirs. A girl I had been in school with, Marlene Dodd, managed to get one and she brandished it triumphantly on the bus on the way home to Inverness. She did well to get one, as she must have been the smallest person at the gig!

My all-time favourite Who song, 'I Can See For Miles', was particularly memorable. Standing so close to the band and hearing the guitar intro at that sound level, along with the drum intro, was incredible. Keith was using his twin bass drum Premier kit with the coloured fluorescent 'The Who' logo, with 'The' on one bass drum and 'Who' on the other.

My one other memory of the Who gig took place beforehand in a local pub called the Star. As no alcohol was on sale in the Ballerina, The Who's roadies were out for a couple of beers after the sound check. There was an upright piano in the corner of the lounge bar and one of the roadies pulled up a chair and started to play some tunes a la Chas and Dave, so we had a right good sing-song before going to the gig!

7 OCTOBER 1967
BEACH BALLROOM, ABERDEEN, UK

JIM STRACHAN

I took my new girlfriend to see The Who. I was amazed at Townshend's electrifying guitar playing on a Rickenbacker and Entwistle's thunderous bass sound. I'd never heard anything like it before - or since! My girlfriend became the wife and we're now in our 49th year of wedded bliss.

ARTHUR WYLLIE

The tickets cost 15/- (75p). I was there with three friends. The Who were meant to be on stage for an hour to close the night, but they stayed on stage for at least one and a half hours. They played all their hits and several album tracks, very loudly. After they had been on stage for about an hour, they started playing *A Quick One* – which I had never heard before – and this lasted about half an hour. At the end of the night, Pete Townshend smashed his guitar over his knee and Keith Moon kicked over his drum kit. The best performance I have ever seen.

8 OCTOBER 1967
KINEMA BALLROOM, DUNFERMLINE, UK

LINDSAY CARMICHAEL, AGE 18

I saw them perform at the Kinema. There was a story of the band staying in the City Hotel in Bridge Street and Keith Moon being arrested because he was using an air pistol to shoot out some of the old-style Christmas lights which were stretched out between the lamp posts at that time.

21 OCTOBER 1967
NEW CENTURY HALL, MANCHESTER, UK

STEVE BERNING, AGE 15

At school in Bury in the 1960s, pupils were either Beatles or Stones fans. However, as soon as I heard 'I Can't Explain', The Who became my band. The 15-year-old me was thrilled that Friday night as I set off for Manchester. I had managed to get about 20 feet from the stage as The Who came on. Townshend had his twinnecked Gibson SG and Moon his 'Pictures of Lily' Premier kit. When they started, the sound was unbelievably loud. You could feel Entwistle's bass thumping your chest. Their set consisted of their third album, *Sell Out*, earlier hits, 'Heatwave' and Stevie Wonder's 'I Was Made To Love Her'. When I got into school on the Monday, my ears were still ringing!

TED TUKSA

The second time I saw them was at the CIS building in Manchester. The Who did a great set, but were being hurried up by the manager to finish the night. He was shouting from the side of the stage. Pete used his guitar as a cricket bat and smashed all the lights at the foot of the stage, one by one.

29 OCTOBER 1967
COVENTRY THEATRE, COVENTRY, UK

DAVE JONES

They were top of the bill on a Sunday night. Before their act reached its smashing finale it was cut short. At 10.30pm, power to the stage was cut and the safety curtain came down, leaving the audience somewhat bewildered. Sunday night in the '60s - that was the curfew for entertainment to cease! I don't think there was any fuss or protest by the audience, just a bit of moaning. It was what happened at the time, like last orders in the pub!

RAFFERTY BATES

The Who were top of the bill. Before they came on, the Jimi Hendrix Experience were on, and I think The Yardbirds were on as well. Nobody expected what would unfold at the end of the show. The Who were at their brilliant best. It was an amazing performance by the band. All of a sudden, the stage manager drew the stage curtains while The Who were still playing and announced on the tannoy for the band to stop as the show had to stop at 10.30pm. Pete Townshend was not amused.

He said, 'You don't draw the fackin' curtains on The Who, we are The fackin' Who. What gives you the right to do this to The fackin' Who?' Pete and Roger swung on one side of the stage curtains and ripped them down and John Entwistle and Keith Moon did the same to the other side. They then ripped down the side curtains, smashed all the stage scenery and set about all their equipment. The stage looked like a bomb had hit it. The crowd could not believe what they had witnessed, the best and most destructive band on earth living up to their reputation that night.

6 NOVEMBER 1967
TOWN HALL, BIRMINGHAM, UK

LIZ WOLSEY

They were supported by the Tremeloes and third on the bill were Traffic. The Who were brilliant, with lots of energy and Keith Moon on form. At the end of the concert Pete Townshend smashed his guitar and Keith kicked over the drum kit.

ROGER HILLIARD

What a great line up this was – Traffic, The Herd, Marmalade and The Tremeloes - with a top seat price of 12/6d (63p) and headlined by The Who. I listened attentively to the supporting acts and then on came The Who… They shook up the whole town hall with their vibrant music and Keith Moon's stage antics. And then the finale, when Pete Townshend smashed his guitar on the stage and the whole audience went home buzzing. Considering this was probably just one of many concerts The Who played on this tour, Pete must have had a vast collection of instruments if this destruction went on every night!

8 NOVEMBER 1967
GRANADA CINEMA, KETTERING, UK

DAVID ROBINSON, AGE 18

It was probably the first of the two houses they played that night, as buses home to the steel town of Corby did not run particularly late. In retrospect, the bill of The Who, Tremeloes, Traffic, Herd and Marmalade – all with their definitive line ups – was solid gold. There were no weak links in that chain! I'd decided at the time of *My Generation* that The Who were my favourite British band of the '60s, ousting Gerry and the Pacemakers and running alongside the Byrds and the pre-*Pet Sounds* Beach Boys. One of the things that appealed about The Who was that Pete's songs such as 'I'm a Boy', 'Happy Jack', 'Pictures of Lily' and the subsequent rock operas weren't your typical love and relationships pop fare.

Some of their songs I found straightforward to perform using three guitar chords. A mate and I were asked to do 'Substitute' at a church service (don't ask!) and 'I'm a Boy' was the first track our modest local 'beat group' attempted. We didn't last long.

On stage at the Granada, the boys still had the tail-end of their Mod look. We had quite good seats in the circle but, as was par for the course, could hardly hear a thing due to the screams of teenage girls. Luckily, I could lip-read most of the playlist and it included one or two of my favourites, including 'Happy Jack'. They might have included 'Rael' in that set, too, although the logical side of my brain suggests that they wouldn't have included two elongated tracks at that pre-stadium stage of their career, and they definitely did 'A Quick One (While He's Away)'. I remember the ads in the local paper printed the title of a high profile hit for each act above the name of the band, and thinking these were unsubtle, as though we wouldn't know who they were! But I don't think any of the audience cared. For me, it was at least a double header, and probably more.

9 NOVEMBER 1967
GRANADA CINEMA, MAIDSTONE, UK

DAVID STAFFORD

I sat politely through The Tremeloes and Marmalade ('Ob-La-Di, Ob-La-Da', their big number, was never a cue for dangerous over excitement). Then The Who came on. I'd never been to a proper rock concert before, but I knew straight away that this was a proper rock concert. It was like attending a small war. They were thugs – thugs dressed in satin and lace, but still unmistakably thugs. Roger's voice hadn't yet reached its full Rock God potential, but it could menace. He spat 'I Can't Explain' and 'Substitute' all over the audience. There was no sense of fun in Pete's windmilling. It was a job that had to be done, as if the only way to build enough momentum to hit the strings properly was to start high. I'd worried about Keith's defective motor functions and unblinking eyes when I'd seen him on telly. That night, I swear, the eyes had crosses in them, like Tom's after Jerry has smacked him on the head with a bowling ball. I don't recall any of the more restrained numbers like 'Happy Jack' or 'Pictures of Lily', but they finished the set with 'My Generation'. It started like a jet engine and got louder. The small war escalated into something that was genuinely scary. Bits of wood from Pete's splintered guitar flew around like shrapnel. Smoke was pouring out the speaker cabs. Cymbals got frisbeed. Keith managed to kick the entire kit off the riser and into the orchestra pit while stage hands ran on to sort the carnage out. I don't remember much after that, except I was deaf for three days.

10 NOVEMBER 1967
ADELPHI CINEMA, SLOUGH, UK

JUDY MARNES

We couldn't get in as we didn't have tickets so we stood outside until Keith Moon hung out of the dressing room window shining a green light on his face!

The Who return to the USA for a string of eleven dates.

17 NOVEMBER 1967
SHAWNEE MISSION SOUTH HIGH SCHOOL GYMNASIUM, OVERLAND PARK, KANSAS

RICH HOLLOWAY

They played at my high school, Shawnee Mission South. They were the back-up band for the Buckinghams but stole the show, including smashing their equipment, which was pretty radical back then, especially in the conservative midwestern USA.

DAN SMITH, AGE 15

My older sister, Kathleen, was a senior at Shawnee Mission South High School in Overland Park, Kansas. Overland Park was the largest suburb in Johnson County, Kansas and the fourth largest city in the state. Johnson County was an affluent suburban county, just south of Wyandotte County witch mostly included Kansas City, Kansas. Across the state line to the east was Kansas City, Missouri, the largest of the cities in the metropolitan area. Outside of politics, we all considered Kansas City our home town.

Kathleen's best friend, Debbie, lived just behind our house on the next street. Our yards were separated by an old hedgerow, left over from when the land was somebody's farm. Debbie was a fixture at our house and very involved in student council. My brother, Mark, was the pop music expert at our house and had a pretty large collection of rock recordings; all the Beatles records and plenty of Rolling Stones, the Byrds, Buffalo Springfield, the Animals, Cream, Jimi Hendrix and The Who. Mark was my ride to see the Beatles in Kansas City in 1964, so I looked up to him when it came to pop culture.

One day, early in the school year, Debbie was visiting Kathleen and we were all hanging out in the family room. Debbie announced that the student council was going to put on a concert and dance in November. She said that they booked the Buckinghams, a very popular American band with several hits on the radio, and a band called The Who. Mark was beside himself.

Herd pray Townshend will spare his guitar!

ANDREW STEELE

ANOTHER week of fun and hard work, but at long last, we're beginning to get the hang of this touring business. By that, I mean that we're getting used to the unexpected being commonplace, if you get my meaning. Anyway, let's have a look at what's been going on.

We had great audiences for the show up in Newcastle, where both The Traffic and ourselves suffered equipment failure. Once again, we were showered with sweets — we made a small fortune after the show selling them off at one-and-six a quarter! Still on the "sweets" topic — our organist, Andy Bown, was officially awarded the C.D.M. for bravery and fortitude in the face of overpowering odds — he had a cold!

During the Who's act, their road manager stood behind Pete Townshend's equipment trying to stop the speakers toppling over whenever Pete lashed out. But without warning, Pete suddenly started pulling instead of pushing. Everything fell forward with a mighty crash — revealing one mystified road manager to an equally mystified audience.

All was reasonably quiet at Liverpool — until Pete Townshend broke a string during the second bar of The Who's first number. His guitar started spluttering, the rest of the group were taking side bets on when it would actually blow up, but Pete soldiered on to the last number before smashing the guitar over the speakers. One of my prize possessions now is a piece of wood 6 ins. by one inch — all I could find of the ill-fated instrument!

We celebrated our first date in the south — at Kingston — by turning up for the show with diabolical, streaming colds . . . courtesy of our beloved organist. Keith Moon impressed everyone with a startling demonstration of drum annihilation. I managed to nip out front during the show, and was knocked out by The Marmalade — they really blow up a storm.

The Tremeloes were tremendous — a really polished act. Their voices are great, especially Dave Munden. It's hard enough to play drums well, but to sing brilliantly at the same time is really going some. Mr. Munden has my greatest admiration.

At Walthamstow, all the drummers decided to use their own kits, so the stage looked reminiscent of a drum convention. There was some trouble with the P.A. during the second house, and The Dream had to play about 80 bars of music before their voices could be heard at all. I thought they stuck to their guns very bravely, and won out in the end.

The Traffic's percussion number was an absolute gas. This group is very fresh in its approach, and their success is well deserved. Steve Winwood impressed every time. If you think I'm very pro-Traffic, you're dead right — that's why I wore a Traffic fan club badge during The Herd's stage act!

Townshend kicked up a storm on stage yet again, and when he looked like smashing his great Les Paul guitar, Peter Frampton was seen in the wings saying prayers that it would be spared. It seems his prayers were answered, since the guitar was still intact at the end of the evening.

At Nottingham, the Marmalade, the Tremeloes, Roger Daltry and our Gary Taylor gathered in a dressing room for an impromptu session of old and nauseous numbers. On stage, Dave Munden was badly hampered by a broken bass drum skin, but he played masterfully just the same. Townshend arrived on stage playing a guitar bound together with string and tape, but still sounded great.

The Herd were affected by mike failure at one point, and Andy Bown — who was singing at the time — ended up giving a very passable imitation of an enraged gorilla with fleas! Later, in an Indian restaurant, Alan Whitehead (drummer with the Marmalade) admirably demonstrated that he should read up on exotic foods before trying to order. What a mixture!

And that's my lot. Next week, a final round-up on the tou[r] ... ubiquitous Gary Taylor - journalist extraordinaire!

ANDRE[W STEELE]

Stuco Brings the Buckinghams and the Who to South in an Exclusive Concert

StuCo sponsors pop rock groups tonight

Buckinghams will perform

The internationally known "Buckinghams" and THE WHO will perform for nearly 3,500 students at the concert-dance sponsored by the Student Congress this evening from 8:00 to 11:30 in the gymnasium.

The previous act promised to South by a promoter was virtually impossible to obtain from the beginning, but Stuco wasn't aware of this until last week.

Paul Revere and the Raiders were not free until after December and don't play for anything but a concert and expect $7,500 plus 20% of the gate which usually exceeds $20,000. The other groups required approximately the same.

The Buckinghams will sing some of their most famous songs like: "Kind of a Drag," "Mercy, Mercy, Mercy," and "Hey Baby, They're Playing Our Song."

THE WHO, hailing from London, England, will begin their American tour at SMS. Their on-stage act includes the destruction of part of their equipment. This is done to achieve a different, more unusual sound, but also provides for an exciting act.

A limited number of tickets were available for the other Shawnee Mission High Schools to purchase and at publication time, some 200 tickets were still available at $3 per ticket. Tickets may be purchased at the door for $3.

THE MIND-BLASTING MUSIC OF THE WHO will be heard along with the Buckinghams tonight at 8 p.m. in the gym for the StuCo Big Name Concert. Stuco sold several hundred tickets to insure sufficient funds for the group.

SMS Patriot

November 17, 1967

Jr. officers choose 80; committees

Certainly not 'Kind of a Drag'

By Robert Trussell

They still talk about the Johnson County gig.

The Who first appeared in the Kansas City area 21½ years ago—before their official local "debut" at the Music Hall in August 1968, before Woodstock, before "Tommy." And long before they managed the mysterious transition from contemporary commercial band to rock legend.

No, they were just young Brits with an attitude when they opened for the Buckinghams at Shawnee Mission South High School in 1967. It was Nov. 17, a Friday night, and only a few weeks after "I Can See for Miles" hit the American charts.

"South's Student Congress planned and organized successfully the first big-name band concert ever to be presented at Shawnee Mission district high school," the 1968 Heritage yearbook reported. The official crowd count was 3,500.

"The concert, held in the S-M South gymnasium, opened with the music of the well-known local group, Bobby Soul," the yearbook recounted. "Later, the two nationally-known bands performed for one-hour periods. The Who arrived in Kansas City directly from England, where they became internationally known for destroying their equipment at the end of each performance . . ."

In 1967 few bands were as different as the Who and the Buckinghams. The Who were the cutting edge of mod fashion from England. They wore ornately decorated jackets, sashes and ruffled shirts. They seemed dangerous and unpredictable.

The Buckinghams were Americans who adopted an anglicized name to cash in on the British invasion. They scored with a No. 1 hit in 1967, "Kind of a Drag," and followed it up with "Don't You Care," which rose to No. 6. Their music was feel-good pop, and they wore matching uniforms with lapels wide enough to land radio-controlled airplanes on.

the Who—minus the late Keith Moon and featuring the hearing-impaired Pete Townshend on acoustic guitar—return to Kansas City on an over-hyped world reunion tour that celebrates the band's 25 years in show business. A reconstituted version of the Buckinghams, working the nostalgia circuit this summer, will play Aug. 18 at Crown Center Square.

Chris O'Brien, the 1967-68 senior class president and an organizer of the concert, recalled that school officials, worried about damage to the gymnasium, made the Who promise not to tear up their instruments at the end of the set.

"They pushed over some amplifiers and stuff," said O'Brien, who lives in Wichita.

But others, all of whom still live in the metropolitan area, remember it differently.

"Actually, he (Townshend) destroyed his guitar," said Craig Williams. "They went bananas. They had smoke bombs. Pete Townshend destroyed his guitar, because a friend of mine got a piece of the guitar neck. Keith Moon knocked over his drums. Townshend was the really destructive one. Entwistle dropped his bass while it was still on."

Williams, like others at the show, took a keen interest in current British music but couldn't have cared less about the Buckinghams.

"It was real exciting at the time," he said, "because I was really into the British bands. I couldn't stay when the Buckinghams came on, because they were just such a letdown."

Dick Daniels and several friends drove to the Downtown Airport to greet the band. The musicians piled into a limousine, and the students followed them to the studios of WHB-AM radio. They traded English and American cigarettes, and Daniels had each member of the band autograph a *Playboy* centerfold. His brother later cut it into pieces to use in a collage.

"Townshend smashed up his guitar and he threw it out in the crowd," Daniels said. "One of my friends caught it, and glued together—like it was a previously smashed-up guitar."

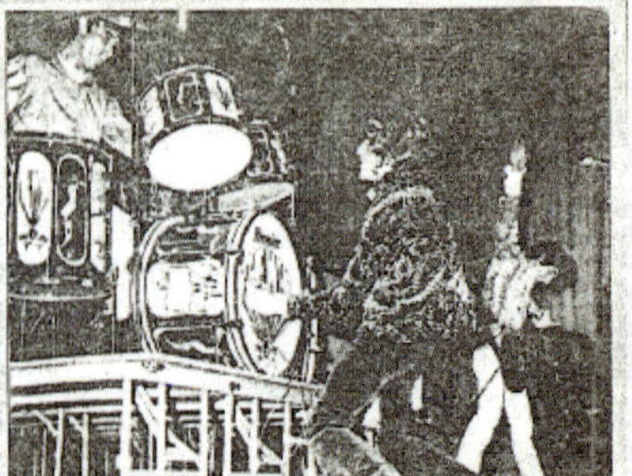

When the Who performed at Shawnee Mission South High School in November 1967, Keith Moon's "Pictures of Lily" drum kit included the words "Patent British Exploding Drummer." In typically flamboyant poses on the gym stage are singer Roger Daltrey and guitarist Pete Townshend. (photo courtesy of Dick Daniels)

Some said that high-school jocks were turned off by the Who and walked out. Others said there were two distinct audiences—those who came for the Who, and those who liked the Buckinghams. The way Daniels remembers it, the crowd thinned out after the Who's performance.

"When they played, everybody was just jammed up to the stage and nobody was dancing," he said. "Then when the Buckinghams came on, the small crowd of people that stayed started dancing. Suddenly it became a dance instead of a show."

Dan Smith, then a ninth-grader and novice drummer, slipped into the gym ...

"I found myself positioned (so that) I almost had my chest pressed against the gym stage about 6 inches from Pete Townshend," he said. He was amazed by the panels picturing nude women worked into Moon's drum kit and recalled Townshend tossing his guitar neck in pieces into the crowd.

"You could see the gym coaches freaking out because here was this guy they didn't know tearing up the gym floor," he said.

Few who saw the performance realized that it would be remembered as a historic moment.

"We certainly didn't realize the significance of it at the time," O'Brien said. "I would guess that was the cheapest they were ever paid."

Clockwise from top left: *Record Mirror* clipping from Doug Oldham; press cuttings from Dan Smith.

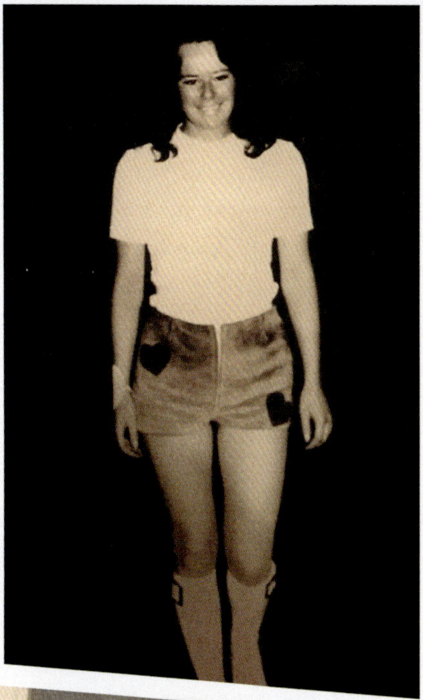

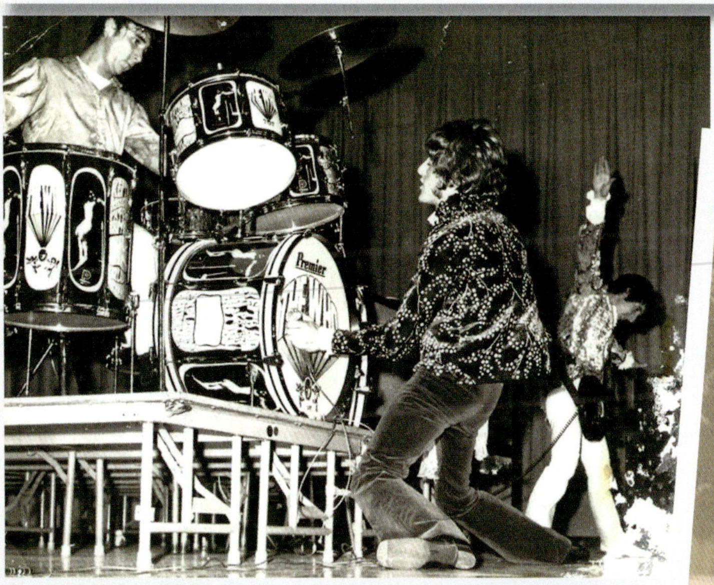

Clockwise from top left: Chris Mason (right) saw The Who at York University; Bill Harding bumped into the band in the corridor post-gig; Jill Morrison remembers Keith trying to reach her with his drumsticks; James Baddock saw a bill featuring The Who, Free, Joe Cocker and the Small Faces; The Who at SMS - photo Daniel Smith; Cheryl Malone saw The Who at Walthamstow Granada several times.

To him (and me) The Who was a much bigger deal that the Buckinghams, in spite of their lesser fame at that time. Mark knew they had played the Monterey Pop Festival that summer in California with the likes of Janis Joplin and Jimi Hendrix, all getting ready to explode on the music scene.

The problem was, this was going to be a school function. Only students at the four high schools in the Shawnee Mission School District would be allowed to attend. As word got out to friends of friends around the city, the cool kids began conspiring to get in, by hook or by crook. Mark was in college and I was still in junior high school. Undaunted, we gave Kathleen money with an order for four tickets, assuming we would figure a way in.

I asked a cousin who attended Shawnee Mission East High School if I could borrow his student ID. They were just printed on card stock with no photo back then. I practiced his signature for days, as though I would have to prove who I was at the door. I knew that nobody would know me or my cousin and that I would probably get in, unchallenged.

Kathleen was a member of the National Honor Society. But she was also a teenager who didn't always plan ahead. Invited to go with Debbie and some of the student council members to the old Kansas City Municipal Airport to greet the bands when they arrived in KC, Kathleen rode along. When requests for autographs were made, Kathleen offered the tickets to the four members of The Who. They politely signed the back of the tickets. When she returned home, she gave me the one signed by Keith Moon, since I was a drummer and a huge fan. I showed that off to my friends at school the next day. I was the envy of my musician friends, until one of them asked how I was going to get in and still keep the autograph. It was then that I realised my sister's mistake!

I rode my bicycle to the show. Arriving at the door, I showed the ticket to the student who was collecting them and asked if I could keep it as a memento. He said no. I would have to surrender the ticket or I couldn't get in. Unwilling to risk missing the opportunity to see The Who, I opted to say goodbye to Keith's autograph and get my skinny self inside to see local history be made.

Entering the gymnasium, I could see Bobby Soul was on stage playing to a full dance floor. Bobby Soul was a Kansas City band of white kids with greasy pompadours playing James Brown, Motown and the like. They were very popular around town.

When they finished, the mood in the room changed. The Who made it to the stage, dressed in the latest Mod fashion. The audience began to move forward. Being small, I slipped through the crowd and made it to the front of the stage. Pete Townshend was standing in front of a stack of amplifiers, They kicked off their set with 'Can't Explain' and the audience was captivated. Keith beat the daylights out of his kit, which had the naked form of a woman repeated on the drum shells and double bass drums and which took up the centre on a drum riser. Roger Daltrey began to swing his microphone in large circles over his head. In contrast, John Entwistle stood basically still. Having read an article about teenagers losing their hearing from loud music that week, I was convinced that I would be deaf before the Buckinghams did their set. After a couple of songs, I slithered back to the back and headed for the gym bleachers where I found my brother, Mark. He was having a great time.

When The Who finished and the Buckinghams took to the stage, the concert reverted back to a dance. They were very good, but an anticlimax after Pete Townshend had just destroyed his guitar and Keith Moon had kicked his drums apart.

The Who were a huge success. They played 'I Can See for Miles' during the show which made the top ten on Kansas City radio by Christmas. Probably every student there went out and bought The Who's *Sell Out* album that winter. To this day, I still get told that the Who playing at my high school is a bullshit story. Fortunately, the internet and smartphones make it easy to whip up proof of the event, including photos of the concert on pages of the Shawnee Mission South Class of 1968 yearbook. I saw The Who again in 1968 at the Kansas City Music Hall and in 1970 at Freedom Palace in Kansas City. Both were great shows, but playing my high school was special.

18 NOVEMBER 1967
COW PALACE, SAN FRANCISCO, CALIFORNIA

BOBBY ASEA

By the winter of 1967, I was somewhat of a veteran concert-goer, mostly due to the fact that my older sister would let me tag along with her and her girlfriends when they went to see the Beach Boys in concert. After two or three Beach Boy concerts between the years of 1964 -1965, I was fortunate enough to see the Rolling Stones in December 1965 with my best friend and we were all on our own. It was a wonderful feeling to be able to do this at the not so ripe age of twelve years! Fast forwarding to the Christmas holidays of 1967, my Christmas wish list consisted mostly of records by some of my favourite bands. I remember one night my family and I were Christmas shopping at a department store called White Front. Naturally, I had to drag my parents to the record section to show them what record albums that I wanted for Christmas. Lo and behold, once we arrived there, we discovered that the store was having a special that offered a free concert ticket with a purchase of a record album. The concert was to be held at the Cow Palace in San Francisco, 50 miles from where we lived. On the bill were The Sunshine Company, Sopwith Camel, The Association, The Everly Brothers, The Animals and The Who.

Originally, I was just going to show my folks what records I wanted and they would possibly purchase them at a later date so I could be surprised on Christmas morning. That plan got shot to hell when I begged them to buy a couple of records so that my twin sister and I could go to the concert. To our delight, our parents agreed to buy two albums right then and there so my sister and I could score tickets to the show. We were thrilled, and somewhat surprised that our folks were going to allow us 14-year-olds to attend a show so far from home.

When concert day came, it was my older sister (who'd taken me to see the Beach Boys in concert) and her boyfriend who drove us from San Jose and dropped us off at the Cow Palace. Even though I had heard of all the groups, I was most excited to see the Animals and The Who. We had very good seats on the main floor. The show opened up with The Sunshine Company, then the Animals; not the original Animals but Eric Burdon was there and he was fabulous!

The Who followed the Animals and they were on fire. Among the songs that they played were 'My Generation', 'Happy Jack', 'I Can't Explain' and 'Substitute'. But 'I Can See For Miles' stands out. It was their latest hit from their most recent album, *The Who Sell Out*. It was a short set but filled with high energy. Pete was doing his trademark windmill motion, Roger was tossing his microphone in the air and catching it, Keith was recklessly pounding on his drums like a madman while always staying in time, and John stood firmly in place holding it all together with his dynamic bass playing. There were many highlights during their set but it was the climax that stole the whole show. This was still the period when the band would destroy their equipment at the end of the set and we were treated to their display of violent madness. It was quite entertaining to watch Pete and Keith go ballistic on their instruments. Broken drums and guitars littered the stage as they stormed off in victory.

In the years that followed, I attended many Who concerts including the one where Keith Moon passed out during the show and the rest of the band had someone from the audience come up on stage and finish the show with them. As great as each and every one of them were, the first time that I saw them at the Cow Palace will always remain my favourite.

19 NOVEMBER 1967
HOLLYWOOD BOWL LOS ANGELES, CALIFORNIA

HARVEY KUBERNIK

In 1967 they're coming to town. I go with my friend David Wolf and we get second row box seat tickets (in the days before the world was rigged). That would never happen today. It's kind of a blur to me. But it was frantic. After seeing the Everly Brothers and The Association and their very well constructed, beautiful harmony pop songs, here comes The Who and it's 'My Generation' and Roger Daltrey's doing that microphone deal. I'd never seen anybody be so aggressive and strident in his playing as Pete Townshend. Keith Moon was in hog heaven because he was playing in Hollywood. He's playing in a venue with 18,000 seats. They're on the stage where Sinatra and The Beatles and everybody has played. It isn't like you're seeing Oasis in a club in Manchester. They're starting off in an 18,000 seater on a package show out here. It was really something.

18 DECEMBER 1967
PAVILION, BATH, UK

JOHN LEIGHTON

It was a fantastic show. I was down at the front. My ears have been bad ever since – but it was worth it!

8 JANUARY 1968
SILVER BLADES ICE RINK, BRISTOL, UK

JOHN MOGER, AGE 16

I was still at school but any pocket money I had went on watching bands, especially the old 'package' tours. I saw The Who about five times during the 1960s, including at the now demolished Silver Blades Ice Rink in Frogmore Street. I was a regular visitor to places like the Bristol Corn Exchange, Colston Hall and Bath Pavilion. Almost every band in the country (and from the US) would gig at some time or another in one of these venues. The Bristol Locarno Ballroom and Silver Blades Ice Rink were part of one complex and relatively new, so hadn't established themselves yet on the gig circuit, although I do recall seeing the Yardbirds and the Move at the Locarno, which had a revolving stage and (then) state of the art lighting.

I've no idea who thought it was a good idea to stand hundreds of people on an ice rink, but it's possible the gig may have been moved from the Locarno Ballroom, which was situated in the same building, due to technical problems. Anyway, this was pre-health and safety, so we gathered round the stage and waited for our rock heroes to appear. They were late starting – no surprise there – but once they did, they were brilliant. Amazingly, there were no covers on the ice so the combined body heat of the crowd started to melt the ice. By the end of the gig, we were standing in an inch of freezing water. But it didn't matter – we'd seen The Who! It goes down as one of the most unusual gigs I've been to. It was winter and just as cold in the ice rink as outside, although we warmed up as the show progressed!

JOHN RUDGE

We couldn't understand why the ice rink was used but there was a rumour that they'd trashed their dressing room the year before and so the Locarno manager banned them from ever appearing there again. I've since heard the Locarno was double-booked that night but I prefer to believe the trashing ban story! My mate caught a drumstick at the ice rink. Moonie was always breaking them and throwing them at the crowd. I remember the ice was bloody cold to stand on. I don't think they wanted people on the ice with no skates but we went on anyway. You can't stop hundreds!

11 JANUARY 1968
ASSEMBLY HALL, WORTHING, UK

JOHN FEEST

My friend Pete Wadeson was in a band called Total that supported The Who on this occasion and Pete Townshend wanted to borrow his guitar, pledging to pay for any resulting damage. My friend sweated throughout the act. Fortunately Townshend didn't damage the guitar, much to the other Pete's sanity!

12 JANUARY 1968
ROYAL BALLROOM, TOTTENHAM LONDON, UK

PAULINE LEVER

I had Keith's drum stick with teeth marks on it. He just lobbed it straight into my lap and I shoved it down my dress for safe keeping.

The Who travel Down Under in late January, performing eight dates in Australia and New Zealand.

11 FEBRUARY 1968
STARLIGHT BALLROOM, CRAWLEY, UK

DAVID GOODWIN

We saw them at Crawley Starlight. They were exceptionally good. They came off the stage and walked across in front of us. Moon's eyes were staring everywhere. He just bumped into us and had a laugh and said 'come on lads, come and have a drink' but the whole thing was gobbledegook really.

16 FEBRUARY 1968
UNIVERSITY, SHEFFIELD, UK

PAUL BRUCE HADEN

Because I was brought up in Sheffield, the only way to find out what was happening on the music front was by reading music papers like *Melody Maker* and *NME*, which were weekly, and *Beat Instrumental*, which was monthly. I'd been going to gigs from quite a young age as my dad took me to a few of the rock 'n' roll package tours that went around the country in the late 1950s and early 1960s. My first gig was Gene Vincent and Eddie Cochran. Radio Luxembourg was a source of new music and I used to listen nearly every night. I was by then playing guitar, although I'd played classical violin from the age of seven. I think it was the overall raw sound of The Who, and particularly the guitar, that drew me to them.

I first saw them in Chesterfield in a small club in early 1966. My girlfriend's older brother could drive and was also a fan. We next saw them at Barnsley Town Hall and then in 1967 at Sheffield City Hall on a package tour, where the support acts included Traffic and The Herd. At the uni gig, because the stage was quite low and we were sitting on the floor quite near the front, the whole experience seemed much more intense. The sound was better, presumably because we were hearing a lot of the stage sound and not the PA sound.

The Who are off to North America again, playing 22 dates before returning once more to the UK.

24 FEBRUARY 1968
WINTERLAND BALLROOM SAN FRANCISCO, CALIFORNIA

NEIL FAUGNO

It was an interesting line up – The Who, Cannonball Adderly and The Nice. The Nice were boring, Cannonball was cool and The Who were fantastic. This show was set up like a dance with a very large dance floor. The Who finished with 'My Generation' and people were urging them to destroy their equipment. Pete made a comment about 'how much this stuff cost' but that only made the crowd cheer louder. Well, Pete complied but really looked pissed off and he walked off, leaving just Keith playing his drums like only he could. Keith eventually kicked over his drum set but I really felt that his actions were a big 'fuck you' to the crowd urging him on.

23 APRIL 1968
MARQUEE CLUB, LONDON, UK

GERRY ALLINGTON

I saw them three times at the Mecca in Stevenage – nobody local called it by its correct name, the Locarno Ballroom. I was in my last year at school. They were my idols and didn't disappoint. Their records were good but live they were fantastic. I recall an article in either *Melody Maker* or *Sounds* about how, after one of those gigs, John injured his hand punching a framed picture of Joe Loss in their dressing room. Aah, happy days!

They often kicked off a show with 'Substitute' which got everyone rocking from the start. I saw them about 14 times in all up to about 1971, including at the Civic Hall in Dunstable, Brunel University with the Crazy World of Arthur Brown, The Alan Bown Set and others, at the Roundhouse and at the Saville Theatre, when Vanilla Fudge were second on the bill. Best of all was at the original Marquee Club in Wardour Street, which ended with equipment wipe-out and Pete shoving two guitars at the same time into the very low stage ceiling. It cost 25/- (£1.25) entrance. My ears were ringing for days afterwards.

At the end of June, The Who are again off to North America.

28 & 29 JUNE 1968
SHRINE AUDITORIUM
LOS ANGELES, CALIFORNIA

IRA KNOPF

I saw The Who five times with Keith. The first time they were sharing a bill with The Crazy World of Arthur Brown and the original four-piece blues line-up of Fleetwood Mac, all for $3.00. Their set consisted of 'Substitute', 'I Can't Explain', 'Summertime Blues' and 'My Generation' and ended with the destruction of their equipment. At Santa Monica Civic Auditorium that August, the set list included 'I Can't Explain', 'Summertime Blues', 'Fortune Teller', 'Happy Jack' and 'My Generation' and again they destroyed their equipment. After the show, I saw someone with Pete's destroyed Fender Strat body and part of the neck. Lucky guy!

In June 1970, they played Anaheim Stadium. This was a day-long concert featuring Blues Image, John Sebastian and Leon Russell. The Who performed *Tommy* in its entirety along with 'I Can't Explain', 'Summertime Blues' and 'My Generation'. This time there was no destruction of their equipment.

I saw them again on December 9th, 1971 at the LA Forum. Songs performed included 'Baba O'Riley', 'Bargain', 'Behind Blue Eyes', 'Won't Get Fooled Again', 'I Can't Explain', 'My Generation' and 'Pinball Wizard'. Pete's guitar kept going out of tune between songs, so rather than destroy it he opted for a back-up Gibson SG, which stayed in tune for the rest of the show.

March 1976 was again Anaheim Stadium and another all-day concert. This one featured Chaka Khan, John Sebastian and Little Feat. The Who's selection of songs included 'Squeeze Box', 'I Can't Explain', 'Pinball Wizard', 'Behind Blue Eyes', 'Baba O'Riley', 'Won't Get Fooled Again' and 'My Generation'. Sadly, this was to be the last time I saw The Who with Keith Moon.

10 JULY 1968
STAMPEDE CORRAL, CALGARY, CANADA

KEITH ROWLEY

The Who headlined the Calgary Stampede in 1968 and my brother John and his wife Rita went backstage to meet up with Roger. They had filthy old ice hockey dressing rooms to change in and there was no security to stop anyone wandering around backstage. John and Rita went a few years back to see The Who in Winnipeg and tried to see him again but this time there was major security in place, so no luck.

14 JULY 1968
MUSICARNIVAL, CLEVELAND, OHIO

RICK MAROUS

I loved The Who from the beginning. My second album ever was *Happy Jack* (I believe it had a different title in Britain) and my first stereo album was *My Generation*. They were my favourite band in the Sixties and Seventies. I saw them several times but the first time was 1968 at a theatre in the round in a tent called Musicarnival. I was 16 and a roadie for the opening act which was Cyrus Erie, an early band with Eric Carmen (who did 'Hungry Eyes' from *Dirty Dancing*). We were taking the equipment off the stage when we were asked if The Who could borrow some speakers, mics, etc. Since it was our stuff up on stage, we decided to stay up there with it. I was getting Keith Moon's sweat on me (it was a tiny stage) and was loving every minute of it. I think Pete was really upset about the sound system or something, because he started smashing stuff early including some of ours.

21 JULY 1968
OAKDALE MUSIC THEATRE WALLINGFORD, CONNECTICUT

HENRY MCNULTY

In 1968, *The Hartford Courant* didn't cover pop and rock music shows, except as police stories. As a summer intern, I saw that the lack of serious pop music coverage was an opportunity, so I approached then city editor Irving Kravsow with a proposition: how about if I reported on, and reviewed, major pop and rock acts that came to Connecticut – on my own time? It wouldn't cost *The Courant* an extra cent. That was an offer Kravsow couldn't, and didn't, refuse. But, he added, he wasn't going to assign photographers to concerts; they had better things to do. That was fine with me. I brought along my camera, and now, half a century later, I have my own amateur but evocative photos of some of those who played here.

I saw The Who and Herman's Hermits at the Oakdale Theatre. In those days, meeting the performers was easy. I didn't need an ID or a backstage pass. I let the promoter – often someone about my age – know that I'd be there; identified myself to whoever opened the stage door and the next thing I knew I was face-to-face with genuine rock stars, most of whom turned out to be more than willing to talk with a reporter, and to let me photograph them.

I rode along with Herman's Hermits from a Meriden motel to the Oakdale, interviewing them and taking photos on the way. At the theatre, the band was greeted by a bunch of fans; in the front were several mothers and fathers, wheeling their children with severe disabilities closer to their idols. Peter 'Herman' Noone said that this was a common practice at concerts.

The Who warmed up for their Oakdale show, in what was then a rustic dressing room, by consuming most of a bottle of MacPherson's Cluny scotch. A pal had told me that lead guitarist Pete Townshend's right index finger was deeply scarred as a result of his so-called 'windmill' style of playing, and I persuaded him to let me photograph it. He got a kick out of the idea, saying he had never thought his finger was all that newsworthy.

2 AUGUST 1968
SINGER BOWL, FLUSHING, NEW YORK

JOHN KOEGEL

The Doors headlined, performing on a revolving stage which broke down partway through their show. It was a wild performance that led to a well-documented melee when the security staff and police tried to end it early. The opening act was called Kangaroo. The Who opened with a song about angels and devils I had never heard before. It was 'Heaven and Hell'. They also played 'Summertime Blues', 'Young Man Blues', 'Magic Bus' and 'My Generation'.

4 AUGUST 1968
MELODY FAIR
NORTH TONAWANDA, NEW YORK

DENNIS THOMANN

It was *The Who Sellout* tour, and when John, Keith, Pete and Roger emerged, the sold-out crowd erupted in screams and cheers. The *Magic Bus* album had come out about six months prior. I, along with my brother Tim and a few friends, were up front. They began with 'Magic Bus'. Roger's voice was so powerful and in between singing he would toss the microphone high in the air, catching it just in perfect time to sing the next verses. He repeated this with a few other songs as well. The sound system was perfect and the band and audience were thoroughly enjoying themselves. The next song was a Jan and Dean cover, 'Bucket T', which Keith sang. Being a drummer myself, I was totally mesmerised by his amazing drum rolls and performance. They went on to perform their hits like 'Substitute', 'The Kids are Alright', 'I Can't Explain', etc. but when they got to 'My Generation', something wild and crazy happened that nobody was prepared for. Pete, doing his wild trademark rhythms and jumping high in the air, came to the front of the stage screaming, then turned towards his highly-stacked amplifiers and ran towards them, doing a flying drop kick into them. Result? Nothing!

He looked furious and came back to the front of the stage, more determined than ever, and then repeated his drop kick but with double the force and landing his kick higher. This time, the speakers went tumbling down. Immediately, the rest of the band followed suit and began smashing their equipment as well. Drums were flying everywhere and Pete was violently smashing his guitar onto the stage. My buddy Dave got a big chunk of his guitar and my brother Tim got Keith's drum stool. It was an unbelievable show that I will never forget. Unfortunately, as we were leaving, a roadie took the stool back from Tim, but Dave still has that chunk of Pete's guitar on the wall above his stereo to this day!

10 AUGUST 1968
JAGUAR CLUB, ST CHARLES, ILLINOIS

DANIEL TEAFOE, AGE 13

If one saw the them in concert in the late Sixties or Seventies, it's possible you had a 'profound experience' of the transcendental kind. The Who could take you to places your mind didn't usually go. Having seeing the band many times over the past 50 years, and in many incarnations, the show worthy of claiming bragging rights for took place at the Jaguar Club in St Charles, Illinois – my home town. The Jaguar, once a roller rink and then a used car dealership, was a popular music venue at the western outskirts of the Chicago area. It was a groovy place to hang out, where acts on the summer concert circuit with a hit single or two appeared. It also served as a showcase for local talent. The intimate space was festooned with florescent-coloured murals, psychedelic posters, strobes and blacklights. The announcement of The Who playing there drew great excitement. I couldn't believe it! In my little town? I heard them on the radio. Saw them on TV. They touched a nerve in me. 'My Generation' was an anthem. 'Magic Bus' was cruising up the charts.

On show day, I was among the first in line at the door, with my 'that was a lot of money back in those days' hard-earned four dollars. Once inside, I went straight for the stage, firmly planting myself on the cold hard concrete floor. Front row centre, within arms' reach of the three-foot-high stage.

After the two opening acts finished their brief sets, their stage gear was taken away, revealing The Who's equipment. I thought how cool Keith Moon's double bass drum kit looked. But it was Pete Townshend's scorched and battered stack of Marshalls that startled me a bit. As in 'I think this is going to be intense'. Otherwise, the staging was unadorned save for a few flood lights and a follow spot. Very basic. There were no monitors. The only microphones on stage were for vocals. No microphones for the stacks of speakers, no microphones for the drums. What you got in the end was in-your-face, grab you by the throat, kick you in the groin, straight-from-the-source, raw and unfiltered Who. All within spitting distance. This is about as close as you would ever get to seeing The Who play in your garage.

Without fanfare, after a polite introduction, the band took to the stage. The latest sensation from the British Invasion was here. The Who have landed and have something to t-t-t-talk about. Roger Daltrey, looking dandy in velvet trousers and a suede shirt, said 'thank you. Just getting the balance sorted out. We're not used to playing in places with quite such low ceilings. We'll play for ya, anyway.' On behalf of the audience, Townshend's tendency to 'turn up the amplifiers so they can't hear themselves think' was obvious at the very first chord he strummed. 'This one's called 'Can't Explain'.' For the next 66 minutes, the band was in full throttle, focused and ferocious, well orchestrated, youthfully defiant and exuberant. Punks. Taking no prisoners. Apologising to no one for nothing. The set list was a collection of rarely played tunes, then current crowd pleasers and new songs. The set included 'I Can't Explain', 'Fortune Teller', 'Tattoo', 'Heaven and Hell', 'Young Man Blues', 'Daddy Rolling Stone', 'Summertime Blues', an 18-minute long 'Magic Bus', 'Boris the Spider', 'A Quick One (While He's Away)' and 'My Generation'.

There was also relaxed and humorous band member banter in between songs, whether it was to introduce the next one, or Pete's explanation of his mini-opera. Visually, the band was thrilling. Having only seen them perform a song or two on television, suddenly there they were in full feature-length mode. By then their meaty, beaty, big and bouncy stage personas were becoming legendary. I was gob-smacked by their presence from the get go. It was all a heavy dose of sensory overload, sending quivers down my backbone. I wanted them to play all night.

If you listen to a bootleg of the show, in a quieter moment during 'A Quick One' you can hear a girl in the crowd say 'uh-oh'. I'm guessing that was her response when she saw the cops come into the club. Through the side door on the left came a battalion of the local's finest, lining up in front of the stage. The police presence was puzzling, distracting and a bit unnerving, given the climate of the time. In 1968, the world was in turmoil. Townshend announced, 'We've been asked to finish now, so we'll play our last song, called 'My Generation'.'

In an instant, the audience rose to their feet and rushed the stage. Simultaneously, the cops leapt up and locked arms. I became pinned against the stage but managed to wedge my head between two of the uniformed guards to get an unobstructed view of band and of the wreckage about to take place. 'My Generation' was played with a vengeance. And in the end, amid the smoke bombs, strobe lights, feedback and mass hysteria, there was Daltrey helping to kick over the drum kit as Moon firmly planted his boot through the bass drum heads. Entwistle, meanwhile, continued playing off to the side. As for the coup-de-grace, the cheap plywood stage floor was no match for Townshend's guitar as he tried to desecrate his instrument. So, like a slugger in the batter's box taking a few measured half-swings, he took aim at an overhead pipe with the body of his Les Paul knock-off. Chunks of wood went flying, Pete did a pull up on the pipe and rammed his foot into the crumpled ceiling. Before we knew it, The Who were gone, thank you and good night.

As the stunned crowd, including myself, started to slowly file out of the club, I nonchalantly reached over onto the stage. I got my hand on a splintered chunk of broken guitar just sitting there. But the roadie guy came up to me and said politely, 'oh no ya don't'. Shucks, that would have been a treasured belated birthday present to myself. If turning 13 years old involves a rite of passage of some sort, then seeing The Who at the Jaguar was one hell of an initiation.

16 AUGUST 1968
SELLAND ARENA, FRESNO, CALIFORNIA

BRUCE WOODWARD

I wasn't up front like some of the other concerts I've attended. It was notable in that they were still destroying their kits. That was wild! I didn't see them again for various reasons (marriage and child raising) until 1996 on their *Quadrophenia* tour. I took my 14-year-old daughter with me that night and to several other shows over the years. I was at the show at the Shoreline Amphitheater in the Bay Area right after John died, as well as a show there a year or two previous. And I've seen them at the Hollywood Bowl several times, at the *The Who Hits 50!* concert in San Francisco and several since. The last time I saw them was with the orchestral backing in 2022. That was a great concert. When they came through Fresno in 2007, Pete mentioned from the stage that they had played there about 40 years ago. I was in the front row and held my hand up for him to see that I was there. The Who are the best live rock and roll act I've ever seen, better than Led Zep and Hendrix.

The Who leave North America in August and in October are back on the road in the UK.

11 OCTOBER 1968
UNIVERSITY, YORK, UK

BILL HARDING

By the time I heard about it, tickets for this gig had all sold out. Luckily for me, the girl next door had a cold and couldn't go. Two or three hundred of us piled into Derwent dining room. I met up with a couple of friends and we supped a few Newcastle Browns. Big mistake! 'Magic Bus' had just been released and I distinctly remember Moonie's magnificent drumming in the wonderful live version. Townshend kept looking at him nervously, as if he expected him to fall off his drum stool. My bladder held on as long as it could and finally gave out.

I rushed to the loo and could hear the yells as the concert ended. Bugger. I ran back down the corridor just as the band was leaving the stage. Daltrey was first, followed by Moonie. I stopped dead and realised I was standing next to the dressing room door. I was a few feet from Daltrey and was about to speak when he said 'what the fuck do you want?'. He thumped my chest and turned to his left into the dressing room. I said something like 'what did I do?'. Moonie gave me a huge grin and spread out his hands as if to say 'it's nothing to do with me, mate!'. He disappeared into the dressing room, followed by Pete and John. It was more of a thump than a punch, but I always tell Who fans about it. I'd love to buy Daltrey a pint and find out if he remembers the incident. I don't blame him as he obviously thought a bloke running towards him presented a threat.

My diary entry for that day reads:

Good day, except for the weather. Spent most of afternoon in refectory. In evening, Stella's ticket for THE WHO! FANTASTIC! Tried to catch a Moonie stick during 'Magic Bus'. To bog after floods of Newcie Brown. Missed last song. Face to face with band as they came off. Roger thumped me in the chest! What!? Moonie gave a cheeky smile and big shrug. Should have said something! Bugger! Bed at 1.

I have a couple of rehearsal rooms and a few years ago the band Mostly Autumn moved in for a couple of weeks. I soon learned their guitar tech is a friend of Daltrey's. I told him the story and he said I'd hear back from Roger. Sadly, I never did.

JOHN HARRIS, AGE 18

This was in my first week as a first-year student. The university had only been founded five years earlier and was still very small. Langwith College dining room was also very small for such a major band. My diary entry for 11 October 1968 reads:

An absolutely outstanding evening. The set list included 'Shaking All Over' with three-part harmony on the chorus line, and the whole of 'A Quick One (While He's Away)', as well as most of their hits.

During 'My Generation', Daltrey slipped and the music temporarily halted before Townshend led them back into an amazing climax, in which he raced athletically up and down, forwards and backwards; shook the lighting staging behind Moon; threw his guitar spinning into the air, then caught it neatly and continued playing; and finished by throwing his guitar against the wall behind him, kicking his amplifier over it, and jumping on top before walking off. Moon kicked his drums over; Daltrey smashed his mike against the cymbals. Entwistle, after an hour of truly excellent bass playing, left the stage calmly. A great fifteen shillings (75p) worth – the most incredible group performance I have ever seen.

CHRIS MASON

I was an undergraduate, studying history at the University of York and went to both The Who's concerts there. At the 1970 concert – and I should have had more sense by then – I managed to position myself rather too close to the speakers and was suffering from partial deafness for the next two or three days. They were already a big name. It now seems truly remarkable that, with an act which more befits a stadium, they should be doing gigs in a hastily converted college dining room, but that is the way it was then. What was then Langwith College Dining Room was the venue for numerous concerts involving big names. (In October 1967, I attended a Freshers Week concert performed by Peter Green and Fleetwood Mac, who were last minute stand-ins for John Mayall and the Bluesbreakers.)

Although I enjoyed the music of The Who, I was not a particular fan. In the cosy confines of Langwith Dining Room, their seemingly anarchic guitar smashing finale seemed pretty over the top and I did wonder about illegal substances. However, when I saw the band for a second time in 1970, the same routine was reproduced and was clearly tightly choreographed. It was a bit of a USP! That aside, such standards as 'Substitute', 'My Generation' and 'Pinball Wizard' were delivered with great power. They were just very good. And Pete Townshend's nose looked just as impressive as it did on television.

PETE MORTON

I was living in Sheffield where I saw lots of live gigs in clubs and pubs (Joe Cocker was a regular performer). It was rare for York to stage a gig, even more so the university. I went with my mate, Mick Bates (who was disappointed when the support band, Spooky Tooth, failed to appear as he had their latest record), and our girlfriends. The place erupted when The Who arrived on stage. They were extremely loud and Keith Moon's drumming was something I had not seen before. You almost expected him to go through the drum skin as he was hitting it that hard. Keith Moon had been drumming on a raised platform and he kicked all the drum kit over. At the same time, Pete Townsend was smashing his guitar on the stage until nothing was left. I've seen anything like it, before or since.

19 OCTOBER 1968
CALIFORNIA BALLROOM, DUNSTABLE, UK

PETE WRIGHT

They still had the big Marshalls then. I had a car by this time and I parked outside. A bloke came on stage and said 'would the owner of car registration number so-and-so,' which was me, 'please move it.' And I thought 'Sod it, I ain't going out there now.' And The Who came on and, afterwards, I went to get in my car and there was a policeman standing there and I got done for all sorts of things – wrong side of the road at night, no lights. I got fined £7, which was more than a week's wages.

The Who embark on a nine-date UK theatre tour with a changing bill that includes Free, Yes, Joe Cocker and headliners the Small Faces. Keith appears at Clerkenwell Magistrates Court the same week, charged with being drunk and disorderly. The magistrate tells Keith, 'We don't want you playing in traffic anymore, Mr Moon,' to which Keith replies, 'Absolutely. They already have a drummer.'

8 NOVEMBER 1968
WALTHAMSTOW GRANADA, LONDON, UK

CHERYL MALONE

It all started with 'My Generation'. I was 14 and it was so different. I had been a Beatles fan and never really interested in anything remotely rock, but I went out and bought the record for 7/6d (37p) and I played it non-stop. It was the era of the *New Musical Express* and I learnt more about The Who, and especially the lovely Roger Daltrey. Soon my school ruler and desk were emblazoned with his name. I joined The Who fan club through which I acquired a pen friend. Rosalyn was based in the exotic location of Ealing, which to a 14-year-old seemed miles away. The great thing about Rosalyn was that she lived near Shepherds Bush, The Who's stomping ground, and may even have met them! We stayed in touch for years afterwards.

When it was announced that The Who were to play at our local cinema in November 1967, I drove my mum mad saying I wanted to go. I was still at school so my Mum, bless her, queued up at the box office in her lunch hour to get tickets. The tickets were 15 shillings (75p) for seats in the stalls. The other acts were The Herd, The Tremeloes, The Kinks and The Marmalade. I still have my tickets and the programme.

The next year they played the Granada once again. This time Mum came up trumps and we were rewarded with front row seats. Not that we sat on them – we stood on them throughout, screaming. They were billed with The Crazy World of Arthur Brown, who all but set light to himself, but that was all by-the-by. The whole time we couldn't wait to see The Who. Roger Daltrey was iconic in white fringed leather jacket, bare-chested with a large crucifix. The mic was swung out into the adoring crowd and magically retrieved. 'I Can See For Miles' was belted out at ear-damaging volume. The atmosphere was magical, and more than 50 years later, I can still remember it vividly. Pete did his guitar smashing whilst Moon was true to form on the drums. It was electric. We screamed, we shouted, we went crazy. We walked home afterwards chatting to others in the audience, glorying in the evening.

They came to the Granada once more after that and I saw them there again. I wasn't on the front row this time but the performance was still electric. I have seen them many, many times over the years since. Although there is sadly just the two of them now, they are still brilliant and can still whip their audience into a frenzy. I last saw them at the O2 a few years back. I usually have to go with my friend's husbands, as my female friends have all now defected to Michael Buble.

9 NOVEMBER 1968
ADELPHI CINEMA, SLOUGH, UK

DENISE HARPER, AGE 16

I had my first pop concert experience at 15 watching the Monkees at Wembley in July 1967, then went to a few concerts at the Slough Adelphi. I lived in a small village, so attendance at these shows depended on whether I could still catch a bus home afterwards as my parents didn't drive! I saw The Who at the Slough Adelphi in 1968. I know we were all waiting to see if Pete Townshend smashed a guitar on stage, as per his reputation at the time.

10 NOVEMBER 1968
COLSTON HALL, BRISTOL, UK

WAYNE PURSEY, AGE 12

I was still in school. I'd heard that they were going to be on at the Colston Hall and told my friends, who told me that I'd missed it. I told them 'let's go to the Colston Hall anyway. There may be posters or something.' When we got to the hall, chalked on an A frame blackboard was 'The Who, The Crazy World Of Arthur Brown.' They were playing two houses that day. It was ten shillings (50p) a ticket. I now had a big dilemma. That was a lot of money to me and I was sure my parents wouldn't be able to afford it. To my surprise, my mum gave me the money straight away. When we got into the hall, there was what seemed to be a chrome drum kit that went right across the stage. In front of it was a normal size drum kit. I later found out it was played by Carl Palmer (later of ELP fame) when he was with the Crazy World of Arthur Brown.

I really can't remember seeing the other members of the band because, when Keith Moon started playing, I had never seen anything like it. At the end, he kicked the whole kit over. When I got home, I made a pair of drum sticks out of some wood from my mum's clothes horse and I have been messing about with drums ever since.

18 NOVEMBER 1968
CITY HALL, NEWCASTLE-UPON-TYNE, UK

JILL MORRISON, AGE 17

My friend Lesley and I went to see The Who. The main event were the Small Faces. We were sat on the balcony, which seemed miles from the stage, and we were the only people screaming for The Who. Keith Moon was trying his hardest to throw his drumsticks at us but couldn't quite reach. If only!

RUSSELL WILKES

I saw the group several times in the late Sixties and early Seventies. In 1968, I saw them as part of a very big tour at Newcastle City Hall with the Small Faces, Joe Cocker, Arthur Brown, the Mindbenders (no Wayne Fontana, but including Eric Stewart and Graham Gouldman, later to form 10cc) and an unknown band called Yes. Everyone only played two songs. There were two shows that night. It was probably the last big tour ever undertaken and the place was packed. It was a great atmosphere. I can't remember what they played but I do remember it was a great night. The City Hall isn't a huge venue. If you're down near the front, it's fantastic.

19 NOVEMBER 1968
PAISLEY ICE RINK, GLASGOW, UK

JAMES BADDOCK, AGE 18

The Who were the headline act on probably one of the last UK package tours where you had several bands on the same bill. They were supported by Free, The Mindbenders, Joe Cocker and the Grease Band, The Crazy World of Arthur Brown and the Small Faces, who were billed as 'special guests'. Each band was limited to about 25-30 minutes on stage, although The Who probably had nearer 45. It meant about three hours' worth of music, which wasn't bad for a 12/6 (62p) ticket.

I travelled up from Ayrshire with about half a dozen mates, one of whom had brought along his younger sister. She was a rabid Small Faces fan and had threatened to tell their parents what he had been doing with his girlfriend unless he took her along.

The ice rink had been mostly covered over in front of the stage, but the venue was still pretty cold, especially at rink level. We were up in the gallery to the left, looking down on the stage from about 30 yards away. The line up was pretty impressive, although none of us had heard of Free at the time. The stage was set up with every band's equipment on it, one in front of the other, so that at the end of each set their amps and speakers were removed, enabling the next band to go straight on. After the opening acts, there was a short break before the Small Faces came on and that's when the screaming kicked in, especially from my mate's sister, who deafened us all. I especially remember a rocking version of 'Tin Soldier'.

And then – finally – it was The Who. They did not disappoint. Even then they were an amazing live band. They'd been touring for most of 1968, gradually writing the songs that would form *Tommy*, but I don't remember any of them being featured at Paisley. Songs that I do remember were 'Substitute', 'I Can't Explain', 'My Generation' and finishing with an extended version of 'Magic Bus', where they were joined onstage by the Small Faces who mostly hit various percussion instruments.

Pete Townshend was in classic arm windmilling mode. Roger Daltrey had honed his microphone whirling act to perfection, swinging it around his head on its lead and sending it curling out over the audience before pulling it back just in time to sing the next line. John Entwistle just stood over on the left-hand side of the stage, playing rock solid bass while Keith Moon's arms seemed to be flailing everywhere without ever missing a beat – and yes, he did destroy the drum kit at the end.

Apparently the police were waiting to interview Moon after the gig. The Who had been performing in Newcastle the night before and Moon had taken it into his head to steal a mannequin, as you do, and stuff it into the boot of his Rolls-Royce to drive over to Paisley. But he'd left one of the legs dangling out of the boot and the police had received phone calls about a dead body in a car boot.

By later standards, the sound quality wasn't anything special. You couldn't really hear the Small Faces anyway for the screaming. But the actual performances across the board were top notch, especially from The Who, although there may well be a hint of rose-tinted spectacles here. It was nearly 50 years ago, after all. All in all, it was well worth the money.

22 NOVEMBER 1968
CITY HALL, ST ALBANS, UK

PETE WRIGHT

There was a massive queue outside. I went straight to the front and said 'is this for tickets only?'. He said 'mate, we're sold out.' So I hung about until everybody had gone in and the security man running the show and the bouncers seemed to go back into the shadows a bit. There was just an old age pensioner on the door and I said, 'What's it gonna cost me to get in, mate? This is my band.' He said, 'Go in the bar and buy a drink' and I went in there and he came up and he said, 'Just give me 12/6 (62p), same as everybody else.' I got the money out and his hand was shaking. It was probably more than he earned for the night. They were doing 'A Quick One (While He's Away)'.

7 DECEMBER 1968
UNIVERSITY, BRISTOL, UK

JOHN FLETCHER

I saw them at Bristol University Union where they put in a very presentable but not amazing performance, and I speak as an admirer of their LPs of those days. I had already seen groups like the Stones, John Mayall, Cream, Yardbirds, Hollies, Animals and Them. They finished with the usual destruction of guitars! I saw The Who again relatively recently at the NEC and frankly found them loud and boring.

14 DECEMBER 1968
BUBBLES CLUB, BRENTWOOD, UK

JOHN HALES

Bubbles was an old converted cinema next door to the railway station in King's Road in Brentwood that this guy had converted into a nightclub. He got The Who ridiculously cheap, for next to nothing, on an old contract. I was a drummer playing progressive rock on the college circuit. At the same venue we supported The Herd, The Nice, The Easy Beats, and Small Faces with Peter Frampton as special guest just before they broke up and formed Humble Pie. And we had The Who. It was about the time of 'Magic Bus', because they did that in their set. I stood in the wings about ten or 15 feet away, just watching Keith Moon from the side.

When our road crew set up all our stuff, a couple of them knew The Who's road crew and they came back and said 'you want to keep your eye out because I know a couple of them blokes and they make their money up by nicking other people's equipment, like mics and stuff like that.' And sure enough the lead singer had bought a couple of new Shure mics and we did have one did go missing. Roger Daltrey's mic used to look like a massive great ice cream cornet. He used to swing it round his head and chuck it out into the crowd. When the band finished, he put it down on the stage and someone we knew cut the lead and had it away. When everyone was getting packed up, we came to get our stuff back and let him have that mic back. This was all just between the road crews. It was good, meeting all the bands. The Small Faces, Keith Emerson from Nice. They were all good gigs, but The Who was probably the highlight.

21 DECEMBER 1968
GAIETY BALLROOM, RAMSEY, UK

PETER WOOR

A feature of this old dance hall was a very low ceiling and we came out afterwards deafened. I remember the very chilly ride home on my friend Ray Banyard's scooter from this Fenland town back to Cambridge.

19 JANUARY 1969
MOTHERS CLUB, BIRMINGHAM, UK

MAUREEN STOBBART

Mothers was a music club over a furniture shop on the High Street in Erdington and between 1968 and 1971 it was the best club in Britain. Over 400 acts performed there including Pink Floyd, Family and Led Zeppelin and, in 1969, The Who. My boyfriend and I were both still at school, we had very little spending money and we were too young to get into Mothers. We sat in the Milk Bar, opposite Erdington Parish Church and adjacent to Mothers, and listened to The Who, who were notoriously loud, all evening – or at least as late as we could, as I had to be home before 10pm.

JOHN PATRICK BYRNE

I saw The Who six times and they're the best live band I've ever seen. There was a capacity crowd for this show. It was so hot the condensation was running down the walls, the bar ran out of beer and we all stripped to the waist and used our t-shirts for towels. Halfway through The Who's first set, Keith Moon passed out and Roger and Pete had to carry him bodily backstage. 40 minutes later, they were all back on stage as though nothing had happened. It was a tremendous show!

1 FEBRUARY 1969
UNIVERSITY, NEWCASTLE-UPON-TYNE, UK

RUSSELL WILKES

The final time I saw them was at Newcastle University. I wasn't a student but on two or three occasions I managed to get tickets for the student union. It was a very small and intimate venue and I was only a few feet from the small stage. If I was to go back into that room now, I wouldn't recognise it. They put on a great show and it's the only time I can remember Townshend smashing a guitar up and Keith Moon kicking the drums over. Those in the very front had to get out of the way because the drums came out into the audience. I had a pint in the bar beforehand and I can recall Roger Daltrey also being in the bar and chatting to people. Remember the outfits Roger used to wear, with all the tassels, and the long hair and him swinging the mic about? Well, he was standing at the bar dressed in that jacket, having a chat with whoever it was.

8 FEBRUARY 1969
CENTRAL LONDON POLY, LONDON, UK

NIGEL MOLDEN

In 1969 I was studying at the Polytechnic of Central London, UK and had been elected Social Vice President. I booked the band to appear for a 45-minute set for a fee of £450. Tickets were eight shillings (40p) in advance and twelve and sixpence (63p) on the door. The event took place in the gymnasium of the Main Extension Building in Little Titchfield Street and was completely packed. The date was less than three months before the launch of *Tommy* and their set included all the hits, plus the classic rock and roll numbers that they always performed towards the end of the show. I introduced the band and had the opportunity to talk to Roger Daltrey briefly in the toilet just before the performance. Not many people can say that! I have also been told that a recording on a reel-to-reel tape machine was made but since lost to posterity. Certainly, I have never heard it.

14 FEBRUARY 1969
LANCHESTER COLLEGE, COVENTRY, UK

GRAHAM AUCOTT

There was a lad sitting in front of the speakers, when they were the loudest band in the world. He was shouting, 'Smash! Smash! Smash!' And when the number finished, Daltrey went over to him and said 'I'll fucking smash you in a minute.'

14 MARCH 1969
CORN EXCHANGE, CAMBRIDGE, UK

PETER WOOR

They were just bringing out *Tommy* and played some material from that ground breaking album. I can remember Pete Townshend coming into the hall and making an acid comment about the lack of people in there. A year or so later, they would be packing out stadiums all over the world.

22 APRIL 1969
CASINO CLUB, BOLTON, UK

DAVID ALMOND

It was Bolton's student rag week. The Casino Club was on Crompton Way. It was an old cinema-type building. They were on the verge of bringing *Tommy* out and they played one or two of the songs off Tommy. Daltrey had that jacket with all the tassels on.

TOM CASEY

I was a semi-pro drummer in a band called The Answers, while also working for the L.E. Agency at Hindley and it was me who booked The Who to play at Bolton Casino for the Bolton Students Union annual bash. Not being totally stupid, I had the presence of mind to put The Answers on with them as support group. Townshend broke a G string part way through one number, and he actually changed it during the song whilst Moonie, Daltrey and Entwistle carried on regardless, and without the audience noticing. This confirmed to me then that John Entwistle was the best bassist in the world – next to our own bass guitarist Dennis Shuttleworth! I also had the presence of mind to wrap up my own Ludwig set of drums following our set before Moonie started his antics in destroying drum kits.

CARL RUSSELL, AGE 21

The Casino Club was a cinema originally. It had a balcony, but they'd taken out the downstairs seating and there was a bar at one end and a stage at the other end. It was quite near private houses. When Slade played there, they actually stopped them from playing because they had that many complaints from neighbours nearby. In the end it got turned into a supermarket.

I went with a couple of mates. Pete had the white boiler suit and the flailing arms on the guitar and there was Roger with the permed locks, throwing the mic out to the crowd that were round the stage. In fact, I think he hit somebody with it. He kept doing that. And obviously Keith was on the drums and John was just stood still. But it was a great night. They played 'Pinball Wizard' but the showstopper for me, which they liked to do on live shows, was 'Summertime Blues'. I would probably put The Who third after The Beatles and the Stones for best in the world as far as rock groups go. The Beatles had quite a short life and you couldn't really call them a touring band as such but the Stones – well, they're still at it, aren't they?

The Who also appeared at the Cromwellian Club on Bank Street in Bolton prior to that, probably in the early to mid-Sixties. I didn't see them there then, but a friend did and got one of Keith's drumsticks.

25 APRIL 1969
STRATHCLYDE UNIVERSITY, GLASGOW, UK

JOHN CHARLES MORTON

I played with them at Strathclyde University. It was the start of the *Tommy* rock opera tour. The name of my band was Happy Ever After but we were changing our name to Snow, so I'm not sure which name we were billed under. We were up there in the afternoon and so were they, and we were sharing a changing room. Daltrey was there in the afternoon. We spoke to them all. Obviously, Keith Moon was crazy. We had a four bar. We'd made one out of wood. Our road manager was a joiner and his electrician mate had made one out of wood. We'd had it for six years. It was six double sockets, and they pestered us all day to buy this off us. We were a professional band. We were a Scottish band but we'd moved to the north east to get more gigs and we needed it for ourselves. We were set up at the other end of the hall from them. We did our set and they asked us if they could come and play our last song with us. I had Pete Townshend, Keith Moon and John Entwistle backing me while I sang 'People Got To Be Free by The Rascals'. At the time, I didn't think it was a big deal.

26 APRIL 1969
COMMUNITY CENTRE, AUCHINLECK, UK

JEAN FERGUSON, AGE 18

People came from all over and the hall was packed full. One thing I remember is that no one was dancing. Everyone was so engrossed with The Who they just stood and listened. You could have heard a pin drop. People still talk about that night yet my family find it hard to believe that it happened, or that I was there!

ROBIN LEES

I was lucky enough to play lead guitar in the Merry Macs band, the warm up act in April 1969. We were a large band, and probably termed a show band like some of the Irish show bands of the Sixties. The venue where The Who performed also had a lot of other Sixties acts including The Troggs, David Bowie, The Tremeloes, The Hollies, The Move, Herman's Hermits, The Searchers, Dave Dee, Dozy, Beaky Mitch and Tich, The Love Affair, Amen Corner, Kenny Ball and his Jazzmen, Marmalade, and The Cream. It was a sign of the times then that, to get established, groups had to perform in many different venues and made their money more from record sales. Touring just increased their popularity. What struck me was that most groups sounded as good as their records – there was no computer enhancement of recordings back then. My stand-out memory is the amount of amplifiers and speaker cabinets that were on the small stage for The Who. They were Marshall cabinets – two high and four per instrument. They took up the full width of the stage. The sheer volume was tremendous. I used a Vox AC30 which generated 30 watts. The Who must have had hundreds of watts!

ALEX WILSON

I was a miner but also played drums for local band the Merry Macs, who opened the show and were the resident twelve-piece band with three brass, piano, bass, two drums, two guitars and four vocals. It was a great time at the Community Centre with not only The Who but all the big-name groups at the time appearing there – The Tremeloes, who were at number 1 in the charts at the time of their appearance, The Searchers and Dave Dee.

I knew who the group were – I'd seen them on TV – but it wasn't really my kind of music. Fans came from as far away as Glasgow and paid ten bob to get in. The Who were excellent in terms of sheer stage presence. I can't remember the entire set but they played all their hits and it's impossible to forget the single 'Pinball Wizard'. We were waiting to see what happened at the end because they had a reputation for smashing up their stage equipment. We weren't disappointed. At the last number they knocked over their PA speakers and smashed their guitars and drums.

Keith Moon had a really unusual technique. Normally, you'd hit the top of the cymbals but he'd strike the edge and sticks would fly everywhere. He went through dozens of drumsticks during the gig, while I'd make one set of mine last months.

At the end of the night, I was speaking to Keith Moon and he asked if I needed any sticks or drum parts so I said yes. He was being sponsored by Premier Drums who supplied him with all his gear and that is how The Who could smash their gear – they were being sponsored by PA companies and guitar companies! He gave me about 30 pairs of sticks and some accessories and a bass drum pedal. Both lasted me for years. Playing with them brought back memories of that great night. I still have the bass drum pedal to this day.

RAY LORIMER, AGE 17

I was home on leave in Cumnock as a junior boy soldier, having joined up two years earlier as a 15-year-old. I remember getting a ticket locally and went along with a now deceased friend after some pre-gig under age tanking up on the McEwan's Export. The Community Centre was packed, it was a Saturday night and the teens came in from all over Ayrshire. The Who were unbelievably brilliant and I can still remember 'My Generation', 'Substitute', 'Happy Jack' and 'I Can See For Miles' being blasted out. The noise was deafening and the atmosphere in the packed out Centre was incredible. I also vividly remember them smashing up their kit, which was just unbelievable. That night there was no room for dancing, which was the norm on Saturday nights – it was truly a gig!

There was also a big police presence, as these Saturday night concerts at the Centre attracted local gangs and much fighting with knives at the time between Cumnock and Auchinleck youths. I remember getting a late bus back to Cumnock in the early hours, calling in at the back door bakery for warm rolls and making myself scrambled egg at about two in the morning. I was still pinching myself and couldn't wait to get back to Aldershot to tell my mates I had watched The Who live in - where? Auchinleck!

JAMES NICHOL

I was there that night along with my girlfriend Catherine Andrews, my twin brother and his girlfriend Grace McNeish. It was a fantastic evening, The Who were brilliant and they did smash up their equipment after the gig.

MIKE FISHER, AGE 15

I went with my 18-year-old brother. We travelled from our home town of Ayr in a minibus with about six others. We arrived early and it was decided we would all go to a local pub for a couple of pints. I had never been in a pub in my life but was handed a pint of lager and lime. I loved every second of the experience but was terrified the police were about to walk in at any second and arrest me for underage drinking.

One of the supporting acts was Pure Greed, an excellent local rock band, and the drummer was a good friend of my brother. We asked him a few days after the concert if he got to meet the members of The Who back stage and he told us the following funny story:

Backstage, the drum kits of the Merry Macs, Pure Greed and The Who were lined up together for easy access to the stage. The drummer of the Merry Macs (who were a tartan-clad big band) walked over to Keith Moon's drum kit, flicked his finger on one of the cymbals and then leaned over with his hand cupped behind his ear to listen to the quality of the sound, whilst knowingly winking and nodding at Keith Moon with a thumbs up. Keith Moon then proceeded to walk over to the Merry Macs drum kit and started destroying it, kicking the bass drum and knocking over the entire kit. He then also cupped his hand behind his ear, winking and nodding to the Merry Macs drummer with a thumbs up.

The concert was nothing short of amazing and since then I have seen them another five times. A couple of years after they played in Auchinleck, a show was announced in Glasgow. So that I could queue up for tickets when they went on sale in the morning, I travelled to Glasgow to stay with family the night before. However, when I arrived at the train station the evening before I saw that a queue had already formed and I just joined on at the end. Ticket sales were supposed to start at 10am the next morning. However, they brought that forward by a few hours because of the size of the crowd. It got totally out of control with a few shop windows smashed, ironically by the people that arrived late. The good news was that I did get my tickets and was treated to another amazing concert.

RONNIE WHITELAW

My friends and I were a wee bit late in arriving from Mauchline. However, when we got off the bus there was an amazing sound coming from the Community Centre as The Who were in full force. Entering the hall was an incredible experience. There were rows of speakers on top of each other, Keith Moon's drumsticks were in orbit and Roger with the Kit Carson jacket on was in fine voice, ably backed by lead and bass… 'My Generation' – wow! Much better than Jimmy James and the Vagabonds the week before…

MATTHEW HAMILTON, AGE 16

As an Auchinleck lad, born and bred, it was amazing. Unlike my sisters, I was allowed to go to the 'dancing'. I left school at 15 and went to college to complete a year-long pre-apprenticeship course. I joined Massey Ferguson as a toolmaker that year too, so it was a big year. I saw a number of bands at Auchinleck – Jimmy James and the Bandwagon, Brian Poole and the Tremeloes, Herman's Hermits and more – but The Who were the most memorable. From Keith Moon wrecking the drums to Pete Townsend smashing up his guitar, they had real attitude. They also had a great sound, and to me and my mates and sisters who were there also, it was just like listening to their records – only much better. The place was packed as you would expect. I note from looking at the billing now that it was 12/6p to get it. I somehow thought it was £1. But I don't suppose I was even thinking about change when I handed over my quid!

The warm up band was The Merry Macs, a really popular local band made up of great musicians and a fab lead vocalist Wilma Telnet and 'Big' Samson. I don't know whether that was his real name! They were like a dance band with smart suits and trumpets and trombone, etc. The contrast between them and The Who couldn't have been greater. The Who were great. They were controversial, they had everybody jumping about and afterwards everyone leaving was raving about the performance.

After engineering, I joined Tayside Police rising to the rank of Chief Superintendent. I had the pleasure of being the Operational Commander in charge of *T in the Park*, a festival for 70,000 fans near Kinross. Guess what I was in charge when The Who headed the bill in 2006. I did a few TV interviews at the event for BBC Scotland and managed to get some time off with my wife to watch their set. They were brilliant as always.

WILLIAM LOGAN, AGE 18

I went with friends. It was a wonderful night. There was supposed to be a support band but The Who played all night, playing all their hits including *Tommy*. Some people may wonder why a wee mining village like Auchinleck could attract such big name bands, but I recall that there was a lot of gangland trouble in Glasgow at the time, and as a result it was deemed off limits to touring bands. Knowing they wanted a venue in the west of Scotland, a Mr Rafferty from Auchinleck saw an opportunity to bring them to our village community centre, where they wouldn't be exposed to any trouble. It certainly paid dividends for us young guns in East Ayrshire, as we were privileged to see many groups from the Sixties on our doorstep. I first saw The Searchers, for 3/- (15p), and many bands followed.

27 APRIL 1969
KINEMA BALLROOM, DUNFERMLINE, UK

ALAN HILL

I'm pretty sure it was one of the very early occasions when they performed songs from *Tommy*. The Kinema was absolutely packed and there were a number of busloads through from Glasgow. The Kinema's bouncers did not stand for any nonsense and a few of them were ejected in the customary Kinema manner. Pete Townshend effectively ran through the *Tommy* story with a short monologue between each song. I can remember him introducing one song with an anecdote about Tommy's conception and a quip about Tommy's father being like British Rail and 'not pulling out on time'.

JOHN FOSTER

I saw The Who play the Kinema in Dunfermline twice. One time, Roger Daltrey and Pete Townshend stood at the bar and had a pint with the locals before they went up on stage. They appeared there just before *Tommy* was released so it must have been one of the earliest renditions of *Tommy* live. Keith Moon was wearing a New York City policeman's cap and a black leather jacket. After the gig, we were outside the venue just waiting to go home and this large gold vehicle appeared like something out of a space programme. It was Roger Daltrey's new car that he'd imported from the States. He came out, got in and did a wee tour around the streets, just to try it out.

1 MAY 1969
RONNIE SCOTT'S JAZZ CLUB, LONDON, UK

NIGEL MOLDEN

As a result of booking The Who at Central London Poly, I received an invitation to the launch reception for and first public performance of *Tommy* at Ronnie Scott's. It was my introduction to Ronnie Scott's, which I thought was an excellent venue and somewhere that I very much like to visit to this day. The volume of the music was extraordinary. I was seated in the middle of the club, on the front row of the raised level and only a few yards in front of Pete Townshend and his stack of speakers. It was quite a long performance and I remember the rock and roll finale. After the show, I went to Klook's Kleek in West Hampstead to see Deep Purple. My ears were ringing for two days!

May 1969 sees The Who in the USA and Canada again.

9 - 11 MAY 1969
GRANDE BALLROOM, DETROIT, MICHIGAN

JIM BIELECKI

After playing some familiar favourites, I recall either Pete or Roger telling the audience they were now going to play some tunes from their new album, *Tommy*. As we were hearing brand new music, we just sat back and enjoyed the show. I have no memory of the songs they actually played, but I believe this was the American debut of songs from *Tommy*. Joe Cocker was the warm-up band that weekend. Looking back, that as probably the best show I ever saw at the Grande, with The Who and Joe Cocker on the same bill all for a few dollars.

FRAN DWIGHT

It was a Sunday, the third night of their three-day show there, and as a result there weren't many people in attendance. Either that or we got there early enough that we got preferential treatment. I don't have memory of this, but being with Jeep Holland often opened a lot of doors. Jeep and I went to see the show together. (I 'worked' for him at A2 Productions for a short time when I was 18, basically a runaway from home. And by 'worked' I don't mean slept. He was always a gentleman with me. I spent a lot of time typing contracts there. I remember typing one for the Stooges, which forbid Iggy from having physical contact with the fans. But I digress....) I know there were other people in the Econoline van that night, but I don't recall who.

THE WHO TO APPEAR AT CENTRE

On Saturday evening, the Community Association are staging a big beat show in the Centre featuring one of Europe's top groups, T.V. and recording stars, The Who. Nearly all the records released by this group have climbed high in the charts and some of their earlier hits included "My Generation," "Substitute," "I'm A Boy," "Pictures Of Lily" and "I Can See For Miles." Their latest disc, "Pinball Wizard," is in the Top Ten at the moment. One feature of this group is their superb stage act, which is highlighted by the drumming of Keith Moon. On the same bill are top local band, The Merry Macs, and a group who are rated among the best in the district, Pure Greed.

Clockwise from top left: Mothers Club, Erdington; Peter Woor (left) recalls a poorly attended gig at Cambridge Corn Exchange; the Auchinleck gig attracted press highlighting the 'big beat show'; the Merry Macs supported The Who in Auchinleck - photo Alex Wilson; Ray Lorimer, here with sister Lorna, saw The Who in Auchinleck.

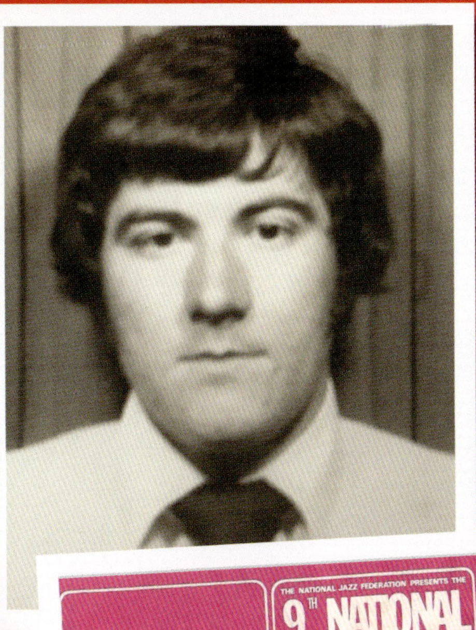

Second Edition of Programme. All artists subject to return of contract

9th NATIONAL JAZZ, BLUES & POP MUSIC FESTIVAL PLUMPTON RACECOURSE Nr. LEWES, Sussex

Friday 8th August 8 - 11.30 p m Tickets 15/-
THE PINK FLOYD
SOFT MACHINE
EAST OF EDEN · BLOSSOM TOES
Keith Tippett Jazz Group
JUNIORS EYES · THE VILLAGE

TRAVEL: By road about 45 miles from London. Take A23 or A22(A275) turning off at B2116. Special Southern Region Trains. SPECIAL LATE SERVICE back to Victoria and Brighton.

Saturday 9th August ☐ 2 Sessions
☐ Afternoon 2 - 5.30 p m Tickets 10/-
BONZO DOG BAND
Roy Harper
THE STRAWBS · BREAKTHRU'
JIGSAW · PETER HAMMILL

For Special Party or TRAVEL RATES and all enquiries contact the NJF Secretary at the MARQUEE. 01-437-2375

☐ Evening 7 - 11.30 p m Tickets £1 The Jazz Sound of
THE WHO · CHICKEN SHACK · FAT MATTRESS · JOHN SURMAN
AYNSLEY DUNBAR · YES! · The Spirit of JOHN MORGAN
KING CRIMSON · GROUNDHOGS · DRY ICE
Introducing from Belgium THE WALLACE COLLECTION

Sunday 10th August ☐ 2 Sessions
☐ Afternoon 2 - 5.30 p m Tickets 10/-
THE PENTANGLE
Long John Baldry
RON GEESIN · JO-ANN KELLY
MAGNA CARTA · NOEL MURPHY

For advice on TENT HIRE and details of camping facilities contact NJF Camp Secretary at 01-437 6603

☐ Evening 7 - 11.30 p m Tickets £1 The Blues Sound of
THE NICE · THE FAMILY · London Cast of 'HAIR' · CHRIS BARBER
KEEF HARTLEY · ECLECTION · Mick Abrahams' BLODWYN PIG
CIRCUS · HARD MEAT · AFFINITY · BABYLON
Introducing from Holland CUBY'S BLUES BAND

FESTIVAL VILLAGE ——— Open all day to Ticketholders
Including mornings and between shows — Coffee Shop — Discotheque
Book and Record Shops — Equipment — Clothes — Souvenirs — Dairy Shop for Campers

To NJF BOX OFFICE, MARQUEE, 90 Wardour Street, W1
Please send me the undernoted tickets for which enclose a cheque/postal order for ______
also enclose a stamped addressed envelope

FRIDAY (8th) ______ @ 15/- Evg
SATURDAY (9th) ______ @ 10/- Aft ______ @ £1 Evg
SUNDAY (10th) ______ @ 10/- Aft ______ @ £1 Evg

SPECIAL TICKETS (IN ADVANCE ONLY)
WEEKEND (Sat & Sun) ______ @ £2
SEASON (Fri, Sat & Sun) @ £2.10.0

Clockwise from top left: William Logan was at Auchinleck; Robin Bell was up in the gods at the Royal Albert Hall; Plumpton running order - photo Kevin March; Gerry Balcikonis was short of cash because he was paying for his scooter on HP; Plumpton flyer - photo Kevin March.

As a child of the sixties and a great fan of rock 'n' roll, I was keenly aware of all the music going around, so The Who were just one of many to me. But *Tommy* had been released by then, and we listened to the entire album on the ride from Ann Arbor to Detroit. It was being played on the radio, I guess because they were in town. It was pretty cool. I might have been tripping, I can't be sure. When we got into the theatre, it was sparsely populated and I distinctly remember easily finding seats in the second or third row, centre. My memories are fuzzy after that, except that when Daltrey came out in a flesh-coloured loincloth, I thought for a minute he was naked! This would have got him arrested immediately in those days, as would have any of the seven deadly swear words. The cops were always on hand to monitor the heathens. That's about all I remember, except how good the show was. They performed *Tommy*, start to finish. Fucking amazing.

17 MAY 1969 (USA)/23 MAY 1969 (UK)

***The Who release their rock opera album,* Tommy.**

HARVEY KUBERNIK

I thought the drums were under-recorded on *Tommy*. I was impressed by the scope of it but I'd already heard *Village Green Preservation Society* by the Kinks and I thought Ray Davies was already doing this kind of themed rock opera work. That's not to take anything away from The Who. But I thought there was something wrong with my AM or FM radio when I heard *Tommy* the first time, at least side one of it. The drums weren't prominent. Now I'm older I realise someone was trying to tell a story and there were horns and all kinds of things. And guitars and the drums were a tad unrecorded because it was supposed to be done that way. That front cover was all over town. Townshend wouldn't even be able to put out an album like *Tommy* in the politically correct world we live in now. He would be accused of exploitation of challenged people, where he was showing the heroic journey of Tommy. I remember it confused the media initially and he had to really keep talking until people understood he wasn't exploiting or mocking or making fun of the hero in his story. He was showing us the victory lap. We didn't give a fuck about any of this. We thought the music worked. It leapt out of our car radios and our transistor radios. They were coming to town every year. And *Tommy* sounded great.

25 MAY 1969
MERRIWEATHER POST PAVILION
COLUMBIA, MARYLAND

CHRIS ALVORD, AGE 18

I was a senior at Wakefield High School in Arlington, Virginia and travelled about 40 miles to attend the concert. I had been a Who fan since first hearing 'I Can't Explain' on the radio and their following hits 'My Generation', 'Substitute' and 'I Can See For Miles'. Merriweather Post Pavilion is an open air venue with a covered area and massive lawn seating. My friends and I were on the lawn close to the stage and had a great view of the band and stage. The sound was perfectly balanced and loud. My friends and I all buzzed to see the 'new' Yardbirds. Zeppelin had an incredible rousing opening set and we shared the sentiment that no one could top that performance. Boy, were we wrong. The Who followed and opened with 'I Can't Explain' and ended with 'My Generation' and then 'Magic Bus' with the destruction act. We heard a lot of the *Tommy* album performed. 'Pinball Wizard' was a standout along with personal favourites 'Happy Jack' and 'Boris the Spider'. Pete was wearing a white jump suit and impressed us with his jumping leg kicks, windmill guitar strumming and other antics. Roger was wearing a fringe vest, which was open with just his bare chest under it. He did his famous microphone swirling over his head. John was rather subdued and not moving much, except during his bass riffs. Keith was behind his drum kit so we really didn't see much of him but we sure did hear his drumming. We had been impressed with Led Zeppelin's performance but The Who took it to another level. They were much tighter and polished but still had the raw energy and knew how to play to the audience.

I also have less fond memories of seeing The Who later that year in November at Georgetown University's basketball court, McDonough Gymnasium in Washington, DC. The acoustics were horrible and it seemed to be a shorter set list.

JUDY GREENBERG

It was a beautiful evening at the Merriweather Post Pavilion. Led Zeppelin were the opening act, with a very young and bare-chested Robert Plant. I was there with my high school boyfriend but the real reason for us to be there was to see The Who perform *Tommy*. Led Zeppelin were pretty much nobodies. The crowd just milled around smoking dope during their set. It was dusk and the crowd really didn't pack in until The Who took the stage. My little sister became the Led Zeppelin fan in the family but I'm not even sure she had their first album then. The Who were great!

MAC MCMULLEN

The Who did the whole *Tommy* album and Led Zep did their whole second album along with most of their first. To this day it was the best show I've seen!

LEE SMITH

I came for Bonzo, and left during the first Who song, because I was never a fan of Moon's playing. When The Who took the stage, Daltrey said, 'We'd like to thank Led Zeppelin for what they did to you!' We looked at each other and said, 'What did they do to us?'. Psychedelics may have been involved.

SLIM MANICOTTI

I met Robert Plant a few years ago at a funky old grocery store in a not-so-great section of Nashville. He was in line behind me and nobody recognised him. I asked him about that Who show at the Merriweather. He told me they didn't want to do the show; they thought they were better than The Who!

5 JULY 1969
ROYAL ALBERT HALL, LONDON, UK

ROBIN BELL, AGE 22

I was studying engineering at South East London Technical College. I had been to the free Stones concert in Hyde Park that afternoon before going to the Albert Hall with a couple of housemates from college. We could only get in to the very top of the hall, right up in the standing circle, so we could move around a bit up there but it was a very long way down! I remember peering through the balcony railings and seeing Roger's buckskin fringes and Moonie's mad drumming.

GORDON HEATH

After seeing them at the Trade in Watford in the early days, I saw The Who live on two more occasions. While I was at university from 1965 to 1968, they headlined the bill at the student union dance one Saturday night. I bought my ticket and looked forward to a good night. People danced to the warm up groups and then The Who came on and started their set. But because their music was not really stuff that you could dance to, the dance floor slowly emptied and I was left standing there with only a couple of dozen others, such was the lack of enthusiasm for the boys. They still gave a great, professional performance but my own enjoyment was diminished.

Then in 1969 they appeared at the Royal Albert Hall, sharing the bill with Chuck Berry. Chuck closed the first half and was well received by an audience that included large numbers of Rockers in black leather biker gear. When The Who came on, these rockers were still chanting 'we want Chuck' and it was clear they were not going to go away. They roamed around in the aisles and threw coins at the group and abused some fans, who were headshaking in the boxes higher up in the hall. I was down in the stalls, as were the Rockers. It got quite ugly and the police arrived in force and spread out around the place, which calmed things down. All the while The Who carried on performing, although I thought a few times that they were going to have to run for it!

MICK NORWELL

I was sitting just to the left of the stage. Chuck Berry was the group to perform before The Who. He played a few songs and all of a sudden Hell's Angels, helmets and all, lined up along the front of the stage. Chuck came on for an encore and the crowd loved him. The Who came on and the crowd wanted more of Chuck. Coins were being pelted at The Who. Daltrey swung his mic the way he does at the fans and they eventually were escorted away and out of the venue. The Who carried on performing a perfect set and one to remember. I can always remember the stage equipment they used. It was called Hiwatt, which you see little of now.

GUðBJÖRG ÖGMUNDSDÓTTIR

We had been to see the free Rolling Stones concert in Hyde Park which became a memorial concert for Brian Jones. But my Danish friend and I had tickets to see the Chuck Berry and The Who double bill at the Albert Hall, tickets we had bought months in advance, when the idea of the not-to-be-missed free Stones concert wasn't even born. We arrived at our entrance to the Royal Albert Hall entrance at least 20 minutes late and the men at the door seemed agitated. But to our relief a lot of people were late arriving from the park, so the concert had not yet started.

We found our seats upstairs with a great view of the stage. I had initially wanted seats on the floor downstairs but I could see these were really good seats. It wasn't long until Chuck Berry started playing. We were amazed that a man in his forties was still rocking out like that. He played all his hits one after another and kept doing the duck walk across the entire length of the stage. The audience was rocking and rolling with him. After his set there was an interlude before The Who.

Many people downstairs with floor seats started protesting as soon as Chuck stopped playing. It turned out there was a large number of Teddy Boys who all had floor seats and wanted more old time rock and roll. Teddy Boys – and their girls – were usually ancient (in their thirties, at least!) and had grown up with rock having been born in the Fifties, with Elvis Presley, Chuck Berry and all the rest of the older great rockers. They wore tight jeans and leather jackets and had brilliantine in their short hair, which they slicked back showing long side burns.

It became clear when The Who took the stage that the Teddy Boys and their girls were not going to stand for 'long-haired hippies' playing and they started shouting and screaming. There was pandemonium downstairs and I thanked my lucky stars I didn't have seats there. It got worse. They threw things at The Who and began ripping up the chairs and throwing them about too. Roger Daltrey got something thrown at him and received an injury to his forehead. It wasn't serious, and The Who tried to calm people down by stating Chuck Berry was their hero too and that they had roots in old time rock and roll. They played 'Summertime Blues" by Eddie Cochran to prove their point. It took a long time to calm things down but eventually The Who were able to continue with their set.

They performed with great intensity and professionalism. I was enthralled, listening and watching their fantastic performance of their best songs, among them the mini opera, 'A Quick One (While He's Away)'. Then they launched into *Tommy* and played their great opera almost in its entirety. I'd never seen such a performance as theirs: Roger Daltrey in his suede-fringed pants and jacket, swinging the microphone around him like a circus entertainer; Pete Townshend's fantastic hand swings while playing his guitar fantastically and energetically, now and again jumping straight up into the air to underline his powerful playing; John Entwistle playing the bass impeccably and singing high note back ups but not moving around as much as the others; and, last but not least, Keith Moon – I had never seen drumming like he did drumming. And he also sang! He had the biggest drum set I had ever seen and the biggest grin on his face. He played the drums intensely and like a mad man. I loved watching his different expressions as he pounded the drums. At the end of the set, he kicked and threw all of his drum set all over the stage.

After this fantastic day, my friend and I were exhausted and stopped by a coffee shop before catching the last Tube train home. We both fell asleep aboard the train and missed our stop by two stops before we woke up! We had to hitch a ride home.

DAVE LEE

My friend Hugh and I were going to the Rolling Stones' free concert in Hyde Park so took an overnight coach from Stockport to London. Arriving at Hyde Park in the early morning, we decided to walk round to the Albert Hall to see if we could get tickets for one of the two *Pop Proms* shows The Who were playing there later that day, alternating as headliners with Chuck Berry. We had no trouble getting really good seats for the first show.

The Stones were still playing when we set off on the short walk to The Who concert and when we reached the Albert Hall, we could still hear them. But as we went through the doors of the Albert Hall, this changed to the amazing sound of the harmonies at the end of 'I'm a Boy'. The Who had already started playing!

Our seats were in the sixth row and many seats around us were empty. After playing some of their earlier hits, The Who launched into playing the whole of *Tommy*, which had come out a few weeks before. It was an inspired performance and Roger's singing was the most powerful singing I had ever heard. I took some black and white photos on my 35mm camera, and I couldn't help noticing that Roger didn't seem at all happy with that and kept glaring at me. I've heard him say since that he sometimes used to aim his swirling microphone at people he didn't like the look of, so I was lucky that I was perhaps just out of range.

Melody Maker reported that Pete was wearing his trademark white boiler suit, but their review was based on the second show. In the show we saw, he was wearing a blue t-shirt. There was no equipment smashing, and even though I saw The Who many times in the 1970s, I didn't see Pete smash a guitar until 1989!

People who have only seen The Who in more recent times may not realise just how loud they used to be. 'Deafening' has never been a more apt description. I've stood quite close to a Vulcan bomber when it took off, and it wasn't as loud as The Who! A few months later, I saw The Who in Manchester and travelled back to Leeds on the overnight mail train, as I had my French Dictation exam the next morning – my marks were unexpectedly poor because I couldn't hear the examiner properly when she read out the text that we were expected to write down.

20 JULY 1969
PIER BALLROOM, HASTINGS, UK

ANDRÉ PALFREY-MARTIN

The Who had just released their album *Tommy* and came back to Hastings to play a warm up show for their appearance at Woodstock. They were fantastic and loud and I wandered home in a bit of a daze. When I arrived home about one o'clock on Monday morning, I found my parents still up and watching a live television broadcast from Cape Canaveral. Two men had landed on the moon. No one had mentioned it and I could hardly believe it. Afterwards, it was strange to think that this historic event was being witnessed all round the world and we were on the pier, not giving this momentous event one thought.

28 JULY 1969
WHITBURN BAY HOTEL, SUNDERLAND, UK

KEITH SCOTT, AGE 20

Me and my three mates from work went. When we first arrived, about an hour before the show was to begin, we got in the door and there was a big reception area with a lot of people standing about chatting. Somebody said, 'Ah. there's Pete Townshend coming through the door.' Pete walked in with one or two of his entourage and they were standing chatting about ten or 15 yards away from us. I said 'I'm going to go over and shake his hand and just say hello.' I went over, we had a quick hello and he said 'do you live locally?'. I said I did. And he said, 'Do you know anybody who's selling anything?'. I instantly knew what he meant. As it happened, we knew a lad who was also called Peter. He was a student at Leeds University and we used to buy some stuff off him. I said, 'Aye, as a matter of fact I do. I know somebody who might be able to help you out if you want something.' He said, 'I would appreciate that' and I said 'just give us five minutes'.

Now I knew Peter was in because I'd seen him earlier. I ran through the reception area and into the stairwell. He was halfway up the stairs with his bag, a rucksack affair, on his shoulder. I told him what had happened and I took him back down and got them together, as it were. I introduced them and left them to it. And I spoke to Peter about an hour later and I asked him how things had gone. I said, 'Did you make a few bob?' He said, 'I've got nowt left. They took everything.' I said 'What? Everything?'. He said, 'Aye, just about. They emptied the bag.'

That night they did a 15- or 20-minute version of 'Magic Bus' and Pete dedicated that song to me. Not by name. But at the start he said 'the next song we're going to do is the 'Magic Bus'. And it's for our mate over there in the corner,' and he pointed across to where I was standing. Obviously, nobody in the audience knew what was going on, but we did.

There was one other highlight of the night, performance-wise. Keith Moon had a white t-shirt on with a bull's eye on and, halfway through the gig, the t-shirt was literally saturated in sweat and sticking to him. He pulled it off over his head, held it at full arm's length above his head, wrung it out and proceeded to drink the sweat out of the t-shirt. The roar in the crowd nearly took the roof off.

2 AUGUST 1969
WINTER GARDENS, EASTBOURNE, UK

GERRY BALCIKONIS

I went with my friends Ray and Gary. Being on apprenticeship wages meant that we were skint most of the time, plus I was paying for my Lambretta on HP at the princely sum of £2.2s (£2.10) a month! I wore the Parka a lot of scooterists wore in the era, with an army-issue roll cap and scarf. The scooter was yellow and midnight blue with gleaming chrome crash bars and, because the GT had a quick turn of speed, I wouldn't load the bike with a load of mirrors, as some of the lads had, due to wind resistance. But despite having no money, we were desperate to see The Who.

Ray came up with the idea of arriving backstage at the venue and asking the roadies if we could help carry in the equipment from the pantechnicon, securing places to watch the group in return. On the day we duly turned up at the venue, spoke to the roadies and, to our amazement, they agreed to our suggestion. After lugging in heavy boxes, etc., we were told to hang around backstage whilst the concert started and, when the curtains had been drawn, to go to the front of the stage and jump into the crowd.

We decided instead to climb up the spotlight gantries and watch the concert from there, hidden by the glare of the lights. However, we weren't prepared for the sheer volume of the noise the speakers blasted out. So, when The Who opened up with 'I Can't Explain', I nearly lost my grip whilst holding the gantry. We were very relieved to climb down at the interval and jump into the crowd. The ringing in my ears lasted for days. But that hour watching, listening and clinging on for dear life was brilliant – and unforgettable!

4 AUGUST 1969
PAVILION, BATH, UK

STUART THOMSETT

I had washed my hair and we got there a bit late. They had closed the doors so we stood outside listening. When it got to the last number, the fire doors opened and a tsunami of bodies escaped the building. We went in to sweat profusely and enjoy the final song!

7 AUGUST 1969
ASSEMBLY HALL, WORTHING, UK

JON SAVAGE
I saw them in a small church hall in Worthing the day before the Plumpton Festival. They were so loud they took the top of my head off for three days.

9 AUGUST 1969
9TH NATIONAL JAZZ AND BLUES FESTIVAL PLUMPTON, UK

STEVE DAVY
I remember it as an outstanding and breathtaking performance. They played a lot, if not all, of *Tommy*. Daltrey was wearing a light-coloured leather jacket with long tassels and swinging the microphone by its lead a lot. I sat out on the ground not too far back and had a good view of the stage. I remember the weather being very good and it was one of those performances that had an exceptional magic about it. I played bass with a group called Steamhammer, who played on Sunday. We were more successful at the 1970 festival, when press reports suggested we upstaged Family.

IAN EVEREST
My first ever music festival. They did all or most of *Tommy* and Roger Daltrey sang 'from Soho down to Plumpton….' during 'Pinball Wizard'!

ANDREW WELLS
My parents had a house in a small village about three miles west of the racecourse and, if I was in the garden, I could hear that festival from the garden. It was that loud. My friend and I went to see The Who. They were the star act. You know that line he has in Pinball Wizard about 'from Soho down to Brighton he must have played them all'? Well, he changed Brighton to Plumpton!

SANDRA HARDY
I was 17 or 18 and went to this three-day festival with my first proper boyfriend. It was miles away, at the other end of the country. Appearing were Pink Floyd, Roy Harper, Family and Soft Machine. The Who sang the whole of *Tommy* and I remember Roger Daltrey in his fringed jacket swinging the microphone round. I also remember was Chris Barber. His jazz was amazing – I'd never heard anything like it.

Plumpton Festival - photos John Funnell.

PLUMPTON FESTIVAL

PLUMPTON top): the Deep Purple

And so on to Audience, one of Friday's best acts. They put an awful lot into a short time. A hand drum solo from Tony Connor, some amazing electronic sax sounds which made one horn sound like six from Keith Gemmell and some nice vocal and guitar work from Howard Worth.

Fat Mattress followed with a tight set but sounded rather like "just another heavy band." This was their first gig since their reformation and they promise well for the future. They made way for **Tony McPhee and the Groundhogs**, one of the most improved groups this year with the release of their "Thank Christ For the Bomb" album. Tony has a good blues voice, which he uses to the best advantage when he picks up slide guitar and solos.

Steamhammer, were the best of the night — including bill toppers Family. They received the first standing ovation of the weekend and unavoidably caused the first sniff of ill-feeling through lack of encores.

In contrast, bill-toppers **Family** were disappointing. "Weaver's Answer" and "A Song For Me" — two family favourites (groan!) — were well received but Roger Chapman, idiot dancer supreme, appeared bored with the music and everything else. Hurling the mike stand in all directions, his face contoured in apparent anger, he stalks the stage like a man possessed. It was a pity they didn't come over better, for last year they were one of the big hits at Plumpton.

A dissatisfied crowd left for their tents or cars when the evening's entertainment was over. Dissatisfied because of the lack of encores — Family were allowed a

M.M. 15 Aug. 1970.

The Groundhogs continued to prove that they are a much-improved band before Steamhammer produced one of their finest sets —they really excelled and lead guitarist Martin Pugh seems to get better with every gig.

Top-of-the-bill Family are

week ending August 15, 1970

NEW MUSICAL EXPRESS

PLUMPTON SUCCEEDS WITH GOOD MUSIC

THOUGH it didn't attract the vast claustrophobic multitudes that the national press take great delight in playing the guessing-numbers-game with the NJF Festival again proved to be a most pleasant weekend in the fresh green Sussex countryside for all those who ventured forth.

As in past years, this event has always endeavoured to present much that is good in contemporary British music. And this, the 10th anniversary sustained the expected high.

Report by RICHARD GREEN and ROY CARR

Audience was a big hit on Friday with a blend of jazz and blues that earned a prolonged standing ovation at the end of the set. Screaming Jay Hawkins' "I Put A Spell On You" was given a new treatment that was not as wild as the original but equally as interesting.

Keith Gemmell played an amazing clarinet solo during his own composition "Ebeny Variation" and drummer Tony Connor equalled this on "House On The Hill" when he played a long solo without sticks. Keith used a triple echo tape on that number to give his sax a freaky sound which the crowd got well into.

Because Rare Bird's gear was late, Fat Mattress swapped places on the bill and showed that the addition of an organ has really improved the group's sound. "Naturally" was followed by "I Don't Mind" which featured a nice bit of interplay between the organ and lead guitar and Mattress featured a much longer version than normal of "Mr. Moonshine".

For this number, Neil Landon and Jimmy Leverton took it in turns to sing lead and occasionally sang harmonies. The song developed into a wild, spontaneous thing which was very good and there were outbreaks of dancing in the crowd.

As the shadows drew long over the racecourse, Steamhammer who are a tremendous attraction on the continent received a home-grown reception worthy of their stature.

Introvert

In Martin Pugh, the Hammer have a guitarist who by nature of his introvertness hasn't as yet received the same attention that has been heaped upon far less proficient players. Matched to vocalist Kiernan White's second lead, they produced some very fine moments in "Suppose To Be Free" and Mick Bradley's drum feature "When Your Friends Have Gone." By way of a trailer for their next album, they climaxed with a rousing fast shuffle called "Ridin' On The L & N," which eventually resolved itself as a Boogie, with Steve Davy pumping out a powerful bass line, and the entire audience leaping to it's feet.

It was only a tight schedule that prevented a well earned encore, before they handed the stage over to Family.

Being the final act, Family had to work extremely hard to follow Steamhammer. Family must be one of the very few bands to which the terminology "original" has any real significance.

All-British Plumpton goes ahead

DESPITE the threat of a High Court injunction, the National Jazz Federation is to go ahead with its plans to hold its tenth annual festival, this year at Plumpton race course, Sussex.

The festival already has a huge line-up of all-British talent, and is to take place on August 6, 7, 8 and 9 despite the threat from Tory MP Martin Madden.

Groups approached to take part so far include Family, Groundhogs, Steam Hammer, Third Ear Band, Quatermass, Patto, Clark Hutchinson, Fairport Convention, Strawbs, Elton John, Granny's New Intentions, Daddy Longlegs, Chicago Climax Blues Band, Gracious, Da Da, Edgar Broughton, Black Sabbath, Jackson Heights, Hardin-York, Hard Meat, East of Eden, Audience, Incredible String Band, Matthews Southern Comfort, Brian Davison's Every Which Way, Vandergraaf Generator, Pink Fairies, Wishbone Ash, Slade, Colosseum, Humble Pie, Yes, Juicy Lucy.

Clockwise from top left: Dennis Dunaway opened for The Who in Detroit as a member of the Alice Cooper Band; Leo Mullen recalls an audience member 'mooning' at the Bristol show; Plumpton cuttings from Stephen Davy.

JOHN FUNNELL

We travelled to the racecourse site in my friend's Morris Minor soft top car. We only had about five miles to go so we thought six of us in it would be okay, but we picked up some interesting characters on the way, male and female, and by the time we arrived in Plumpton there were 13 of us! The Who were one of the highlights of the weekend, of which there were many. Their set, which was pretty loud for the time, was similar in content to Live at Leeds and their Woodstock appearance. I remember in particular 'Summertime Blues', 'Shakin' All Over' and 'Magic Bus'. As far as all us fans were concerned, it was a fantastic festival but it only lasted one more year. The weather was good but local complaints soon finished it off; it was too close to the village of Plumpton.

KEVIN MARCH

I remember it being a warm evening and standing at the back on an incline looking down on the stage. Roger was strutting his stuff in his tassels. I also had the honour of seeing Chicken Shack on the same evening. Tickets for the whole weekend were two pounds and ten shillings (£2.50)!

GUðBJÖRG ÖGMUNDSDÓTTIR

Me and my French boyfriend decided to go to the Saturday concert. I still have the pink pamphlet so I can tell you the afternoon session cost 10 shillings (50p) and the evening session cost £1! We chose to go on the Saturday because The Who were headlining in the evening. My boyfriend had a little yellow sports car so we drove down there and managed to get lost on the way. We stopped for directions and finally found the festival grounds. A lot of people were camping out there and there were also lots of tents with all kinds of groovy merchandise, even one with a fortune teller. It was a hot, sunny day and people were sitting on the grass enjoying the music and we soon joined them.

During one set, possibly the band Jigsaw, a mystery drummer joined the band unexpectantly and incognito. He had a large brown paper bag over his head. Everyone soon realised due to his antics and playing that this was none other than Keith. He did some fantastic drum playing but mostly fooled around, running on and off stage. At one point, he came on stage with a bucket full of water and threatened to empty it over the heads of the band members. After he'd finished playing, he pushed and kicked the drum set all over the stage and emptied the water bucket over himself. He still had the paper bag on his head. Then he was led to the front of the stage by one of the band members, introduced with great bravado as 'Peter Townshend!' before finally taking the brown paper bag off his head. It was the highlight of the day. People around us who had been camping there since Thursday told us that Keith Moon had come along with his own tent and had been drinking and enjoying himself with the other campers for a couple of days.

The evening line-up for the festival featured twelve acts. As a result, nobody apart from The Who played a long set, but I especially remember King Crimson and Yes. Then The Who headlined. There was a seated enclosure right in front of the stage and my boyfriend knew the people at security. They let us into the enclosure and we managed to get front row seats. The Who astounded me with their professionalism and pure quality of performance. In my memory, they played only music from *Tommy* that night, but I was over the moon to witness that and haven't forgotten it to this day. As when I'd seen them at the Royal Albert Hall in July, Roger Daltrey was again wearing his now legendary fringed suede pants and jacket, singing his heart out and doing amazing tricks with the microphone line. Pete Townshend was at his best playing the guitar like a madman, swinging his arm and jumping into the air. John Entwistle played great bass lines and Keith Moon was no worse for wear after his afternoon adventure and played incredibly. They just launched into *Tommy* and played without any interruption. It was an unforgettable event to witness. They finished by smashing up their gear and hurling their drums and amplifiers all over the stage. After the festival and late in the night, we drove on to Brighton and got a room for the night, exhausted but very, very happy.

ALAN POWELL

A minibus went from our youth club in Ellesmere Port, Cheshire. The bill was fantastic and comprised The Who, Chicken Shack, Yes, The Bonzo Dog Doo Dah Band with Viv Stanshall and Neil Innes, Family, the Strawbs, Roy Harper and many supporting acts. We had a great day and The Who were astounding and in top form. In December 1998, we went to see Stan Webb's Chicken Shack in a small club in Chester. After the gig, we were lucky enough to have a drink with Stan who was great company. He told us that he, Viv Stanshall and Keith Moon went out on the town in Brighton that night. All three of them were famous party animals and they'd got into all sorts of trouble, each egging the other on in to more and more outlandish behaviour. Sadly, both Keith and Viv are no longer with us. Maybe Stan will write his memoirs one day and let us know what went on!

In August 1969, The Who played the Woodstock Music and Art Fair aka The Woodstock Festival.

17 AUGUST 1969
WOODSTOCK, BETHEL, NEW YORK

STEVE DOCKENDORF, AGE 17

My first exposure to The Who was when 'I Can't Explain' rattled my little GE clock radio. They seemed to have the energy of The Kinks, but with smoother vocals. Shortly after I acquired the *Tommy* album, I discovered that my local library had high-end phonographs and headphones, presumably for listening to the classical music in the library's collection. I had the bright idea of taking this new double Who album off my stereo that only played the left channel, and listen to the whole thing straight through at the library. It was as close to heaven as I'd ever been, although I remember being afraid that people walking by would hear what was coming out of the headphones and send me home.

In May of 1969, I saw them at Merriweather Post Pavilion in my home state of Maryland. I was positioned about 25 rows back and directly in front of the stage right PA speaker stack. It was the loudest sound I'd ever heard. I was thrilled to hear a number of songs from *Tommy*.

In August of 1969, I took the five-hour car trip to Woodstock with my then girlfriend and I was again thrilled to hear *Tommy* played live. The spell was momentarily interrupted when Abby Hoffman took Pete Townshend's microphone to plead the case for imprisoned revolutionary John Sinclair 'rotting in prison'. Pete manually forced him off the stage. And just as abruptly, the show went back on as though nothing had happened. My favorites, 'Pinball Wizard' and 'We're Not Gonna Take It' helped to make The Who's performance one of the most exciting of all the acts at Woodstock, as well as one of my fondest musical memories.

30 AUGUST 1969
2nd ISLE OF WIGHT MUSIC FESTIVAL ISLE OF WIGHT, UK

GERALD CLEAVER

Between 1969 and 1970 I saw them about six times. The first time was the 1969 Isle of Wight Festival, where the story goes that they asked for more money, the promoters refused and they said 'okay then, we want to play in the afternoon so that we can go back to the mainland and play another gig in the evening'. So they flew in by helicopter on the Saturday afternoon, played what for them was a short hour-long set and flew out again. They'd just played Woodstock and they spent their whole set talking about Woodstock, how Joe Cocker was on the bill later and that he was fantastic and how we should all stick around and watch him.

MIKE TUCKER

There were an overwhelming number of people and few facilities. I'd never experienced anything like that before, with a far distant and not very big stage. There were no screens and nor was there a PA system that could reach everyone. Daytime performances were difficult to see unless you were in the front third of the crowd, which was pretty much impossible. Night time was better. But I remember Pete in his trademark white boiler suit and an amazing amount of frills on Roger's clothes.

7 SEPTEMBER 1969
COSMOPOLITAN CLUB, CARLISLE, UK

JOHN BELL

All the men had to form a security cordon around the stage to stop the chicks from rushing the stage. Us real fans could not get in because of the strict suit and tie policy that was in force at the Cosmo, but Roger Daltrey came out closely followed by Pete Townshend. Roger had a quick chat with us and wished us a pleasant evening. Keith and John must have been engaged with the Carlisle chicks as there was no sign of them. The sound outside was excellent!

UNKNOWN, AGE 17

The Cosmo is gone now but it was a club in the south of Carlisle, on a council estate called Harraby. A bloke called Les Leighton ran it for years. You could get a thousand people in there. I didn't know anything about *Tommy* because I came from a big family and we didn't have a record player. We couldn't afford LPs. But I knew from the *NME* that they were doing a tour of *Tommy*. I remember going up to the club with my friend on the Sunday before to buy the tickets.

When we were queuing up outside for the gig, there were two Rolls-Royces parked outside and my mate looked in the window of one of them. Down by the handbrake there was a wad of notes – hundreds of pounds in a roll – with an elastic band around them.

We went in and got to the front. It was a very small stage, probably two or two and a half feet high. You could step up on to it. We were going to be stood right in front of Townshend. I went to the toilet before it started and John Entwistle and Roger Daltrey came in. I was having a slash and Roger Daltrey was stood beside me, with his bare chest and in his fringed leather jacket. He said to me, 'Alright mate, here for a good night?'

In the audience was a guy from Carlisle who was always well turned out in a three-piece suit and with lovely hair. He was a bit odd. Everyone from round Carlisle knew him. When Keith Moon was playing, he kept dropping his drumsticks. There must have been twelve or 15 drumsticks lying around in front of the drums, and this guy in the three-piece suit climbed onto the stage and bent down and started picking the drumsticks up. Townshend must have thought he was going to have a bit of a go at Keith Moon, so Townshend just turned his guitar over his back, got this bloke, headbutted him and threw him back into the crowd. And everybody cheered. I've never seen anything like it. I felt sorry for the guy, because he wasn't the full shilling.

When we were leaving at the end, there were people asking girls if they wanted to stay back for a drink. One of my mates from school, Stan Richardson, worked behind the bar at the Cosmo at the weekend, and he said they brought all these girls into the bar and The Who came in, and they were drinking with the roadies and got up to all sorts with the women until two in the morning. The Who were the dog's bollocks.

21 SEPTEMBER 1969
FAIRFIELD HALL, CROYDON, UK

CHRIS SMITH

After Leeds in 1966, I saw them again when I was a student at Ealing Art School. I'd formed a band called Smile with a fellow student called Tim Staffel. We had a band outing to see The

Who perform *Tommy* in Croydon. The other guys in the band were Brian May and Roger Taylor and we took along our other college pal, Freddy Bulsara. There was a lot of constructive criticism of the gig on the way home in the van. Personally, I thought The Who were magical and it was a magnificent performance. As musicians, we all learned a thing or two that night.

On 10 October 1969 The Who commence a five week North American tour.

11 OCTOBER 1969
GRANDE BALLROOM, DETROIT, MICHIGAN

DENNIS DUNAWAY, ALICE COOPER BAND

In the mid to late Sixties, as a high school teen in Phoenix Arizona, I was lying on my family's living room floor and The Who came on television. Pete threw his guitar into the crowd and my parents went on and on about 'how could he treat a perfectly good instrument that way?' I thought it was the coolest thing I'd ever seen.

On 11 October 1969 the Alice Cooper Group opened for The Who. We had chickens onstage and created a feather storm with pillows and a CO2 fire extinguisher. The song was 'Black Juju' and when we were walking off stage, I told Neal Smith that his drums sounded exceptionally thunderous. Then our roadie told us that Keith was backstage playing his kit along with Neal.

The venue was an old movie theatre with a perforated screen, which you could hazily see through. I squeezed behind the screen and sidestepped over unused stage lighting until I was directly behind Keith, who was set up at floor level with no drum riser. Nobody could see me, but if the screen hadn't been there, I could have placed my hand on the back of Keith's head. With my face pressed to the dusty smelling perforated screen, I watched The Who play their entire set. They were on fire that night. Between songs I could hear them talking to each other, but it wasn't about the show. They were cursing at each other.

17 OCTOBER 1969
HOLY CROSS COLLEGE WORCESTER, MASSACHUSETTS

JOHN FARLEY

My roommate's brother was on the school's entertainment committee so I got to watch this show from the front row with my (now) wife. Daltrey was wearing the fringed jacket and swinging the mic, which was all taped up so it wouldn't fly off. Townshend was slinging chords, doing windmills, etc. It was just after *Tommy* broke and the set was a nice mix of *Tommy* and pre-

Tommy tunes. As a fairly mediocre bass player myself, I thought Entwistle was calmly holding down the bottom with remarkable speed and dexterity. The only things moving were his fingers. Moon, on the other hand, was a percussive dervish, hitting everything that wasn't moving!

1 NOVEMBER 1969
VETERANS MEMORIAL COLISEUM COLUMBUS, OHIO

MICHAEL ALWOOD

We'd often go around the back of the building and try to meet a band after their show. But the night of the *Tommy* show, someone asked 'should we go back around?' and it was a unanimous 'no'. We were all tired. We were in the line to leave Vets Memorial parking lot, in a yellow VW bug, when a station wagon pulled up alongside us in the queue, honking the horn. I was riding shotgun. I rolled down the window and the chap driving yelled, 'Hey, where can you get something to eat around here?' I told the guy the only place was Jack and Benny's, at the corner of Broad and High (their slogan was 'food cooked in butter'). Daltrey, who was riding shotgun himself, leaned past the driver and yelled, 'Are you guys going to eat as well?' I looked quickly at the other guys and they all nodded. I leaned out the window and said, 'Sure, we could eat.' So Daltrey says, 'Well, you guys drive there and we'll follow you.' We drove to the diner.

We were in the diner when Keith walked in, sat down at the counter and started eating mustard by the spoonful, straight out of the little glass dispenser. Then, after we'd eaten, I was chatting with Townsend on the sidewalk and Keith came out of the restaurant and started slamming salt and pepper shakers on the concrete. He must have had 20 of them.

During the evening, my friend Greg was sat in the shotgun seat of The Who's station wagon. I was in the back. Greg reached down to the floor of the station wagon, pulled up Daltrey's fringe leather eagle jacket and gave me an eyebrows-raised sign as if to say 'should I take it?'. I said, 'Um, no.' I'm glad I did. I'm pretty sure that thing's in the Rock and Roll Hall of Fame in Cleveland now.

2 NOVEMBER 1969
GEORGETOWN UNIVERSITY WASHINGTON DC

PATRICIA MARX, AGE 17

I was about to see The Who for the fourth time in two years, this time at McDonough Gymnasium at Georgetown University, and this would be the second time I saw them perform

Tommy that year. Outside it was hot, humid and raining, but inside it was standing room only and abuzz with excitement. My friend and I had excellent seats in the centre, fairly close to the stage. I counted 14 amps and 24 speakers and it was loud. Keith Moon was using his silver drum kit. When The Who came on stage after 10pm, they were obviously in a very good mood, and whenever Roger wasn't singing he was laughing. Keith and Pete did a Laurel and Hardy routine.

The Who took command of the stage immediately and went straight into the John Entwistle number 'Heaven and Hell', which was their concert opener in those days. This was the first time I saw Pete in his white boiler suit, and also the first – and last – time I saw Roger in his spectacular buckskin outfit with fringe, fringe and more fringe. Some of the fringe looked to be three feet long. They played for an hour and 35 minutes and, in addition to doing nearly all of *Tommy*, including 'Sally Simpson', they played their versions of 'Young Man Blues', 'Summertime Blues' and a very delicious 'Shakin' All Over'.

Quite a few people outside the gym were trying to break down the doors to get in and Pete dedicated *Tommy* to them. At the end, everyone was dancing and the aisles were packed. They finished not with 'My Generation' but a long jam session that included parts of *Tommy* and other songs. Pete didn't smash his guitar. There was no encore despite the crowd calling for more. I was flying high on natural adrenalin and went to school on Monday morning without having slept a wink.

16 NOVEMBER 1969
ONANDAGA COUNTY WAR MEMORIAL SYRACUSE, NEW YORK

JOHN OLMSTEAD

They said it was the last time they were going to do *Tommy* live, and played another 15 or so songs after *Tommy*. The show was about three hours long. They stopped playing mid-song because police were expelling people for dancing in the aisles. Pete said they'd come there to do a job and wouldn't continue until the people who'd been expelled were let back in. He used the wait to tell us that, despite the rumours, his friend Paul McCartney was very much alive. The audience members were readmitted, The Who started playing again and the audience went wild. Oh, and a policeman walked in front of the stage and was hit by one of Keith's drumsticks. Intentional or not, it was definitely a crowd-pleaser!

Returning from North America, The Who perform a short UK tour.

4 DECEMBER 1969
HIPPODROME, BRISTOL, UK

NIGEL CORTEN

My wife Pat and I saw this tour, which was unofficially billed as 'The Last Big Gig of the Sixties', in Bristol. We queued for about an hour to get in and ended up with a balcony seat overlooking the stage. On the support bill were The Crazy World of Arthur Brown, Joe Cocker and the Grease Band, The Alan Bown Set and The Mindbenders, who in a month or two turned into 10cc. When the roadies were setting up The Who's stage kit, I remember one fellow nailing down about eight tom toms in front of Keith Moon's drum kit.

Once on stage, they played for over an hour, which was pretty unusual for those days. The Kinks, who we'd seen at the same venue, were louder. There was not a lot of screaming from the crowd; we were all a bit awestruck to see such a big band. They did all the singles, and I remember Townshend saying 'on our next number, Keith is playing lead drums'. It was 'Happy Jack'. They also played a few album tracks, and Entwistle's 'Boris the Spider' was memorable. Moon was magnetic and played the drums like he did on the TV, with that high wrist style. Most stunningly, the whites of his eyes were super white. They didn't wreck their guitars at the end, but Moon jumped from his kit and ripped a few of his nailed down tom toms from the stage and tossed them around.

I kept the ticket in a jacket for a few years but it disappeared over time. Shame, as entrance was 19 shillings and sixpence or 97p. That's pretty good value by today's standards for a line-up like that.

WAYNE PURSEY

I remember Pete Townshend in white boiler suit apologising because he had a cold. During the show, somebody threw an orange smoke bomb onto the stage. Then someone in one of the boxes took his trousers down and showed his bottom to everyone. Pete said 'so, did you see the pimples?'. You could hear the bass tuning up on Queen's Square beforehand. It's a fair distance from the Hippodrome.

LEO MULLEN, AGE 14

A member of the audience did a 'mooner' over the side of a box on the right-hand side of the stage. I saw this quite clearly from where I was sitting in the balcony. There was uproar in the Hippodrome when security were going to eject the culprit. Eventually the situation settled down, the culprit returned to his seat and the concert carried on. I remember the concert being very loud and absolutely brilliant. Roger Daltrey was in his jacket with the long fringes and somehow swinging the microphone at length on a cord whilst singing.

I also saw The Who at Bath Pavilion and was taken with my friend by my dad in his black Morris Minor car. I can't remember the date but I do remember not having a ticket and climbing in through the toilet window at the side of the Pavilion. That was in the days when I could fit in through a small window. Again, I remember the concert being extremely loud and fantastic. We climbed up on top of the speaker stacks!

5 DECEMBER 1969
PALACE THEATRE, MANCHESTER, UK

STEVE BERNING

The second time I saw them they were supported by the James Gang, with Joe Walsh. They played what I now think of as their *Live at Leeds* set – *Tommy* in its' entirety, 'Summertime Blues', 'Shakin' All Over', 'Young Man Blues' and an extended version of 'Magic Bus'. As an aspiring guitarist, Townshend was my hero. But what strikes me retrospectively was that my eyes kept getting drawn back to Moon. He was arguably then at his peak and drove them on like a madman. Even when he wasn't drumming, he was acting out each song. Having seen hundreds of gigs in my life, this remains number one.

TONY MICHAELIDES

Seeing The Who perform what was the first and is still the best rock opera, *Tommy*, was indeed a piece of history and remains one of the finest shows I ever attended. I saw The Who another three times over the next 18 months and they never disappointed, yet the show they put on that night was so different to anything else I'd ever seen. Just for a band at that time to attempt anything like *Tommy* was unique. A 'rock opera'? What the hell was that? The thing I remember most was the sheer power of the band and how much they looked like they were loving every minute they were onstage.

12 DECEMBER 1969
EMPIRE THEATRE, LIVERPOOL, UK

ADE FELTON

Because I went to Padgate College, we had access to Liverpool, Manchester and Lancaster unis and would regularly travel to other unis to see bands. Keith Moon used to kick the drums over. And they'd smash their guitars up. It was so rehearsed it didn't look exciting. You didn't think 'wow, they've really taken off'. You just thought 'this is what you do at the end of every act'. And the way the drums went over, he could have stamped on it and made a hole in it, but he didn't. But the guitar got properly smashed. It just looked very rehearsed.

12 DECEMBER 1969
REGIONAL COLLEGE OF TECHNOLOGY LIVERPOOL, UK

PAUL BARTLETT

I was studying for a degree at Liverpool Regional College of Technology and got involved with the Guild, or student union. It was based on the top floor of a 1960s-built block that faced on to Byron Street, which is a very wide road linking the old and new Mersey Tunnel entrances. The refectory was also on the top floor and was where the gigs were staged. A number of students did the setting up – clearing tables, building the bar and the stage and so on. We used very good quality desks borrowed from various senior staff offices in the building to form a stage. The refectory had a relatively low ceiling, and a fire certificate for 700 occupants. In exchange for free entrance, security was provided by a hired team who wore proper old-fashioned uniforms. Usually, there was one dog available. I don't remember there ever being any trouble.

On this particular evening, the Bonzo Dog Doo-Dah Band were playing the refectory. The Who were also in Liverpool, playing at the Empire. The Bonzos arrived unusually early, and with a considerable quantity of stuff, including two drum set ups. We learned that, unexpectedly, Aynsley Dunbar was to use the extra drum set up. I remember Neil Innes hammering a wooden foot stop into the top of a very fancy desk and swearing about not expecting to play in such 'fucking awful places'. The Bonzos then asked if they could play late, as they wanted to catch the first half of The Who gig. This was fine with us as we had our regular support act – a brilliant and very heavy band called Stackwaddy – and knew they would play for hours if asked.

The Bonzos returned as promised and did their usual set, full of playfulness with Viv Stanshall's beautiful lead. Sets in those days typically lasted no more than an hour. And then most of The Who turned up, minus Pete Townshend. The Bonzos stayed on stage. The Bonzos' second drummer was Sam Spoons (Martin Ash) and he readily gave his seat up to Keith Moon as Sam preferred larking about. And then we were off – for some hours! I'll admit I don't remember much detail, apart from a drum battle between Moon and Dunbar which lasted about 25 minutes.

I don't know when it finished but I remember it was very late, with all the band and few of us helpers having a drink in the bar until gone 2am. What we did about security I have no idea. They were paid by the hour and, apart from the bands, were the major expense of these gigs. On Saturday, the college was closed but we were able to go in to clear up and return the desks to thWe learnt from the college security that the residents of the adjoining Gerard Gardens were very angry, not appreciating the amount of noise that had come from the largely glass-walled eighth floor refectory until the small hours. Years later, I learnt that Stanshall and Moon were good friends, often drinking together in the Sgt. Peppers club in Staines. I also read that the Bonzo Dog Doo-Dah Band and The Who only ever played together once. I think that was in Canada. Well, admittedly not all The Who played our college. But did they battle Aynsley Dunbar anywhere else?

14 DECEMBER 1969
COLISEUM THEATRE, LONDON, UK

JOHNNY FOLLON

What a colossal performance it was! Daltrey's voice singing *Tommy* was mesmerising. 'Pinball Wizard' and 'See Me, Feel Me' were incredible sounds. And it was probably revolutionary at that time, them appearing at an iconic theatre world renowned for mainstream opera.

MICHEAL O'GEALLABHAIN

It was good music, well played with a very strong rhythm. But it was very, very loud. Uncomfortably loud. And unfortunate subject matter.

19 DECEMBER 1969
CITY HALL, NEWCASTLE-UPON-TYNE, UK

JOE CHIPCHASE

Newcastle City Hall was packed. The group were on top form, with the vocals being outstanding. This was no doubt due to the banks of speakers on the City Hall stage. What sticks in my mind is that Keith Moon stotted (ie. bounced) a cymbal edgeways off the stage into the audience. Hopefully, nobody was hurt. Despite their reputation, no guitars were smashed up but I think Keith Moon kicked his kit over at the end. You could tell who had been at the concert later that evening as people headed for home – they were conversing in shouts!

ROB GRIMES

I had a ticket in the cheap seats, upstairs in the balcony. They were not the best but standing up along with everyone else you got a good view. I can remember a huge wall of amplifiers and Keith Moon sat in front with the biggest drum kit you could imagine. They are the loudest band I have ever heard. I remember nicking a huge poster advertising the concert off a nearby building. It went on my bedroom wall.

RUSSELL WILKES

This time it was songs from *Tommy*. It could have been exclusively *Tommy* songs. I don't think they played any hits.

4 JANUARY 1970
RED LION, HATFIELD, UK

JOHN MEARS, AGE 20

Keith moved in opposite me in Winchmore Hill towards the end of November 1969 and bought a house directly across the road. When I first met him, it was snowing and I heard a load of bottles being smashed outside and wondered what it was. I went to look out the window and there was this guy standing in the middle of the road wearing leopard skin underpants and nothing else. A woman at the front door of the house was throwing bottles at him. It was Kim (Keith's wife) and they'd had a row and it had got a bit out of hand. So I opened the front door and he saw me and said 'do you mind if I come in for minute?'.

My old man was in at the time and he was a bit like Moon in that he loved his booze, and Keith told us how they'd had an argument and things didn't look too good and Dad said 'well, come up to the bar and we'll have a drink.' We had a bar at the top of the house. Dad gave him a dressing gown and he went up there and spent virtually all night up there talking to Dad. And as a result of that he got to know Dad well. After that, he had a few parties and we went over there and got to know him.

And then Neil died.

On 4 January 1970, Keith's driver Neil Boland was accidentally killed when Keith, Kim and others were visiting a pub in Hatfield and their car was attacked by local youths. Neil got out of the car to remonstrate with the youths and was dragged under the vehicle. Keith was reportedly at the wheel of the car but the death was later judged to be an accident.

JOHN MEARS

They went to an opening at a place in Hatfield and that was down to my Dad. My Dad knew the owner and he wanted someone to open it and Dad mentioned Keith Moon and they said 'great'. And they went down there and that's when the accident happened. Neil got dragged under the car. When they got back, I'd left a note on his front door saying 'party time', thinking he'd come over and celebrate. And when they eventually got back, I heard a big commotion outside and wondered what was going on so I thought I'd leave it. Next day it was front page news.

About two weeks later, he was he was having his first party with the same old mates – Legs Larry, Jimmy McCulloch, Jack McCulloch, Thunderclap Newman and a few other people – and he came over the road and invited my old man across. And my old man was out so I said I'd go over. I was working for my old man at his furniture factory in Hatfield, which was a long way away. I was sick of it and I spent half the night telling Keith how bored I was with it all and he said 'well, we'll see what we can do'. And the next morning he was kicking everyone out and he said 'look, I've got to get into the office and you've got a motor.

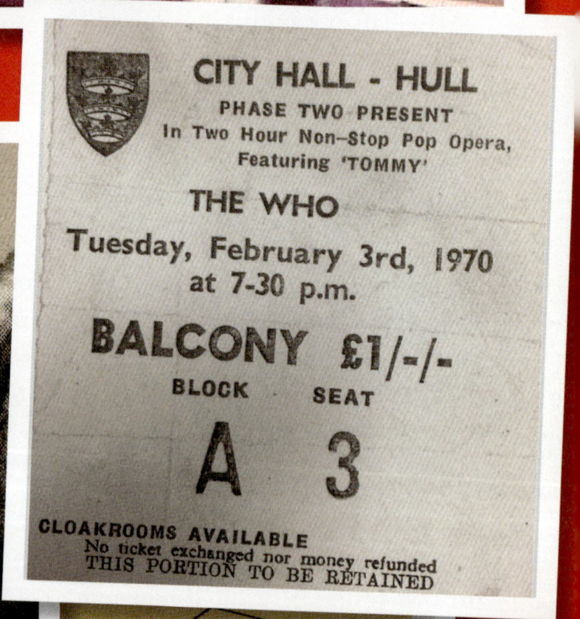

CITY HALL - HULL
PHASE TWO PRESENT
In Two Hour Non-Stop Pop Opera,
Featuring 'TOMMY'

THE WHO

Tuesday, February 3rd, 1970
at 7-30 p.m.

BALCONY £1/-/-

BLOCK A SEAT 3

CLOAKROOMS AVAILABLE
No ticket exchanged nor money refunded
THIS PORTION TO BE RETAINED

Clockwise from top left: John Mears found himself living opposite Keith Moon; Keith at the Crown and Cushion hotel - photo John Mears; Sheila Stark's Hull ticket; Dave Lee was Live at Leeds; Keith backstage at Leeds Uni - photo John Mears.

Clockwise from top left: Keith with John Mears' father - photo John Mears; Keith with John Mears' father - photo John Mears; Keith with wife Kim - photo John Mears; Keith's Winchmore Hill house in 2017; Keith with John Mears' father - photo John Mears.

Would you mind taking me in?' I said 'no, not at all.' It was a Saturday so I didn't have to go to work and so I drove him in.

We got to the Track office and he said 'come up and meet some people.' So I went upstairs and met all the guys up there. And he said, 'Could you do me a cheque for about three thousand five hundred?' The guy did the cheque out, gave it to Keith and Keith gave it to me. He said, 'Listen, if you fancy a job, you can drive me if you go and buy me a Roller. I want a Silver Cloud Mark 3.' It just knocked me for six. I said 'I'd love to work for you.' 'Well, go and buy a Roller and bring it round to the house. I'll get one of the guys here to take your car back home and take me home with it.'

So I went up to Owen and Son. They only had one in there for three grand – a green one. I took the car back and Keith took one look at it and said 'I don't like the colour. Do you know anyone that does spray jobs?' I said, 'Yeah, I know a couple of people in Southgate that have got a garage' and he said 'well, take it there and get it sprayed'. I said 'what colour?' He goes, 'Er, lilac.' I had a bit of a laugh and said, 'No, what colour?' He said, 'Lilac. Get it sprayed lilac.' So that's what I did.

That night I had to tell the old man that I'd finished working for him. He didn't mind, because the business was going downhill. And that all conjoined into him wanting to get something else and ending up with him buying a hotel with Moon.

A couple of weeks after I'd been working for Keith, Dad had a party. He always had parties at the weekend, with people back from the pub, and he invited Keith over. Keith was talking about hotels all that day, saying 'it's about time I had one of my own'. And he started talking to the old man 'do you fancy going in on a hotel with me?' So they started looking and visiting places together and they came up with the Crown and Cushion (in Chipping Norton).

When I was working for Keith, we went there once or twice a month because at the time he was doing a lot of gigs. He was either in the States, or that year was the university gigs all over the country, *Live at Leeds* and all that sort of stuff. But when we had a spare weekend, we'd take Mandy and Kim and go and spend the weekend down there. And, of course, he had loads of parties. That's the reason really why the hotel ended up having to be sold. Because he never paid his bill. He'd invite all these people down, free drinks and all that, and it would take months to get the money from Track.

The normal routine if he had a day off was that he'd get up at about twelve, go into London to get some money from Track, go to the A&R Club in Wardour Street and meet all his mates up there and start drinking. I didn't drink so much because I had to drive, obviously, but I'd have a few. That would go straight through to knocking out time and then we'd all go down the Speakeasy until that shut at about four o'clock and then I'd drive him home. And if he had another day off, he'd go through the same thing again. It was constant party time. He hardly spent any time at home. He was always out on the razzle.

The first few weeks I worked for him he was still getting over Neil and it was playing on his mind something chronic. The depression was terrible. He'd get back from a club and then he'd disappear into the front room. I was in the kitchen making a cup of coffee one time and I went in the front room and he was lying on the floor, mouth half open and frothing, with this white stuff coming out of this mouth and a bottle of pills by the side of him. Kim had warned me that he did things like that for attention, and when I got to him I opened his mouth and the pills were all in his mouth. He hadn't swallowed them. I thought then 'she's right what she's saying'.

I had to get him up, get him to drink water and walk him round. It was Mandrax in sleeping pills and they were deadly if you had too many of them. He did that twice over that month. He didn't know what to do with himself. He was a different man. The jokiness in him didn't come back for about another month. Those times were very dark for the first two months after Neil died. But when he perked up, he was back to his old self.

One day, we'd gone somewhere for a few drinks – I think it was with the McCulloch brothers and Legs Larry – and he took us into a costumiers. We all got dressed up. Legs Larry and the two boys were dressed up as hoods from the 1930s with hats and plastic machine guns. He gave me a gorilla outfit, so I was driving the car in a gorilla outfit. And he did himself up from head to toe as a vicar. He had the bald head, the dog collar, the bible and everything. The gag was that he would walk down Shaftesbury Avenue and I was supposed to drive up, screech to a halt and the boys would get out, drag him to the car and drive off. Shaftesbury Avenue at that time of day was packed, with all these people looking round. So we drove off and Keith had his head out of the window, shouting, 'Obscenities! Obscenities!' We got to the end of the road and there was a copper standing there, with his hand out to stop us. He obviously knew it was Moon's car, because everyone did in London in those days, and the window came down and he goes, 'Hello, Mr Moon, I thought it was you. We've had reports that a vicar was shouting obscenities out of a car having just been abducted.'

On the third day I was working for Keith, he said 'we'll go and meet a mate of mine'. And my eyes nearly popped out of my head when we got there because it was Ringo. We got invited into the house. Ringo was in the front room, laying floor tiles.

I ended up meeting Ringo's driver and PA at the time, Martin Lickett, and we became really good friends. He knew I was going through a lot with Keith. It was having a devastating effect on me, trying to keep up with him. I wasn't getting sleep. I lost a lot of weight. It was very difficult and I was only 20 – I didn't have the skills that I've got today. So, at the end of that year, Martin said to me, 'If you've had enough, why don't you come and work at Apple? I've got a spot for you driving if you want it.'

So I spoke to Keith when we were at the Crown. He said, 'Dear boy, if that's what you want, no problem. I can always get someone else to drive me.' And that was it. It was just before the end of 1970 and I went straight into Apple and started there.

I did a lot with Keith over that year. We went to Copenhagen. And then there was *Live at Leeds* and the Isle of Wight. So I got into all the really good gigs that they did and I think they were the best gigs that they'd ever done. Especially *Tommy* – it was fantastic.

16 & 17 JANUARY 1970
THÉÂTRE DES CHAMPS ELYSÉES PARIS, FRANCE

OLIVIER COIFFARD, AGE 15

I was blown away when I heard my first rock single, 'Summertime Blues' by Eddie Cochran. I first heard The Who in December 1967 with the French 45 'Mary Anne With the Shaky Hand'/'I Can See For Miles', which I listened to on my sister's best friend's Teppaz Oscar Stereolux. In January 1968, I discovered *The Who Sell Out* and was fascinated by its cover and the poster that came with the English version. These songs, interspersed with radio jingles, took me on a journey. I had just turned 13.

My father loved to listen to the radio, and particularly the France Inter station. In May 1969, I was listening to *Pop Club*, presented by José Artur, when they played the entire double album, *Tommy*, which Artur's assistant, Patrice Blanc-Francard, had selected. They said Pete Townshend's work was sure to become a major record in the history of rock music. My parents bought me *Tommy* and I listened to it regularly that summer. And I was lucky enough to see The Who on my fifteenth birthday the following January, when they played two dates in Paris as part of their European tour.

My older brother got me the ticket. As soon as I entered the theatre, I felt a special atmosphere. The excitement of the adults around me increased as the start of the concert approached and the atmosphere gradually became more electric. For the next two hours, I felt like I was on a cloud. I really felt the extraordinary power of this band on stage, the enormous bass sound of John Entwistle, the virtuosity and madness of Keith Moon on drums, the uninhibited vocals of Roger Daltrey with his fringed jacket and using his microphone as a lasso, and the incredible jumps and the rage of the guitar riffs of Pete Townshend. They played almost all of the tracks from *Tommy* followed by 'Summertime Blues'. The concert ended with a 15-minute long version of 'My Generation'. Nothing was ever the same for me after that. In that one evening, I entered the Who religion.

Four months later, *Live at Leeds* was released. It had been recorded on February 14, 1970, barely a month after the fabulous concert I attended. It's the most valuable and vital Who live album I own. Although I know it by heart, every listen still gives me tremendous shivers of happiness today.

27 JANUARY 1970
BEAT CLUB, BREMEN, GERMANY

STEPHEN DAVY

I briefly met Keith Moon. It was whilst my group were in Bremen, Germany recording some numbers for the TV programme *Beat Club*. The Who were also there, recording parts of *Tommy* for the same TV show. We went to a nearby night club and were sitting there upstairs, sipping some lagers. During the evening, in walked Keith Moon and bassist John Entwistle. They sat down at the next table and recognised us from the studio earlier. They came and sat at our table, bringing a bottle of wine which Keith had smuggled into the club hidden under his coat. He introduced himself as Keith, speaking in a very educated voice, and shook each one of us by the hand. He made conversation while John sat there in complete silence. This lasted for a little while and then we went on our different ways.

Deciding that they don't want to listen to the 80 hours of tape recorded on the 1969 US dates for a possible live album, a performance at Leeds University in February 1970 is recorded on the Pye mobile studio. The subsequent album, Live at Leeds, is released with minimal overdubbing.

14 FEBRUARY 1970
UNIVERSITY, LEEDS, UK

GERALD CLEAVER

Daltrey knocked me gently out of the way when they had done their sound check. They came marching out through the crowd who were queuing to get in. It was a good-humoured exit, but they did move us out of the way.

The person I was sharing a room with at the university was a drummer in a band. He was adamant he was not going, because Keith Moon was 'a bloody rubbish drummer.' Afterwards, he wanted to know what I thought of the concert and said, 'I walked around the back of the refectory and they were playing some song about Christmas' – it was the track 'Christmas' from *Tommy* – 'and I was listening to the drumming and I have to admit it was bloody good.' He apologised. Keith Moon was the right drummer for them and their sound.

The Leeds University social secretary who booked them got into trouble with the student union. The termly gigs had an overall price ceiling of £5, ie. around ten shilling (50p) average price. The Who cost around ten shillings and sixpence (52.5p), which was above that. I recall some really cheap gigs after that – Mott the Hoople and Elton John were both 3/6d (around 17p) – to bring the average cost of tickets for the term down.

DAVID HICKES

I'm a professional photographer and took pictures of The Who 'Live at Leeds'. I have several pics of them on stage and also a couple of the audience. I wasn't there long, as I had to wire pics to the Sunday papers.

DENNIS APPLEYARD

In the mid-Sixties, the university's student union had Saturday night gigs all through term time in the Refectory and the smaller Riley Smith Hall. The bookers were really astute and we heard lots of cool music. I saw up and coming bands like Elton John, Joe Cocker and a very early gig by the Faces. The main hall featured bands like Free, The Move and Fairport Convention. The admissions policy varied every year. Some years it was open and on others it was students only or guests signed in by a student. As a junior clerk in an insurance firm, this could be problematic and I admit I resorted to forgery and blagging on occasions.

When The Who were booked, we acquired our tickets and waited for the band to appear. In those days long waits were normal. I went for a pee and heard a commotion from one of the stalls. And then Keith Moon tumbled out. I do not know if he was pissed, on something or just clowning around but he thought it was hilarious. As the night wore on, we heard that it had been cancelled and was going to be rearranged and so we shuffled off. That was the night Pete says he ran out of petrol! Would you believe the garage attendant wouldn't take his guitar as payment? A while later, we queued on a Sunday morning for tickets for the gig which was recorded as *Live at Leeds* but they sold out before we got to the front of the queue.

BRYAN BENNION

I saw them at the Refectory with my mate Steve Hardy, who came up with his girlfriend to see them. It was the gig where *Live at Leeds* was recorded. I had forgotten that Steve had been up to Leeds but he has a better memory than I have. He even remembered the flat I rented in my second year at Leeds University. I couldn't.

DAVE LEE

The weekly 'hops' at Leeds University were a seemingly endless stream of now legendary groups. Week after week we saw groups such as Led Zeppelin, Deep Purple, Fleetwood Mac and many others, but excitement reached a peak when we heard that The Who were coming to play in the Union Refectory, which held about 2,000 people for concerts on Saturday nights – quite a small venue by modern standards – and where we had meals during the rest of the week. It was billed as The Who's very last performance of *Tommy* ever. That seemed strange as it hadn't been out all that long, and not surprisingly they played it again the very next day in Hull! And carried on playing it. But at the time it was quite a shock announcement. It would have left a big gap in the two-hour non-stop performances they were now doing. Another shock was that the tickets were going to cost ten shillings (50p) – double what we normally paid. It doesn't sound much now, but at the time you could just about get a week's meals for that.

On the day of the concert, we got to the Refec so early that we were among the first few in the queue, standing right up again the doors. After a while, the doors opened briefly and Roger Daltrey and John Entwistle appeared, and pushed past us to get out.

Although they were called hops, it was usual to sit on the floor for student concerts, and for this one The Who had stipulated that everyone must remain seated at all times. When we were finally allowed in, we ran through to the refectory and claimed a very good spot right near the front – so close that I can hear myself cheering on the album. As everyone now knows, The Who were on brilliant form. But they seemed to me to be on the same brilliant form at every gig around that time. *Tommy* seemed ideal for live performance, more than anything they have brought out since, and the sound that just the four of them made was frightening. Many of the wonderful songs they have come up with since have needed tapes and/or extra musicians for live performance.

I didn't manage to catch one of the many drumsticks that Keith launched out into the audience, but afterwards I did find the metal discs that flew out of Roger's tambourines as he hit them so hard. It's still amazing looking at these and thinking about the sounds they made, on one of the most celebrated live albums ever.

About ten days before the *Live at Leeds* album was released in the UK, a message came over the union building loudspeakers that they had some pre-release copies available for sale at the reception desk. I've still got mine, stamped with the Leeds Union stamp and the date, 13.05.70.

Only a short time after the Leeds University gig, I saw The Who again at an even smaller Leeds venue, Cinderella's discotheque. It was so small that the width of the stage seemed greater than the distance from the stage to the back of the room. As usual, we had to sit on the floor. I don't think many people know about this concert and I can't find any mention of it in the various books or online. Of course, they played *Tommy* again.

MALCOLM TEDD, AGE 15

I became aware of The Who when 'I Can't Explain' was a hit in 1964, and liked all of their hits, but it wasn't until 'Pinball Wizard' came out in 1969 that I was truly knocked out. I couldn't wait until Christmas Day that year to receive my present of *Tommy*, and I wasn't disappointed. My older brother was in his first year at university and asked me if I'd like to come up to see The Who live at Leeds Uni. I couldn't believe my luck – my first ever gig and still the best. I got Pete Townshend's autograph and was later blown away (and deafened) by the brilliant show. I couldn't believe it when a couple of months later they released the live album to prove wrong any of my doubters as to just how fucking brilliant they were that night.

15 FEBRUARY 1970
CITY HALL, HULL, UK

SHEILA STARK

My husband and I saw The Who at Hull City Hall. I still have my original ticket. The hall was packed, standing and balcony. We were front row balcony, above the stage and with a good view. Our ears were buzzing for about two days afterwards.

TONY WARD

I remember the recording vans outside recording the concert which I believe was mixed as The Who *Live at Leeds* album as the recording at Leeds wasn't too good. I sat on the balcony and thoroughly enjoyed it as that was the real Who, Keith Moon and all.

27 APRIL 1970
CIVIC HALL, DUNSTABLE, UK

PETE WRIGHT

Dunstable had a lovely venue, the Civic Hall, which has been knocked down now. It was only built in the early Sixties and it was gone by the late Seventies. I took this girl with me and we parked my car and we were walking across this car park. There was a massive juggernaut there – The Who were in the money by then - and Roger Daltrey was walking back from it. All I had to do was walk over there and shake his hand and I just didn't feel I could, you know what I mean? And this girl with me, she would have given anything to give him a hug or something. And she thought 'no.' In those very early days, you'd go to these clubs in London like the Marquee, and The Who would be at the bar surrounded by 16, 17-year-old girls and you felt, if you pushed through them to shake hands, that people would think you were a poof. I just regret it so much, not meeting them when I had the chance.

It was all sitting on the floor stuff that night. They came on and it was Roger Daltrey in his tassels and Pete Townshend in his white boiler suit and all the Hiwatt amps. And Pete leapt in the air and his guitar was as dead as a dodo. But the rest of the band sounded very good, and Daltrey started singing 'Can't Explain' and Townshend realised his guitar was dud and slung it on the floor and kicked all three of these Hiwatt stacks over. Someone came running on stage to try and calm him down and he took a swing at them. They managed to grab his arm and then three or four people came on and they just manhandled him off the stage. The rest of the band walked off.

They got all the gear set up again. Roger, Keith and John came back on stage and Pete came on a bit later. They had a bit of a sound desk on stage and he went over there to the sound desk and threw a few fucks into him, and then came back and picked his guitar up and carried on. That was the very, very best I ever saw them. They played a blinder.

And after that you're talking about buying tickets from touts. You'd ring the Astoria, Finsbury Park or something and they'd say 'sold out, mate' at nine in the morning on the day they went on sale. And you'd go up there and buy a ticket off a tout.

1 MAY 1970
UNIVERSITY OF EXETER, EXETER, UK

MIKE WATTS

I had joined the social committee just in time for The Who concert. The social secretary, Rod MacSween (later to become a legend of the music agency world), gave me the job of minding the Green Room and making sure the band were fed and watered. Roger Daltrey had driven himself to Exeter and arrived in the early afternoon and could be seen happily wandering around the student union building, causing heads to swivel. Townshend and Entwistle arrived together, followed, not long before curtain up, by Keith Moon who bounced out of his chauffeur-driven Rolls sporting a gorilla mask. I left the dressing room at one point to collect some drinks and returned to the unmistakeably pungent smell of ripe bananas. Moon, it appeared, had come armed with a bottle of concentrated banana essence, the stuff you might use to flavour a cake, and had sprayed it across the room, mostly in the direction of Daltrey, who was not at all happy and was chasing the drummer around the room.

The show itself was fantastic; opening with a string of Who classics – 'I Can't Explain', 'Substitute', 'I'm A Boy', 'The Seeker' and a cover of Mose Allison's 'Young Man's Blues'. This was the *Tommy* tour, and the heart of the set was dedicated to the album - from 'Overture' through 'It's A Boy', 'Acid Queen', 'Pinball Wizard', 'Smash the Mirror!', 'I'm Free' and many more. The band gave an absolutely brilliant performance, encoring with Johnny Kidd's 'Shakin' All Over', Eddie Cochran's 'Summertime Blues' and 'My Generation', and while Townsend attacked his speaker cabinets, Daltrey indulged in his trademark microphone swinging on an ever extending lead, perhaps more closely to Moon's grinning face than usual!

Walking through town the following morning, I passed the rather posh Rougemont Hotel and there in the car park was Moonie's Roller, with the gorilla mask leering out of the back window.

9 MAY 1970
UNIVERSITY, MANCHESTER, UK

BILL WHITE

I saw Bruce and Baker with Graham Bond and Clapton with John Mayall at the Blue Moon Club in Cheltenham. Being a Mod, I was more into seeing The Action, Spencer Davis and the Steampacket. The Action definitely had the credibility over The Who with the Mods, although I don't know why they were compared. I saw The Who once during the *Live at Leeds* tour but by that time, I was deeply into jazz and pretty snobbish with it. I went extremely reluctantly but my girlfriend wanted to go. It was absolutely fantastic, and still one of the best live shows I've ever seen.

15 MAY 1970
LANCASTER UNIVERSITY, LANCASTER, UK

BARRY LUCAS

I was Social Secretary at Lancaster University, having been a student there since 1968. My first gig as Ents Sec was in May 1970 with The Who. The fee for bands around that time, like Deep Purple and Led Zeppelin, was £350. But we were paying The Who £1,000. The student union were going fucking apeshit. They tried to stop us booking them. I got the contract in the post before they could stop us.

16 MAY 1970
UNIVERSITY OF YORK, YORK, UK

DAVE LEE

I sometimes went to gigs at York University, which involved a train ride and an early morning arrival back in Leeds. And it meant an additional round trip a couple of weeks before to buy a ticket, but when I heard that The Who were going to play there, I went straight off to get a ticket. It must have been different in the South of the country, but in the North it was always very easy to get tickets for The Who. It was hard to find anyone else who really liked them. In my home town of Stockport, I only ever found one other fan and we went together to any show The Who did in Manchester.

On the day of the York concert, I arrived really early. As I walked around outside the venue, it seemed as though the only other people there were The Who. Keith Moon's Rolls-Royce was parked outside, and for some reason he decided to move it, driving off very suddenly with a roar of spinning wheels and squealing tyres! Roger Daltrey was walking around in a long psychedelic cloak, looking with interest at the lake that was there in the campus. A bit later, I followed the unmistakable sound of Pete Townshend playing an acoustic guitar, and went up some external steps to the first floor of a building where I was on a balcony, right outside a door where the playing was coming from. Suddenly Roger came out and stood right next to me and looked down over the balcony, then he looked at me and went back in. Seconds later, a guy came out to tell me, in very clear terms, to go away!

The concert was in a room that seemed to be a large lecture theatre, with typical steeply-tiered single rows of seats. It followed the same two-hour format of the two concerts I had seen in Leeds earlier in 1970, but I particularly remember it as the first time I had seen them play 'The Seeker', which had been released as a single in March. During the show, Roger mentioned how impressed he was with the lake they had there on the campus – maybe he was already thinking about developing his own trout fishing lake…

TONY SHAWE

I was often in York for half-term holidays from boarding school in Richmond, Yorkshire. One half term, my father showed up, which was rare (he was always travelling) and one evening, he suggested we go to the cinema and handed me the *York Evening Press* to check what was on. On or near the cinema page I spotted a tiny classified advert which read, in summary, 'for one night only, The Who, York University.' I was already a huge fan and could hardly believe it, so I went with my father, him full of scepticism and dressed in his military blazer and regimental tie.

The concert took place in a very large lecture hall with the seating on a steep slope.

My father and I took seats at the back. Roger swirled his mic high into the air and caught it on the way down. He was going through his goldilocks phase with a suede, heavily fringed jacket and bellbottoms while Pete was in a white boiler suit with DMs, playing the red Gibson SG. Keith and John were in their usual roles, left and centre back. The music was a blend of familiar *Tommy*, a few singles and *Who's Next*. I may have a few of these details a bit wide of the mark, but it remains a powerful photographic image from an elevated angle to the right of the stage. I never saw them live again, although I did bump into Pete at record label party at The Venue in Victoria in London many years later. I often wondered why they showed up in York almost incognito when they were such a big band, A friend says it was a rehearsal for the *Live at Leeds* tour.

STEVE ROGERS

I was in a band and doing theatre work when I heard The Who were on at Central Hall at York Uni. I had a night off so had to go. They were on with Wishbone Ash so it was going to be a good one. After Ash had done their gig, The Who just strolled on, picked up their instruments and started. It was bloody loud! Their set was the whole of *Tommy* and several old hits. They were on for about three hours and it was one of the best concerts I've seen. They were on form and you could tell they were enjoying it and playing well. Roger Daltrey was top man in his fringed jacket and big hair. He was superb, as was Keith Moon. It was a superb show and a pleasure to hear and see.

JOHN SIMPSON

It was one of the venues on their tour of universities including the Refectory at Leeds University where they recorded the *Live at Leeds* album, a concert at which I was also at. At the

Leeds concert, my friend caught and kept one of Keith Moon's drumsticks. At the York concert, they played the same set as is on *Live at Leeds*. They were superb and sounded much like the album. I remember walking to the venue and passing Keith Moon's psychedelic Rolls-Royce being filled up with petrol at a garage on Lawrence Street.

June 1970 sees The Who back in the USA for a 22-date tour.

14 JUNE 1970
ANAHEIM STADIUM, ANAHEIM, CALIFORNIA

TOMMY CARRASCO

That was the first time I ever witnessed nudity and open drugs at a concert. Everybody smoked pot, but hallucinogens were rampant there. They played their *Live at Leeds* set. It was five dollars entrance fee, and three and a half hours of raw energy. Blues Image, John Sebastian and Leon Russell with *Mad Dogs and Englishmen* opened. Amazing!

22 JUNE 1970
MUNICIPAL AUDITORIUM, ATLANTA, GEORGIA

RICK FREEMAN

I paid $6 for my ticket. Joe Walsh opened the show but in my excitement at seeing The Who I was anxious for them to finish their set so that The Who could take the stage. Back then, it seemed as if it took hours for them to remove the opening bands gear. The wait was worth it. When the lights dimmed, the place went 'wow'. Most of the audience seemed surprised when they opened with 'Heaven and Hell' – I know I was – yet it worked. Hearing Entwistle singing was an unexpected treat, and Pete proved he was a marvellous guitar player. Just the sheer energy of three guys playing and sounding like six is something I still remember. I honestly do not think I clapped or said a word because I was spellbound. All of them seem to be trying to be the lead. Four or five songs went by in a blur. Then they announced *Tommy*.

It has been 53 years since that concert, but I still feel the visceral raw power of them.

The banter between Pete and Keith made me think they should do a comedy show together, it was so entertaining. The friend who came with me had also attended the Rolling Stones show the year before, and we were both in awe. We had a good-natured rivalry when it came to music. If one of us bought an album that the other didn't have, we would rag each other about how good it was, regardless of whether it was good or bad. I would buy it because he had it. Unfortunately, we both wound up with a few albums we only played once or twice. But that was not the case when it came to the Stones, The Beatles and The Who.

Seeing The Who in 1970 is something I will always cherish. They were the best. No one could touch them. They played the same venue the following year, but tickets sold out so fast that I was not able to buy one. This was the era of standing in line for hours or taking a change and trying to buy one over the phone. Just getting someone to answer was a nightmare. Years later, I was able to get backstage at a Deep Purple show as I had known Steve Morse since his early days playing with The Dixie Grits. They changed their name to The Dixie Dregs. Steve and I were talking about shows we attended in the late 1960s and earlier 1970s. He mentioned seeing Cream in Atlanta. I told him I couldn't get anyone to drive me to the show, but I did see the Stones in 1969 and The Who in 1970. He told me that he and his brother were at the Who show. Small world.

25 & 26 JUNE 1970
TAFT THEATRE, CINCINATTI, OHIO

GARY EPPERSON

I got down in the orchestra pit, climbed up on some scaffolding and had my elbows on the stage not more than ten feet away from the band. I even caught one of Keith Moon's drumsticks as he threw them out into the audience. Things got wild with the crowd at the end of the show when the band commenced destroying their equipment!

29 JUNE 1970
MERRIWEATHER POST PAVILION COLUMBIA, MARYLAND

DENIS GOULET

MPP is a cool little amphitheatre that probably holds 14,000 including some fixed pavilion as well as lawn seating. But the venue was overrun and police later estimated that 20,000 showed up. Our seats were centre stage and about 30 rows back on the aisle. We were totally stoked. I had bought tickets with the expectation that my very pregnant wife would have dropped our baby on the date due, three days before, and that she'd be sufficiently recovered to go with me. The show was slated to start around 7.30pm.

I got off work and made it back to the apartment and my wife, my cousin and good friend piled into the car for the normally quick trip up Route 29. It was hot, very hot. I must have asked my wife 50 times if she really wanted to deal with the walk once we got there, given the heat and the crowd. But there was no way she was staying behind. We got to within a mile of Merriweather and traffic came to a standstill. But we were still 45 minutes early and there was no concern at the time that we'd miss anything. After sitting in the car and not moving an inch for ten minutes, we noticed people walking up from behind us and there was no doubt that, if we wanted to see The Who, we were going to have to hoof it from that point.

I wedged the car onto the shoulder and off we set. It probably took 30 minutes to get close to the gates. When we got close enough to see the fence that surrounds the centre, it was apparent that the crowd was having none of the fence and ripped it down. It was at that point a free concert.

I was constantly worried that my wife was going to start downloading that baby. She was already three days overdue and all of that excitement couldn't help. But she was relentless. She led the way past the mob on the lawn. We lost track of my cousin and friend and ploughed toward our seats. When we finally got there, they were – of course – occupied. She looked at the two people and said 'out!'. They said 'right, where are we supposed to go?'. Then they saw her giant pregnant belly and got up and moved on. We had missed maybe half of the first song. We were treated to the best Who show I would ever see. Show over, we marched back to the abandoned car and went home. Our daughter was born eight days later. If she was a boy, I would have named her Tommy.

4 JULY 1970
AUDITORIUM THEATER, CHICAGO, ILLINOIS

NICK VERBIC

I saw The Who seven times between 1968 and 1970. The first time I saw them they were the opening band for Herman's Hermits, which is almost as crazy as when Hendrix opened for the Monkees. Seeing them at the Chicago Auditorium in July 1970 is one of the top three concerts in my life. I've seen more bands than I can remember. None of them played with the energy of The Who with Moonie.

29 AUGUST 1970
3RD ISLE OF WIGHT MUSIC FESTIVAL ISLE OF WIGHT, UK

ALAN WATTERS

I hitchhiked down from Scotland and, just outside London. got a lift down to Portsmouth in Roger Daltrey's Rolls-Royce. One of The Who's management team, possibly the road manager, was driving and he told me lots of stuff about The Who that people wouldn't generally know – like how he took every new guitar for Pete Townshend apart and then bolted it back together again so when Pete smashed it up on stage, they could salvage some bits and put them back together.

ALAN BUTCHER, AGE 17

This was my first ever festival, although I had seen a number of their London gigs at the Marquee Club and the Lyceum. It was Saturday night and I had been there three days so I crashed out before The Doors played and only woke up to the sounds of The Who. The band played the rock opera, *Tommy*, plus the hits and were the best band on the whole weekend, alongside Rory Gallagher's Taste.

GERALD CLEAVER

When they returned to play the Isle of Wight Festival, they played a long set partly to make up for the previous year. They seemed to go on forever and they sounded superb. I was there with my girlfriend and she just couldn't believe what she was seeing. The 1969 set had been a shorter set and we'd been a long way away.

If you hadn't already realised why The Who were so popular in the 1960s and 1970s and why nerds like me would see them up to four or more times in any one year, as I did in 1970, quite simply The Who were an exciting live band. They put on a stage show to entertain their audience, and engaged their audience by talking to them, by looking at them and giving the audience something to look at on stage. There were many other bands on the road, but many were scruffily dressed, some did not talk to or look at the audience, and some had zero stage presence. Light shows and effects were sometimes used to entertain the audience, but The Who did not need these; they were showmen and were leaping about and showing off, etc. The only big effect they used at that time was a huge searchlight shining out over the audience at the 'listening to you' refrain at the end of *Tommy*, which always got a big response.

I think they used it at the Isle Of Wight in 1970 for the first time. I can still recall how entranced my then girlfriend was by the sight of Roger Daltrey, long curly hair, dressed up in his cowboy fringed jacket, swinging his microphone on a long lead out over the audience like a lasso. Nobody else was doing this then. No one else does now. Keith Moon was playing the drums as if he was an octopus, arms flailing everywhere, eyes bulging, cheeks puffed blowing away. As for Pete Townshend... well, you know about him!

PAUL BRUCE HADEN

My girlfriend and I had been to a couple of smaller festivals with a group of friends, but the Isle of Wight was on a whole different scale. It was a bit of a trek so we took my girlfriend's car and set off a few days before to make sure we got on a ferry. The scale of the festival was mind-blowing. Supposedly there were more people there than the 500,000 at Woodstock. I think we just about managed to see every act, or at least hear them, as we lay in our tent. Fortunately, the weather was fabulous.

The Who came on very late. It must have been the early hours of the morning. Because the air was still at that time of night, the sound was crystal clear with none of the wind-blown phasing that often occurs at outdoor gigs. My favourite memory of the set was the intro to

'Pinball Wizard'. When John's bass came in, the ground seemed to shake. I've been a sound engineer both live and in studios all my life, so it's sounds that move me. In comparison with today's sound systems, the PA at the Isle of Wight was tiny, but for the time it was enormous and also made by WEM, who were pretty good.

The atmosphere when The Who were on was fantastic. Everyone seemed to be singing along and it was as though they lifted the crowd, who had sat there patiently for hours. The Who's set was one of the best I'd seen from any band and certainly the best I'd seen them play. The DVD of the gig is good but it doesn't entirely capture the visceral sound of the band or the atmosphere of such a huge crowd. It really was a case of 'you had to be there'.

MICHAEL STOKES, AGE 16

I have seen The Who many, many times. The hundredth time was in April 2017. One of many gigs I remember with great fondness is the 1970 Isle of Wight Festival. I had persuaded my parents to let me go. I told my parents I was going with two friends; I lied. I had been a fan since the age of eleven and had already seen them a couple of times, but this was the big one so I travelled from Bristol to the Isle of Wight. I'd never seem so many people at a gig before and I was so far back they were only just visible, but boy could you hear them! The sound was out of this world. Loud would be an understatement. They started with 'Heaven and Hell', John Entwistle in his bones costume, Daltrey looking cool and mean, Moon looking like Moon and Townshend looking mean with his white boiler suit and Doc Martens. It was loud and full of energy until the third song and then, somehow, they stepped up a gear.

'Young Man Blues' was so good I honestly thought my lungs were going to explode. I could not get my breath – this was something else. It was aggressive and so full of energy. I remember looking around me at the time and seeing that people were just mesmerised by the sheer power coming from all four members of the group.

They went into *Tommy* and again held the audience in the palm of their hands, and when it got to 'See Me, Feel Me', a massive searchlight came on and it was an amazing moment. I believe this was a defining moment of the band's career; they were at the top of their game.

I went back to my tent to find it had been stolen along with all my stuff. All I had left were my train tickets back home, a small amount of money and the clothes on my back. I stayed to watch Jimi Hendrix but was so exhausted I fell asleep and slept through the whole performance. When I got home, I don't think I stopped talking about The Who. The rest of the festival didn't matter. I was hooked for life.

RICHARD DIXON

I lived in Belgium until 1970 so my first live concert was the Isle of Wight with my cousin. *Tommy* was playing as the sun came up whilst my cousin slept next to me in his sleeping bag. He has always maintained that The Who were amazing! I took my daughter to Hyde Park some years ago, having given her The Who's greatest hits. Whilst waiting for them to come on, Lucy asked me when I first saw them. I was telling her about the Isle of Wight and was overheard by a 40-something couple who started bowing to me. My street cred with my daughter rose astronomically!

MARTIN JONES

This concert was proof to me that they were the best live group in the world, bearing in mind over a period of time I saw all the top groups apart from The Beatles. They played at around 2am at the festival and played a set which included most, if not all, of *Tommy*. Given the sound system, the quality of performance was staggering. I remember paying £4.50 for a weekend ticket which was never checked and which I wish I'd kept!

TONY LANGFORD

Me and a mate hitched down there with nothing but the clothes we were wearing. On the first night on the way to the south coast, we slept in a ditch in fertiliser bags we had found. We huddled around a generator at night at the festival.

MIKE MURTAGH

By the time The Who appeared at the Isle of Wight Festival, there was a tendency to get blasé about the plethora of top-quality, legendary bands. You had to weigh up whether you wanted to sleep or eat or see some classic band. I reached that point with The Who. They were always regarded as an OK but definitely second-order band in the progressive music pantheon. Then came *Tommy* and their gig at Woodstock and suddenly their star was in the ascendant. Well, not for me. I needed sleep and sloped off outside the arena (I could still hear them, of course), lay in my sleeping bag beside a van and tried to doze off. Not for long though. The van caught fire and some were going frantic trying to clear the area before it blew. Most, however, like me, were too bloody shattered or stoned to move and so we accepted our likely fate until the arrival of the fire brigade. Apparently, it was one of The Who's greatest performances.

The Who play a handful of European dates and are then back on the UK tour circuit for the remainder of 1970.

Clockwise from top: the Isle of Wight Festival captured by Paul Bruce Haden; Claus Stenhøj saw The Who in 1970 and 1972; Ian Dalgliesh was at the Mayfair; John Oldroyd was at the Locarno in Leeds; Steve Rogers remembers The Who playing for three hours at York and being 'bloody loud'.

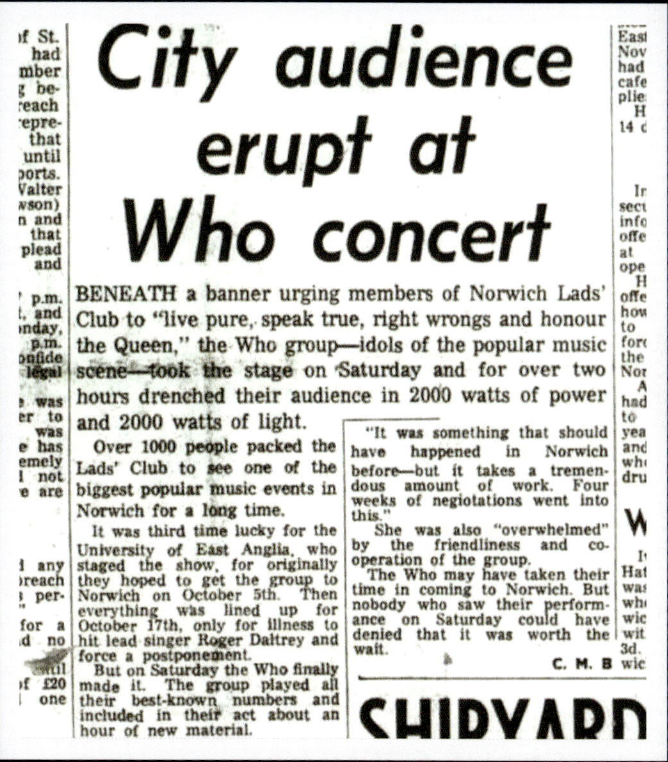

City audience erupt at Who concert

BENEATH a banner urging members of Norwich Lads' Club to "live pure, speak true, right wrongs and honour the Queen," the Who group—idols of the popular music scene—took the stage on Saturday and for over two hours drenched their audience in 2000 watts of power and 2000 watts of light.

Over 1000 people packed the Lads' Club to see one of the biggest popular music events in Norwich for a long time.

It was third time lucky for the University of East Anglia, who staged the show, for originally they hoped to get the group to Norwich on October 5th. Then everything was lined up for October 17th, only for illness to hit lead singer Roger Daltrey and force a postponement.

But on Saturday the Who finally made it. The group played all their best-known numbers and included in their act about an hour of new material.

"It was something that should have happened in Norwich before—but it takes a tremendous amount of work. Four weeks of negiotations went into this."

She was also "overwhelmed" by the friendliness and co-operation of the group.

The Who may have taken their time in coming to Norwich. But nobody who saw their performance on Saturday could have denied that it was worth the wait.

C. M. B

Clockwise from top left: Tony Langford was at Norwich Lads Club, an 'odd choice of venue'; Norwich Lads Club review; Robert Kelly managed to miss the Who gig at Norwich Lads Club; Ashley Smith couldn't believe how poorly attended the Scarborough gig was in December 1970; David Nobbs remembers 'Won't Get Fooled Again' being played ahead of it being released.

20 SEPTEMBER 1970
FALKONER CENTRET TEATRET COPENHAGEN, DENMARK

JOHN WADLOW

I only saw The Who once. It was part of a 28 date European tour they did that year. I've always remembered the classic look of the band at that time – Townshend with his paint-splattered white boiler suit, Entwistle with his famous skeleton suit and Daltrey with his long-fringed jacket. It was a long set; they played 29 songs that night, most of *Tommy* but also some of their big hits, including 'I Can't Explain' and 'My Generation'. I remember being shocked by the sheer volume of the band. It was the loudest and most energetic gig I'd ever been to. The band were incredibly tight and all of them were superb, particularly Pete Townshend. It's one thing to hear him on record and quite another to see him live. It's definitely one of the best gigs I've ever been to and that includes seeing Jimi Hendrix at the Royal Albert Hall.

CLAUS STENHØJ

The Who had visited Denmark in January for a show at the Royal Theatre (Det Kongelige Teater), which only seated 1,100 people. Most of the tickets were reserved for VIPs. I was too young to get permission to even think about queuing up. In September they returned and played almost the same set as at the Isle of Wight about a month before. They played 'Water' and 'I Don't Know Myself' as new songs, and some songs from *Tommy*. I looked on in awe as Keith threw his drumstick in the air during 'Christmas' – and caught it! The band were so loud that I had to clamp my hands over my ears for 'My Generation' and 'Magic Bus'. No one thought of ear-plugs then.

In August 1972, The Who came and played two more shows in Denmark, on the 20th and the 25th. In between, they did a show in Sweden. They stayed at the Sheraton Hotel in Copenhagen, and on Keith's birthday (August 23th), he did the prank with the waterbed in the hotel elevator. Ticket prices were very cheap back then but, aged 16, I had no income so only saw one show. I remember Roger smashing two tambourines to smithereens by banging them together in 'Baba O'Riley'. Me and my mates left our seats and went up in front of the stage.

I also saw The Who in the '90s on their *Quadrophenia* tour, but that wasn't so great. I remember PJ Proby accidentally dropping his mic when he was supposed to sing his part in 'The Punk and the Godfather'. Embarrassing...

6 OCTOBER 1970
SOPHIA GARDENS, CARDIFF, UK

PHILIP GOODRIDGE

I couldn't get a ticket and couldn't get in. But The Who were that loud I stood and listened to them from outside the venue.

7 OCTOBER 1970
FREE TRADE HALL, MANCHESTER, UK

COLIN JOY

A totally different Who played the Free Trade Hall in 1970 – they were bloody loud! The main emphasis of the tour was to capitalise on their appearance at the Woodstock and Isle of Wight festivals, and to bring their showpiece *Tommy* to the stage. The album when originally released was not to everyone's cup of tea, but, live, it was a masterpiece mixed in with The Who's back catalogue of stage favourites.

Townshend had his trademark hand swinging guitar playing down to a tee, Daltrey was throwing his microphones high in the air at every opportunity, Moon's drumming was over the top and Entwistle occasionally moved. Not too much – but he moved! The problem was the band got louder and louder, but the set seemed to go on forever as they played the full *Tommy* album, with all the instrumentals. It was a good night which took no prisoners. They did 34 songs in all. It was a long, long deafening night.

10 OCTOBER 1970
UNIVERSITY OF SUSSEX, BRIGHTON, UK

JOHN SCHOLLAR

A few times, Keith would ring me up and say 'what you doing tonight?' I'd say 'not a lot' and he'd say 'come up and see the gig' and I'd drive up there in my little sports car. When they did the university tour, when they recorded Live at Leeds, we went to the show at Sussex University outside Brighton. I rang Keith up and he said 'come down in the Rolls with us.' So we drove over to his house and he'd left a great big note on the front door saying 'sorry, mate. I've got to pick somebody up. See you in Brighton.' We got there and walked up to the main entrance and said 'we're with Keith' and the bloke said 'yeah, everybody says that mate. No ticket? You're not getting in.' Then Keith turned up in his Rolls and gave me a big hug and I said 'we've got a problem, mate. They won't let us in because we haven't got tickets.' He said 'what?' and called for the manager.

The manager came out and Keith said 'my mates can't get in without tickets and they haven't got tickets. Well, if they don't get in, I ain't coming in. Have you ever seen The Who without a drummer? They're crap.' So the manager agreed to let us in. Now, a crowd had gathered by this time and Keith said to the crowd 'has anybody here not got a ticket?' And half a dozen said 'we ain't got tickets.' And Keith said to the manager 'and they're my mates as well.'

13 OCTOBER 1970
LOCARNO BALLROOM, LEEDS, UK

GERALD CLEAVER

As soon as they got *Tommy*, Pete started playing in the boiler suit. I think for the Locarno gig he got it tie-dyed, possibly by John Sebastian at the Isle of Wight Festival. It was quite a shock. I'd only ever seen him in this plain white boiler suit and there he was looking quite garish. It was the *Tommy* set. They'd start with the singles and 'Young Man Blues', then *Tommy* and then come back for 'Summertime Blues'. I never saw them smash up their equipment. The couple I went with had rowed and he'd ripped the tickets up in a fit of pique. They turned up at the door with the tickets sellotaped back together and had to blag their way in.

JOHN OLDROYD

The Mecca ballroom was situated in the Merrion Centre, Leeds. The support act was a band called the James Gang, whose leader was Joe Walsh, later to join The Eagles. They must have been good because I went and bought their LP, *The James Gang Rides Again*, which I still have. The Mecca had a huge wooden dance floor with seats around the outside and a seated balcony. There was no hysteria and no rushing towards the makeshift stage. Everybody just sat on the dance floor or in a seat and enjoyed the music. The quote of the night came from Pete Townshend just before they were to play songs from *Tommy*, when he said 'and I as a composer'. It sounded unusual coming from a rock star. You normally think of them as songwriters.

18 OCTOBER 1970
LEWISHAM ODEON, LONDON, UK

DAVID SUMNERS

I liked The Who, and always enjoyed their TV performances, especially on *Ready Steady Go!*, but had never bought an album or single or considered myself a fan. I knew 'Pinball Wizard' but hadn't listened to the rest of *Tommy*, released the previous year. I'd only been to a few local concerts, seeing such acts as The Searchers, Screaming Lord Sutch, Geno Washington and the Ram Jam Band, Cliff Bennett and The Rebel Rousers and Desmond Dekker. In September 1970, I was sitting on the train on my way home from work when the train pulled into Lewisham station. The station overlooked the Lewisham Odeon, which was advertising the fact that The Who – 'The Greatest Rock and Roll Band in The World' – would be playing there. On impulse, I jumped off the train and went and bought a couple of tickets. Having had to fight for every ticket since, I'm still amazed I could walk up and buy them.

The day came around, and I took my girlfriend, who was a Tamla Motown and soul fan. The James Gang, featuring a certain Joe Walsh, was supporting them, and were impressive. I remember the growing anticipation waiting for The Who, who came on stage quite late. The lights went down and as they came on stage from the right, I remember Pete Townshend in his white boiler suit and Dr Martens leading the way on tip-toes, holding his guitar. Following him was Keith Moon doing a forward somersault, with Roger Daltrey and John Entwistle following.

They went straight into 'I Can't Explain' and the energy from the start just blew me away. I confess I can't remember the setlist, but *Tommy* was a big part of it. I was totally mesmerised, but I don't think my girlfriend was so impressed. The show finished, and as I looked at the debris-strewn stage I knew something in me really changed that night, dramatic though it sounds. The next day I went out and bought every Who album and remember driving my mum mad by playing *Tommy* continuously for the next month.

I've since seen them perform in excess of 40 times, the pinnacle being the gigs at The Valley. Charlton have been my team since I was ten, so they were such special events, and I later became a director of the club. Our manager at that time, Alan Curbishley, is Bill Curbishley's brother, so I managed to get invites to a few gigs. Even though I'm now over 70, I still attend all the UK tours.

DEN BOUNDY

They were fantastic and put on a standard but spectacular trademark performance. Keith Moon was his usual manic self, Roger Daltrey was swinging his microphone around his head and Pete Townshend was jumping up and down while flailing his guitar like a windmill.

24 OCTOBER 1970
STUDENTS UNION, SHEFFIELD, UK

COLIN BEARDSHALL

The cost of tickets was £1.50. The usual price of concert tickets was £1.00, which I paid to see bands such as Pink Floyd, Deep Purple and Family. And Sheffield Students Union Hall is quite big but nothing compared to a concert hall or arena. This being so, the show was comparatively intimate, with the audience sat cross legged on the floor for the full three or four hours. A new band, The James Gang were first on. The flyer said that Pete Townshend really rated this band's guitarist, Joe Walsh, and he didn't disappoint, playing with much skill and attack, all the time contorting his face in the best guitar gurning manner. The James Gang got a good reception from the audience and I for one went out to buy their record the next week.

The Who were delayed that night. A roadie or the tour manager came on stage at one point to ask if anyone had seen Keith Moon in any of the local pubs. It must have been an hour later that The Who took the stage, Pete in white boiler suit, Roger in open-fringed shirt and John in leather skeleton biker gear. Moonie crawled on stage on all fours, bottle of brandy in hand, and took his place behind the kit.

The set they played was pretty much the same as the *Live at Leeds* and Isle of Wight sets, both of which took place earlier that year. They opened with 'Heaven and Hell' (unless I'm remembering the Isle of Wight DVD!). I know for sure they introduced a new song called 'Naked Eye' and did 'Young Man Blues', 'Water' and 'Summertime Blues' as well as most of *Tommy* and a selection of hits such as 'The Seeker', 'Substitute' and 'My Generation'. I was sat pretty close to front centre of the stage, which had been augmented with refectory tables across the front, and remember thinking they might collapse under one of Pete's jumps. I also remember flinching every time Roger swung his mic, thinking it was going to fly off and hit me on the head.

The show ended about 1am which meant I and my mates had missed the last bus home, about 15 miles away. We set off walking and did about eight or ten miles before flagging down a taxi. We were tired but buzzing after seeing the then best live band in the world. It was well worth £1.50 of anyone's money.

26 OCTOBER 1970
TRENTHAM GARDENS, STOKE-ON-TRENT, UK

ALAN GOODWIN

I went with my wife. It was a ballroom gig and standing room only. On the night, Keith Moon's drums remained intact. During the interval, we went for a drink in the upstairs lounge bar and found ourselves sat on the next table to the group and their entourage. Contrary to their perceived image, they were very well behaved. Apart from their star status, you wouldn't have realised they were one of the country's leading groups.

29 OCTOBER 1970
HAMMERSMITH PALAIS, LONDON, UK

GREG COYNE, AGE 15

I saw The Who the first time at the Hammersmith Palais for a gig that was limited to just 300 tickets, or so we were told. I paid black market prices to get the tickets, which was a lot of pocket money! Me and three other mates got there early and were right at the front of the stage. As the concert began, I climbed up on to the stage, far right. I was recording the gig on a small tape recorder and the gig was amazing. It opened with 'Heaven and Hell' and went right through *Tommy* and finished with 'Magic Bus'. Pete even shouted some obscenity into the tape recorder microphone for me. At the end of the gig, he smashed up his Cherry Red SG guitar right next to me. The SG body was lying smashed up next to me on the stage and I grabbed it and made a dash for it. But an eagle-eyed roadie grabbed me and ripped the body out of my cradled arms. You can't imagine my disappointment. I subsequently wrote to Pete to tell him and hoping he would take pity on me and send me a smashed up body but I didn't get a reply. (If you are reading this, Pete, I would still love one.) That one gig made me a Who fan for life. As for the recording of the gig, it came out really well, but I lent it to a mate and never got it back. I did buy a t-shirt of the gig from a seller outside and still have it somewhere. I wouldn't be able to get it over my head now.

21 NOVEMBER 1970
UNIVERSITY, LEEDS, UK

GERALD CLEAVER

I think they were better the second time they came to Leeds University in 1970. The first time I'd gone with fellow students, and the second time with my then girlfriend. She was coming up to see me and I managed to get tickets by a fluke. I'd not been around when the tickets first went on sale and they'd sold out. But the next day they found they had ten they'd forgotten to sell and I just happened to be walking past the counter when they made the announcement in the student union. I was first in the queue. This was probably the loudest I ever saw them. My ears were ringing as I was walking back to where I was staying and were still giving me some discomfort several days afterwards. (Since then, I've started being more careful about where I stand.) It was only after that that I started seeing them in seated venues and it wasn't the same. If you got excited and stood up you were sometimes made to sit down again. I don't think their music is music for sitting down and nodding to.

26 NOVEMBER 1970
MAYFAIR, NEWCASTLE-UPON-TYNE, UK

IAN DALGLEISH

On the date they were first due to play, only two of them turned up so the support act, Curved Air, did an extended set. As we left, it was announced that we would get a ticket for the rearranged date. The wide boys left early, got their tickets and then ran round the back to sneak in the fire escape door and leave again with a couple more!

5 DECEMBER 1970
THE LADS CLUB, NORWICH, UK

DAVID NOBBS

The venue was fairly small and wider than it was long. The music was so loud you heard it twice – once when it came towards you and then again when it bounced off the rear wall! I had met Roger Daltrey earlier that day. I worked just down the road from the Lads Club. I was an apprentice engineer so was the company dogsbody and was sent out to the corner shop to buy some tobacco for my boss. Roger was in there buying some cans of Coke. He was my hero at the time but I was too shy to speak to him. We just nodded to each other. I still regret not speaking to him.

TONY LANGFORD

It was a very high energy gig and they did a lot of the stuff on the *Live at Leeds* LP. My abiding memory is the volume. I don't think I ever went to a louder gig. The Lads Club was a bit of a strange venue. I don't know why they didn't use the UEA LCR.

ROB CRANTHORNE

It was a brilliant performance - with no guitar smashing! I was, and still am, an amateur photographer and in 1970 I had a Zenit E camera with a 58mm Helios lens, which I took to the gig loaded with high-speed Ektachrome film. I shot a number of photos from the audience, some more successfully than others.

ROBERT KELLY

I bought a ticket in 1970 for a gig at the University of East Anglia, which was due to be held on

5 October. A short time later it was postponed and rearranged for another venue, the Norwich Lads Club. But I made a mistake and thought it was a week later! So I missed the gig but I still have the postcard-sized ticket. It cost one pound and five shillings (£1.25).

6 DECEMBER 1970
FUTURIST THEATRE, SCARBOROUGH, UK

DIANE BAILEY, AGE 16

I went with friends to see them. We were seated in the second row, directly in front of the band. Roger Daltrey had a habit of swinging his microphone around in the air and I could not believe it when it actually landed in my lap! I was stunned, and my friend and I did a little scream into the microphone, before Roger hauled it back on stage, grinning at us as he did so. I remember a lot of screaming and Keith Moon going at 100 miles an hour on the drums, his face completely wrapped up in what he was doing. He really did have a wild man look about him.

It was over all too soon, but not before they trashed all the equipment, sending us and all the other people lucky enough to see them wild. What a night it was. I saw The Beatles before The Who, but I was too young really for that, and Black Sabbath and Deep Purple when they were just starting out. But the concert by The Who was the most exciting of them all. I can still see a young girl giggling into a microphone looked on by a grinning Roger Daltrey!

IAN DAWSON

I was at university but some of my peers were at the Tech and I went along with them. For me, it was quite a big gig to attend, having missed out on the Sunday night one night stands of the early to mid-Sixties at the Futurist – the Beatles, Stones, etc. Young teenagers did not have the cash for such events, although my sister and my wife both managed to get to many of those events through complimentary tickets given to theatre staff and shopkeepers carrying publicity posters. The Who was also priced at a comparatively low level for the time, costing me no more than I was paying to see lesser bands like Renaissance, Caravan, Hardin and York.

The Futurist Theatre was owned by the Robert Luff Organisation, who ran *The Black and White Minstrel Show*. They generally ran the summer season shows and an occasional out of season week-long booking. The Who were not booked by them, but by the Scarborough Technical College student body, which organised regular dances and concerts at both the college and outside venues. I believe the concert was subsidised by accumulated profits. The concert was well attended but far from being a sell out. It was a large provincial auditorium with a 2,150 capacity that was geared up for high season tourist shows rather than out-of-season events in a modest-sized town. Pete Townshend commented on the audience's enthusiastic and appreciative response.

CHRIS HAMLIN

I was a student of Scarborough Tech and a roadie for the night! My group of friends at Tech included Paul Woodhead, then Social Secretary and in charge of entertainments for the college. I remember being in the small group of people influencing Paul in decisions about Tech Dances and this one was the climax. The budget was the largest ever, £4,000, and to economise on costs a number of students would volunteer to roadie. In return for some extremely hard work, lugging amps, cabs and flight cases up the back stairs, six of us got tickets and seats for a rendition of *Tommy*. Memories include Keith Moon's entrance in a full gorilla outfit and the stage being strewn with plectrums and broken drumsticks afterwards. I had many souvenirs of the night, still have a couple of the plectrums (bought from Manny's Music in New York).

MIKE HOLLIDAY

I went with fellow students Rod Parker (sadly no longer with us) and Rob Hart. The drink beforehand was probably in the Toby Jug, a long-gone bar on The Crescent. We sat on the right-hand side of the stage, three rows from the front, and in the seats somewhere around D6. Entwistle was his usual calm self. Townshend was fairly reserved with just a few guitar bounces off the stage. Moon was spellbinding and absolutely brilliant, and Daltrey did his usual stage show. He lost the mic off the end of the lead whilst doing his trademark microphone swinging and it hit a young lady in front of us on the front row fair and square in the stomach. I think she thought she had bagged a good trophy but it was retrieved within seconds by a couple of roadies.

GUY JIBSON

They finished with a shortened version of *Tommy*, which ended on such a high that an encore just could not be expected.

PAUL MURRAY

I've still got the newspaper clipping. There was The Who and there was a support band called Spread Eagle and underneath it said 'and Scarborough's top DJ Paul Murray'. It was 17/6 (87p). It was originally booked for October. A pal of mine was the main one in the student union, and they did quite a few gigs over a period of a couple of years – Black Sabbath, Free. The Who was the biggest one that they did, cost-wise, and apparently there's still talk at the college of the loss that one made. At one point they weren't going to go on stage and Pete Townshend kicked off because it wasn't a complete sell out.

All the four band members turned up in different vehicles. I think Entwistle was in a Citroen. And there was a Range Rover, an old Jag and something else. There were a couple of artics for the gear. They had a 2,000 watt WEM PA system. I've got an amp which is 2,000 watts on its own now, but back then the biggest amp you could get was 100 watts. They looped them from one to another to another. They had 20 amps with 20 sets of speakers, from either side of the stage. That's why they needed an articulated lorry. And they had an entourage of 30 or 40, including a lot of Americans, because they'd played Woodstock only about twelve months earlier. It was a hell of an entourage with them.

I remember the rider was amazing; it was all booze. They had a bit of an argument because on the contract they said they wouldn't play within 50 miles of Scarborough and they'd been in Middlesbrough. They reckoned that Middlesbrough was 53 or 54 miles away and Dick Kilburn, who booked them, said it was 48 miles away.

DENIS PICKUP

I went into Bernard Dean's music shop on St Thomas Street the day before the concert to see if there were any tickets left. I remember saying exactly that to the assistant who replied with a laugh, 'How many do you want?'. There were about six of us, seated about ten rows back, with nobody in front of us and very few around us. The gig had no advertising and I remember looking around and seeing something like 300 – 400 there in the 2,000-seater Futurist. It was obviously a financial disaster, and the union were paying it off for years. The Who were great, as you would expect, but I wondered what were they thinking as they played to a near empty hall after all the massive gigs they'd performed.

ASHLEY SMITH, AGE 17

It was a strange gig, because so few people turned up. I couldn't believe it because they were massive. They'd done Woodstock and all that sort of stuff. It was so surreal, when you looked back behind you and saw all those empty seats. It was unbelievable. I kept the ticket, pinned to a copy of *Live at Leeds*, and I had a nice album collection, but you get into your teens and you start selling stuff to go out to nightclubs. I'd love to still have it.

15 DECEMBER 1970
MAYFAIR, NEWCASTLE-UPON-TYNE, UK

RUSSELL WILKES

The Mayfair had a small circular stage, but in the early Seventies, they got some really big acts, like Led Zeppelin and The Who and had a huge specially-constructed stage that took up half the dance floor. The Who went on for about two hours. They did 'Ohio', (the Neil Young song) which was about the National Guards shooting four students dead in America and I think they did all their hits. It was a great night!

20 APRIL 1971
HURST, BERKSHIRE, UK

VAL MABBS

I went to interview Roger at his house, the interview appearing in the *Record Mirror* on 8 May 1971. He had a nice house down in the country, before he bought and moved into Holmshurst Manor in East Sussex. I travelled up there by train and then was picked up at the station by one of the guys that worked with him in his beautiful Jensen Interceptor. I went down to his home and we sat out in the garden there and had a chat. He was a very nice guy.

7 MAY 1971
TOP RANK SUITE, SUNDERLAND, UK

BILLY HUTCHINSON, AGE 19

I was with five friends. It was a packed house and everyone was sitting on the floor. In my estimation, there were approximately 7,000 people in an average dance hall. I can't remember who was supporting them. It might have been Jethro Tull with Ian Anderson? Pete smashed his guitar into Keith's bass drum. They sang 'Substitute', 'Magic Bus' and 'My Generation'.

HENRY RACE, AGE 17

I saw them at the Top Rank Suite but everybody knew it as the Rink. It was just next to Park Lane bus station. Everybody played there in their prime – the Stones played there in the Sixties, The Beatles played there twice, Deep Purple and Free.

The other big venue in Sunderland was the Mecca ballroom. Local promoter, Jeff Docherty, put Sunderland on the map. He put on The Who at the Bay Hotel in Whitburn, just outside of Sunderland. It was the back room of a local hotel and Jeff Docherty used to rent it out on Friday nights. He'd been working there as a bouncer. I didn't go because it was three or four miles out of Sunderland and a bit of a logistical nightmare to get there. Then Jeff Docherty moved to the Mecca Ballroom, which was bigger than the Bay Hotel. He brought Led Zeppelin to Sunderland, Pink Floyd, Ginger Baker's Air Force. The Mecca Ballroom was the big venue in Sunderland for live music.

I was still at school. You just piled through after school. It was very much a communal, social kind of thing, going to see bands. If you were going to see gigs at City Hall in Newcastle, that was a sit down thing and you needed a ticket. It was a proper 2,400 capacity seated concert hall. But for the Mecca and the Rink, you could just turn up. I went with my girlfriend at the time, Alison. Five or six of us used to go and see bands even though we were only 17. We'd seen the *Woodstock* film and saw phenomenal scenes of The Who live and were thinking, 'Will Townshend smash up his guitar at the end?'. We were really quite gassed at the prospect of seeing The Who. My friend Ian Anderson was there, John Malarky, who we always called Muff for some reason, and Stephen Barry. We'd gone into the back room of the pub, the posh bit, and were sat there just being daft teenage kids, drinking our lager and lime, when in walked Daltrey and Entwistle with their guys. There were probably five or six of them.

We were completely overawed and we didn't go and say 'hi' to them. Daltrey was asking at the bar if they could buy a bottle of brandy. They wanted to try it first, and Daltrey took a swig from a glass and he said, 'This isn't good stuff. Go into the cellar and get me out a bottle of good stuff. I'm not paying for that.' A group of them just sat in the corner and drank their brandy, having a good crack. This was in a pub only three minutes away from the venue. We didn't say a word to them. We were frightened to even make eye contact.

We left soon after they did and walked back down to the Rink. By that time there was a fairly hefty queue and we realised that the white Rolls-Royce being driven backwards and forwards was Keith Moon's chauffeur-driven Rolls Royce. Keith had his body out of the back window and he was waving and shouting. 'Fucking hell, it's Keith Moon!'

I remember Townshend was being quite rough with his SG, but he didn't smash it. He had his white boiler suit on and his monkey boots. They were still playing bits of *Tommy*.

JOHN SANCASTER

50p – that's what it cost to see the greatest ever rock band. I was about three feet away from the pure unadulterated rock music. My friend John managed to grab Keith's drum stick as he flung it and I managed to get John Entwistle's plectrum. As if that was not the ultimate way of ending the night, we went round to the back of the Top Rank which then led to the back of the Odeon. It was there that we saw Keith, Pete and John and were lucky enough to get their autographs. Roger had gone off before them so we couldn't get his. The pen I gave to John was spring-loaded and it sprang just as John was going to sign. What a nightmare! But John opened a car boot, proceeded to look for a torch and then looked on the ground for my pen top, which he found. He then gave me his autograph, which I still have to this day.

JOHN MCCLUSKEY

I was there at the Top Rank. The ticket price was 50p!

13 MAY 1971
MAYFAIR SUITE, BIRMINGHAM, UK

GERALD CLEAVER

My girlfriend and I went and it was packed. This was the only show where I saw any instruments broken. It was a lot of new material which became *Who's Next*, which hadn't come out yet. Pete probably broke the neck of the guitar while he was playing it, or it was already damaged. But he dropped it when he finished and it just broke across his knee. It was the first time I'd seen them do some different tunes; they were trying to get away from just playing *Tommy*. They were doing things like 'Behind Blue Eyes', which no one had heard before, 'Water', which they'd done at the Isle of Wight, and they did 'I Don't Even Know Myself'.

14 MAY 1971
MOUNTFORD HALL, LIVERPOOL, UK

JOHN HARDY, AGE 19

There were no chairs so we sat on the floor. It was a great set. Moon was nuts, as usual. They smashed up the equipment at the end. They knew how to put on a performance. I also went to see them in Melbourne in 2004. Roger and Pete were as good as ever.

23 MAY 1971
CAIRD HALL, DUNDEE, UK

IAN DOBSON, AGE 16

This was a warm up show for a forthcoming British tour. *Who's Next* had been recorded and they were planning on going on the road on the back of this album. A number of songs on the album used synthesiser and performing these live involved using pre-recorded passages which I believe The Who wanted to test out on stage before embarking on the main tour. What better venue to do this than a backwater like Dundee? I attended the gig with my friends Graham and Harry, both sadly passed on now. Although the Caird Hall was on the tour circuit for most bands, this was special and caused massive excitement among us when the gig was announced. Graham was a massive Who fan and beside himself at the thought of his heroes playing the Caird Hall. The ticket price was £1.00, which was a fair outlay for a schoolboy at the time. I borrowed the money from my father and had to pay him back at five shillings (25p) per week out of my pocket money. Hence it took me a whole month to fund the ticket price – but it was worth it!

The show was on a Sunday night and prior to the gig we went to Forte's Cafe decked out in our flares, t-shirts and greatcoats. This was the event of the year and we were buzzing. I still have a very bad photo of us in the café, holding our tickets and beaming broadly. It was a fantastic show. I don't recall there being a support act. They played mostly the new numbers from *Who's Next* in the first half of the show and followed by excerpts from *Tommy* and a couple of numbers from *Live at Leeds*. I have a memory of them playing 'Magic Bus', which was a real highlight. Townshend wore his white boiler suit, Daltrey his fringed jacket, Keith was very animated and Entwistle was his usual enigmatic self, standing in the background pumping out the bass lines.

Security wasn't what it is today. If you knew your way around the Caird Hall, it was possible to get down to the dressing room area. After the show, the three of us blagged our way backstage and I managed to get the autographs of Townshend, Daltrey and Entwistle. Keith Moon wasn't there, but when we left and went round the back of the Caird Hall, we spotted a pink Rolls-Royce parked in Shore Terrace. On approaching the car, there was Keith Moon sitting in the back with his driver/minder in the front. We went over and Keith rolled down the window and signed autographs for us to complete the set. He was quite chatty and took the time to speak to us, which made our night. I sold the autographs a few years ago to a memorabilia company and got £300 for them. Little did I know at the time that my £1 ticket outlay would prove to be such a lucrative investment.

The *Melody Maker* used to have a letters page and they would give an album to the author of any letter published. I had drafted a letter to them slagging off The Who for various things. I had mainly written it to annoy my mate Graham (the massive Who fan), as it was all about 'favourite band' rivalries in those days. I had the letter in my pocket that night and I got their autographs on it as it was the only piece of paper I had on me. I remember being terrified that they might turn the paper over and spot the nasty things I was saying about them!

I saw many bands at the Caird Hall in the 1970s, including Zeppelin and Bowie, but the Who gig always stood out as one of the best. I saw them again at Parkhead, Glasgow a few years later and was blown away. But nothing beats seeing a band of that stature in your own backyard.

RODDY FERGUSON

It was the day after Scotland got beat 3-1 by England and a wet Sunday night in Dundee. Heavy, heavy rain. The reason I remember it is that I was standing on stage. Townshend had a white boiler suit on with big brown boots. Moon, at the back of his kit, had a big gong. In the 1960s, most cities had Mods and Dundee, just like any other city, had a lot of Mods. The boys in Dundee used to go to a coffee bar and play Small Faces and The Who. But this mob seemed to enjoy the B-side of 'My Generation' which was called 'Shout and Shimmy'. And these guys were going in the town and they were singing it all the time, and people assumed there was a gang. Because there was a lot of gang culture in Scotland at the time. Anyway, I got to know quite a few of these guys and we went to see The Who, and me and some of the yobs, as you might call them, went and sat right in the front seats. The people were coming in and saying 'excuse me, that's my seat' and we were telling them in no uncertain manner to 'eff off'. So the doormen came over but they didn't know what to do because, the brother of one of the guys I was with had a bit of a reputation in Dundee. They didn't want to eject us, because they didn't want to fall out with his brother. As a compromise, one of them came up with the solution. 'Do you want to stand on stage?' 'Yeah, nae problem.' So me and me mates were standing right beside them, actually on the stage, watching The Who.

GERRY FORTE, AGE 19

I was very much into underground music as it was called back then. My favourite band was (and still is) Led Zeppelin, who we also saw a couple of times at the Caird Hall. But my good friend's favourite band was The Who. I liked them but they were basically a '60s pop band to me, and not an underground band like Led Zep, Deep Purple, Tyrannosaurus Rex, Jethro Tull, Genesis, Yes, etc., all of which we'd seen come to the Caird Hall. I liked all the 'flashy" guitarists of that era, and to me Pete Townshend was basically just a chord thumper. But my mate loved them so when it was announced that they were coming to the Caird Hall I decided to go with him.

We solicited another of mate's mum (who became my mother-in-law) to stand in the queue for tickets at Largs music shop in Whitehall Street for us as we were all working the day they went on sale. She stood in line for hours for us and got the tickets for my mate, my other mate and his sister – now my wife of 44 years!

Our tickets were up on the second tier level, right above the right hand side stage as you faced the stage. In fact, it was directly above the amplifiers, speakers and other sound equipment on the stage, which was manned throughout the concert by a dedicated sound engineer who we could see and watch easily. He proved to be an integral part of the concert.

This was the *Who's Next* tour and some of the material had not been released yet. It was evident to me from the get go that this was not the pop group Who of the '60s – they were doing something different. They went on to play a lot of their well-known songs and all of the tunes that went on to become classics from *Who's Next*, which has become one of my favourite albums of all time. It was the first time that I had seen and heard a sound engineer use the equipment to play back the recorded loops of music as the band were playing live. That loop of recorded music turned out to be 'Won't Get Fooled Again', which we all became familiar with very soon afterwards.

We were all blown away by The Who's performance. It is one of the best concerts I have ever witnessed, and (chord thumper) Pete Townshend's compositions and use of sound were ground breaking for the time. We all thoroughly enjoyed their performance and it became a benchmark for us throughout the years. I can't listen to anything from *Who's Next* without a fond memory of that concert. We were at a lot of great concerts in the Caird Hall around that time, and this was right up there with the best of them, if not in fact *the* best!

JACK LORD, AGE 18

The concert I saw was part of their 'small city' short UK tour to phase out *Tommy* and introduce new material from *Who's Next*. The tour was a major surprise. I still recall sitting at home on study leave, with Radio 1 on, and the DJ saying, 'The Who have announced a short tour of smaller venues, and will be playing X, Y, Z… and Dundee.' His voice implied 'where?' and I was wishing 'pause and rewind' was available!

The Caird Hall was a 2,300 seat auditorium with perfect acoustics and a very busy venue in the early '70s, with a regular flow of artists on an early upward spiral. But the bigger artists didn't usually come further north than Edinburgh and Glasgow, so this was a major event for us. With no mobile phones, no internet, and hardly any of us even having a landline, a gathering in our local was required to allocate responsibility for the box office visit. I worked 100 yards from the Caird Hall, so it may have been me. My pals were all students.

I recall the immediate feeling of a huge level of energy from the band, probably only ever replicated by the punk phase in smaller venues, and of hearing a few of my favourite tracks from *Live at Leeds*, still a couple of songs from *Tommy*, and the whole of *Who's Next*, especially the magical 'Baba O'Reilly'. The encores were a blur of old hits, but they (almost predictably!) went well over the normal 'lights out' time. Our last bus home was 10.55pm and at 10.45pm my pals all got up to go. But I said, 'They're doing another encore – I'm not leaving yet,' and I stayed. This final number was 'Water', the perfect number for Daltrey swinging the mic about his head, Townshend's flailing right arm and Moon spraying himself, the stage and front rows with water fountains from huge gulps of bottled water, while half a dozen sets of sticks flew through the air. Guitars and drums remained undamaged.

As soon as it was over, I ran for the exit, down the huge sandstone steps, through the underpass and down the street to see my bus pull out of the terminus. I had no money for a taxi, so had to walk five miles home. My blistered feet were very sore, but I was absolutely convinced I'd made the right decision to stay to the end.

After this tour, The Who rapidly became a huge arena band, and I've never again been anywhere close to where they've played, but of the dozens of concerts I was lucky to see in my youth, that raucous night at the Caird Hall is easily the stand out for me. 'Baba O'Reilly' was my first mobile ringtone. It used to drive some colleagues bonkers if I'd left my desk and my phone rang, as it played the entire track – all seven minutes of it!

IAN MCALLISTER, AGE 20

It was a Sunday night. The sound was good. They obviously played all the songs that people wanted to hear. I was upstairs in the Caird Hall so probably seated. There are two specific things that I've always remembered about that gig. There were coloured lights on the lighting rig on the stage behind Keith Moon. He had bottles of water by the side of him, and I remember him tilting his head back during a song, taking a big swig of water and then spitting it high up into the air. As the water cascaded back down through these coloured lights, it created a rainbow effect. The water was then landing on his drum skins which bounced back up as he was playing the drums.

They obviously felt obliged to sing 'My Generation'. Townshend pointed out that he hated the song. He introduced it by saying, 'This is 'My Fucking Generation'.' I remember thinking 'oh, that's not very nice'. They didn't play the whole song, just a few verses. And then they went straight into another song. So they felt they'd done their bit for the fans. Even at that young tender age, I thought it was a bit dismissive. Other people might have thought it was funny. I didn't think that was very nice. They were a rock band. Townshend – he was quite coarse. But as a rock band perhaps they thought the audience wanted them to be coarse.

The only other thing I can remember is Daltrey swinging his mic around on his lead and the amount of gaffer tape to secure the mic onto the lead.

JOHN WALLACE, AGE 20

I was first and foremost a Beatles fan but I absolutely loved the music of The Who. My favourite track is the album version of 'Won't Get Fooled Again', because Townshend was getting into socio-political stuff and it's the most amazing track. The Caird Hall is a lovely building. It's got all these cornices and all that sort of stuff. But it's a venue that has had criticism over the years from rock bands about its acoustics. If you're playing acoustic music with a 60-piece orchestra, the acoustics are beautiful. But if you're listening to a rock band, you have to be facing the stage to appreciate the music.

Post Woodstock, people were getting into festivals and bands were having to have big, big PAs. The word at the time was that The Who were one of the loudest bands in the world, because the PA system was something like 10,000 watts. I saw The Beatles at the Caird Hall in 1963, and they were playing with eight Vox AC60s and a 100-watt PA system. I was only twelve years old. It was my birthday. And there was too much screaming going on.

The Who took it up a notch in 1971. My pal and I had bought tickets. We'd queued for them. And on the day my pal phoned me and he said, 'I'm stuck out of town with work. I can't make it.' So I was sitting there like Billy No Mates because I couldn't do anything with his ticket and I'm thinking 'this is going to be effing loud'. But it was no louder than any other concert at the Caird Hall. It was a great gig. I could not tell you what the set list was, but they did stuff from *Tommy*. They did the classics, the whole range. And there was some humour. They were starting up on a number and Moon said, 'Excuse me, Mr Townshend, what key are we playing in?' And they had to stop the number. And I'm sure Townshend said 'B flat.' A drummer doesn't need to know the key. It was a piece of theatre.

And there was another point where Townshend unplugged his guitar and said 'we're going to do an acoustic number'. Now, how do you do an acoustic number in a venue that seats 2,400 people with an unplugged electric guitar?

Townshend played Gibson SG 200s and just before the end of the concert, when he knew all hell was going to break loose and Moon was going to trash the drum kit, the roadie brought out another guitar for him. It was almost like a disposal guitar. He had a few precious Gibsons and a few SG 200s that he wasn't too concerned about. When he broke the guitar, it wasn't the guitar he'd actually been playing the gig with.

But then again, Ian Paice of Deep Purple used to do the Keith Moon thing, where he would just walk out of the drum kit, and Ritchie Blackmore would pull over a Marshall stack, a Marshall 4 x 4 with a Marshall amp on top. But if you looked at the stack that Blackmore pulled over, there wasn't a light on it. It wasn't plugged in! It was all showmanship. And The Who was a little bit like that.

1 JULY 1971
ASSEMBLY HALL, WORTHING, UK

JOHN PARSONS

I was there introducing them when they did their trial run the first time they ever played 'Won't Get Fooled Again'. They're my favourite band of all time. The first time I saw them was in the Florida Rooms at Brighton Aquarium, before they were well known. I think they were called the High Numbers then. The next time was at the Assembly Hall when Fred Bannister was putting them on. I worked with them three or four times at the Assembly Hall and it always used to be absolutely packed. It was 7/6 (37p) to get in. Fred used to put the bands on there and I used to do the announcements. I used to do the continuity and put records on. It wasn't a disco. There was no such word as disco in those days.

We would go in the dressing room and have a chat. Fred would leave four bottles of drink in the dressing room and they were all gone by the end of the show. They used to like their drink. Keith Moon turned up in his Rolls-Royce. He was an absolute nutcase but a nice guy.

I had the Assembly Hall booked that night in 1971 for myself, but Fred Bannister got in touch and said, 'Look, they want to get out and do one gig. They've always liked Worthing. Can you let me have the hall?' I forget what band I'd booked but I managed to rearrange it. Fred booked The Who. My ears were still whistling for about three days afterwards. I'm sure that's what's given me a hearing problem.

They were very loud. They had a whole new set of WEM amplification. It was massive. It took the whole stage up. They had a reel-to-reel tape recorder which they used for the intro to 'Won't Get Fooled Again'. I remember the manager going on and switching it on. They couldn't stop people coming in there. In the end they just had to open the doors. I reckon there were about 2,000 people in that hall that night. It was only supposed to hold 1,000 but I just lost count. It was absolutely heaving. There was water running down the walls because it was so hot. It was probably the best night ever there.

At the end of July 1971, The Who are off on another month-long tour of the USA.

2 AUGUST 1971
CENTER FOR THE PERFORMING ARTS SARATOGA SPRINGS, NEW YORK

KEVIN M KNAPP, AGE 13

I went with my brothers. The Who broke the attendance record with 35,000 people there, a record that still holds today. They were touring right after they put out *Who's Next*. The crowd was shoulder to shoulder and they were the first band to play there where they had to put a big screen outside so that everyone on the lawn could see the stage. It was an excellent show. Pete had his Esso jumpsuit on and, of course, smashed one of his guitars.

3 AUGUST 1971
THE SPECTRUM PHILADELPHIA, PENNSYLVANIA

GAIL THOMPSON MOYER

I remember Roger swinging the microphone, Keith being totally crazy and the instruments getting destroyed at the end of the concert. I went with a whole bunch of people from work, the Prudential insurance company. We drove all the way down to Philly from Newark, all the way back up that night and then came home to Pennsylvania the next day.

12 AUGUST 1971
PUBLIC MUSIC HALL, CLEVELAND, OHIO

ANDREW MIKULA

This was my first major concert and The Who were absolutely my favourite band, touring in support of *Who's Next*. It was pretty early in the tour. Cleveland was one of their favourite places to play in the States and they gave a show to beat all shows. They started out with 'Love Ain't For Keeping', with Townshend jumping around all over the place, Daltrey doing the lasso whip with his mic cord and Moon flailing away like a madman. I was in the upper balcony and you could feel the balcony vibrating, both from the loudness of the band and people stamping their feet and screaming. In the encore, after they closed the regular set with 'Won't Get Fooled Again', Townshend smashed his guitar on stage during 'My Generation', something I read he had stopped doing for a while. Moon kicked his drum set over and there was smoke everywhere. It really looked a lot like the closing of their set at the Monterey International Pop Festival movie. It was the wildest thing I ever saw in my life and I was absolutely physically drained from the experience.

13 AUGUST 1971
HARA ARENA, TROTWOOD, OHIO

MIKE ALLEN

My then girlfriend Sherri and I double-dated with my high school friends, Tom and Carol, to go see The Who on their *Who's Next* tour, the first rock concert for all of us. We loaded up in my '66 VW and started driving through the trees of Ohio. I took a short cut, got lost and was trying to make up time in pouring rain. But we made it. It was general admission and standing room only on the main floor. We were 75 feet back from the stage and the excitement and the energy of the crowd were amazing. The lights were off. The only thing you could see were the orange lights on the amps. Then the hypnotic beginning of 'Baba O'Riley' started… a one-minute opening of electric piano until Moon's drums started and then the explosive intro of the guitars. The lights came on and you could see the guys coming down from the sky. They had timed their leap with the lights coming on. It was great to have bought the album early and to know the lyrics and the songs to sing as we watched them being performed.

14 AUGUST 1971

The Who release* Who's Next*, featuring songs such as 'Won't Get Fooled Again' and 'Baba O'Riley', which are to become automatic set list choices from this point forward.

BARRY BELOTTI, AGE 12

In the summer of 1971, *Who's Next* came out. I was in seventh grade and my music teacher, Mr Dee, had an old reel to reel tape deck. We'd go into his music class and he used to play music. He was an old hippy. He wore a flowered tie and a three-piece suit and was bald as a cue ball. The kids would make fun of him. But I listened. I liked him. Music was a big part of my life and I went on to play drums myself.

He put this reel-to-reel on and he said 'now, you kids, I'm going to play something from a British band called The Who. This is a record that just came out and it's called *Who's Next*.' And he introduced the members and did a little background, and he pressed the button and he played the whole thing. He would stop the song and explain about the ARP synthesiser. He was getting really into it.

Kids were sitting in the back and passing notes but I listened to the whole thing. So the class ended and I walked out to the door – and he used to stand right at the door as the kids would exit – and I said to him 'Mr Dee, where can I get this record?' He said 'Lechmere Sales, Barry.' Back then, that was it. There were only a couple of places you could buy a record, and so I ran home and told my mom.

My father worked for the Boston Herald, in downtown Boston, and Mom said 'call your dad.' So I called my dad: 'Dad, on your way home can you go to Lechmere Sales and pick up this album? It's by a band called The Who and it's called Who's Next. So he gets home, he brings the record home and we had spaghetti dinner, and then I put it on the big stereo console that my parents had. That was my introduction to The Who. And there's a photo of the twelve-year-old me holding my copy of *Who's Next*.

Another class, a few weeks later, Mr Dee plays the whole of Tommy and he explains it. 'So this is the wicked uncle Ernie… This is where the followers start to rebel…'. He was such a story teller. I went back to thank him years later, after I got in with the fan club. He was still there, at the school. And I was able to thank Pete one night as well. I always felt like they were writing about me. But Townshend more than anyone. Especially *Quadrophenia*.

18 SEPTEMBER 1971
OVAL CRICKET GROUND, LONDON, UK

ALAN BUTCHER

I was here to see at least three of my favourite bands. The Faces and Mott the Hoople had been excellent and The Who had to follow them but The Who were (and are) the greatest live band in the world ever. I remember Pete Townshend sliding across the stage whilst Moon attacked the drumkit and threw broken drumsticks out to the audience. I was lucky to catch one half of a drumstick as I was down the front. Easily my favourite ever concert.

ROBBIE LATHAM

My friend's mum worked for EMI in London and that's how I got the tickets. It was a brilliant night. The stage was at one end of the ground. The Oval holds quite a few thousand people. It was an evening performance and the weather was fine. From what I remember, they all wore white boiler suits.

RONALD D ROWLANDS

This charity gig also featured The Faces, Atomic Rooster, Eugene Wallace, America, Mott the Hoople, Quintessence, Lindisfarne, Grease Band and Cochise. Keith Moon came onstage brandishing a cricket bat. He then proceeded to use the bat as a drumstick for the first number. I was up on stage and have never seen a group work a crowd like that. The smashing of the guitar was the only way to bring concert to an end. I was lucky enough to get a large chunk of Pete's Gibson SG guitar.

MIKE WINTERS

I hitched it from Southport to London with a mate to watch The Who at the *Goodbye Summer* concert. It was in aid of famine relief for Bangladesh and also to provide some much needed cash for Surrey County Cricket Club. The journey down was great, as after making our way to Knutsford Services, we got a lift on an empty coach that dropped us off in the centre of London. It was in the early hours so we found an all-night café before heading off to the Oval later that morning. The tickets were, bearing in mind that The Faces, Mott the Hoople, Atomic Rooster, Lindisfarne and others were also appearing, ridiculously cheap at £1. Introducing the acts was Jeff Dexter who was a London club DJ. We were told that The Who had a new sound system and, after The Faces set, Jeff Dexter said, 'If you think that was loud, wait until you hear The Who. They'll be rocking to them in Paris.'

They were brilliant. They played several songs from *Tommy*, with 'Pinball Wizard' going down a storm along with 'Won't Get Fooled Again'. Townshend had stopped smashing his guitar for a while but in answer to requests from the crowd he shouted, 'You want my guitar? Alright then you can fuckin' have it', and totally wrecked it. Pretty much as soon as he started, Keith Moon, who Townshend always said was a 'great joiner-inner', simply stood up and walked through his drum kit as though it wasn't there. Pure mayhem and everyone loved it.

I can't remember what time it all finished but everyone left the ground peacefully which, given the numbers – it was later reported that there were over 30,000 there – was quite something. It was late afternoon the next day before we got back home to Southport, having spent most of the night at Scratchwood motorway services. I've seen The Who since but that was the only time I saw them with their original line up. I'd seen the Stones (who were also brilliant) in Liverpool only a week before, but they were completely outshone by The Who.

PAUL BASS, AGE 16

This was my first big outdoor concert. It was a great day and I enjoyed most of the acts. Then the Faces came on and were brilliant, playing Rod's new song 'Maggie May' and really getting the crowd going. Rod even auctioned his leopard skin suit. I thought 'nothing can follow this' and then the announcement came 'all the way from Shepherd's Bush...' and The Who came on stage. I think Keith played the first number with a cricket bat. They ran through some of the early singles, which really got the crowd going. By the time they played 'Won't Get Fooled Again' I had forgotten there was a band called the Faces. The Who were in a different league altogether.

GER O'DONOVAN

I was just out of school from Cork and a mate from school had gone over to England earlier in the summer. There were 14 of us in a two man bedsit in Ladbroke Grove. We had a German guy, an American guy and people from my village in Ireland. We 'hot bedded'. The Who were phenomenal. A guy called Jeff Dexter was the DJ and I remember he was kitted out in cricket

The Who erupt in Caird Hall

Scientists' conception of the world diminishing to a "global village" was demonstrated last night as The Who, heroes of Woodstock, Isle of Wight, Monterey and countless other giant contemporary music venues, chose Dundee's Caird Hall as the stopover for a "new act" workout.

Not a seat was to be had in the hall, and the 2500-plus audience waited expectantly for the band, who had travelled up from London to Perth by chartered plane earlier in the day.

The huge scaffolding erected at either side of the large stage housed dozens of coloured flashing lights, and Scots group Poets, who preceded The Who, got an added lift throughout their act as the lights lent themselves sympathetically to some of their more delicate numbers.

These included selections from Crosby, Stills, Nash and Young, Santana, and a classic entitled "Yours is No Disgrace," penned by Yes.

An impressive start to the evening by Scotland's top group, but no match to the resounding acclaim generously awarded to The Who when they appeared onstage.

The stage was made to appear small with the amount of equipment the group have accumulated to lavish the best of sound on their admirers.

Fresh material

A whole batch of newly-written and previously unrecorded material ensued, including "Love Ain't for Keepin'," "Pure an' Easy," "Time Is Passing," "Bargain," "Too Much," and "Gettin' In Time Blues."

The group, Pete Townshend, Roger Daltrey, Keith Moon and John Entwistle, laced these new numbers with "Pinball Wizard" and "See Me, Feel Me," from "Tommy."

Then on to "My Generation," which flowed excitingly into "Magic Bus," with Roger Daltrey on harmonica.

Thus, The Who, with their stage act reckoned to be the most exciting ever in rock music history, showed as a group just how tight and together they are.

Action routine

Pete Townshend with his gyrating, jumping-in-the-air-while-playing routine, Daltrey with his full, raging voice, Moon with his comical-clown drummer antics and quiet dignified Entwistle with his bass riffs — all these attributes give the group a rippling, magic-dream quality which abounds with technical brilliance.

Twenty years or so from now, when all the youngsters in the Caird Hall are middle-aged, I'm sure the shattering effect of having been a Who guinea pig will still remain.

At the end of "Magic Bus" the audience, which had been erupting frequently after each number, erupted volcanically.

Thus much feet stamping and hand-clapping later The Who reappeared to give an encore rendering of "We Won't Get Fooled Again" which included a played back tape, recorded at Pete Townshend's private studio, which gave a cascading background effect to the improvisation of the group.

Backstage after the show the group admitted that they had got "good vibrations" from the Dundee audience on this their first concert tour for a year.

Pete Townshend said that the encore number gave them special satisfaction as the tape sequence took "months and months to work out."

Pitlochry Theatre's birthday treat

A concert in the Pitlochry [F]estival Theatre last night by [th]e B.B.C. Scottish Symphony [O]rchestra conductor James [L]oughran celebrated the [Th]eatre's 20th birthday and [ho]noured the 14th anniversary [of] the death of the founder, [Jo]hn Stewart.

A packed house attended the [co]ncert, part of which was [br]oadcast.

The programme opened with [th]e first performance of William [W]ordsworth's "Spring Festival [Ov]erture," dedicated to the [Th]eatre and its present artistic [director] ...

Clockwise from top left: Caird Hall gig review; Ian McAllister remembers Pete Townshend being less than enthusiastic about 'My Generation'; Barry Belotti with Pete Townshend; Paul Bass was at The Oval.

RECORD MIRROR, November 13, 1971

LIVE! International

he Who

AINBOW THEATRE, NSBURY PARK: The 10 are a group who viously never forget their ots, and still include an d Marvin Gaye number om their early Marquee — ffectionately known as e tent" — days, just to mind everyone. 'I Can't xplain', their opening mber is an indication of s, as is their somewhat aggerated cockney chat, ough entertaining it is.

'Substitute' had Roger ickly warming the dience and roaring about e stage, and by the time ey reached 'Summertime ues', Townshend was aping characteristically ngside him. But despite e Who's efforts the dience failed to respond enthusiastically as might expected, although their ran to almost two hours d included a wide range material. 'Baba O'Riley' s perfectly timed with oe backing, and Roger king up harmonica; and proved to be one of the favourites for me. The atmosphere on 'Behind Blue Eyes' a dramatic and mellower number for the Who was somewhat broken by Mr Moon crawling around the stage, and presenting his usual funny antics, though he provided some nice rhythms on 'Magic Bus'.

The light show throughout the act was handled well and blasted the audience with brilliant white and coloured lights during the inclusion of numbers from the 'Tommy' opera. As the set ran on several of the audience left, presumably to catch buses and trains, which brought the comment of "You can't leave now, this is an opera" from Pete.

No Who performance would seem complete without the rendering of 'My Generation', which after several calls from the audience, finally emerged, and proved to be worth waiting for. Even now it still sums up what the Who, with their driving rock style and straight from the bel quips, are all about — eve John Entwhistle, i dramatic black, look somewhat revolutionary a he pounds out som excellent bass lines.

Best part of the audienc were on their feet as th group left the stage - though they didn't returr and seemed not to b entirely happy with th venue — not that anyon could complain at the lac of an encore after such stint on stage. — V.M.

Clockwise from top left: Val Mabbs' Rainbow review for *Record Mirror*; Nig Greenaway (far left) recalls Keith Moon being outside the Reading University gig and giving the band a less than favourable review; The Oval cricket ground; The Who in action in Charlotte, North Carolina - photo Jack Garrett; Mike Winters hitched to The Oval from Southport.

gear. The Faces were really good but, my God, The Who blew them away. During 'See Me, Feel Me', which is a powerful, powerful number, they had big searchlights behind them which they shone out onto the crowd. The fists went up, the hands went up. It was a bit like the film you see of those Nazi rallies. They had the audience absolutely in the palm of their hands. If they'd said, 'Let's go and invade somewhere,' we'd have gone.

28 SEPTEMBER 1971
FREE TRADE HALL, MANCHESTER, UK

CHRIS KETTLETY, AGE 16

I only saw them the one time but it was one of the best concerts I've been to. Although I liked The Who's music, my sister and future brother-in-law were the bigger fans. My sister went to get the tickets in Manchester. On seeing a very long queue, she very cheekily asked if she could push in about three people back from the head of the queue. That is how we managed to be sitting in the middle of the front row. Brother-in-law to be went prepared for a loud concert, with ear plugs at the ready! They opened with 'Baba O'Riley', Keith donning headphones to listen to the backing track, and played a lot of their back catalogue and at one stage I turned to my sister and said, 'I hope they play 'My Generation'.' I'm sure Roger then said, 'Just for you, 'My Generation'.' The energy, musicality and atmosphere were wonderful, made so much better by being so close to them. On the night, my brother-in-law to be caught Roger's tambourine. I asked him to give it to me as a bridesmaid's present when they got married in 1972. I still have it!

2 OCTOBER 1971
UNIVERSITY OF READING, READING, UK

NIG GREENAWAY, AGE 20

My mates and I all lived in Reading and went along to a lot of gigs at the university. We were all just starting work and were not flush with cash. Some of us were doing further education so NUS rates were welcome. People from the town could go to events anyway, but had to pay a higher price. I had a mate who was a printer and the NUS cards didn't have pictures on them, so we all became 'students', even those who only studied music at the University on a Saturday night and sometimes at the disco on a Friday!

Who's Next had been out for a couple of months. I recall having the single of 'Won't Get Fooled Again' in a picture sleeve which I purchased after seeing it performed in the 'album spot' on *Top of the Pops*. I didn't get the album until later due to the aforementioned cash shortage.

For once, the curtains over the large windows down one side of the student union hall were left open so those that couldn't get in could see from outside. We heard some commotion from outside and later heard that someone had come up behind the crowd outside, saying 'The Who are a load of shit.' This caused the fans out there to turn round to set about this guy, and then they realised it was Keith Moon!

Inside the hall, we were all waiting for the band to come on when a hand with a hammer appeared over the wall of amps and started laying into them – that was Keith again. I've seen them at least eleven times since, but that was the only time with Keith and the band has never been so effectively introduced on any of those later occasions!

18 OCTOBER 1971
GUILDHALL, SOUTHAMPTON, UK

JEFF LEWIS

The Who demanded a top of the range bottle of brandy, which was not mentioned in the contract when I booked them. The said bottle would have cost more than two weeks of my student grant money so I refused to buy them one, pointing out that their £1,000 fee was the highest the students union had ever paid any act (later eclipsed by the £1,200 we paid Captain Beefheart on Cup Final Day, May '73). The Who got quite snotty, particularly their lighting manager John Wolfe who, with his gleaming bald head, was an intimidating figure. I stood firm against them despite all sorts of threats but the sell-out gig went ahead and they played a brilliant, savage set. It was probably the first time on that tour that they had played sober.

20 OCTOBER 1971
ODEON, BIRMINGHAM, UK

GERALD CLEAVER

We saw them at Birmingham Odeon. We were right down the front, on the left-hand side, and there was obviously a problem that we weren't aware of, which was that the PA wasn't working. Because we were down the front anyway, it was so noisy that we didn't notice. We were looking round, saying 'What's the problem? It sounds perfectly good to us.' And then the PA kicked in and we were almost knocked over. We then realised you didn't need the PA. You could see this big grin on Keith Moon's face because he knew what had happened.

22 OCTOBER 1971
OPERA HOUSE, BLACKPOOL, UK

NICK MOORE

I went with my mate Phil Crowther to see their last ever gig in Blackpool. We had managed to blag two tickets from a lad at Blackpool Tech by swapping them for my original copy of Black Sabbath's first album! The gig was absolutely fantastic. Daltrey was lashing his hair and jacket fringes around in gay abandon, Entwistle actually moved once or twice, and Moonie was an absolute thrashing loon. Townshend was strangely subdued for the first 15 minutes, but after exchanging 'pleasantries' with two or three ignorant, swearing hecklers, he told them to go fuck themselves and then instantly switched to his imperious, windmilling best!

The whole gig was utterly superb and all of us in the crowd worked up a proper sweat by dancing like idiots – much to the chagrin of the house staff. My everlasting memory has to be when Moonie launched a drumstick into the crowd and I caught it. That stick took pride of place on my misused homework desk for at least three weeks. Sadly, the lure of a copy of *Live at Leeds*, signed by all four lads, and complete with all the original tickets and memorabilia, proved too tempting and I swapped it. And, no, the album ain't for sale. I swear that my ears didn't stop ringing until we saw Led Zep at Preston Guild Hall in 1973. Them were't days lad!

JEFF CALVERT

I lived in Morecambe then and a group of about 15 of us got tickets but, as we couldn't drive, we travelled on public transport – Ribble Buses as it was then – to Blackpool. I remember wearing my brand-new Ben Sherman shirt which, for those who remember that brand, were usually stripe or sometimes check in design. This was plain white and I thought I looked 'the business'. Not everyone believed it was genuine as it was plain so I repeatedly had to show the label to convince them. The concert was superb and Roger Daltrey with his flowing long hair was incredible, as was the volume! I remember seeing something fly through the air so I ducked out of the way, not realising that Keith Moon had launched one of his drumsticks into the audience. Someone three rows back got a great souvenir! It was a great day out and a fantastic concert for my first gig. I saw Roger Daltrey a few years back, when he hit the road doing the *Tommy* tour. He can still do it and was again fantastic!

PETER DOONEY, AGE 16

At the tender age of 16, I was sat quite near the front and the noise and visuals felt like nothing I'd experienced before. Right at the end Roger Daltrey threw his tambourine into the band pit in front of the stage and I ran forward, dived over the barrier and made a grab for it but another young man had exactly the same idea. We struggled and fought for a few minutes but I came out the victor – the proud owner of Roger's tambourine. I've travelled a lot since and somewhere along the way it was mislaid. Not to worry. I still have that wonderful memory.

24 OCTOBER 1971
TRENTHAM GARDENS, STOKE-ON-TRENT, UK

MICK FARR

We were a group of four lads aged 14 and 15 who attended Who concerts in 1971, 1973 and 1975. We were working class lads who happened to pass the 11 plus so went to grammar school. We had very little money in comparison to some at 'Grammar' so we tended to excel in sports and trying to outdo those with plenty of money and assets. As a kid, I had heard 'Substitute' on the radio and was always fascinated by the lyrics, never quite working out what sort of 'suit was made out of sack'. I always found the stuttering in 'My Generation' slightly weird, probably because there were a couple of kids at junior school who did stutter. However, 'Pinball Wizard' got me hooked.

Were we Mods in 1967 and 1968? A couple of years earlier, we had seen the fighting at Brighton and elsewhere and I had two older uncles who spoke about it. One was a Teddy Boy and the other a Mod. From what I saw and heard, I felt more inclined to be a Rocker. However, then the Parka appeared in the provinces. We bought them purely because of the fur around the hood and they were warm. Going to football games in those days was a cold affair. A Parka, and plastic bags inside your socks, kept you warm.

Everyone had a Parka and then the trouble started. The school confiscated them from anyone who turned up in one. 200 were impounded in one day out of 600 pupils. My mother was furious, mainly because of the cost and because she had bought it in the belief that it was a useful piece of clothing and nothing to do with gang warfare.

The Parka quickly disappeared to be followed by the 'original skinheads'. These were lads from the local secondary modern. They hated us and we hated them. They liked music performed by black artists, which morphed into Northern Soul, and we decided we hated black artists and chose a more 'psychedelic' code of dress, with a lot more denim and leather. Well, what we could afford, which wasn't much. I would have died to be able to afford to buy a pair of Levi jeans or Sta Prest. We could not, however, have our hair long. School had its own barbers for those that did! Finally, the original skinheads ended up on the football terraces and became proper nasty skinheads and we spent two years running from them until Slade came along and gave them a band to latch onto. We were shocked when one of us acquired a BackTrack album featuring The Who on one side and Slade on the other.

For my 14th birthday, my mum and dad bought me *Live at Leeds* out of a catalogue. I played it a lot and in particular 'Magic Bus'. From the paraphernalia inside the sleeve, I learned who The Who were. There was even a copy of their Woodstock contract. I had never been to a concert before and we read The Who were coming to Trentham in October 1971.

We walked. It was almost five miles but this was nothing to us as we regularly walked to Stoke City home games, which was three miles, and we would do anything to save what money we had. We were eventually let in. It was a Sunday, so we had been queuing outside the Gardens for some time. We walked past three or four huge lorries, which must have brought the band's equipment, and a very large Bentley motor car parked almost outside the main entrance. The statue on the front grille of the car was missing and I thought 'were all Who fans thieves?'. In later life, I learned the statues on Bentleys and Rollers were retractable.

I had been to Trentham Gardens before but never in the ballroom. It seemed huge. It quickly filled up. It was hot and the crowd noisy. Then they came on. Christ - the noise. The energy! It was louder than a plane taking off. They played a lot of *Tommy*, *Who's Next* and *Meaty Beaty*. The latter came out at the same time and I bought it some weeks later. I had a part time job, cleaning glasses at the bar at Port Vale Football Club, so for once I had a little bit of my own money.

Townshend, wearing white overalls, kept putting his microphone on the floor and dropping from a jump fully onto his knees with an almighty bone-crunching thud. Was he nuts? Towards the end, he pulled his trouser legs up to reveal two large knee protectors. Roger was all fringes and hair and microphone spinning and it took me a couple of Who concerts to realise the microphone was stuck on with a great deal of tape and that there were always a couple of spare microphones laid across the front of the stage in case they broke.

It was the energy I remember the most, and the smashing up of equipment at the end. Funnily, it seemed the right thing to do. The only disappointment was that they either did not do 'Magic Bus' or it was not as good as on *Live at Leeds*. And there was a bit too much *Tommy*.

30 OCTOBER 1971
ODEON, NEWCASTLE-UPON-TYNE, UK

HENRY RACE

I was there with two pals from school, on the front row of the balcony. We had a great view. I'd just bought myself a portable tape recorder with the shittiest mic ever and I recorded the show. I sellotaped the little mic to the armrest, although I missed the last 15 minutes because I could only afford one tape and it ran out. On the tape you can hear a 17-year-old me say, just before they came on, 'It's fucking marvellous when they star.' I digitised the recording and uploaded it to a file sharing site and about 10,000 people grabbed it.

It was the *Who's Next* tour. They played numbers like 'Won't Get Fooled Again' and 'Baba O'Riley'. Moon was playing with the backing tracks in his headphones and Townshend, taking the mickey, said, 'Oh, Keith finished before the tape. Most nights the tape finishes before him. So well done Keith.' I think he was playing Les Pauls by then. He had five customised Les Pauls numbered one to five, and was wearing his white boiler suit again.

PETER SMITH

They were at the height of their powers in the early '70s and easily one of the greatest rock bands in the world – and they knew it. I went to buy tickets on the morning they went on sale, only to find that the queue was absolutely massive. I joined it but soon began to realise that I had little chance of scoring a ticket. The box office opened and people started to emerge with their tickets. One guy came down the queue with a few spares, offering to sell 50p tickets for £1. Unwilling to take my chances in the queue, I bought one. It was a rear stall ticket, and not a particularly good seat, but I was in! I was delighted and counted the days to the gig.

The Who had just released *Who's Next*. It had started out as *Lifehouse*, a multi-media project symbolising the relationship between an artist and his audience. Townshend developed his new ideas for the concept in his home studio, using lots of synthesisers, and a series of experimental concerts were booked for the Young Vic in London. However, the concept proved too complex to implement and it eventually became a much more straightforward rock album. This tour featured the first live performances of 'Baba O'Riley' and 'Won't Get Fooled Again', both played with a synthesiser backing track.

I arrived at the Odeon in time to catch support band Quiver, who you could rely on to warm up the audience. The Who exploded on stage to a massive roar from the audience, and for 90 minutes or so played a loud, incredible high energy performance. The opening songs of 'Can't Explain' followed immediately by 'Substitute' just can't be bettered. Townshend commented on the 'Baba O'Riley' backing track, saying, 'We've been waiting for the day that we'd stop playing before the tape finished, and this was it!'

'Magic Bus' included a lengthy jam, with mouth harp from Daltrey and much arm swirling by Townshend. 'Won't Get Fooled Again' had recently been in the charts and was a crowd favourite, and a personal highlight of the concert for me. Townshend closed by throwing his guitar in the air and letting it crash to the stage, even though the audience, me included, were shouting 'smash it, Pete!'.

4 – 6 NOVEMBER 1971
RAINBOW THEATRE, LONDON, UK

VINCE JORDAN

It was the opening night at the Rainbow and The Who were the first band to play the theatre when it changed its name. I was sitting 13 rows from the stage, bang in the middle of the auditorium. Can-can girls brought The Who onstage after support act Quiver had finished. The Who played a great set, including many tracks from *Who's Next*. 'See Me, Feel Me' had the now customary searchlight illuminating the theatre and my ears were ringing for three days after the concert. It's still the best gig I've ever been to.

VAL MABBS

I was lucky enough to meet The Who and see them in later years, primarily because I worked for *Record Mirror*. I saw them when they opened the Rainbow Theatre, formerly the Astoria, in Finsbury Park. That's one I definitely know I went to – a great concert. In later years, Keith used to spend time at the London pubs that we frequented. For all that he could be crazy I thought that he was a really nice guy. He taught me how to drum paradiddles, which I had no idea of before. That was nice.

The Who finish 1971 with another American tour.

20 NOVEMBER 1971
CHARLOTTE COLISEUM
CHARLOTTE, NORTH CAROLINA

JACK GARRETT, AGE 14

I and brothers Tommy and Harry Graham drove to this show in my friend's yellow 1968 Karmann Ghia four-speed. It was the dead of winter and freezing cold but we made the two-and-a-half hour trek without complaint because these guys were at their peak and we were fanatics. We played Who cassettes all the way and arrived well ahead of time. The concert was a sellout, although some seats were still available on the day of the show. I remember the tickets were $4.50, $5.50 and $6.50. We bought well in advance and opted for the most expensive ones, although the three of us still ended up with nosebleed seats at the top of the arena.

I was determined to get a decent recording of the concert and smuggled a friend's battery operated 'portable' reel-to-reel deck under my heavy winter coat. This went undetected for the entire show, even when I used a flashlight to flip the reels. Unfortunately, it was a loaner and I didn't realise you had to press play *and* record to get it to work. Imagine my disappointment when we tried to play it back on the return trip and discovered both sides of the tape were blank.

The concert was the loudest I've ever attended and opened with 'I Can't Explain' and 'Summertime Blues'. There were some sound problems and feedback during the first few numbers and the crowd was ordered to sit down at one point. I remember they played an extended version of 'Baby Don't You Do It', 'Magic Bus' and several numbers from *Tommy*. They closed with 'Naked Eye', which we found an odd choice. The crowd went wild when they performed 'Won't Get Fooled Again'. The blinding spotlights were behind the band, creating a great silhouette effect.

While they were always my favourite band, this was to be the only time I would see The Who in concert. I was in the audience at the Greensboro Coliseum on August 2, 1974 for the Eric Clapton show when Pete Townshend and Keith Moon were brought onstage for the encore. They performed 'Badge' and 'Little Queenie' with Clapton's band. Earlier in the show, Vivian Stanshall brought Moon onstage and he smashed a toy guitar filled with cuts of raw meat. Moonie, who was wearing an Army camouflage jacket and blue jeans, swept the cold cuts into the audience and the concert continued.

9 DECEMBER 1971
THE FORUM, LOS ANGELES, CALIFORNIA

PAUL JOSEPH

I was in high school, living in Glendora, so it took about an hour to get there. I was totally blown away at how these four guys sounded. It was if the heavens opened up and poured forth an indescribable energy. Keith Moon was a show unto himself, a blur of motion and joy. Pete Townshend seemed to be upset with a roadie near the top of the show as he was yelling at someone off stage. It went on for a couple of minutes, with Pete looking displeased about something, pointing at this or that on the stage while he was yelling. Other than that, it was The Who, as you'd expect them to be, astounding in every way. I know that I'll not witness again, anything that even comes close to what I heard and saw that night. They were truly amazing.

12 & 13 DECEMBER 1971
CIVIC AUDITORIUM SAN FRANCISCO, CALIFORNIA

JIM FORSTER, AGE 14

It was the first concert I attended in the big city. I was a huge Who fan and I remember threatening my father that I would ditch school to get a ticket. He went on his lunchtime and got me what may have been the last ticket available because he could only get one. I think the cost was $5.50. I saw them more recently in 2006 and paid $225! Back then, I was too young to drive so I convinced my brother to drive. The show was incredible and Keith was a jovial, acrobatic clown. Pete was still into jumping high in the air and often landing on his knees. Roger had mastered the mic swing and his voice had not begun to show the slightest wear. I think they were probably at the peak of their ability to perform at a very physical level of high energy. This show still rates in the top five of all the concerts I have attended.

My brothers both saw The Who in the late 1960s. My mom was an opera fan so one year my brother gave her the *Tommy* album for Christmas!

15 DECEMBER 1971
SEATTLE CENTER COLISEUM SEATTLE, WASHINGTON

STEVE MYERS, AGE 19

I and my friends gravitated to the English rock groups as superior to our American counterparts. I had followed The Who since 1964; they were the equal of the Stones in the second tier behind 'the lads'. Since I was not a wealthy lad, I pawned my darkroom enlarger to afford the trip up from my home in Portland, Oregon. It's about a three-hour drive and I went up in my 1965 blue and white VW bus. I was far from the stage. It was packed, loud (of course) and a damned fine show. Driving back home post-concert, I stopped at a light and the band's limousine glided through the intersection right in front of me. I honked and waved and Mr Townshend shot me a thumbs up from his seat by the window.

1972 sees John working on his second solo album in April and May. The Who are recording at Olympic Studios in London in May and June.

AUGUST 1972
HOLMHURST MANOR, WEST BURWASH, UK

KEITH ROWLEY

Me and my (now ex) wife Beverley, and my brother John and his wife Rita (who were on holiday from Canada) were invited to Holmshurst Manor, Roger's mansion in East Sussex, just after his daughter Rosie Lea was born. Roger had just paid £30,000 for the house, but it must be worth several million pounds today. I remember that Roger needed a pen for something but couldn't find any in the house so we had to troop down to his local pub, The Kicking Donkey, to borrow one!

In August, the band embark on a European tour.

9 SEPTEMBER 1972
FÊTE DE L'HUMANITÉ, PARC PAYSAGER DE LA COURNEUVE, PARIS, FRANCE

OLIVIER COIFFARD

In front of a 400,000 audience, The Who made their debut on the biggest stage at the Fête de l'Humanité. They seemed very happy to be there. But at the start of 'Long Live Rock' a blackout plunged the whole concert into darkness. The band left the stage. Pete Townshend returned to the main stage with a megaphone in an attempt to explain to the audience that the band would return as soon as the issue was resolved. But alas, after ten minutes, the electricity still had not come back on and the rain slowly began to fall…

NOVEMBER 1972
MORGAN STUDIOS, LONDON, UK

DENNIS DUNAWAY, ALICE COOPER BAND

Keith came to the *Billion Dollar Babies* recording sessions. He was wearing novelty glasses like the Groucho Marx model with the big eyebrows and moustache, but the nose was a limp penis. Lots of other musicians showed up – Donovan, Harry Nilsson, Rick Grech, Marc Bolan, and Flo and Eddie – and it turned into a super jam. Harry was too drunk to walk a straight line but he was playing piano and singing surprisingly well. Everyone sounded great except Keith, who kept falling off the drum stool and couldn't come close to keeping time. However, he did manage to keep it together enough for great renditions of 'Bang a Gong' and Harry's song, 'I Want You To Sit On My Face'. Everything else was sloppily incoherent, although Keith had everyone dying laughing.

1973 sees The Who buy an old church hall in Battersea and start recording their new album,* Quadrophenia, *whilst Ramport Studios is taking shape. The Who tour* Quadrophenia *in late 1973.

28 OCTOBER 1973
TRENTHAM GARDENS, STOKE-ON-TRENT, UK

STEPHEN BOSSON

I went with my best friend Neil Buckley. We were both in our early twenties. We both loved

The Who and had bought *Tommy* and *Who's Next*. It was a cold, dry midweek evening and the concert was a sell-out. This was the first Who venue of the UK *Quadrophenia* tour – other legs included Wolverhampton and Manchester before dates in London. Pete had already stated in the press, prior to the release of the album and the start of the tour, that he wanted to fine tune their performances by first visiting the 'lesser provinces' so that when performing in London, they would be at their peak. This was a typically caustic Pete comment and controversial at the time.

Trentham Gardens was quite an intimate venue and The Who's massive PA system was quite intimidating. The show opened up, highlighting Roger's long all blond curls, whirling mic and tassels, Pete's windmill guitar actions and attitude, John's stoic but brilliant bass and Keith's quite sombre but eye-catching drumming.

After the first songs from *Quadrophenia*, you could sense the frustrations of the crowd and the band, who it seems were having problems translating the complex structure of the studio sound and performing it live. Pete was changing his multitude of guitars very frequently. The crowd were by then calling out for more familiar Who songs, including 'Magic Bus', a song I personally wasn't aware of.

Townshend got so fed up with the interruptions that he abruptly stopped mid-song and, very angrily and swearing loudly, said 'we are not playing 'Magic Bus'. We are trying to educate you Philistines!'. They carried on playing a selection of songs from *Quadrophenia*, finishing with 'Bell Boy', with Keith Moon's vocal solo being sarcastically applauded by Townshend.

The second half of the set started with The Who playing their back catalogue, which received a very enthusiastic response from the crowd. They ended the set with 'Magic Bus', and I saw for the first time why the big concert song, that included solos from all the band members, was such a crowd favourite – a brilliant end to a controversial concert. So – no smashing guitars, Moon stayed conscious throughout and Daltrey and Townshend didn't fight. Simply the best live performance I've ever seen in over 50 years of going to gigs.

MICK FARR

We are the guinea pigs. We will be the first people to hear *Quadrophenia*. By now I had bought a few Who albums and learned about their so-called Mod roots. This was a painful, muddled concert because we did not really understand what Townshend was on about. It took years, until the film came out, before we did. There were no breaks in the music. There was a weird backing tape with sounds of the sea and seagulls which reminded me of *Sgt. Pepper's*. And that was crap as well. One of our brethren had bought The Beatles' famous album and we could not understand why anyone thought it was any good – we wanted short, rocky songs not long-winded stories.

The tape kept breaking down and we all found out who Bob Pridden was. He was being tortured on stage by Townshend as band and sound technician were not in harmony. A couple of years ago my dad, in his mid-eighties and still with us, spotted and bought me The Who *Live at Hull*. It was made the night after *Live at Leeds* as a back-up. The Hull recording had been kept by Bob Pridden all those years and it was he who released it. He was right – it was better than the Leeds concert.

As a result of seeing *Quadrophenia* live, I never bought the album and still don't own it. But after the film, and later Oasis, I started wearing Mod regalia and 'inherited' (it was left at our house by one of my son's friends – they were 15 or 16 when Oasis appeared) a 1962 Canadian fishtail Parka which I wore for a while and still wear at parties for a laugh. So, did all of this Mod culture and all these stories influence me? Yes, they sure did.

29 OCTOBER 1973
CIVIC HALL, WOLVERHAMPTON, UK

ROB TITLEY

In the 1970s I had the privilege of seeing The Who three times in concert in consecutive years. On the first occasion, the ticket cost £2.20 and I had front row balcony seats. The *Quadrophenia* album had been released three days previously and the band played a large amount of material from what was at that point in time a relatively unknown album. It didn't matter as the crowd went crazy right from the beginning.

GERALD CLEAVER

One of the best times I saw them was with a group of friends, on the *Quadrophenia* tour. I know the band themselves didn't like it as much. We hired a bus from Leamington Spa because there were so many of us, and we got the timing wrong so had to hang around afterwards until the bus came back to pick us up. I got to speak to Entwistle. He had a chauffeur who looked quite like him. They'd got three or four limousines outside – they obviously travelled separately. Entwistle came out first whilst we were all chatting to his chauffeur. He came over and joined in the conversation. I can't remember anything about the conversation other than that he was very friendly. People were very polite and there was no screaming or shouting or 'I love you John' or anything, so he was quite affable and happy to join in the conversation. And then he got into the back and off he went at great speed.

They weren't happy with the tour. This was the second or third date on the tour.

They got a drum riser for Moon which lasted the first date. It just didn't work for them. They needed him on the same level and close to them. They had played *Tommy* so long they knew how they were going to present it and they knew what they were going to say. They hadn't worked out how they were going to explain *Quadrophenia*. I think Daltrey just wanted them to play it and Townshend wanted to explain it, so they had that bit of tension between them. Like a lot of his ideas, Townshend knew what he was on about but he couldn't always put them across for people to hear and understand, and not everyone wanted to hear that. The album had only just come out and it's another long work and another one where they had tapes. There was meant to be quadraphonic sound, but that didn't work. But, having said all that, it was one of the best times I saw them. Perhaps all this tension meant they were really giving it some.

One of the things that set The Who apart is they were very, very funny. They were usually quite chatty but very good at deflating each other or pricking each other's pompous comments, usually Townshend. But whoever was being pricked didn't mind. It was part of the show almost. The way that Moon used to rattle the drum kits and pretend he was introducing the orchestra and wave his arms about. And he'd always play up. If he threw the drumsticks in the air and actually caught them on the way back down, which was rare, he'd always have a big grin on his face and they'd all look at him. They had a tremendous banter. They were very, very funny. On stage they had a good joke, a good laugh.

1 & 2 NOVEMBER 1973
KING'S HALL, MANCHESTER, UK

LESTER MCILWAINE, AGE 18

I grew up in Northern Ireland during 'The Troubles'. My only exposure to commercial music was via Radios Luxemburg and Caroline and (of course) BBC Radio 1, with the usual practise of listening to a cheap transistor radio under the bedclothes at night. In the early '70s, I discovered the Pound Club in Belfast where I spent a lot of time watching live music. I managed to catch Rory Gallaher (Taste) and Van Morrison when they were on the rise. I lived in Lurgan, Co Armagh, about 20 miles away, and used to go down to Belfast on the train on Saturday afternoons without my parents' knowledge. They were avid churchgoers and, apart from my age and the violence that was prevalent at that time, would have been horrified to know what I was up to. They forbade my elder brothers (both considerably older than me) from listening to Elvis, Cliff, etc. and that Devil's music better known as 'rock 'n' roll'.

I first saw The Who on *Top of the Pops* doing 'I Can See for Miles'. I had to nip over to my neighbour's house on a Thursday night to watch it; my parents wouldn't countenance it in our house. Then came 'Pinball Wizard', which prompted me to go out and buy *Tommy*. I was hooked. I was saving my money to buy a motorbike but my folks wouldn't let me have one so I tortured them by buying my first hi-fi system (deck, amp, speakers) and installing it in my bedroom. I left Northern Ireland in October 1973 at the age of 18 to study civil engineering at the University of Manchester.

When the *Quadrophenia* tour was announced, the Manchester shows sold out really quickly but I was lucky enough to score a ticket for 50p from one of my classmates who couldn't go. The venue was the King's Hall, Belle Vue. It was pretty tacky but big and pretty well organised. It's long gone now. I was still very new to the whole live concert scene and absolutely blown away by the energy, the volume, the clarity and the sheer power of the band's performance. They opened with 'I Can't Explain', then 'Summertime Blues' and 'My Generation' in quick succession. Then Pete stepped up to the microphone and, casual as you like, said 'We're gonna play our new album now.' And, of course, it was in quadraphonic sound.

The waves started crashing from the back of the venue behind us and they launched into

'The Real Me'. I'd heard *Quadrophenia* before the concert and was already loving it. It's a technically and musically brilliant album and I was amazed how they managed to reproduce it so well in a live concert. I was completely transfixed and got totally lost in the music, with one fantastic number after another. (I have a musical ear; my parents sent me to classical piano for seven years. I hated it and told my teacher I wanted to play blues and ragtime. She was appalled. I stopped going to lessons, using studying for O-levels as an excuse). I was completely stunned by the end of the show and raved about it for days afterward; I drove my mates round the bend. That concert cemented my status as a Who fan. I still have some crappy Instamatic photos I took during the concert...

I remembered hearing about the Mods and Rockers on the BBC news while still growing up in Northern Ireland (I love that soundbite on the album!) so the *Quadrophenia* storyline was easy for me to follow. I then made it my business to learn as much as I could about the band and get hold of as much of their music as I could. A certain enterprising chap several years older than me had set up a record store called Virgin Records within walking distance of the Engineering department and I spent a lot of time there. There were a lot of shops around Manchester even back then, but Virgin was always that all-important 20p cheaper for an LP.

STEPHANIE THOMASON

I was introduced to the music of The Who when I first became a Mod and member of the famous Manchester Twisted Wheel Club and, of course, The Who were the group of the Mods. I was very lucky to see The Who several times in the Sixties. I lived in Manchester and they appeared at a number of different venues in the area at that time. Being fanatical about them, I would usually turn up at the venue with a friend at least two hours before the doors opened so we could be first in and head straight for the front of the stage, where we had the best view in the house, but of course we would come out at the end of the show with our ears ringing! One of my favourite memories is of the time we saw them at Belle Vue. As usual, we were right at the front of the small stage. We couldn't have got any closer and, at the end of a fantastic show, Keith kicked over his drums and Pete decided to demolish two amplifiers with his guitar. The top one toppled over and came crashing down towards us and my friend and myself had to jump back and run pretty sharpish. Now that's something you don't easily forget from a Who show! I can also recall many instances of dodging Keith's flying drumsticks at the end of each show and picking one up, along with a plectrum of Pete's - they were treasured possessions!

In 1967 I went on a trip to London with three friends and couldn't wait to get to Wardour Street, where The Who's fan club was based. I remember running up some stairs to the office and bursting in hoping to find any member of the group there. Instead, a bemused Chris Stamp patiently explained 'the boys' weren't there! We tried the Marquee the following evening thinking they may be playing there, but no luck there either. But I didn't come home entirely empty handed after I bought a pair of pink crushed velvet trousers exactly the same as Roger's from a shop where I heard he had got his from, on the King's Road, London. Wow, I thought I was the bee's knees!

5 – 7 NOVEMBER 1973
ODEON, NEWCASTLE-UPON-TYNE, UK

BILL MONKS, AGE 18

I saw them for the first time at Newcastle Odeon on Bonfire Night 1973. There weren't just fireworks outside that night but fireworks on stage too when problems with the backing tracks on some of the *Quadrophenia* songs led to Townshend hitting one of the sound engineers and walking off stage. After a short delay, they were back and performed a blistering set.

PETER SMITH

The Who were calling at Newcastle Odeon for three nights. Demand for tickets was high with people queuing overnight. I queued in the snow for several hours, getting quite poor seats upstairs for myself and a group of mates. We knew from reports in the press that The Who were planning to play the entire *Quadrophenia* album. We weren't familiar with it, so although we were looking forward to seeing The Who, we were a little unsure how much we would enjoy material that was totally new to us.

Support came from Kilburn and the High Roads, featuring Ian Dury, who wore a Teddy Boy drape jacket. Their music was pub rock-cum-rock 'n' roll. They went down quite well considering. The Who came on stage and started with 'I Can't Explain', 'Summertime Blues' and then 'My Generation'. They then proceeded to play *Quadrophenia* and got as far as '5.15' when things began to go wrong. The backing tapes they used to play along with weren't working correctly, and apparently not at all during '5.15'. Pete went crazy, totally losing it. From upstairs, we could see him shouting at someone to the side of the stage; he then started punching the guy and smashed his guitar to the floor of the stage. He started ripping wires out of their equipment. Roger, Keith and John were just staring at him, wondering what on earth he was doing. The theatre obviously realised that something was going seriously wrong, and they dropped the big white safety curtain.

We sat in darkness for 15 or 20 minutes until the band reappeared. The Who launched into 'Magic Bus' followed by a lengthy jam (possibly including 'Spoonful') and finished by playing 'My Generation' for a second time. Pete was in a wild, strange mood swearing at us all, calling us 'fucking bastards'. I recall being very upset with him and shouting back at him, as did many others. He then smashed his Gibson guitar, threw one of his amps to the ground and Keith crashed through his drums, knocking them all over the stage. They received 'thunderous applause' as they left the stage.

My friend John remembers the gig thus: 'We were sitting downstairs to the right of the stage and I can remember seeing Townshend going off to the side of the stage a couple of times and that something was up. Listening in the audience, I could not hear anything amiss. Then after about half a dozen songs he went off stage and I think hit the guy on the soundboard. I swear I saw sparks and he stormed off. The rest of the band were stunned and for a few moments did nothing and then went off stage. Similarly, the crowd did not understand what was happening and for a while was silent. Then I recall the safety curtain came down and the crowd began to boo. Not sure if things were thrown at the curtain. After what seemed like a long time, although perhaps it was only five minutes or so, with the crowd getting very restless, the band began to play 'Magic Bus' with the safety curtain still down. Once the crowd began to cheer, the curtain was raised and they continued with 'Magic Bus' and then 'My Generation' and I think that was the end of the show.'

It had been a strange, surreal and brilliant night! We went home on the train, everyone talking about what we had just witnessed. I remember planning to go along to the next night's gig and trying to buy a ticket outside, but didn't. I wish I had!

JIM ROBSON

All appeared to be going well for the first part of the show. They came on and kicked off with 'I Can't Explain', 'Summertime Blues' and 'My Generation'. But we knew something was going wrong as they started to play tracks from the new album, *Quadrophenia*. We heard later that the backing tapes weren't working correctly causing Pete Townshend to lose it. You could see him shouting at a soundman at the side of the stage, which turned out to be Pridden. It turned into a scuffle with punches being thrown. Pete just went mad. He smashed his guitar on the floor of the stage and then ripped wires out of the mixing desk and amps. As all this was going on up on the stage, the fire curtain was brought down and we all sat in darkness for 20 minutes or so until The Who reappeared. They played a few songs but you could tell Pete was still furious and was swearing at the audience calling us 'fucking bastards'. He then smashed his Gibson SG guitar, threw one of his amps to the ground, and Keith joined in, knocking his drums all over the stage. Quite a night!

IAN POTTS, AGE 14

I met the band outside their hotel in Gateshead on the same night that Pete Townshend went on to famously smash the stage up. Me and a mate, both 14 years old at the time, heard they were staying at the Five Bridges Hotel just up the road from where we lived. As we had tickets for the Tuesday gig, we thought we'd pop along. There was no one around but just as we were about to leave a guy came out and asked if we were waiting for the band. On us saying yes, he said 'do you want to ride in their car?' pointing to a big Jag in the car park. Dead right we would! It turned out he was only going around the corner to get petrol but we couldn't believe it, riding round the block in The Who's motor. It turned out the guy was the road manager. Five minutes later, we were back round the front of the hotel. We got out and he opened the boot and then dished out these posters of Keith Moon lying naked on a bed. Then, best of all, the band came out, all four of them chatting away and signing the posters along with my ticket for the 6th and my *Who's Next* tape cover which I had brought with me. Sadly, two of the band are no longer with us and the hotel is no longer a hotel, but my memories are still with me all these years later.

COLIN PETERSEN, AGE 15

I've seen The Who a number of times, most recently in 2014 at Newcastle Metro Arena on the 50th anniversary tour, the first big gig my son went to; he was transfixed, especially as the tickets were four rows from the front. However, I saw the original *Quadrophenia* tour. In those days there was no internet, social media, etc. as we have now and no buying tickets a year in advance. You found out who was touring by word of mouth or via *Sounds*, *Melody Maker* or *NME*. You normally had to buy your ticket in person at the box office, so for a group like The Who this meant an early start.

I was still at school. I'd started going to gigs at 13, my first being Free at Newcastle City Hall, and seen the likes of Deep Purple and Led Zeppelin. The Who would be the biggest band I'd seen at that time of my life. My friend Jim and I caught the first number 39 bus from Washington to Newcastle at 4.45am, but when we arrived at the Queen's Cinema where the tickets were being sold, there was already a vast queue snaking away from the entrance. As we walked along the queue, we saw a group of school friends including Dave, with whom I still attend gigs today. We stopped and talked to them and, as no one protested, absorbed ourselves into the queue, significantly forward from where we should have been. Dave being Dave, he bought tickets for all three nights. Jim and I plumped for the third night. I think our rationale was that Newcastle was the beginning of the tour, or very early on, and any glitches would be addressed by night three. Little did we know about what glitches would occur on night one and how prophetic our thoughts would be!

On the morning after gig one, we attended school avidly awaiting a report from Dave. He told us about the backing track problems and the fight between Townshend and the sound engineer, with Moon joining in. He said the gig was great in some parts, shambolic in most. On the morning of gig three we awaited his report from the previous night. A bit subdued, he said, as if they were playing it ultra-safe and not what you expected from The Who. Off we went on the Wednesday evening, a quick pint or two in the Man on the Moon and then off to our first ever gig at Newcastle Odeon.

I can't remember the set list other than the whole of *Quadrophenia*, which I hadn't heard before, plus the other tracks you might expect, such as 'Won't Get Fooled Again'. The atmosphere was electric and the audience so, so excited. The band? Awesome. It was if they'd thought about the previous two nights and said 'fuck it, let's go for the jugular'. They were very much in their prime at that time: Daltrey shouting, screaming, caressing the lyrics, prowling the stages; Townshend all pent-up anger, aggression, a vast array of emotions absolutely flooding out in his playing and singing; Moon mesmerising, a whirlwind, not the best but still the most exciting drummer I've ever seen; and Entwistle, an un-moving presence for much of the time but with mesmerising bass runs. It's probably the best Who gig I've attended, although a few others run it close. We thought the support band, Kilburn and the High Roads, were poor. Later they morphed into Ian Dury and the Blockheads!

BRIAN DICKINSON

Myself and friends queued all night outside the Queens Cinema for tickets going on sale the next day. It was bitterly cold and I recollect stealing early morning milk from the adjacent office doorways. My then girlfriend brought us soup on her way to work – which was the least she could do since I was getting her a ticket! Our tickets were for the second night. I believe that there had been an altercation between Pete Townshend and one of the roadies on the first night. Great concert!

BRIAN GOULDEN

They played the *Quadrophenia* album at the Odeon on Pilgrim Street. I can't remember much about it other than they played *Quadrophenia* and they were good. They were very exciting. I was about 24, 25. I'd heard the album, I knew somebody else who had it, and it was played every day at work.

JOHN ROBSON

I first heard The Who in junior school when 'I Can't Explain' came out. I thought it was The Kinks and I remember saying to a lad in my junior school 'that Kinks new record – great, innit?'. He said, 'It's a band called The Who.' I first saw them on the final night of their visit to Newcastle on the *Quadrophenia* tour in 1973. I queued all night and it started to rain about 6 o'clock in the morning. A guy got right to the front of the queue and started pushing in and a copper got him by the hair and dragged him out. I thought, 'You've waited all night for a ticket and you've let yourself down like that.'

On the night, we were eight rows from the front and all of a sudden found ourselves on the grand piano in the orchestra pit, right at the front. Me and one of my pals got a drumstick each. We nearly got Pete Townshend's guitar because it was smashed to bits and lying on the stage. My mate leant across the stage and nearly got his fingers on it before a roadie came on the stage and kicked it away. I've got the drumstick framed with the tickets on the wall at work. My mate hasn't got his drumstick any more. His mother threw it out. She thought it was just a scrap bit of wood.

11 – 13 NOVEMBER 1973
LYCEUM, LONDON, UK

WAYNE PURSEY

Me and my friend Malcolm queued outside for 15 hours to get in. The queue became massive as the day went on. I remember being cold and uncomfortable because that was a long time in the queue.Some girls in the queue had come from Australia to see Yes but couldn't get tickets. When the doors opened, the queue became wider and dangerous. People were pushing, and if you fell you would have been crushed to death; that's not an exaggeration. People were looking out of surrounding office blocks to see what the commotion was about. I can't remember what we paid for the tickets.

We eventually got into the Lyceum. Roger Daltrey said that if the crowd didn't move back and stop pushing, the show would be stopped. The lighting rigs were moving. I wanted a closer look at Keith Moon and so I said 'excuse me, excuse me' etc. and managed to get to the front of the stage. I was staring at Keith Moon and he was staring back. He looked rough and unshaven, like someone who hadn't slept for days. I noticed drum sticks all over the floor. I was disappointed, as I thought he caught the ones he threw in the air. He then did a very impressive paradiddle around the kit. At that point, I thought I'd better not get separated from my friend so I made my way to the back of the hall.

After the three Lyceum shows, The Who fly to the US for a handful of American shows.

20 NOVEMBER 1973
COW PALACE, SAN FRANCISCO, CALIFORNIA

BOBBY ASEA

It had been a few years since the last time I saw them, in 1968, and I was very excited to hear their new songs in concert. It wasn't too far into the show before it became noticeable that Keith Moon was off on his playing. As the set progressed, he became worse at his playing, to the point where it got Pete's and Roger's attention. They continued to play even when Keith started to wobble in his seat. A roadie appeared and attempted to hold Keith in place in order for him to keep playing. Finally, it seemed that Keith was okay and the roadie left. At one point, Pete crossed back to the drum kit and it looked like he was trying to help Keith with his playing. But when they were playing 'Won't Get Fooled Again', Keith couldn't hold up anymore and collapsed into his drums. He was carried off the stage and left everyone in the house baffled and concerned. Roger and Pete addressed the audience, offering the explanation that Keith must have had eaten something bad that made him sick, and saying they would come back again in the near future to make up the show once Keith got better.

Apparently, that idea didn't seem like it was going to work so instead Pete asked if there was anyone in the audience that could play drums. I had gone to the show with my best friend, who happened to be a very good drummer, and we thought that this would be an unbelievable opportunity for him to play with The Who. Unfortunately, our seats were not close enough to the stage to make our way there before the hordes of others who rushed the stage. It wasn't long before some lucky guy was asked to join the band onstage. For obvious reasons the show lost its spark. They had to play some songs that were not some of The Who's strongest, and musically the show went downhill. Not long after this, it became known that it wasn't food poisoning that did Keith in that night. It turned out that his use of drugs and alcohol before the show that was to blame.

PAUL HUTCHINS

I was supposed to see The Who at Wimbledon Palais once. Keith Moon would always overdo things, like drugs and things and he was obviously incapacitated so they cancelled the gig that night, a Friday, and they said 'keep your tickets and we'll reschedule the gig' so it was all a bit mad. Everybody was all chanting 'where's The Who?' and they had to come on and say Keith Moon was inebriated and he couldn't come on. I'm not sure how often that happened. I'm sure it happened again on other tours. There was one time in America where he was so ill that they asked the audience if there were any drummers in the audience and a guy went up and did the whole gig with them.

STEVE ROZZI

I saw The Who perform at the Cow Palace in San Francisco the night Keith Moon couldn't finish the show and the band asked the audience if there was anyone in the audience who played the drums. This kid jumped up onto the stage and finished their set without missing a beat. He was blowing people's minds, including the other band members! He knew every song and didn't miss a beat.

MARTY MATHIS

You know what they say – if you can remember the Sixties, you weren't there? Well, insert the Seventies for me. As an innocent white suburban kid, I remember being wide eyed by the San Francisco culture of freaks and costumed people and open sexuality. I remember, too, the revolutionary quadraphonic speaker system set up, with half the speakers located behind the audience. During the intro to 'Won't Get Fooled Again', I swear I could see the notes passing me and bouncing back towards the stage.

22 & 23 NOVEMBER 1973
INGLEWOOD FORUM
LOS ANGELES, CALIFORNIA

MICK HICKS

I was management with The Wherehouse record store chain at the time and was at the after-concert party at the Sheraton Universal. My main recollection of that is having a five-minute chat with Roger Daltrey in the buffet line up. He was wearing a t-shirt with BB King's album cover *Indianola Mississippi Seeds* on it. Roger was very friendly and down to earth. I told him how much I enjoyed his solo album, *Daltrey*, that had come out earlier in the year and he appreciated that. I asked him about a song I hadn't heard before and which they played earlier that evening,

'The Naked Eye'. As *Quadrophenia* had just been released and I asked what the next record might be like. He told me the next release would be a collection of unreleased tracks. Sure enough, *Odds and Sods* came out next summer. It was cool because the next day at the record store I was able to tell a customer that was a Who fan and that 'I was talking to Roger Daltrey last night and he told me their next album was gonna be a collection of unreleased tracks'.

I saw an empty chair at the table Pete Townshend was sitting with Harry Nilsson so sat down for what might have been 30 seconds. I told Harry how much I loved his standards album, *A Little Touch of Schmilsson*, and Pete how much *Who's Next* meant to me. They were gracious and friendly and Pete asked my name. Then I got up and left. I vividly recall Keith in his gold lame suit going from booth to booth, drink in hand, introducing himself. He sat down at our table briefly after welcoming us with ''ello mate!'. I don't recall seeing John Entwistle there.

HARVEY KUBERNIK

I ran into Keith Moon in 1973 at the Century Plaza Hotel. I was doing a little bit of rock writing for the Hollywood press at the time. He was with Dean Torrance, of Jan and Dean, and Harry Nilsson. In *Sixteen* magazine or *Melody Maker*, Keith would still talk about surf music, so I bought him a t-shirt from the Con surf board company. It was a shop on Pico and Santa Monica Boulevard. He really flipped out because he was a surf guy and liked the wild abandonment of surf music. He wore that t-shirt on stage when they encored one night at the Forum in 1973, and I was invited to the party after. That was kinda cool.

25 NOVEMBER 1973
MEMORIAL AUDITORIUM, DALLAS, TEXAS

ALAN MCKENDREE, AGE 17

I first saw them two or three days after the infamous Cow Palace Keith collapse. I remember feeling a twinge when I heard the line 'like to help you son, but you're too young to vote' during 'Summertime Blues' because, alone amongst all the uni friends I was with, I *was* too young to vote. A friend had acquired tickets and we drove up in a group from San Antonio, a five-hour drive from Dallas. They were really good seats considering the place and time and our relatively 'newbie' state of fandom... about 20th row, slightly right of centre on the floor. I didn't get floor tickets again until 1989!

I don't remember any reference to Keith's 'problem' of a few nights earlier. He seemed fully recovered, as they played all the music I loved and I don't remember being drawn to him wondering 'what's wrong?'. It being very early in my Who career, I was focused almost totally on Pete as I revered him as the author and, so I thought, primary musician.

At the end of the show, Keith jumped out from behind his kit and one entire leg of his Levi's was missing, from the bottom of the pocket on down. This was immortalised in a backstage photo by Tom Wright. A friend remembers Roger having bad mic problems and Pete offering Roger his mic. Roger apparently described Dallas as the only bad show of the tour. It was my *only* show – and I was blown away! It was an epiphany for me. The difference between live and recorded Who was like seeing a different animal, the difference between a sedan and an F1 racecar.

The songs from *Quadrophenia* came and went, along with other great songs, and towards the end there were a couple of *Tommy* selections. I'd memorised *Tommy* and went in expecting to hear them more-or-less as they were recorded. On about the third repetition of the increasingly frenzied 'listening to you' chorus in 'See Me, Feel Me', a bank of Klieg airplane landing lights along the back of the stage, which had been dark through most of the show and which I hadn't even noticed, went on the audience full force and hit me right in the face. Pete, as songwriter, was communicating to us, the audience, maybe even to me. It was no longer Tommy singing to his muse, it was The Who, the band, saying they were listening to us and drawing strength and inspiration from us. That change in perspective showed me there was much more to The Who than I had imagined, and set the course for a lifetime of appreciation of them.

The Who finish 1973 with five London shows, one at the Rainbow and four at the Sundown Theatre, Edmonton.

18, 19, 20 & 23 DECEMBER 1973
SUNDOWN THEATRE, LONDON, UK

DAVE BAGNALL

This was probably the best Who performance I ever witnessed. It was one of those occasions where everything was perfect. It was only a week or so before Christmas and so everyone was up for it. My mates were students and lived in London, so I went down and spent the weekend there. Everything just gelled. It was not a big venue and the floor was stepped, like in a cinema, so wherever you stood you got a great view. All the anoraks had queued for ages and got in the front, but it didn't matter. Wherever you stood, you got a great view and everything was just perfect for it.

IAN MCKEAN

I was living in Farnborough and made my way up to Edmonton via coach and train. We arrived about four hours early. Babe Ruth opened who were great, but when The Who came on there was a big rush towards the stage and me and my mate got squashed up in front of Entwistle. It was very hot and Daltrey was handing out plastic cups of water. They played most of *Quadrophenia*, which had only just come out. Townshend made some joke about not recognising people and said he even sent his own mother away at the stage door because he *did* recognise her. He was in his Spike Milligan mode. They did an encore (the only time I ever seen

Ian Potts' poster of Keith Moon; Colin Petersen (left) was at the Newcastle gig;
Ian Potts chose not to model in the style of Keith; Linda Sweeden was at Charlton; Bobby Asea was at the infamous show where a fan stepped up from the audience to drum in place of an incapacitated Keith.

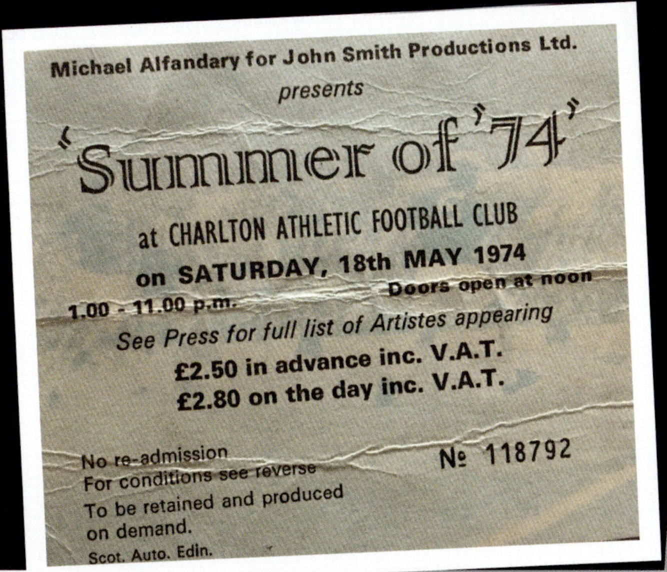

Michael Alfandary for John Smith Productions Ltd.
presents

'Summer of '74'

at CHARLTON ATHLETIC FOOTBALL CLUB
on SATURDAY, 18th MAY 1974
1.00 - 11.00 p.m. Doors open at noon
See Press for full list of Artistes appearing
£2.50 in advance inc. V.A.T.
£2.80 on the day inc. V.A.T.

No re-admission
For conditions see reverse
To be retained and produced
on demand.
Scot. Auto. Edin.

№ 118792

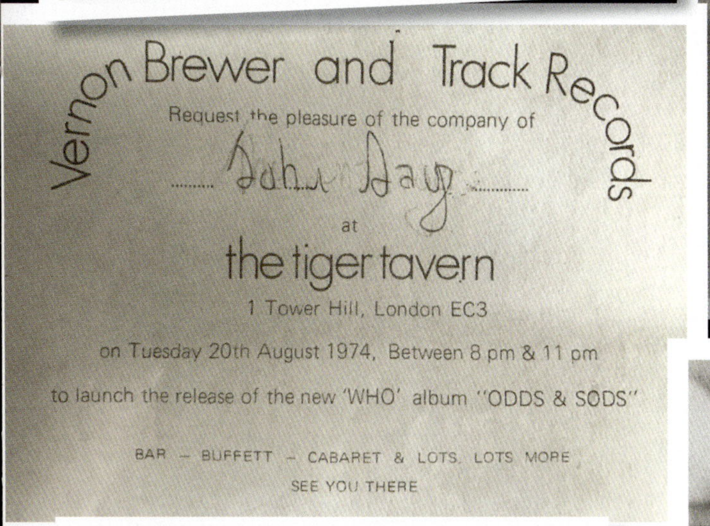

Vernon Brewer and Track Records
Request the pleasure of the company of
....
at
the tiger tavern
1 Tower Hill, London EC3
on Tuesday 20th August 1974, Between 8 pm & 11 pm
to launch the release of the new 'WHO' album "ODDS & SODS"

BAR – BUFFETT – CABARET & LOTS, LOTS MORE
SEE YOU THERE

Clockwise from top left: Charlton ticket from David Almond; Glenn Fearons saw *Tommy* being filmed in Portsmouth; Marc Librescu saw The Who at MSG in 1976; Dylan White was at Charlton in '74 & '76; John Parsons' *Odds & Sods* invite.

them do one) and Townshend smashed his guitar (the only time I ever saw that). The encore went on for about 40 minutes. My parents had driven up to Edmonton and had to wait forever while they played it. I was very excited and was saying how Townshend had smashed his guitar, but my dad was none too pleased. He'd had an accident in the car just prior to me and my mate coming out of the venue.

10 FEBRUARY 1974
PARIS EXPO PORTE DE VERSAILLES
PARIS, FRANCE

OLIVIER COIFFARD

I arrived at 10am although the concert wasn't scheduled to start until 5pm. An increasingly large crowd gathered outside the gates and security decided to let the early arrivals, including me, in. I found myself at the foot of the stage, on Pete Townshend's side. They started with 'I Can't Explain', 'Summertime Blues', 'My Wife', 'My Generation', 'The Real Me', 'The Punk and the Godfather' and '5.15' before a power failure interrupted the show for a quarter of an hour during 'Sea and Sand'. After 'Drowned', Pete Townshend angrily smashed his Gibson Les Paul Deluxe. It was a pleasure of hear Keith Moon sing 'Bell Boy' and then we got 'Doctor Jimmy', 'Love Reign O'er Me', 'Won't Get Fooled Again', 'Pinball Wizard' and 'See Me, Feel Me'. The group got a huge ovation and after a ten-minute delay they responded to the crowd by coming back to play an encore of 'Substitute', 'Magic Bus', 'Naked Eye'/'Let's See Action' and 'My Generation'. It was dark when we came out. The Who had played for almost two and a quarter hours.

In February 1974, nine weeks of production commence on the film* Stardust*, sequel to the film* That'll Be The Day*. Starring David Essex as Jim Maclaine, Keith Moon reprised his role as the drummer in Jim's backing band, The Stray Cats. One scene aims to recreate the hysteria of Beatlemania, with the Stray Cats in matching suits.

17 MARCH 1974
BELLE VUE, MANCHESTER, UK

DONNA SULLIVAN, AGE 12

I was an extra in *Stardust*. David Essex was the lead singer in the band so we all had to dress in Sixties gear. I was at church that morning, so everybody was like 'what's she wearing?', and then I had to go to this gig at Belle Vue. So we're all in the audience, everybody's really pent up, and the producers were saying 'don't forget to scream, don't forget to scream!'. Keith Moon came on stage first, playing the drummer. Then the other people in the band came on, and then David Essex, playing the part of Jim McClaine. Everybody was a massive David Essex fan and so everybody was going bananas for David Essex and screaming 'David!' The producers were running up and down, going 'it's Jim! It's Jim!', so we had to scream 'Jim!' But Keith was throwing his drumsticks into the crowd and then everybody started getting into Keith and going 'Keith! Keith!'.

18 MAY 1974
THE VALLEY, CHARLTON ATHLETIC FC LONDON, UK

JEFF BERRY

The weather was a little grey going up by train with friends, but when we got there it was dry with sunny intervals. The Who were top of the bill with the artists that preceded them including Lou Reed, Humble Pie, Bad Company, Montrose, Lindisfarne and Maggie Bell, who I wasn't the biggest fan of. I can't remember what order the artists played in but it was a fun day out. I was boozed up but not too drunk.

TONY BROWNSON

This was the first of 14 times I've seen The Who. No one comes close to them. Talking about this gig in an interview, Pete said his first impression was that the crowd was very aggressive. Well, it was very hot, the only thing to drink was gallons of cider and so most people were pissed. I was at the front and I've never seen so many fights. The Who were brill. However, I think Pete was pissed too!

MICK BROPHY

The best £2.50 I ever spent. I had no money, so the concessions running out didn't bother me, and although there was some unrest in the crowd, I didn't notice any of the violence. I don't remember much about anything around me – apart from it being sunny – as I found a really good spot, close enough to see the sweat, and was mesmerised all-day by the great line-up. As a Free and Mott the Hoople fan, Bad Company did it for me and Stevie Marriot kicked ass, almost stealing the show.

Come The Who and I was absolutely gobsmacked! I knew most of the songs, worshipped Townshend's songwriting and loved the records. But live they were something else. Tremendous power, uplifting rather than bone-crunching, and I didn't know where to look next. Haymakerguitars? Whirling-dervish microphones? Every cymbal at once? Or the serene bass man with the mad spider fingers?

The whole thing seemed on a knife-edge. Later reports talked of sound problems but I didn't notice any, and I remember some moments when the band seemed like they were collectively mind reading their cues for the changes. It was inspiring. It was exhausting. It sucked me in deep. Then it was over. An hour plus felt like 15 minutes and I was on such a natural high afterwards I can't remember how I got home that day.

A few weeks later, a pal suggested my birthday drink location to be the pubs around Twickenham. After a few pints, and much blithering on from me about Charlton, 'would you like see Pete Townshend's house?' seemed like a great idea. So down a path by the side of the Thames staggered the two drunken numpties. 'That's Pete Townshend's house!' he slurred. And so it was, complete with a tall guy with a instantly recognisable proboscis having a chat with next door at the end of their respective gardens. What I wanted to say was 'Mr Townshend, you are God and your band changed my life last month. Please can I shake your hand?' What I actually said was, 'Oh shit! It's him!' and we legged it.

ROB TITLEY, AGE 16

The second time I saw The Who was at Charlton's football ground for the *Summer of '74* show in front of an 80,000 crowd. The price of the ticket was £2.50 and, living in Birmingham, I made the trip to London to meet up with my pal who was studying at Canterbury University. I recall Roger Daltrey twirling his mic and Pete Townshend dressed in white Oxford bags and Doc Martens and him whirling away on 'Baba O'Riley' and 'Won't Get Fooled Again'.

LINDA SWEEDEN, AGE 16

I was a schoolgirl. My fellow classmates were into The Jacksons and The Osmonds, swooning over Donny! My friend Denny and I were different. We loved rock music and couldn't get enough of The Who. Denny's older brother said they were appearing at Charlton's Valley football ground. We begged him to get us tickets. They were on sale for £2.50. I only had a pound but promised I'd pay him with next week's school dinner money.

The day of the concert arrived and we caught the train from Hitchin to King's Cross and the Tube on to Charlton. I'd never seen so many people. I was scared but buzzing with adrenaline at the same time. I felt so grown up! We got into the ground quite early, but the football pitch was filling up fast. We sat down on the grass and claimed our space about ten deep from the stage. We had no food or drink, just a can of Coke on the train. I guess we hadn't thought that one through.

There was a heavy smell of dope in the air and the midday sun was beating down on my bare arms. There was no sun factor protection in those days. On came Montrose. I'd never heard of them and they were loud but good. Next came Lindisfarne and I can remember the crowd getting involved singing 'we can have a wee wee, we can have a wet up the wall!' from 'Fog on the Tyne'. Bad Company were next and I loved Free and Paul Rodgers' voice so I loved them. Then there was Lou Reed sporting bright bleached yellow hair but I only really knew 'Walk on the Wild Side'.

Humble Pie and Steve Marriott were amazing. I looked around and noticed the crowd getting thicker and thicker. It was more than ten deep in front of us now, and every little gap was filled up. I was desperate for a wee and a drink, in that order, but if we separated, we would never find each other again! But we had to go, so went together. Maggie Bell was on and we didn't care about missing her. When we came back, we just had to push and weave our way to the front. There were two huge burly blokes stage centre, right at the front. I was a tiny blonde just about five foot and my skinny friend was not much taller. I cheekily asked them if we could sit in front of them as there was no way we would be blocking their view. They agreed and started chatting us up. We didn't mind as we had the best view of all! It seemed to take forever waiting for The Who. They came on at about 8.30pm and we'd been there since midday! The sun was going down as they exploded onto the stage with 'I Can't Explain' and, my God, I was truly in heaven. Tears of joy streamed down my face. Roger was even more gorgeous in real life than on camera! He wore what looked like two chamois leathers laced together, showing off his amazing bronzed torso. At that moment I fell in love!

They did a couple of covers and then launched into my all-time favourite, 'Baba O'Riley'. I screamed as one of the burly chaps lifted me up onto his shoulders. I was flying high, almost face to face with Roger as he twirled his mic round and caught it every time! The lights turned blue and I guessed what was coming – 'Behind Blue Eyes'. I burst into tears again as I felt every word. The crowd went crazy singing along to 'Substitute' and 'I'm a Boy'.

After 'Tattoo', serious John in his glittering emerald green jacket did 'Boris the Spider', his deep voice matching his mesmerising bass guitar. A few tracks from *Quadrophenia* followed, with cheeky Keith Moon played his part singing 'Bell Boy'. I remember trying to count his drums. I'd never seen such a big drum kit, complete with gongs! 'Won't Get Fooled Again' was the song of the night for me. The energy on stage was phenomenal. Pete was windmilling like crazy, Roger was marching on the spot and, as the song built up to a crescendo, Roger let out the scream of all screams – 'yeeeeaaaahhhhh!' His voice penetrated my every cell as the burly chap behind me picked me up and threw me in the air like a child! After 'Pinball Wizard' came 'See Me, Feel Me' and, as I was only feet away, I imagined Roger was singing just to me. I put out my arms as if to try and touch him. Oh, how I wished I could...

They went off stage and the crowd stomped and shouted, 'More, more, more! Who, Who, Who!' To the crowd's delight, they came back for another six songs including '5.15', 'Magic Bus' and, of course, 'My Generation'. As all good things, the day had to end. We were on a high. It took ages to get out of the ground. It was gone midnight when we finally reached the Tube station it was closed. We were tired, hungry, thirsty and sunburnt and we had to walk across London to King's Cross station. But we were happy!

LESTER MCILWAINE

The next Who gig I went to was at The Valley, where they headlined. A bunch of us caught the train down to London from Manchester the night before and slept in an alleyway, not that we slept much. Somewhere in Greenwich around 7am on the day of the concert, we found a transport café and I scored two sausage sandwiches and a mug of tea strong enough to dissolve a spoon. That set me up for the day, which weather-wise was a bit of a scorcher. The line-up was Montrose, Maggie Bell, Lou Reed, Lindisfarne (whose act I was happy to sleep through with the aid of several beers), Humble Pie, Bad Company and The Who. I'd seen Montrose a week or two previously when they supported Status Quo in Manchester. Bad Company hadn't been together very long but you'd never have guessed it as they gave a great performance. There was quite a delay before The Who finally came on stage. Their performance wasn't quite as good as the show I'd seen in Manchester the previous October, but they were still great, probably because they did a bit less *Quadrophenia* and more older numbers. By now I had realised what an amazing bass player John Entwistle was.

RUPERT BOBROWICZ

I moved from England's smallest county to London in 1973 so I could attend gigs.

I wasn't disappointed! The Who live at Charlton 1974 was a whole afternoon and evening full of music at Charlton Football Ground, and well worth the experience with a wonderful selection of bands. I'd always wanted to see The Who, especially after hearing *A Quick One*, *Tommy* and *Who's Next*. They were the highlight of the day's festival with mad Keith on drums, windmill arms Pete Townshend, skeleton Entwistle and the mic swinging Roger the Daltrey! They were there live on stage as the daylight faded and I had to get nearer the front to be closer and see them through the crowds. But the set was not a full set and they left the stage. The atmosphere in the crowd grew ominous as cans flew over our heads. I decided I had to get out of there – it was time for a sharp exit and back to my digs!

PETER SMITH

Townshend said The Who selected Charlton for this big outdoor London concert because it had 'particular acoustic qualities' and offered 'excellent views of the stage from the terraces'. I travelled down overnight by coach with two mates, arriving in London early on Saturday morning. We reached The Valley and the ground was pretty full. By the time openers Montrose exploded onto the stage at noon, the place was ram packed. The concert was intended to have an attendance limit of 50,000, but breakdowns in security resulted in many more people getting in and an estimated crowd of 80,000. I ran into quite a few mates from home on the terraces who'd managed to push or blag their way in without paying. The supporting bill was very strong. Humble Pie were pure class. They almost upstaged the main act. There was a long wait before The Who took to the stage. It was a very hot day and there were some fights and a heavy smell of dope, with many people openly smoking joints. Lots of cans were thrown around throughout the day.

The Who started at 8.45pm and played an hour and 45-minute set, starting with 'Can't Explain' and working their way through old classics and a few from *Quadrophenia*. We had been promised quadraphonic sound and large PA speakers were sited around the ground, but the sound wasn't that great. The Who were excellent though, despite Pete later admitting to being drunk and feeling the show wasn't one of their best. The set included a lot of '60s material and several songs I hadn't seen them play before such as 'I'm A Boy' and 'Tattoo'. Entwistle performed 'Boris the Spider' in his deep bass voice and a lengthy encore included '5:15', an extended 'Magic Bus', 'My Generation', 'Naked Eye', 'Let's See Action' and the first ever performance of their slow 12-bar blues arrangement of 'My Generation'.

When the concert finished, it was absolute pandemonium trying to get out through the crowd so a number of us decided to try and climb over one of the fences and one of my mates cut his hand quite badly on the sharp metal top. We pushed our way back into the ground and to the St John's Ambulance post, which wasn't easy as we were walking against all the people leaving. An ambulance sped us to hospital, where we spent most of the night while my mate had his hand stitched. The hospital was full of concert casualties. It was daylight by the time we got out of the hospital. We walked back into central London, made our way to Victoria and caught our bus home. The things you do for rock 'n' roll!

In the spring of 1974, production begins on the filming of Ken Russell's* Tommy. *Roger Daltrey was cast as the lead, Keith played the role of Uncle Ernie and The Who appeared as themselves in concert scenes shot at the Guildhall in Portsmouth.

MAY & JUNE 1974
SOUTH PARADE PIER, PORTSMOUTH, UK

GLENN FEARONS

Before we were married, we would have a week's holiday down in Portsmouth. We took a taxi to our hotel and passed the pier. We saw that the end of the pier was missing. It had burnt down. We mentioned it to the taxi driver and he said 'oh, it's that film crew that's here'. As we were walking around the shops, most of the young people had got 'Tommy' badges on and I kept looking at them and thinking 'what's this 'Tommy' about?'. One day during our holiday, we took a walk down to the beach from up near the castle. We could see a car with a camera on the top, and it was filming. There was Roger Daltrey with Robert Stigwood at the side of him, running along to 'I'm Free'. They were filming that bit in the film where's he's just got denim jeans on. I've got a lovely picture of Roger with Stigwood. Roger's standing with his hands on his hips. He was obviously looking across to director Ken Russell, who must have been saying something to them. I tried to get Ken Russell's photograph but the camera just went dark and there was this big guy stood there who said 'no, you don't take photographs of him'. But I got quite a few photos. Roger Daltrey looked really fit. There

The Who captured in action in Paris by Olivier Coiffard - photos Oliver Coiffard, one of which The Who used in a slideshow

were maybe 50 people there watching it; it made the holiday a little bit more exciting. And then we understood what all the 'Tommy' badges were about.

Despite working on* Tommy*, The Who manage to fit in four New York shows in June 1974.

10, 11, 13 & 14 JUNE 1974
MADISON SQUARE GARDEN NEW YORK, NEW YORK

NEAL FINE

I was a big Led Zep fan in high school. Then in my senior year I saw The Who at MSG. We were on the second level on Pete's side. Before the show I remember telling my friend 'I would rather see Clapton than The Who'. That was the dumbest thing I ever said; these guys changed my life. I never saw a tighter show and Roger and Pete had so much energy. Keith was the only one that recognised our section and he gave us constant eye contact; his drumming was amazing. It was just an insane, magical night. I have seen them about 18 times but nothing matches that night. I also saw them in Buffalo, the day after the Cincinnati tragedy, and you could tell that Roger was struggling. I felt that losing John was a bigger hit than losing Keith. The last time I saw them was in 2004 and the bass player (Pino Palladino) was not even close to John, but who is? I'd seen John in San Diego around '88 or '89 in a small bar or venue, the loudest concert I ever heard, and I saw Roger in 2018 in Saratoga, California. It was a great show, although there was only one song from *Quadrophenia* and he did a few Elvis songs, which was weird, but he sang 'How Many Friends', which is one of my favourite songs ever. And Clapton? I got to see him at Nassau Coliseum in '74. He was drunk as a skunk. It was boring.

1 AUGUST 1974
OMNI, ATLANTA, GEORGIA

RICK FREEMAN

I'd wanted to see Eric Clapton for years, With the help of Pete Townshend, he had finally cleaned up his act and kicked his heroin addiction. His album *461 Ocean Boulevard* was a surprise to those of us expecting another Derek and the Dominos. I liked it, but felt it was a little too laid back. I saw him at the Omni. As with most rock stars of that time, Eric was obsessed with reggae and I was afraid we would have to sit through a set by a reggae band. But the show started off on a high note as out danced an inebriated Keith Moon. As always, he was the show. One paper said he was shirtless but I do not remember that, just his hilarious performance, giving me and others hope for a great show.

Then out stepped EC, totally unrecognisable dressed in jeans, t-shirt and a felt hat. He started off with 'Smile' and the rest of the show was in the same vein. It soon became clear Eric was drunk. At one point, he sat down and leaned against the piano. The show was only ten songs long, and to be honest I would have left if Moon had not made an appearance.

After Eric left the stage, you could see people remaining on the stage. They were planning an encore but what we did not expect was Pete Townshend stepping out to the front of the stage and bringing the house down when he struck his iconic pose. He started playing 'Layla' and then they did 'Baby Don't You Do It' and 'Little Queenie'. Pete did a wonderful Chuck Berry duck walk. The other member of The Who, Moon, was on drums. The problem? He could not stay on the drum stool. Roadies were on each side, but he was swinging his drumsticks at the drum set and missing it, not to mention slipping off the stool. Still, after 90 minutes of a lacklustre performance from Eric, this made the drive worth it. Two members of the best band in the world proved that they were the best.

AUGUST 1974
A HOTEL, LAKE DISTRICT, UK

JULIA PRIOR

We were on a family holiday. Roger Daltrey was in the Lake District filming *Tommy*. As we were all staying in a small family-run hotel, whichever table you were allocated determined where you sat for breakfast and dinner for the duration. We shared a table for the week. Roger 'fell in love' with our daughter Selina and on the last night he wrote a ditty to her on the back of the menu. We had typical Lake District weather so Roger let us have his poncho!

Keith Moon releases his solo album* Two Sides of the Moon *in the USA on 17 March 1975. It is released five weeks later in the UK.

AUGUST – DECEMBER 1974
RECORD PLANT, LOS ANGELES, CALIFORNIA

HARVEY KUBERNIK

Keith Moon was living out in the hills in Malibu. I knew Moonie a bit from the scene. I wasn't a party guy but I'd see him down at restaurants. The rock 'n' roll scene was very small. Once Ringo moved to town, there was a party every night. I was invited occasionally as a journalist from *Melody Maker*. I could be trusted. I really didn't do drugs. I never drank. I wasn't there to take their chicks from them. I knew Dougie then. 'Keith's having a birthday party at the Beverley Wilshire Hotel. Why don't you come by?' I never travelled with an entourage. It was a great way to get a meal.

Keith would want to know about import records. I would steer him and Dougie towards some record stores. There was a British import store. People like David Bowie went in there. They liked seeing their stuff on the walls. They weren't that jaded yet. The American domestic album releases were still a little bit different from the British versions that came out earlier, with extra tracks and different album covers. In Hollywood, you could get both editions if you were a record collector.

I did a half page interview with Keith for *Melody Maker* about his solo album for MCA Records so went to some of the recording sessions at the Record Plant. There was some crazy madness going on there, but I remember hearing a playback of him covering 'Don't Worry Baby'. The guy liked surf music. He wasn't the greatest singer but he had great energy. He really propelled the group.

March 1975 sees the release of* Tommy*, the Ken Russell directed film of The Who's 1969 album.

19 MARCH 1975
MANN'S WILSHIRE THEATRE LOS ANGELES, CALIFORNIA

HARVEY KUBERNIK

Keith Moon invited me to the *Tommy* movie premiere. He saw me and gave me a big hug.

3 – 4 OCTOBER 1975
NEW BINGLEY HALL, STAFFORD, UK

ROY SMITH

There was a stand off between Pete and Keith over playing 'Bell Boy'. Keith was determined to sing it and Pete was refusing to play the intro. Keith got the crowd on his side and after a minute or so of us all chanting 'Bell Boy, Bell Boy', Pete eventually succumbed but played without looking at the audience and afterwards went over and had a not so quiet word with Keith (off mic unfortunately, as I'd love to know what he said!). Rog and John knew well enough to leave it to them and kept right out of it all. The first gig my wife Debs saw, many years before we got together, was The Who at Charlton in 1974. I was impressed when she told me!

MARTIN JONES

They were the first group to play at Bingley Hall and we were able to see them from the balcony, which was subsequently outlawed for health and safety reasons. But it was a fantastic venue. I'm pretty sure they had the first ever laser show that night and despite audience encouragement I don't recall any guitar smashing or drum wrecking. I think the entrance fee was about £2. All the top groups played Bingley. In summer, it was the venue for the cattle show of Staffordshire County Show so it was very barn-like! The crowd noise banging on the walls inspired Queen to write 'We Will Rock You'.

MICK FARR

We could drive by now so off we went to Stafford and a giant cowshed. Later in life I would become a bank manager in Stafford, and Bingley was used for agricultural shows. It could hold around 8,000 people. I was very near the front. I stood next to a 30-year-old Australian who told me his family was wealthy and he followed The Who around the world. It had started when he saw them in Melbourne two years earlier. I thought, 'my God, this was a fan.'

On stage, matters got out of hand. After a few numbers it transpired that the band could not hear each other. Townshend got very, very frustrated and started having a go at Bob Pridden again! Then Roger started singing the wrong song to an intro and, to make matters worse, Keith was drumming a completely different beat. Townshend accused Moon of being drunk, at which point Keith climbed out of his drums and threw a vodka bottle at him. I know it was vodka and empty because I was that close.

Roger broke up the ensuing melee and they carried on, having dismantled whatever they had installed to 'give them more room on the stage'. To me it was disturbing. These were my working-class heroes. They had gone to grammar school like me (except for Roger) and they were arguing and drunk on stage. We'd seen bottles and other things thrown at football matches, but on stage this was seriously dangerous. Bizarrely, towards the end of the concert, Moon apologised to Townshend and us, and it was as if nothing had happened.

I have been a Who fan since 1965. It was the sheer energy at the concerts which was the draw and which is still evident today. They tore down the perspex drum guard at Glastonbury and Hyde Park because they could not hear Zak, a lesson learned many years earlier at Bingley. I have always liked their anti-establishment stance and Townshend's songs, as Roger always now says, were a joy to sing.

PETER SMITH

The Who had not performed since the summer of 1974 as they had been working hard on the film *Tommy*. This tour was promoting *The Who by Numbers*, which had been recorded the previous spring, although the only track they played from it at Stafford was 'Squeeze Box'. Before Who fans descended upon it, Bingley Hall had been used as a cattle barn. Minimal adaptations had been made in preparation for the show. This added an immense amount of character and the venue provided a strange, surrealist quality to the night which enhanced the experience. I attended the second of two nights, driving down to the concert with a couple of mates, all three of us squeezed into my two-seater MG sports car.

This was a set of classic Who. They started with 'Substitute', returned to *Tommy* with a mini-set featuring in the middle of their show, presumably linked to the success of the film, and closed with 'Won't Get Fooled Again'. The show made use of lasers which shone out over the crowd and was billed as 'the first stage act in the world to employ high-powered lasers'. The band were on fire, with lots of mic swinging by Roger Daltrey and arm twirling by Pete Townshend. They played for two hours with no encore. Pete didn't smash his guitar, although the crowd was willing him to do so. Apparently, The Who had used a raised podium for Moon and his drums on the first night, but this didn't work out and was scrapped for the second concert.

6 & & OCTOBER 1975
KING'S HALL, BELLE VUE, MANCHESTER, UK

DAVE THOMAS

We were all 15 years old in 1975. We were right into our rock music in general but one of the lads let me borrow his copy of *Tommy*. I was blown away. It was just an awesome piece of music. We were going to concerts regularly in Liverpool but The Who were on at Belle Vue in Manchester. We got tickets, £2.50. We had to get the train from Lime Street in Liverpool to Manchester Piccadilly. What an adventure as it seemed like the other side of the country! We had to leg it home from school to catch the train in time. I can't even remember how we got to Belle Vue from Piccadilly but we were there in time to get near the front and watch the Steve Gibbons Band as the support artist.

When The Who hit the stage, the place was electric; Pete windmilling those arms around, Moonie smashing hell out of the drums and Roger (I remember vividly) just skimming our heads with that bloody microphone! Big John just stood there, hardly moving as there was mayhem on the stage. I always wondered what was in those two drinks bottles fastened to his microphone stand. I guess one was brandy… It was the first time they played tunes from *The Who by Numbers*. Usually at concerts we'd be disappointed if the music was new and we didn't know every word and every note, but in this case we just loved it, jumping up and down in the crowd at the front and soaked to the skin in sweat.

The next time I had the honour of seeing The Who was the following year in 1976 at Swansea football ground. One of the lads talked his dad into driving us down there. It was an all-dayer so his dad just hung around all day waiting to take us home at night. By this time I'd discovered The Who's music from the '60s, making the experience complete. I've been lucky to see the band on numerous occasions since (sadly with the different line ups) but those two earlier gigs are the ones that stand out, and are musical experiences I'll cherish for ever.

COLIN JOY

This was the last time I saw Keith play. They opened up with 'Substitute' at full volume and a blinding strobe light display and continued knocking out their catalogue of hits, before entering their *Tommy* opera suite, much to the disappointment of the crowd, which was hoping for *Quadrophenia*. Pete Townshend was being heckled by the audience, but he kept his cool. Keith Moon was his usual flamboyant self, emphasising all the words to the songs with his drumming in his trademark style. At one point, he decided The Who didn't need him for some of the songs and he walked off the stage. It was that kind of evening, but they should have played *Quadrophenia* as we all expected. Only 'Drowned' and '5:15' made the set. A very noisy night!

LESTER MCILWAINE

They played Manchester Belle Vue again in October 1975. It was only a day or two into my final year at Manchester Uni so I got tickets for myself and a couple of mates well in advance by posting a stamped, self-addressed envelope and cheque from my parents' house in Northern Ireland. I worked in a cheese factory over there each summer, earning enough money to take off hitch-hiking around Europe and supplementing the money my dad gave me to get through the academic year. As a result, I was probably better off than many of my mates. This was also how I funded my concert-going and beer consumption.

Belle Vue housed a large zoo and also a funfair and you had to pass through both of them to get to the King's Hall. The concert was another amazing show. The Steve Gibbons Band was the support act and I recall that Moon's drumming that night seemed to be even more manic than usual, with him bouncing drumsticks high in the air then catching them without missing a beat and with beer flying everywhere. In complete contrast, Entwistle was standing motionless and almost looking bored whilst thundering out his incredible bass lines. They played a lot of *Tommy* that night, not so much from *Quadrophenia*, plus 'Baba O'Riley', 'My Generation', '5:15' and 'Substitute', and closed as always with my personal favourite, 'Won't Get Fooled Again'. It was a great gig; real intense, hard-edge, unadulterated rock 'n' roll energy delivered by the greatest band in the world.

MARK ELLISON, AGE 15

My very first gig. It was just before my 16th birthday. Times were very different then. People go to gigs at five years old now! I spotted an announcement in the *NME* about tickets going on sale the next day, during the school holidays. I called up my cousin, Jeffrey, a year older than me, and said, 'Who, Who, Belle Vue' because I assumed that we needed to go and queue up for tickets immediately, and that if we waited until the following day, they'd all be gone.

I was supposed to do the household shopping. My parents had gone to work and left me a shopping list, money and some shopping bags, so I left them a note saying, 'I've gone to Belle Vue to queue up overnight for tickets and I'll see you tomorrow. I've taken the shopping bags with me to do the shopping.'

My cousin and I hopped on the train to Manchester and I did the bloody weekly shop. So I'd got two old granny shopping baskets full of fruit and veg and stuff and then hopped on a bus to Belle Vue with it. It was late afternoon when we arrived and there were about six people there before us. So there I was, in the queue with these shopping bags full of groceries and stuff, and we hunkered down for the rest of the night. 15 years old and daft, you know? It was bloody cold overnight, so the food wasn't going to off quickly or anything. We had a bit of a chat with the other people who were there before us, not much because we were young and gauche and not really able to have a conversation with people who were much older – and hairier! And over the rest of the evening and overnight, the queue started to grow and grow. About 10pm or 11pm, the local radio turned up and interviewed a couple of people. Not us. I remember asking the guy behind us in the queue about the buses carrying on all night. Being a local provincial lad, I was used to the buses stopping at ten or eleven o'clock at night, so I said 'when do the buses stop?' and he said 'no, they carry on all night.' I thought that was amazing, that big city sort of thing.

I don't remember a lot then, just being absolutely bored out of our minds for the rest of the night and it getting bloody cold. I just had a big coat but we were better off than some, who were just there in their jeans jackets. There must have been an alleyway or a ginnel or something across the road, because there was somewhere to stretch your legs but, mainly, when you wanted to go for a pee, everyone was getting up and going down the alley throughout the night, including me at one point because I just couldn't hold it any longer. But that was a bit weird, because I remember it was absolutely pitch black.

Anyways, that was the night – absolutely no sleep or anything like that. The box office opened at 9am. I went in and got the tickets but that's when I realised that I don't do sleep deprivation well, because by that point I was barely conscious and I had no idea how I managed to pass over the money for the tickets. If you'd asked me my name, I wouldn't have known it. So that's a common thing for my two Who gigs – a lack of sleep. I couldn't think straight at all. And, when we left, there was a chippy just very close nearby who'd obviously seen a chance here – 'hundreds of people during the night queuing, they'll all be starving' – so this chippy was open at, like, nine o'clock in the morning, so we called in and got chips and gravy. Funnily enough, that's as strong a memory in one sense as the gig itself.

The support on the day was The Steve Gibbons Band and I thought they were just awful. They were pedestrian and lacking in variation and all the rest of it but that might have been really unfair, because I didn't know any of this stuff and PAs were not that good in them days.

The Who, by contrast, just exploded. When you're 15 and your favourite band comes on stage at mind-meltingly high volume, of course it's explosion. I've got in my head that they started with 'Heaven and Hell' but I absolutely know that's wrong. They would have started with 'Can't Explain', then 'Substitute' and then 'Heaven and Hell'. Either way, it was good to hear because it was not something that got a lot of play. And then it was just a classic Who set of the period – the highlights of *Tommy*, the highlights of *Who's Next*, things like

'Magic Bus' and 'My Generation', all dropped in there. It was an absolutely classic set of the period and I loved every moment of it.

They were very famous in those days for not doing encores but there was still this an absolutely massive clamour for one. People were saying afterwards that this was the best they'd seen them for years. You could see, off the side of the stage, Keith Moon was kind of gesturing as though he was ringing a bell, trying to get 'Bell Boy' chants going or whatever, and there was every indication that they would actually, unbelievably, play an encore. But they didn't, and the house lights went on and everything, and I'd arranged a lift home so we left. And in the car, the local radio that was reporting on the gig said that the band had wanted to play an encore – which was very, very unusual – but that Belle Vue management wouldn't let them back on because they'd run over time. Which is a bit sad, isn't it?

15 & 16 OCTOBER 1975
APOLLO THEATRE, GLASGOW, UK

MICHAEL MALONE

I'd been listening to The Who since 1972. When I heard that tickets were going on sale for the October gigs at the Apollo, I queued out all night, listening to bootlegs on cassette with a great feeling of anticipation as the doors opened. I purchased two tickets for each night for £8 – a bargain, the best I ever had. On the first night, The Who played 24 songs. Highlights for me were Pete using a music stand during 'Squeeze Box' and then Keith standing on his drum kit conducting fans shouting for 'Bell Boy' and Pete telling him (and us) they were not singing it tonight.

After the second gig, I waited round the back and shook hands with Roger, Pete, John and Keith as they came out a door and went straight into a limo. Roger asked if we had been at the previous night's show and, if so, what night did we prefer? I told Roger how, from my vantage point on the famous Apollo balcony, I saw him throw the mic stand into the backstage area and a roadie having to duck as it just missed him.

Since then, I've seen The Who at Parkhead, the SECC, the Hydro, the O2 Arena, and Hyde Park but none of these can beat the first time. Recently, my wife came home from work with a photo of her and Roger Daltrey as he was opening the Teenage Cancer Trust unit at the hospital where she works.

JOHN WILSON

It was the greatest concert I have ever been to. Keith was immense that night. They all were, as you would expect. However, he appeared to be in a huff because, even though there were lots of folks shouting for 'Bell Boy', Keith said to stop shouting for it because 'that particular number isn't in the show tonight'. I remember laughing loudly at that. It was a truly magical night.

18 & 19 OCTOBER 1975
GRANBY HALLS, LEICESTER, UK

DAVE BARBER

They were appearing at the (now long gone) Granby Halls as part of *The Who by Numbers* tour. They were late coming on stage. They had appeared two nights earlier in Glasgow and Keith Moon had apparently been arrested for driving his car into the hotel lobby! Several announcements were made saying that there were doubts as to the band performing because of Moon's absence. Then it was announced that he was on his way and the helicopter had just landed. Rock 'n' roll lifestyle or what?

IAN SMITH, AGE 19

I will always remember Keith Moon arriving late on stage and saying 'I've just been to see my probation officer!' He had in fact been apprehended in Scotland after assaulting a coffee machine at the airport and was then flown down to Leicester by helicopter!

23 OCTOBER 1975
EMPIRE POOL, WEMBLEY, LONDON, UK

ROB TITLEY

This was the final time I saw them. It was the Empire Pool, Wembley – there was no 'Arena' in those days. The ticket cost £2.25 and I made the journey from Birmingham by train. What a gig! They had just released *The Who by Numbers* album and it was a superb show, My main memory is of Townshend whirling away on his Gibson.

KEVIN RICHARDSON

This gig was one of the first I had seen in London and it was fantastic. We drove up on the day and picked up two hitch hikers en route. These guys were huge Beatles fans and we had a big discussion about which was the better band. They had to agree with us in the end that The Who were better, as otherwise we were going to make them get out and walk! At the gig, I remember Keith being suspended in a harness and swung round the auditorium. I can't remember what he was shouting but I think it was something about how uncomfortable his testicles were!

The Who play nine dates in Continental Europe before heading to North America for a further 20 dates.

31 OCTOBER 1975
PHILIPSHALLE, DÜSSELDORF, GERMANY

CHRISTIAN SUCHATZKI

I'd been a Who fan for six years when the band came to Germany in the autumn of 1975 for a few gigs. Still a pupil, I was barely able to afford a ticket for 18DM (approximately nine euros). When I told my friends and school mates that I wanted to be in the front row at a Who concert, they replied, 'Are you crazy? In the front row you'll get hurt by a broken amplifier.' So I took a seat in the second row.

Right after school, I hurried to the concert hall and waited outside excitedly for the doors to open. In fact, it was only one door. A giant man – I think he was a member of the Hell's Angels, hired for security reasons – made the single entrance with his huge body even smaller so that people could only get in one at a time. Everyone began pushing and shoving to get in and it felt quite dangerous situation, but somehow, I managed to be one of the first in.

Inside, things calmed down until The Who entered the stage with a steamrolling performance of 'Substitute' followed by an equally powerful 'I Can't Explain'. I was staggered how four musicians were able to produce such a loud and powerful sound. Keith Moon bashed his drums like there would be no tomorrow, Roger Daltrey's voice was loaded with huge energy while John Entwistle stood in his corner playing a thunderous bass and now and then took a nip from the two beverage bottles which were mounted at his microphone stand. Pete Townshend was in a slightly bad mood.

During the show, he got more and more offended by a few people, probably press reporters or security staff members, chatting in the pit right in front of him. Finally, he took a drinking cup and poured the liquid contents over them while making some enraged gestures in their direction. With 'Squeeze Box' and 'Dreaming from the Waist', The Who played only the two songs from their new album. Nine numbers from *Tommy* followed, accompanied by a stunning green-coloured laser show. When they continued with 'Summertime Blues', the audience climbed on their seats and began going beserk.

The Who's performance culminated in an electrifying version of 'My Generation' and, at the end of 'Won't Get Fooled Again', Roger, Pete and Keith destroyed some of their equipment. The whole stage floor was covered with broken drum sticks, damaged tambourines and unidentifiable pieces if wood. Roger threw some of them into the audience and one of Keith's broken drum sticks came in my direction and I caught it. That was not the only reminder of my first Who concert. I also had a ringing in my ears for two days.

20 NOVEMBER 1975
THE SUMMIT, HOUSTON, TEXAS

JOHN RAMSEY, AGE 17

A few days before The Who's opening American date we (okay, my mom) called the Summit to see if any tickets were available. A lady who worked at the Summit had reserved a bunch of seats on the floor near the front for her daughter's birthday treat. The party fell through, so we scored four seventh row tickets at the last minute. Pure dumb luck. Thanks, Mom!

It was the greatest rock show I have ever seen. When The Who took the stage, people from the back came rushing up the aisles past us in our reserved floor seating. This freaked out my 15-year-old brother, who thought it was very dangerous. I dismissed his concerns, but of course the Cincinnati disaster occurred four years later. The concert has been released on DVD recently, some 40 plus years later.

24 NOVEMBER 1975
THE OMNI, ATLANTA, GEORGIA

RANDY BROWN, AGE 11

I was a huge *Tommy* fan. My sister gave me the album in the early '70s and I just loved it. Then the movie came out and I was floored. It's kinda weird when you grow to love an album and then a movie comes out with reworked lyrics, arrangements and singers, but it was very well done. Ken Russell did an excellent job of directing and pulled together a fantastic cast. After school and on weekends, I helped a guy around the corner with his nursery. He happened to know a lot of people, and he got tickets for *The Who by Numbers* tour. I had seen Kiss in a smaller venue just a month or so before, but seeing The Who in a bigger place – and much, much louder – was amazing. I have seen The Who six times altogether but just that once with Keith Moon and it was so loud. I wasn't much on a lot of their songs at the time, but I certainly caught on to the magic after that.

RICK FREEMAN

This show proved they were untouchable. My wife was four months pregnant with our first son and we had great seats. The opening act was Toots and the Maytals. All English bands were heavy into reggae at this time. Unfortunately, no one wanted to see them and the crowd booed them off stage. Groups like The Who and the Stones really do not need opening acts. Something happened when The Who came out that I had never experienced at a show before. The entire arena was shaking. I thought the seats were going to collapse. Never have I felt such raw visceral energy sweep through a crowd.

They opened with 'I Can't Explain' followed by a heavy dose of *Tommy*, 24 songs in all. At one point, Daltrey missed catching his mic and it flew out into the audience. Some fans grabbed it and sang along. Roger went over to use Pete's mic while security retrieved it. The banter was fun, but it was not as it was in 1970. Pete was more serious than I had seen him before. The last song of the night was 'Won't Get Fooled Again'. Moon's playing on this was stunning. All of them were at the top of their game.

The encore was 'Magic Bus'. Pete was becoming frustrated and angry about something. He kept yelling at his guitar tech and pointing to his ears. As the song went on, he became more upset. I assume he could not hear, something that has plagued them for years. (Roger was always saying he could not hear anything.) Pete finally removed his guitar, placed it against an amp and stormed off stage, shoving people out the way. The rest of the band kept playing and took a final bow without him. I read years later that a journalist with them that night said Atlanta was one of the best shows of 1975. Flash forward to *The Who Hits 50!* tour and the same thing happened, with Pete leaving the stage over sound issues. I guess the human element explains why so many of us love The Who.

27 NOVEMBER 1975
HAMPTON COLISEUM
HAMPTON, VIRGINIA

STEVEN BURGESS

I've been a Who fan since 1966 and have seem them twice with Keith and many times with their different line-ups. Three shows stand out; Central Park in August 1968 (the first), Hampton Roads Coliseum in November 1975 (the best), and Louisville, Kentucky in March 2016 (my last?).

In early 1968 I moved from New Jersey to Erie, Pennysylvania but returned in the summer to see bands. I took a 12-hour trip on a Greyhound bus to the Port Authority in NYC, during which I read *The Graduate*. On the day of the show, my friend Dave and I travelled to the city by train and then walked from the Port Authority to Central Park for the early show. We had no true idea where we were going but found the Wollman Skating Rink, which hosted the Schaefer Music Festival. The Who were backed by Mandala (who replaced the scheduled Crazy World of Arthur Brown). The Who were introduced by either Cousin Brucie or Scott Muni. I don't remember the full setlist, but they played what I expected, including 'Magic Bus' and 'My Generation'. Keith played one of his 'Pictures of Lily' Premiere sets and, of course, destroyed it. The show was short by today's standards, but these were the old days.

In 1968, the stage was more like what any town now would offer for a free summer concert. By Thanksgiving Night 1975, things were much different. They had become the greatest live rock 'n' roll band. They had more lasers at their US shows than in the UK. It seemed like you could almost reach out and touch them. The Hampton show was 24 songs, comprising a great selection of their music. People often ask what it was like seeing The Who with Keith Moon. It's like sex – if you haven't experienced it, I can't explain it to you! This was the first time I heard them perform 'Won't Get Fooled Again' and I knew it would be their closing song and no encores would occur. I remember the audience applauding for their return and thinking 'they're long gone by now'.

The third show of my trilogy, and perhaps my last time of seeing them, was in 2016. I had tickets for their Raleigh, North Carolina show but my dog had to have surgery so I couldn't go. I got tickets for their Washington DC show but it was postponed when Roger contracted meningitis and I couldn't make the rescheduled date. I requested a refund. I told my wife that the closest they were playing was Louisville, so we got tickets for there. The Galt House Hotel is attached to the KFC Yum Center and we figured that if the band was to spend the night somewhere, that would be it. We booked our rooms there, but unfortunately never saw them. I remember telling my wife when the opening chords of 'Won't Get Fooled Again' started that this might very well be the last time we see The Who. Hopefully not.

28 NOVEMBER 1975
GREENSBORO COLISEUM
GREENSBORO, NORTH CAROLINA

VIRGINIA LEE, AGE 12

Moonie had the biggest drum kit I'd ever seen – and it's still one of the biggest I've seen all these decades later. They had a laser light show and it was the first I'd ever seen. We had $11 nosebleed seats. Thank goodness we had my dad's binoculars, because I would have missed so much otherwise.

6 DECEMBER 1975
SILVERDOME, PONTIAC, MICHIGAN

RICHARD E KELLEY

Michigan is the first area in the United States where The Who really took off. Oddly, it was 'Happy Jack' that busted out of Detroit and, as importantly, Windsor, Ontario radio in the spring of '67, becoming the band's first Top 40 hit in the US and going to number one in Canada. The rest of the world caught up, mostly in time for *Tommy*, but Michigan and northern Ohio were ahead of the curve, Who-wise. I know this because Pete Townsend has told me so, repeatedly. Retelling the days of the early Who in Michigan is a part of Pete's stage patter early in the show when the band play Detroit or Grand Rapids. Grand Rapids was a province in the late Sixties, not as hip to The Who, but is still in Michigan and Pete still tells the tale of 'Happy Jack' taking off, followed by 'Pictures of Lily' and 'I Can See For Miles' chasing it up the charts. This while audiences were scooping up tickets to their shows.

I've been privileged to witness the latter day Who many times in recent years but only once with the original line-up. The newly opened Pontiac Stadium was a standard NFL stadium where clever engineers had created a fabric roofing system held aloft by air blown into the building. The first roof succumbed to wind and weather and the replacement had a silver hue that glinted in the sun, leading to it being renamed the Silverdome. Perhaps The Who contributed to blowing the first roof off the place. It was entirely possible given the power and fury of their performance on that very cold Saturday night.

My date was a young lady of determined outlook but with relatively strict parents. Her folks were trying to get her to like Claude Bolling, so they would not have allowed their seventeen-year-old daughter to drive over an hour out of state to see a huge hard rock concert where drugs might be in use, in a foreboding locale like Pontiac, Michigan. We told them we were going to the movies.

We arrived after most of the crowd had entered, meaning we didn't have to wait in the frigid December air to go in. But it was nearly as cold inside as it was out. The engineering to heat such a huge facility had yet to be developed so it was very cold especially higher up where the air blew to keep the roof aloft. This show was to hold the Pontiac attendance record until it was usurped by Led Zeppelin in 1977. The place was packed and the best seats my date and I could find were side stage in the third tier, very far away.

We chilled, literally, for 45 minutes after openers Toots and the Maytals had left. My date was a tiny thing and didn't handle the cold well. Finally, the lights started to go down in the massive room and low stage lighting provided the initial ambience as The Who walked on. A thousand flash cameras vainly tried to get photos but only succeeded in lighting up the band for an occasional split second. I thought I caught a glimpse of Roger Daltrey and his golden, curly mane. Was that Pete dressed in a jump suit adjusting his guitar strap? Then the crashing chords of 'I Can't Explain' cut through the frigid air and the lights came up, much brighter than when Toots and the Maytals had used them an hour earlier. There they were! Townsend crashing down on his fret board, Daltrey swinging his mic by the cord, his leather jacket fringe a-flutter, Moonie flailing as only Moonie flailed and Entwistle standing like a statue. They were very far away and video screens were nearly non-existent at the time. There was some video but not where we could see it. Fortunately, much of the concert was taped so we have it to enjoy today. (A portion appears in the *The Kids are Alright* documentary.)

The Who pulled out all the stops but the one thing they ironically couldn't overcome was that they were not… loud enough! Their sound system was cranked past to point of distortion but the sound just bounced around the cavernous stadium. And there was a delay, so that by the time a trademark Townshend power chord reached our ears, his arm was already at twelve o'clock ready to bring the next one crashing down. This was very disconcerting and, along with the bitter chill, did not lend itself to an enjoyable evening. We stayed for about half the show.

We got through 'Magic Bus', but as the *Tommy* segment began, we took our leave. We were halfway to Detroit before the heater in my old Plymouth finally kicked in.

CAROL DRABEK MOGGO, AGE 18

The place was packed with over 75,000 fans and festival seating and they refused to come on until the crowd backed off in the front of the stage. Once they did come on, they rocked the house. It is one of my top ten concerts.

DENNIS PUTNAM, AGE 19

A few friends and I went together from Royal Oak, Michigan, a half hour away. I remember standing in the cold outside the venue for a while, along with all the other concertgoers. After a time, the lines of people slowly started to move. All of a sudden, the waves of fans began to part to the left and the right. A guy was bent over and vomiting onto the snow-covered cement.

The Silverdome is huge and was jammed full. Eventually the show started with the reggae group Toots and the Maytals. My friend John was really into them. He stood and danced for most of their set. He remembers that I smuggled in test tubes of alcohol. I don't remember this, but it's plausible. The Who eventually took the stage and the show was great! The only song I have a specific memory of was the last one, 'Won't Get Fooled Again'. When Roger Daltrey screamed 'Yeeeeeaaaaaah' towards the end, all these laser lights shot out from the stage in an arc. Tremendous! The band linked arms, bowed, said 'thank you' and left the stage. Sadly, there were no encores but the show was fantastic!

13 DECEMBER 1975
CIVIC CENTER
PROVIDENCE, RHODE ISLAND

KIPP VAN NOSTRAND, AGE 16

That Who show was the best concert I ever saw, and I've probably seen well over a thousand. And you know the amazing thing? It was just another show for them. They basically played the same set that whole tour in '75 and '76. But they were on top of their game, and so good it didn't matter. The show had sold out in three hours several months before, a record at the time. Luckily, my sister worked in public relations at the Civic Center and she secured four free tickets so me and my two besties took peyote and drank many beers before the show. Afterwards, we semi-trashed our hotel room (not even on purpose) and a pair of underpants was thrown out the window, only to land on a wire crossing the street. We were deaf for several days afterwards. It was an epic night.

BARRY BELOTTI

The Who is my band. I worked for a fan club fanzine in the late Seventies which was called *Who's News*. It went from '75 until The Who decided to do their first farewell tour in 1982. I had two friends who started up the magazine. They approached The Who and said that they wanted to start this fan club, this magazine, and The Who said 'oh sure'. And they were dealing with the New York office mainly, here in the States.

The Who said 'what do you need? We'll gladly fund it.' My friend Mark Cohen was 'no, we don't want any money. We're going to do the whole thing ourselves. We just want tickets whenever we want them and a pass to get backstage.' He was an auditor at the time, in downtown Boston and making very good money. He was just doing it out of fandom. Any of the early shows we saw, we were always in the front and at the parties after the show. Keith was my favourite.

They came here in '73 and my mom wouldn't let me go to the show. They came in '75. I was 16. I still didn't have a driver's license but I said 'I'm gonna go see them'. Me and my friend Richie bought tickets and we took a Greyhound bus down to Providence, Rhode Island. It was general admission seating and the first time I was going to see my favourite band.

It was *The Who by Numbers* tour. The show was amazing. Keith Moon came out and did a somersault. My dream had come true. We stayed so that we were almost the last people in there after the show and we watched them break down the whole stage. We were so excited that by the time we left the venue the buses had stopped running back to Boston and we couldn't get home. So I called my dad from a phone booth and said 'Dad, the buses have stopped running.' He said 'call Uncle Louie'. Luckily his brother Louie lived down there and so his brother came and picked us up and we spent the night there and he drove us home the next day.

The Who end the year with three shows at London's Hammersmith Odeon.

21 – 23 DECEMBER 1975
HAMMERSMITH ODEON, LONDON, UK

LESTER MCILWAINE

The last time I saw them was at Hammersmith Odeon, just before Christmas 1975. I recall the shows being billed as 'Merry Christmas from the 'Orrible 'Oo'. One of my housemates (also a fan) lived in Dulwich and invited me down to London to stay with him and his family at the end of term. They played several songs off *The Who by Numbers* and a lot of *Tommy*, probably because the film had been released a few months before. The Odeon was the smallest venue I saw them play. They were wonderfully loud as usual and played a great set, but I remember coming away feeling that some of the usual excitement was missing, although I couldn't put my finger on what it was. Maybe it was just because the venue was comparatively small. We walked the nine miles back from Hammersmith to my mate's house in Dulwich after the show as the busses had stopped and we couldn't get a taxi to take us! But at least my ears were ringing.

I had opportunities to see them after Moon died but couldn't bring myself to do it. Kenney Jones didn't seem like a good fit to me but it seems he was actually pretty good in the end, eg. on the album version of 'Who Are You'. When Entwistle passed away, I was equally devastated. I've seen some of their gigs on TV with other drummers and bass players but it's just not The Who I loved.

KEITH CARPENTER

I saw them at Charlton football ground in the mid-1970s. Roger Daltrey and Pete Townshend stole the show that day. It was pouring down and they both used the rain to slide around the stage. I also saw them at a Christmas party concert at Hammersmith Odeon. It was a raucous concert right from the off, with Keith and Pete appearing to have an argument during the concert. Keith was really on form that night – he was a complete legend.

GERALD CLEAVER

I went to a couple of their Christmas shows. At one of them they had Graham Chapman, of *Monty Python* fame, as the support act. He got a lot of stick. He either wasn't very funny or people were expecting The Who. He wasn't on long before Keith Moon came out, picked him up and carried him off. I think the two of them were friends. The programme was a calendar. I've got another Who programme which is made up to be like a Playboy magazine. And the centrefold is Keith, stark naked.

The Who by Numbers *tour continues into 1976.*

9 MARCH 1976
BOSTON GARDEN
BOSTON, MASSACHUSETTS

JOHN RUSIN, AGE 17

I was a 17-year-old kid. I'd seen The Who for the first time three months earlier, in December '75 at the old Civic Center in Springfield, Massachusetts and walked out of there saying 'what the hell was that?' I'd never seen the likes of it. I had an older brother who'd seen the Tanglewood show in 1970, the *Who's Next* tour in Boston and a couple of nights on the *Quadrophenia* tour. I was an Allman Brothers fan but he said to me 'these guys are major league and the guys you have seen are minor league. You've got to do this.' The tickets were $8.50 when every other ticket was $4.50. It's the best $8.50 I ever spent!

At the last minute, me, my older brother (who's since passed away) and a good friend of mine decided to go to Boston. Between us we had $105 dollars. We didn't have tickets but there were tickets around at the Springfield show – not many, but we got in so we weren't thinking much of it.

But we parked at the old Boston Garden and there was not a ticket to be seen. There were people standing on the sidewalk with cardboard signs saying 'I will pay $100 for a Who ticket'. The whole city was ready for The Who that night. It was a very uptight atmosphere outside the show. People were stressing out, including myself. I was just about to turn 18. I'm totally into this band and I've got to see them one more time. This was back in the day when you could bribe the security guards, so we went up to a security guard and emptied our pockets out. 105 bucks. The first guy turned us down but another guy saw what was going on and said 'c'mere, c'mere' so we went 30 feet down and he took the 105 bucks and we got in. I wasn't the only one that got in without a ticket. The guards were all on the take that night. The Who were already in the middle of 'I Can't Explain'.

45 minutes prior to this, somebody had lit some trash up under a seat on the balcony level in the Garden. It delayed The Who from coming out for about 45 minutes, giving Keith Moon 45 more minutes to do his thing. Maybe he just had too much time to do himself in. If the show had gone off on time, it might not have happened.

We were scrambling around trying to get a seat when they went into their second song, 'Substitute', and that's when I noticed that Townshend and Daltrey kept glancing back at Moon, and that the song was starting to go off. There might have been some anger going on, some tension. But this was only my second time of seeing them, and I didn't know if this was normal or not. But as the song went on, the drumming kept getting more and more off. About halfway through it became really sloppy. They finished the song and two roadies went over to the drum kit. I don't remember if Moon fell down, but I do remember them holding onto him and standing him up. Moon's knees kept going, and before I knew it, they took him away. Entwistle said 'we'll be right back' or 'we're gonna talk this over' or something and the whole band went off.

Remembering the Cow Palace show in '73, when Scott Halpin came out of the audience and played with The Who, people started chanting 'get another drummer'. But Daltrey came out and said, 'Keith Moon is very, very ill. He's got a bad flu.' Obviously it wasn't the flu, it was an overdose. The place started getting a little crazy. Daltrey said, 'He probably can't go on. We're going to talk to the promoter about getting another date –' and I think he said – 'the night after next if we can.' Daltrey was being reasonable. 'Your tickets will still be good.' But at that point it was obvious that The Who were not coming back out and people started giving him a hard time. He said 'that's fine, then – we won't come back'.

After Daltrey walked off the stage, the lights came on and it was like 'oh my God, it really is done'. All I could think about was 'I don't have a ticket!' The place was very hostile after that. Boston fans are not the most pleasant fans. But they came back three weeks later, April 1st, and I was there. And after they did 'I Can't Explain' on April 1st, I remember Daltrey said 'thanks for waiting for the encore.' I've seen The Who 60 times now. All three of my kids have seen The Who countless times with me. That night, I only saw one and a half songs.

BARRY BELOTTI

Six months after I saw them in Providence, they came to the famous Boston Garden, which has been torn down now. There was a late snowstorm going in. A water main broke, up on the second-floor men's room, and it leaked all the way down, right into the lobbies. And these guys are throwing sawdust down so people don't slip and everybody's tracking the stuff around. Toots and the Maytals were the support band. And Jamaican music in 1976, with the anticipation of a Who crowd, just didn't work. All of a sudden, fruit and everything else is thrown at the stage and poor Toots, who I became a fan of years later, is behind Pete's Marshall amps and he's waving a white towel. He was booed off. And then, waiting for The Who to come on, there's a fire in the loge section. Back then, you could still smoke indoors, so some popcorn wrappers caught on fire or whatever. They pulled the seats out and they put the fire out.

Finally, The Who come on stage and they jump into 'I Can't Explain' and 'Substitute' and Moon passes out over the drums. He's out! I was in the promenade section, just about four rows up off the floor. I could see up above everybody's head. Everybody's wondering what's going on and Townshend comes up to the microphone and says 'our drummer's sick.' He's out of it

And Roger comes out and 'we're gonna have to come back tomorrow.' And all of a sudden, the Boston crowd starts booing. 'Noooo! Whaddyatalkinabout?' 'Well, our drummer can't go on.' And this kid behind me is really swearing: 'Fuck you, you'd better play.' So Daltrey throws the mic down and says 'fuck you, we won't come back.' He got pissed off at people booing. And I turned around to this kid and I said, 'See? See what you did? This ain't fucking Kiss, you know. This is the bloody Who.'

They cancelled the show. So it was 'hold onto your ticket stubs'. And back then you had the mini little ticket stubs – they weren't the full ticket – and everybody's going through their pockets. My friend Tommy had lost his stub and he was drunk and he was all upset. And then I had another friend, Keith, who found a cigarette packet as he was leaving the show and it had 14 stubs in it and so he was happy because he could trade those in and get 14 tickets! So it was a long three weeks, but they rescheduled for April 1st. They said Moon had a 'viral flu infection', but we knew it was a little more than that. I guess Keith was one of those guys who took things first and asked questions later.

So they came back on April 1st and to this day, and I've seen a lot of rock concerts, it was the most amazing rock concert I've ever experienced. Non-stop energy from the minute they started. They came running on the stage and Roger said 'we won't get fooled again, Boston.' Because it was April Fool's Day.

They just launched into 'Can't Explain' and 'Substitute' and they played the whole show and at the very end of 'Won't Get Fooled Again' – there were no encores in those days – Moon was going crazy and Townshend just raised his guitar and smashed it to smithereens. He threw it way up into the rafters and it came down and he just totally annihilated it. And then Moon kicked over his drums to join in. We were walking back to the train, me and my buddy, and we didn't say a word to each other. That was either because we were deaf from the show or we were in shock. Probably a little bit of both.

CHUCK MYRA

I first saw The Who at the old Boston Garden, for the *Quadrophenia* tour. When the band was about start 'Helpless Dancer', John had put down his bass and was out front with his French horn. There was suddenly a bit of commotion with signals from stage hands and the song was dropped. A dejected-looking John started back to his amp and then stopped, turned around and walked back to the mic. He slammed the French horn onto the stage and then walked back to his amp. I read later that they dropped that song for the rest of the tour. I've always assumed it was an issue to do with the ocean.

I saw The Who, again at Boston Garden, in 1975. Before the show, they had a small fire at the sound board, but the flames were suddenly reaching 50 – 60 feet high. A wave of panic went through the crowd. Fortunately, it was quickly extinguished. I don't remember the opening act, but during the entire set, I couldn't hear the drummer. I was so upset. Would Keith get buried in the mix like this? The Who came on and during the first song, all I could hear was Keith! H did double bass drum rolls throughout the entire first song and I was in heaven. The second song was the same, with Keith again drumming is loud and furious, playing double bass drum rolls throughout. The band was getting ready to start the third song and I was watching Keith's every move. Suddenly, he leant to his left, pushing his hi-hat stand out of the way, and after a few seconds he jumped up and ran off stage. The rest of the band didn't notice.

After a few moments, a stage hand crawled out on all fours across the massive PA cabinets and started yelling to Pete. Pete finally heard him and the guy pointed at the drums. Pete turned and looked and… no Keith. The Who all left the stage and maybe ten minutes later, poor Roger came out to cancel the show and tell everybody they'd be back in six weeks, and 'don't throw your ticket stubs away'. There was loud booing and jeers from the audience. Roger got angry and said, 'What? You want to have poor Keith come out and kill himself?' The crowd burst into cheers but everyone was angry and disappointed… except me! I was thrilled and thinking, 'OMG, Keith really does do stuff like this! How cool to have it happen to me!'. I didn't realise until years later how serious it was, when I read about poor Keith being put in hospital in Florida the next day.

Six weeks later they came back to Boston and completed their show, which turned out to be the last of the tour. They were so happy to be going home at last that they put on an incredible show. Pete even smashed his Les Paul. What a show!

11 MARCH 1976
MADISON SQUARE GARDEN
NEW YORK, NEW YORK

MARC LIBRESCU

My earliest memories of The Who go back to *Tommy*, which was released in 1969 when I was nine. Later, *Live at Leeds* and *Who's Next* became an important part of the lives of my friends and me. By the time The Who released *Quadrophenia* in 1973, I was 14 and we were full-fledged Who fans. I silkscreened The Who's logo onto the back of the army jacket I used to wear and onto my friends' jackets. My friend Tony smashed an old guitar at a local park one evening.

I grew up in New Jersey, just outside of New York City. I was 16 in 1976 when the deejay on New York radio station WNEW-FM announced The Who would be playing at Madison Square Garden on March 10th. Tickets were by lottery. Anyone who wanted tickets had to send a money order to a PO box in New York City. Lucky fans would get tickets in the mail. Everyone else would get their money orders back.

It took two days for mail to reach New York City from New Jersey, and I knew tickets would be sold out by the time my money order could make it to the PO box, which was located at New York City's main post office near Penn Station. I cut school the next morning, rode the bus into New York City, took the subway to Penn Station, and mailed the envelope in the same post office it was going to. My tickets arrived in the mail.

On the concert's scheduled date, I came home from school to the news that they had postponed the show until the following day because Keith Moon 'had the flu'. We headed out to Madison Square Garden the next day after school. Our seats weren't great, but my friend and I paid a guard $10 to move us down a section. The set ended, and the band left the stage. The crowd applauded and then clapped for an encore, chanting, 'More! More! More!'. After 15 or 20 minutes, it looked like they weren't coming back. The audience began slamming the seats up and down. When people started hurling bottles from the top level, we decided to get out of there.

Backstage, The Who had refused to do an encore. The Madison Square Garden management pleaded with them to get back on stage, saying the fans would destroy the venue if they didn't. We were on our way out when the band finally came back on. We turned around and caught the last three songs. This concert was so loud, I couldn't hear for about two days. The *Guinness Book of World Records* certified another show on the same tour as the world's loudest concert.

13 MARCH 1976
COLISEUM, MADISON, WISCONSIN

PAMELA WOODWARD

I never imagined that I would still remember so many details of my first Who concert, 47 years later. It would mark a turning point for me, that drew me out of my teenage depression and pushed me to embrace my happiness. I had discovered The Who the year previously, when I went to my smalltown cinema in central Wisconsin to see *Tommy*. I only went that day because Elton John was in the movie; I knew very little about The Who. But I came away madly in love with Roger Daltrey and wanting to know more about him and The Who. A year went by in which I had been buying every Who magazine and record I could find; living in a small town that wasn't easy!

I always listened to the radio and one day, December of 1975, I heard an advertisement for a Who concert at the Coliseum in Madison Wisconsin, scheduled for March 1976. I was beside myself. My best friend and I wanted to go so badly and we begged our parents endlessly. At first, we were told 'no, it's too far away (2.5 hours), you can't drive, Madison is a huge dangerous city, there might be drugs there, and you're only 16!' We continued pleading. My father only relented when neighbours of ours agreed to drive us there and pick us up after the show. Then we found out the show had sold out (in 15 minutes!) but I was not to be deterred. A very naive 16-year-old, I wrote to the box office at the Coliseum, explained my situation and said that if anyone returned two tickets I would be happy to buy them. To my surprise, someone at the Coliseum wrote back and said they were holding two tickets for me, at $7.50 each. To this day, I'm stunned that they did that, but it was the glorious days before Ticketmaster/Ticketron.

The show was general admission. My friend and I got ourselves down on the floor area, but too far away to really see details. We brought some items with us for them to autograph. Oh, the sweet naïveté of youth. This was also my first rock concert. I remember the awe I felt when watching them on stage, that it was real, my idols in the same room as me. It was magic. The only thing I remember about the openers, the Steve Gibbons Band, is the lead singer twirling a gun. A short intermission followed and then – wham! – The Who hit the stage. I remember Keith Moon somersaulting onto the stage. I was trying to absorb it all. Roger was wearing one of his fringy things and I was mesmerised. This was the one out of two shows that year where they did 'Slip Kid'. That was a powerful, defining night for me. Everything else in my life flowed from that night.

21 MARCH 1976
ANAHEIM STADIUM, ANAHEIM, CALIFORNIA

JERRY CLOUD

This was an all-day show featuring Rufus with Chaka Khan, Steve Gibbons Band with John Sebastian, and Little Feat as the opening acts. The Who were supposed to be on their final tour with Keith Moon on drums as he had developed numerous health issues. The Who had more than double the number of songs on their setlist compared with your standard concert back then. The venue was a 55,000 sell out but another 15,000 to 20,000 showed up outside and broke down a security fence to get in. If you were there you would be stoned, as the marijuana smoke was so thick you couldn't help but get high. (When the grounds crew for the Angels baseball team started watering the field after the concert to ready it for the impending Major League baseball season, they counted over 500 newly-sprouted marijuana plants.) As concerts go it was a real marathon, but we certainly got our money's worth. The Who were just over the top and played their hearts out, putting on quite a show. I believe they were in farewell party mode for the impending retirement of Keith Moon. He wanted to go out with a bang. Not bad for the sum of $10 per ticket!

25 MARCH 1976
SATTLE CENTER COLISEUM SEATTLE, WASHINGTON

BRIAN ZELMER

I had just finished my high school baseball game when one of my teammates, whose family was filthy rich, asked me if I wanted to go. I showered and headed to the concert. We got to the concert about 30 minutes before it started. The ex-girlfriend was there with her other drunk friends and she staggered over, sat down in the chair next to me and started talking but I couldn't understand what she was saying. She proceeded to throw up on her shoes and then pass out in my lap. The concert started and I was stuck in my chair. Everyone around us was on their feet for the entire concert, and every time I tried to stand up to see, she would dig her fingernails into the back of my leg, so I just sat there and enjoyed the music. I remember hearing Keith Moon just beating the heck out of the drums.

The Who perform three shows at football stadia around the UK on successive weekends under the 'Who Put The Boot In' banner.

31 MAY 1976
THE VALLEY, CHARLTON ATHLETIC FC LONDON, UK

SUE STOW

Over the years I went to see them numerous times. Seeing *Tommy* performed live even impressed my then boyfriend (now my husband). Charlton Football Ground was amazing, with one of the first ever laser shows.

PETER SMITH

In 1976 The Who played three massive UK shows at football stadiums in Charlton, Glasgow and Swansea. The short tour was billed as *The Who Put the Boot In*. I attended the Charlton gig, which was rated at the time as the loudest concert ever by the Guinness Book of Records. These were also sadly to be The Who's final UK concerts with drummer Keith Moon, apart from a couple of low-key gigs filmed for *The Kids Are Alright* movie.

I drove a car load of us down to London on Sunday, where we stayed at a mate's flat, and on Bank Holiday Monday morning we drove across London to Charlton and parked in a street close to the ground. When we got to the gates of the stadium, something was clearly wrong. There was a massive crush around the gate, a heavy police presence, and loads of fans were being turned away. Counterfeit tickets had been circulating in London for some days before the show. Thankfully, ours were fine and we eventually made our way through the crowds and into the stadium. The place was completely rammed, even more so than in 1974, with reports suggesting over 80,000 people were in a stadium with a concert crowd limit of 50,000. Eventually the police stopped letting anyone in for safety reasons, and many fans with real tickets were not admitted. As compensation, they were given a free ticket to the Swansea show and free buses laid on to take them there.

It was wet, with rain falling throughout the day. There was not much use for the sun visors given away free by *Sounds* magazine (I still have mine, unworn). There was some violence within the crowd, with fights breaking out on the pitch and the terraces. We waited patiently during a long delay before The Who came on, caused by a few fans scaling the lighting towers in the hope of gaining a better view. The couple of guys who made it up there were told, over the PA, that the show wouldn't start until they came down. Some fans on the pitch started to chant 'get down' and eventually they did.

The Who ran out onto the very wet stage and Roger Daltrey slipped over, going his full length, sliding from one end of the stage to the other. He got up and introduced the band as 'The Who on Ice'. They started with 'I Can't Explain' followed by 'Substitute'. Townshend taunted us all with 'thank you for waiting for us and getting so wet'. Pete continued to make cracks to the audience throughout the evening, and at one point shouted out to stop a fight at the front of the crowd.

It was the same set they'd been playing in 1975, with several '60s classics, a couple from *Quadrophenia*, two from *The Who By Numbers* and a *Tommy* segment, with Keith playing his parts as Uncle Ernie in 'Fiddle About' and 'Tommy's Holiday Camp'. The laser light show, first seen during the 1975 tour, was revealed during 'See Me, Feel Me', by which time it was dark. The lasers shot through the smoke to mirrors on the light towers, with blue beams bouncing around the entire stadium, and red laser beams cutting through them. I'm sure it would seem quite primitive now, but it was impressive at the time. The entire stadium sang along to 'Listening To You' as laser beams criss-crossed the crowd in the darkness. They finished with 'Won't Get Fooled Again', ending with an incredible scream from Roger. We chanted 'We Want The Who' for five or ten minutes, but there was no encore.

It took ages to find the car. We walked from street to street; each one looked the same, and I hadn't noted the street name. Finally, we found it and set off through the crowded streets. At one point, we were sat stationary in a queue of traffic, when a big black limo pulled up alongside. Sitting alone in the back seat was Pete Townshend. We waved but he didn't respond.

DAVE WELLS, AGE 17

My older brother got the tickets somehow. They had lasers for the *Tommy* stuff. I didn't think they were at their best, to be honest. Keith was drunk and Pete may have been on heroin at the time. The highlights for me were Family singing 'Burlesque', the Outlaws singing 'Green Grass and High Tides' and the superb Alex Harvey Band doing 'Faith Healer'. I can't believe it wasn't filmed.

DYLAN WHITE

The first Who album I got was *Meaty Beaty Big & Bouncy*, which was basically all the Sixties singles because they weren't all available any more. *Tommy* was out, but they were on *Top of the Pops* in the early Seventies with standalone singles like 'Join Together' and 'Let's See Action'. That got you into The Who. And you bought *Tommy* because of 'Pinball Wizard' and then there was *Live at Leeds*, and then you got into *Quadrophenia* when that came out, and that was a big, big album that all of us were into. It was all part of that thing about having long hair, because you were no longer a Glam kid.

I started going to gigs in '73. I'd seen Slade and I'd seen Status Quo, and then I went to see The Who at Charlton in '74. I was 16. The only other act on the bill that I knew anything about was Lou Reed. A few of us went but I can't remember much about it.

In '75, I was getting more into them. The played Wembley Empire Pool on 23rd October 1975. Two or three of us went and we were quite a way back. They didn't have screens then, but there was this big thing about lasers. They had three green lasers shining out over the audience which was a bit 'wow'. And later in '75, there was a Who special Christmas show at Hammersmith Odeon. I managed to get a ticket somehow. I must have queued up or bought them from a record shop. I was in the circle. It cost two quid. That was fantastic, because they were close up, much closer than Wembley or Charlton.

I'd bought *Odds & Sods*, and *The Who Sell Out* and *A Quick One* had been repackaged and put out together. And there was the Woodstock album. I remember I had a hat with 'The Who' written on it. In '76 they played Charlton again. There were counterfeit tickets circulating in London and more people turned up than were supposed to. Needless to say, no one knew what was a real ticket and what was a counterfeit. So the ground was absolutely heaving, and it was raining. I went with two or three mates and it was very hard to get anywhere or move about.

And, lo and behold, before The Who came on, some fella decided he wanted a better view and climbed really high up the floodlight pylon. A couple of coppers went after him. There was a big announcement over the tannoy saying 'this show will not carry on until you come down from this tower. The Who cannot come on stage. We cannot proceed until you have come down.' Two or three others might also have started climbing up, thinking it was a good idea. In the end, we were all chanting 'get down, get down, get down' until eventually the fella conceded and came down.

The Who were fantastic, the dog's bollocks. There's no question. They were phenomenal, massive. The front cover of *Who's Next*, with them pissing against that obelisk, showed you they were proper geezers, proper blokes, and not teeny boppers. I've been a Who fan ever since, and still am. I saw them more recently with Zak Starkey on drums and Joe Strummer supporting. What a double bill. Pete and Roger are fantastic. They just keep going.

SIMON WRIGHT

I still have the ticket for this show, which reminds me I paid £4 to see (in reverse order) The Who, Sensational Alex Harvey Band, Little Feat, Outlaws, Streetwalkers and Widowmaker. A half dozen of us arrived early via Mark's Escort van. We had been warned about forged tickets, of which there would turn out to be 5,000 in addition to the agreed capacity of 60,000. Our mums had dutifully provided us with cheese-and-pickle sandwiches and a local offie had furnished a diverse selection of bottles. Problem: taking booze into the ground was forbidden. As the most respectable looking, it was decided that I should be the designated booze smuggler. This proved ill-advised when, after we successfully entered the already overcrowded ground, I got parted from the other five. It also began to rain. With impeccable teenage logic, I decided that if I was going to be wet on the outside I would be wet on the inside too. By the time the others found me, the booze was gone and so was I.

I sobered up as the afternoon wore off, taking in Little Feat, who should have been great but weren't and Alex Harvey, who should have been great and were. By the time The Who appeared, I was sober and ready to be impressed by my first-ever Who gig. This was before video screens so we couldn't see much, but the sound was commendably clear and loud. At 120 decibels the gig made it into the *Guinness Book of Records*. Only three songs were featured from *The Who by Numbers*. The rest of the 90-minute set comprised some early singles, half of *Who's Next* and a great dollop of *Tommy*, the latter introduced by Keith Moon to great effect. We were about halfway back, so missed the rucks that were happening down the front. Listening today to *The Complete Charlton 1976* bootleg confirms that my teenage self was right to be impressed. The band were on prime form – inventive, concise and enthusiastic. The most memorable part of The Who's set was the lasers. No one had seen them at a gig before and they were used sparingly on 'See Me, Feel Me' and 'Won't Get Fooled Again'. Green and red beams arced over our heads, almost adding a roof to the tatty stadium. I suspect the GLC put the boot in on the lasers, as I never saw them again at a 1970s gig. Getting home took about three days, as did seeing the Stones at Knebworth later the same summer, but it was worth it.

5 JUNE 1976
CELTIC PARK, GLASGOW, UK

ROBERT MONTEITH, AGE 21

I first saw The Who at this open-air concert. The tour was called *The Who Put The Boot In*. Also on the bill were the Sensational Alex Harvey Band, Little Feat, The Outlaws, Widowmaker and Streetwalkers, who were booed off the stage. I bought my ticket from a local sports store called Greaves Sports. It cost £4. The doors opened at 12pm and the show started about 2pm. I can't remember who was on first. I'd gone on my own but eventually met a couple of mates there. The best bit was after the keyboard doodling near the end of 'Baba O'Riley'. Townshend came leaping from the right of the stage as he played a massive chord and a huge round light went off as Pete hit the chord, silhouetting him in mid-air.

I remember there was a competition to win the organ from *Tommy*. A local lad had won it but Keith Moon set it on fire!

12 JUNE 1976
VETCH FIELD, SWANSEA, UK

GERALD CLEAVER

They were just tremendously good and there were thousands of people there. I was working and, because I didn't want to worry about missing the last train, I booked into a hotel. The hotel had locked all the doors so that no one could come in for a drink. Of course, they had to let me in and they were very unhappy about it. Most of the people at breakfast the next morning had been to the concert. We were all talking about it and what a great show it was. That was a good show.

MARK ELLISON

This was the third of three weekends when they'd played football stadia; Charlton Athletic one week, Celtic the following week and then Swansea. I got tickets and went with that same cousin I'd gone to Belle Vue with. No queuing this time, as ticket applications were by post. We travelled down overnight on a train with only six other people in our carriage, all males in their teen and twenties and all going to see The Who. When we got there, we joined the throng to get into the ground. We'd got half a dozen tins of dandelion and burdock each and some sandwiches to see us through the day. But we were all frisked and told we couldn't take the cans in. The deal was 'go over there and drink them or they're going in a skip'. They had half a dozen skips which were already overflowing with confiscated booze and drink. We thought, Well, you can't just drink a load of tins of fizzy pop, can you, and then go into a football ground for the rest of the afternoon,' so we just chucked it in the skip. We learned later they wanted to stop people lobbing cans and bottles, as had happened to Charlton and Celtic, where there'd been truckloads of fights fuelled by booze.

We stood near the back. The bands came and went. There was Widowmaker, Ariel Bender's (from Mott the Hoople) band who were just dull. The Outlaws were a kind of Southern boogie, and boring. We'd been looking forward to Streetwalkers, Roger Chapamn's new band, because we knew some tracks by Family, but again they didn't really do anything for me. Tiredness was setting in and PAs just weren't up to it, so unless you really knew the material, you were struggling with a haze of fuzzy noise. I felt sorry for them. Little Feat were an *Old Grey Whistle Test* favourite but didn't work for me. I was just about semi-conscious by this point because of a lack of sleep.

The Sensational Alex Harvey Band where much better. A mate was a fan so I'd heard some of their stuff before. But Alex did this thing where he dressed up as Adolf Hitler and burst through a polystyrene ball and then felt compelled to lecture the audience about how Adolf Hitler was not funny and blah-blah-blah. I remember thinking at the time, well why do you do it then?

There was a lull before The Who and I had started fading really badly. I was just sat on the floor and looking to prop myself up and have a nap. I could barely think, barely speak and I remember in the back of my mind thinking, 'I'm just fucked here because this'll just happen and I might just about recognise that they're on stage but the reason that I'm here is going to pass me by because I'm just too tired.' I was probably also dehydrated because I'd had nothing to drink for 24 hours. When The Who came on stage, I was thinking 'oh, you know, not good.'

And then I heard the opening chords to 'I Can't Explain' and – wham! Bloody hell, I'd never heard anything as loud in my life. It was just meltingly loud. I mean, just two weeks before at Charlton, they'd been clocked at 220 decibels 20 yards from the stage, which at the time was the loudest on record and it would have been about the same. Thankfully, I was a lot more than 50 yards away from the stage but even so it was just devastatingly loud. The rest of the world disappeared in this massive loud thing and it absolutely woke me up so it was just brilliant in that way.

Halfway through, they turned on the lasers which at the time were very new and very cool and very green. It was just another great set, very similar to the Belle Vue one, but with a couple of tracks from *The Who by Numbers* dropped in and for me 'Dreaming from the Waist' was a real highlight. So, again, a classic set of the time, with a bunch of *Tommy* stuff, a bunch of 'My Generation', 'Magic Bus', 'Can't Explain', 'Substitute' – stuff like. Absolutely brilliant.

There'd been sporadic fights throughout the day and I was not happy about that, even though it was a fair distance away from me. I was glad to be at the back, because it was less volatile over there, and I remember Pete Townshend bollocking a bunch of people from the stage because a fight had started in front of the band. He threatened to bring the road crew in to sort them out if they didn't stop. (Because one way of stopping fighting is to introduce more people into the fight!) But it worked, and it marked a transition to much more together crowd. Everyone was much more into the band then and less into their own problems, or drink that they'd had or not had. And there was tons of booze in there, despite the searches.

The other thing is, it rained a lot for the first few acts. It stopped raining for Alex Harvey and stayed dry for The Who. Moonie was always in the habit of cartwheeling or careering on stage, and when he came on he skidded all over the place on his arse because it was just wet. And when they did 'Squeeze Box', he was dedicating it to the people who were leaning out of the windows of the prison opposite. They got a whole day's entertainment. But they wouldn't have got any sleep if they were going to bed early,because it was bloody loud.

John Entwistle could play better than anybody. He was just absolutely non-stop and varied and wonderfully musical in that sense. Moonie was – well, most people thought Moon was great. I did. I thought he was fantastic. Pete Townshend was never the greatest guitarist on earth, but what he did do was make a virtue of his shortcomings, of his inabilities in some sense, and that is remarkable. Hardly anyone does that and he's made a career of it and that is absolutely fantastic. But Entwistle? His hands were flying and the band were just phenomenal.

BRIAN PLEASS

The prelude to The Who was Alex Harvey and his sensational band. 'Delilah' went down an absolute storm. Along and behind one half of the touchline was a cell block of Swansea jail, and in the setting sun the arms and wrists of the inmates waving through the bars of their cells to the backing of 'Won't Get Fooled Again' was a poignant sight. A little later, in the twilight, the twin floodlight towers flanking the stage had maroon smoke canisters activated at their bases, producing thick purplish red clouds which slowly rose and through which brilliant green lasers from the floodlight gantries at the other end of the ground pulsated, in time to the beat of 'Baba O'Riley'.

DAVE SMALE

I don't recall how much the ticket for Swansea cost me, but I'm sure it would have been well under a tenner. Maybe £5? I still have the magazine-style programme, though, and that cost only 50p. My first memory of the show is the task of getting from Bristol to Swansea! My car back then was a rust-ridden 1965 Austin 1100 which had a permanent oil leak. Around the time of the Swansea gig, it also had a leaky radiator, but two mates still decided to risk it with me! We packed the car with as much water as we could carry – gallons and gallons of it in what was a half-size barrel like you see in pubs – and about eight litres of oil as well, just in case! But as it happened, the old car got us to Swansea without letting us down even once.

We got into the stadium, where we were almost immediately offered and all declined some dodgy substances. We then sat in the middle of the football pitch for the whole of the gig, which started at around midday. Swansea Prison overlooked the Vetch Field and you could see movement in the prison windows as the inmates tried to catch some of the gig.

The bands that came on before The Who – Widowmaker, Streetwalkers, The Outlaws, Little Feat and the Sensational Alex Harvey Band – were all superb. I had sneaked a small portable cassette recorder into the gig in my rucksack and recorded the Outlaws as best I could before the batteries ran out. The recording came out very muffled and was not really listenable.

At around 9pm or 9.30pm, The Who came on stage, kicking off with 'I Can't Explain' and 'Substitute'. It was awesome to see them there on stage and they were just how I'd imagined. Keith Moon was a totally nutcase behind the drums, while neither Roger Daltrey nor Pete Townshend stood still for very long. Only John Entwistle stood motionless, watching the others go about their manic moves, as he plucked away on the bass, his fingers constantly moving. We had a wide variety of tracks in the set list, from right across the band's back catalogue, ranging from some of their other 1960s hits to tracks from albums like *Tommy* and *Who's Next*.

As darkness fell, their light show brought an even greater reaction from the crowd, because they began using laser beams which danced around the four floodlight pylons of the football ground and across the pitch with the crowd below just looking up totally amazed. It was all done in time to the music. This was state of the art technology in 1976. They ended with 'Join Together', 'My Generation' and 'Won't Get Fooled Again', which was absolutely fantastic with the laser beams in full flow.

CHRISTOPHER WHITE

I hitchhiked from Sheffield and slept on the beach. The only thing I had with me was cash and a toothbrush. I remember plenty of *Tommy* and the first time I had seen lasers, which were bounced off mirrors on the floodlights. Some students let us sleep on their floor after the concert and we hitchhiked back to Sheffield the next day.

August sees The Who back in the USA for four dates and then in October they are in North America again, playing another nine.

4 AUGUST 1976
CAP CENTRE, LANDOVER, MARYLAND

SETH DONAHUE

Back in those pre-Internet days, finding out information about concerts was very hit or miss. Often the first information came in the form of an announcement on the radio. Sometimes there would be a teaser to let you know there would be an announcement. Sometimes you just had to be in the right place at the right time. I was at the beach for the weekend when the announcement was made on the radio that tickets for The Who at Cap Centre on August 3 were going on sale the next day. Stuck at the beach, I was screwed. The best I could do was a seat in Section 126. But I knew from experience that there was a good chance that once the August 3 show sold out, a second show would be added – especially since the following day was 'open' on the tour schedule. I started calling the ticket office every day from work to find out if and when tickets for a second show would go on sale. I developed something of a relationship with the woman at the box office – not necessarily a good relationship; I don't think she particularly enjoyed my daily nagging.

Late one afternoon, DC was hit by a fierce thunder and lightning storm. It was during that storm that I decided to make my daily call to the box office. Just as I got through to my 'friend', I heard a loud explosion on the other end of the line. Sounding somewhat frantic, the woman said that lightning had just knocked out their power. Anxious to get off the line, she blurted out that tickets for a second Who show were going on sale at noon the next day.

I had to be at work at noon the next day, so I called my buddy Ron, who was working a night shift as a summer job. I told him that before noon the next day he needed to get over to one of the locations where tickets were going to be on sale. This meant he had to get up before noon, which was not his usual practice. The tickets were being sold through something called Ticketplace, which had sales outlets in a local chain of department stores. Ron dutifully trundled off to the nearest Hecht Company location the next morning.

There was one person in line ahead of him. At noon sharp, without waiting for anyone in line to ask for anything, the ticket agent started printing out tickets. She printed out eight tickets. The first three were front row centre. The next five were in the 25th row. The price per ticket was $8.75. There also were tickets available behind the stage for $7.50. The young woman ahead of Ron asked the price of the Who tickets and, when the ticket agent told her, she said she wanted the cheaper seats, leaving the three front row centre and five 25th row tickets sitting on the counter. Ron snatched up all eight tickets.

On the day of the concert, we faced a question: who would get the front row and who the 25th?We figured we could easily squeeze four of us into the front row and decided we would operate in shifts. Ron would get to be up front for the entire show since he was the one who got out of bed to get the tickets. I would take the front for the first part of the show but trade places and move to the 25th row for the second half of the show, since I'd seen the band more than the others (including the night before).

At the show, a fellow I recognised as a regular at the record store I hung out at was in the front row next to our seats. He had the *Live at Leeds* poster and was jumping around, trying to get the band's attention, as if he thought they'd stop the show, come over and autograph it for him then and there. That obviously wasn't going to happen, but Keith apparently noticed him at the end of one of the last numbers of the band's encore and tossed a drumstick towards him. But Keith's aim was slightly off. Ron, bigger and quicker, snatched the drumstick out of the air. The guy with the poster looked crushed, so Ron turned to him and in an act of generosity that I certainly would not have made, gave him the drumstick. Amazingly, Keith noticed and took two drumsticks, pointed at Ron and tossed them in his direction. But because this move was telegraphed in advance, the folks in the second row lunged forward and Ron came away empty-handed.

But even more amazingly, aAs the show ended, Keith headed off stage... and then paused, turned back to his kit and grabbed one of his cymbals, stand and all, and walked to the front of the stage and handed it down to Ron. I was heading to the front and saw Keith hand the cymbal to someone in the front row, but couldn't see who. When I reached Ron, he was feverishly trying to loosen the wing nut to free the cymbal from the stand, which was being grabbed and pulled by various audience members. Ron got it loose and we surrounded him and got him out of the auditorium with the cymbal wrapped in his arms. Looking back, I could see the crowd breaking the stand into pieces as souvenirs.

In late August 1978, Ron flew back east from LA to be part of my wedding party, bringing the cymbal as a gift. I told him I really couldn't accept it as a permanent gift, and that when he got married I'd give it back to him. We could then trade it back and forth over the years as a way of marking major life events. My honeymoon was a five week cross-country trip. My wife and I ended up in California, staying at Ron's house in LA. On September 8, 1978, I spent the day at the beach. When I arrived back at Ron's house, he met me at the door with a drink at the ready. 'I've got something to tell you,' he said. 'I heard it on the radio. Keith Moon died last night. Here's a drink. And you keep the cymbal.'

Some 30 years later, in July 2008, I was finally able to pay Ron back a little by inviting him to join me at the VH1 Honors Show in LA. It was the first time Ron had seen the band since that night in August 1976. That cymbal now hangs on my wall. But it's not just a cymbal. It's a symbol. Of what The Who has meant to me and what my friends mean to me.

7 AUGUST 1976 GATOR BOWL, JACKSONVILLE, FLORIDA

RICK FREEMAN

I have gotten into arguments with people who were not at this show because I said only a few hundred showed up. They claim three or four thousand. Maybe so, but even if that many came, it still left over 70,000 empty seats. There was a lot of finger-pointing afterwards. Still, it was a great performance. The Who seem to always play better if they are pissed off! The one member who took it all in his stride was Moon. I honestly do not think he cared if it was 75,000 people or 75 people.

They did say that Jacksonville was not a good place to play, but the stadium was packed for the Stones in 1975. When I arrived for The Who, I was surprised by the lack of cars and people. This caused me to fear the show had been cancelled but I went in and they took my ticket. I went to the front of the stage but couldn't see the drums so I moved back. People were slowly coming in. I was a little taken aback that more were not attending. The opening acts came on and played. It seemed to take forever for The Who to come out. The 75,000 capacity stadium looked empty. I could see Pete and Roger with a few guys who looked like promoters. They were pointing at the audience and seemed annoyed.

After the support acts played, it seemed to take forever for The Who to appear. Suddenly, Keith Moon came out and took his place behind the drums. He then stood up and bowed. The rest of The Who came out and played the best show I was able to see with Moon. They had opened the gates and declared free admission. People later said that 30,000 attended but I think it was maybe a few thousand, and only a few hundred during the opening acts. Looking back into the stadium it looked empty. The Who played to the ones who did not come. The intensity of their performance was one of sheer manic energy. It was magical. I never thought it would be the last time I would see Moon.

9 AUGUST 1976 MIAMI STADIUM, MIAMI, FLORIDA

GRIZZ GROSSWALD

My uncle had a friend by the name of Skitch who got my cousin, brother and myself backstage passes. We were 15 to 17 years old. It rained heavily the night before the show and the infield was a muddy mess. We walked into the backstage area. Within minutes someone came up to us and asked 'where the hell did you get those?'. He took the passes from us and made us go into the general admission area. We still got to see the show and it was awesome! It was Keith Moon's final tour.

7 OCTOBER 1976
SPORTS ARENA, SAN DIEGO, CALIFORNIA

MARC DAY

Beneath Keith Moon's drum kit that evening was a Persian rug that the previous day had graced a reception area near his room in a Phoenix hotel. Apparently, Moon was 'accused by another hotel guest of urinating on the expensive carpet... easily seen by anyone walking past the room'. Moon told hotel management that the wet spot had been caused by a spilled drink. 'When told the band would be billed for the full value [of the rug], Moon moved some furniture off the carpet, rolled it up, slung it over his shoulder, and took it immediately to the band's tour bus, using it that night and over the next few dates to anchor his notoriously unstable drum kit.'

The 21-song set included cuts from their newest album, *The Who by Numbers*, including 'Squeeze Box' and 'Dreaming from the Waist', as well as an eight-song medley from *Tommy*.

16 OCTOBER 1976
NORTHLANDS COLISEUM EDMONTON, CANADA

SEAMUS BRADY, AGE 18

It was quite the adventure for a couple of 18-year-olds. We made the seven-hour drive from Saskatoon in a not-very-roadworthy 1973 MG Midget after purchasing tickets in a bar in Saskatoon from a persuasive young woman who had a whole handful of them at $5 apiece. Lots of people snapped them up. When we arrived at the show, we were devastated to learn that the tickets were all counterfeit. Turned away at the door, we were outside with the many other people who had also bought these tickets. It would not have been pretty had the young lady who sold them to us all shown up just then. We did what we had to do and bought scalper tickets. Just as Mother's Finest took the stage, we made it into the show.

I remember The Who as being athletic and funny and it being the greatest concert I had seen at the time, or have seen since. The laser light show was state of the art and the Orange Double Barrel acid that was floating around at the time, and named for its potency, only enhanced the experience. I saw The Who again in 2016 in Saskatoon with the same guy I had seen them with 40 years previous. They were very good but I missed John and Keith.

BRIAN D EDWARDS

I couldn't get a ticket to see them here in Edmonton in 1976, but when we were leaving the arena area, we just about got run over my Moonie's limo. The car stopped by us and Keith Moon stuck his head out and yelled 'you scallywags!' to us and laughed. And the limo drove off.

26 OCTOBER 1976
MAPLE LEAF GARDENS
TORONTO, CANADA

STEVEN RAE, AGE 16

Maple Leaf Gardens was the biggest indoor hockey arena in Toronto at the time. It was home to the Toronto Maple Leafs NHL hockey team, but was also the main indoor concert venue. The Who show was a complete 18,000 sellout and the final show of *The Who by Numbers* tour. They played as a five piece with a touring keyboard player. I went with my friend, Hugh Little. The band and crew were all in a silly mood that night as it was the last show of the tour. They started the show with the house lights still on to surprise the audience. The first tune was 'I Can't Explain'. They also played stuff like 'Baba O'Riley', 'Boris the Spider', 'Squeeze Box' and 'Behind Blue Eyes'. They did a whole section of songs from *Tommy*. The last tune was 'Won't Get Fooled Again'. The entire audience stood for the whole show. The performance was fantastic in every way. To this day it ranks as one of the best shows I've ever seen! It was also Keith Moon's final North American show.

The Who are off the road during 1977. Work begins on* The Kids Are Alright*, an authorised biopic of the band mixing archive footage and newly filmed material. A private concert at the Gaumont State Cinema in Kilburn, North London in December is filmed but the performance from a road rusty band is mostly deemed too poor to use.

1978 sees John mixing* The Kids Are Alright *soundtrack and the band preparing to release* Who Are You*, their first new album for three years. After the Kilburn failure, another private live show is arranged for the cameras at The Who-owned Shepperton Studios.

25 MAY 1978
SHEPPERTON STUDIOS, SHEPPERTON, UK

RUSS PAGDIN

My mate Adam Hope got us both invites via the fan club to this 'secret' gig. We were taken by coach with about 200 other Who fans to Shepperton Film Studios. We got fed like film extras and then were taken into a giant hangar where, sure enough, The Who appeared. They were filming for *The Kids Are Alright* and played 'Baba O'Riley' and 'Won't Get Fooled Again'. They did a few versions, and at the end Pete Townshend said 'fuck it, we're gonna play for the kids' and they did so for about an hour more. It was truly amazing and the memory will stay with me for ever.

After the gig, we were all taken outside for a photo which was supposed to be for the cover for *Who Are You* but sadly it wasn't used. But it is in a Who book. A few months after that, Keith died, which was a massive shock. I saw them a few times after that with Kenney Jones, but it was never as good. I once knocked on Pete's door in Twickenham and he invited us in, which was amazing.

7 SEPTEMBER 1978
WESTMINSTER, LONDON, UK

Having been to a screening of* The Buddy Holly Story *the previous evening, Keith Moon dies as a result of an accidental overdose of the prescription drug Heminevrin, prescribed to combat alcoholism.

BOBBY ASEA

Keith continued to carry on with the drugs and alcohol lifestyle which ultimately led to his demise. When it finally caught up with him, and attributed to the end of his life, I wasn't surprised. In my opinion, The Who were no longer the band that I had come to know and love. Keith's contribution to the music and his drum style could never be replaced.

MIKE JONES

When I heard about Keith's death, I was naturally shocked, but bearing in mind his lifestyle over many years I honestly thought it was just a question of time. When I first saw The Who on Friday night's *Ready Steady Go!* I was blown away by Keith. He came along and simply ripped up the rule books of drumming with a unique style that no one I've ever seen since has managed to match. He was a truly amazing character and drummer.

ROBBIE LATHAM

It was terrible when Moon went. I met his sister. She had a pub and there were all these drum sticks on the wall. She didn't want to talk about him, which was understandable because it was just after he died.

KEVIN RICHARDSON

I was in Majorca on a lads' 18-30 holiday. I had met this girl who was taken very ill and had to be admitted to hospital. Whilst I was in hospital visiting her, I managed to get hold of an

English newspaper where I learnt of the news of Keith's death. I was so devastated they nearly had to find me a bed in the same hospital while I recovered!

LINDA SWEEDEN

I remember the day Keith Moon died vividly. It came on the 6pm TV news. I was hoovering when, out of the corner of my eye, the headlines said 'member of the rock band The Who found dead!'. I dropped to the floor and switched off the hoover to hear, but the BBC were running through the rest of the day's headlines. I felt sick to my stomach. Who had died? How? When? I had to wait for the other 'more important' news to be read before the details of Keith Moon's death were told. They said he died in his sleep, found by his girlfriend. I was in shock. That's not how he was meant to die. He should have died doing something crazy. He should have at least gone out with a bang! In my opinion, The Who have never been quite the same. They were like four very different legs of a table, each one in their own way holding the table up. The four faces of Quadrophenia. What would happen now...?

DERMOT BASSETT

Seeing Keith up close for the first time at The Marquee in 1968 was special, but it wasn't until the latter end of 1968, during the run in towards *Tommy* and beyond, that he really came into his own. That The Who managed to bring *Tommy* to the live stage with just three instruments was a staggering achievement and couldn't have been done without Keith. Taking nothing away from Pete and John, Keith was a phenomenon, filling out the sound in a way no other drummer could have done. Also, the onstage repartee between him and Pete was worth the entry admission alone. Listen to *Live at Leeds* for proof of both.

Eventually, though, we came to the long decline. Keith was always as famed for his excesses and antics as he was for his playing, which is a great shame. Of course, I used to laugh as much as anyone else, but there came a point where I stopped. I started seeing him as a tragic figure and it made me sad to see his powers gradually leaving him. One afternoon, I received a phone call from a friend. 'Have you heard about Keith?' She didn't really need to say anything else – I knew what was coming. I felt the tears in my eyes. I think for the first time in my life, certainly outside of family, I was crying over someone dying.

I only met him a couple of times. In Le Chasse in Wardour Street, a club (well, a room) above a bookies' that was frequented by musicians and roadies. As I walked in Keith, who was standing by the bar, spun round and started shouting at me 'get out, go on get out! We don't want your sort coming in here causing trouble.' We then had a laugh and a drink. Of course, his outburst wasn't aimed at me, just at who walked through the door next. On another occasion, he pushed me off the jukebox, which was in the gap between the two front windows, which were open. The sun was streaming in. Keith said 'just want to do a bit of promotion'. I said 'not that 'Seeker' rubbish'. He replied 'no, this' and selected his and Viv Stanshall's version of 'Suspicion'. I always remember that day and it always makes me smile.

JOHN SCHOLLAR

The last time Keith spoke to me, his mother rang me up when he came back from California. He was staying at the Royal Garden Hotel. His mum said 'ring him up'. I wondered if it was a call for help. He was in such a bad way. I got on the phone and had a chat with him and it was just like old times. He said to me 'I'll get over this problem I've got and we'll get our old band together.' And I said, 'Yeah, we'll go out and have a drink.' He said, 'No, we'll get a pub and go and do a night for them.' He wanted to get back with the old band, just for one night.

9 JUNE 1979
EDINBURGH ODEON, EDINBURGH, UK

PETER SMITH

Only a few months after the loss of Keith Moon, Pete Townshend announced, 'We are more determined than ever to carry on, and we want the spirit of the group to which Keith contributed so much to go on.' This statement was met with mixed reactions from fans, some of whom felt the band should die along with Keith, and others, like myself, who were intrigued to see how they could continue, 'although no human being could ever take his place', as Pete told *Rolling Stone*. Kenney Jones, of the Small Faces and the Faces, would join the band on drums and John 'Rabbit' Bundrick (ex-Free) as unofficial keyboardist for live shows.

On 2 May 1979, The Who returned to the concert stage with a 'secret' gig at the Rainbow Theatre, announced at a few days' notice. One of my mates managed to obtain a ticket and came back with tales of how great they were. A few weeks later, they announced a couple of Scottish gigs; one at the Glasgow Apollo on a Friday night, and a show at Edinburgh Odeon on the Saturday night. The shows were announced in the local press, and both concerts sold out immediately. I talked to my mates, Will and Norm, and, although not having tickets, we decided to drive to Edinburgh on the day in the hope of somehow getting in.

We arrived in the late afternoon, hung around in the pubs near the Odeon and wandered up and down outside the venue, asking any likely looking candidate if they had any tickets to sell. We eventually managed to buy two seats together in row F, six rows back from the stage, and a single ticket a little further back, for £7 or £8 each. Face value was £5 and it seemed a lot at the time, but it seems extremely cheap today!

There was no support act and everyone was very keen to see how this new, post-Keith line-up was going to be like. The Who came on stage, and the first thing I noticed was Roger's very short hair and how fit he looked. They launched straight into a deafening, energetic and thoroughly amazing version of 'Substitute', followed by 'I Can't Explain'. These opening tracks stopped any mutterings of how the band would never be the same again. They seemed to have come back stronger. Townshend was on fire, his arm twirling away as usual, and Roger was swinging the mic around and around. Just like old times. Of course, things weren't the same with no Keith grinning at the back like a cheeky, naughty schoolboy, and we all missed the usual banter between him and Pete. Townsend's infamous edgy attitude was still evident however. After 'Won't Get Fooled Again', he appeared unhappy with the keyboard player and promptly walked across the stage and punched him! Similarly, when hearing some of the crowd chanting 'bring back Moony, he responded 'fuck off Edinburgh!'. The small venue (probably 2,500 capacity), our proximity to the action and the incredible volume all helped in making this a very special night. The crowd went wild, shouting and roaring throughout the whole gig. The Who were awesome and musically, they seemed as good as ever. The Who were back. And they were on fire.

18 AUGUST 1979
WEMBLEY STADIUM, LONDON, UK

PHIL BRENNAN

It was the first day of the new football season and, as the traffic down to 'that London' was always going to be hectic on the day of the gig, we set off the afternoon before. Ten of us in an old transit van, with a few mattresses and plenty of booze in the back. Having survived the journey, we parked the van in a side street in nearby Brent and shuffled off to find some food before ensconcing ourselves in a little pub for the evening.

The weather the next morning was good, so we decided to leave the van where it was and walk over to the stadium. Having found a little café where we enjoyed a half decent fry-up, we topped up our bags with more booze from a local off license, knowing that prices nearer the stadium would probably treble in price. There were already several people staggering around drunk when we got to the ground around midday, but we enjoyed a little kick about in the car park with a group of lads from Leeds. As the game started to become more serious, with a few tasty tackles flying in, there was a huge roar as the gates were declared open, fortunately bringing a premature end to the football match and ensuring that the two groups wandered over to the stadium in good spirits.

As the ground filled up and people were pushing to get as close the stage as possible, there were a few sporadic fights in the crowd, with a couple of people carried out by St John's Ambulance staff. With our new Leeds friends, we were about 20 strong and so never really under threat. Several people were lying on the Wembley pitch having passed out due to over indulgence. This didn't help matters in terms of the pushing and shoving.

First up on stage was former Springsteen sidekick Nils Lofgren, who I didn't really rate although his trick of carrying out somersaults whilst still playing his guitar was impressive. I was really looking forward to Australian rockers AC/DC, having seen them several times over the years including places like the Marquee and Manchester's Electric Circus. This was the first time I had seen them in a stadium and they didn't disappoint. The Stranglers alienated a large section of the crowd by playing pretty much all of their latest album and not playing 'Peaches' or 'No More Heroes', which would have got people up on their feet.

Still, it was The Who that we were there to see and, as this was their first big gig since Keith's death, there was a sense of the unknown about how the set would go down. Any fears I or the rest of the crowd had disappeared as 'Substitute' began. The crowd were up and singing to every word as the band raced through the first few songs in true rock god style. 'I Can't Explain', 'Baba O'Riley' and 'The Punk and the Godfather' were met with enthusiasm around the stadium and Roger Daltrey had the audience in the palm of his hand. The band slowed things down with a superb version of 'Behind Blue Eyes' before John Entwistle took over vocal duties for 'Boris the Spider'. 'Sister Disco' from *Who Are You* was followed by a couple of slow songs, with Pete singing 'Drowned' and Roger performing 'Music Must Change'.

The hits returned with 'Magic Bus' and 'Pinball Wizard' and superb versions of two of my personal favourites, 'See Me, Feel Me' and '5:15' either side of 'Trick of the Light'. The band turned up the noise around the stadium as they rocked their way through 'Long Live Rock', 'Who Are You' and 'My Generation'. I then went to the toilet and the band were well into 'Won't Get Fooled Again' by the time I found my way back to our gang. The band departed the stage and then returned for a two-song encore, the highlight of the show. They played truly magnificent versions of 'Summertime Blues' and 'The Real Me' before taking their bows. It was a triumph in every sense of the word – a gig that lived up to all the hype beforehand, albeit tinged with the sadness that I hadn't managed to see them with Moon behind the drum kit.

PETER SMITH

This was The Who's first big gig with Kenney Jones as drummer and the first time the band were accompanied by a horn section for some songs. A capacity crowd of 80,000 fans crammed into the old Wembley Stadium. I went down to London on an early train with a group of mates, some of whom went off to watch Sunderland play Chelsea. The rest of us made our way to Wembley in time to catch the support acts Nils Lofgren, AC/DC and the Stranglers. AC/DC were the highlight. The Stranglers played mostly new material from *The Raven* album, which didn't go down too well with the crowd. A big fight broke out on the pitch during their performance.

My mates arrived quite drunk and full of stories of how the police had directed them into the Chelsea section of the ground, where all the home supporters were standing. They stood through the entire match, surrounded by hard men Chelsea skinheads, not daring to speak in case anyone recognised their Mackem accent. If Sunderland got the ball, they had to stop themselves from cheering, lest they revealed themselves to the skins. They seemed pretty shaken by the whole experience, but quite proud that they had survived and lived to tell the tale.

The crowd was very mixed; a collection of rock fans, a smattering of Hell's Angels who were camped on the pitch just in front of where we were all sitting, and groups of 'new Mods' in parkas. This was the beginning of the Mod revival and around the time of the release of the *Quadrophenia* movie. One of my mates, who had been to the match and was a little worse for wear, insisted on taunting the Hell's Angels in front of us. Luckily, they started to joke along with him, taking it all in good spirit. The Who started with 'Substitute' and 'I Can't Explain' and played well. Although the sound wasn't good at all, the crowd loved them and gave them a 'returning heroes'-type welcome. I enjoyed the gig, but it wasn't the best time I have seen The Who. We left during the encore to be sure to catch our train home.

NICHOLAS PARRY

Not long after I saw The Who at Charlton, Keith Moon died and Kenney Jones took his place. My sister, Julie, brainwashed by me playing my favourite bands at home when Mom and Dad were out, expressed an interest in going to gigs so we decided to go and see The Who at Wembley. We travelled down overnight in order to get a good spot, about 30 yards back from the stage and in line with the mixing desk. The Who started with 'Substitute'. I have always wondered if that was deliberate, with Keith no longer being there and Kenney Jones substituting for him? 'I Can't Explain' and 'Baba O'Riley' followed. Everything they played was amazing. John Entwistle took centre stage with 'Boris the Spider', more classics followed, and then came a fantastic rendition of the wonderful 'Pinball Wizard', which I had been waiting for. More personal favourites were '5:15' and 'My Generation'. I was so happy to be there. 'Won't Get Fooled Again' closed the main part of the show, after which we just had to have an encore and got 'Summertime Blues' and 'The Real Me'. An excellent show and I was pleased to share it with Julie. We've been to many more concerts since.

1 SEPTEMBER 1979
ZEPPELINFELD, NUREMBERG, GERMANY

VIOLA BOGARD, AGE 17

I had been listening to The Who since I was ten. It was their first tour after Moonie died and my first open air concert. It was a big deal to drive 275 kilometres to see a concert and it took me some time to convince my parents to let me go since it meant camping for two nights and I was the only girl in the group. My dad finally said okay after he found out that one of his apprentices was part of the group. He made him responsible for my well-being - and most likely threatened the poor guy! My favourite album was, and still is, *Live at Leeds* and in particular 'Magic Bus'. To see that song performed live is still one of my best memories.

13 - 18 SEPTEMBER 1979
MADISON SQUARE GARDEN NEW YORK, NEW YORK

JOHN MOGAVERO, AGE 18

I'd become a fan after seeing *Tommy* in 1975. We were dead centre but all the way up at the top tier for this show. These were the first shows to promote the album *Who Are You* after the tragic loss of Keith Moon, and the horn section behind the drum kit was a highlight when they played classic songs like 'Pinball Wizard'.

GREG BRODSKY

I had seventh-row floor seats, dead centre. I had brought my 35mm camera and took a bunch of shots of Pete Townshend punching his tambourine during the opening moments of 'Baba O'Riley' on the parts when Roger sang *fields… meals… fight… right…* etc. Just before Pete hits the first power chord on his guitar – you might suspect where this is going – he flung the tambourine straight ahead into the crowd and right into my open arms. I shook Pete's tambourine for the rest of the night, so can honestly say that I 'played' with The Who at the Garden.

Fast forward: it's 1989 and I'm working at Atlantic Records. Pete is in town to do press for his album, *The Iron Man*, and he signs the tambourine for me.

Fast forward again: It's 2012 and I'm in attendance for Pete's appearance at the Barnes & Noble in Union Square to promote his autobiography. When it's my turn to get my book signed, I show him a picture of the framed tambourine and photo I took of him bashing it. He asks me for the backstory and nods his approval.

10 & 11 NOVEMBER 1979
BRIGHTON CENTRE, BRIGHTON, UK

KEVIN RICHARDSON

After the opening couple of numbers, Roger said 'good evening, Brighton'. He then looked around and said, 'Sorry about the sound quality. They don't make places for rock 'n' roll anymore, do they?'. This got an extremely loud cheer because, of course, he was so right.

16 & 17 NOVEMBER 1979
NEW BINGLEY HALL, STAFFORD, UK

BRUCE PEGG

The New Bingley Hall had to be one of the worst venues in England back in the day; the arena was part of an agricultural showground, a cavernous 10,000-capacity general admission box-like structure that smelled like pig shit. On the night, we got there a little late, and started off quite a way back from the stage. Aside from marking Kenney Jones' first year with the band, 1979 was also notable in Who history for the release of the *Quadrophenia* movie. That, in turn, spurred a Mod revival, so there was no surprise that a large number of attendees were clad in green fishtail Parkas plus suits and ties, emulating the Mod fashions from back in the band's early days. Most of them congregated in a group in front of the stage and began annoying the crowd with their persistent chant of, 'We are the Mods! We are the Mods!'. When the house lights dimmed and The Who came on, many of the crowd around the Mods decided they'd had enough and charged into them, starting a mass brawl right in front of us. The fights quickly spilled out to the sides of the crowd, creating a gaping hole right in front of us. Needless to say, everyone around me surged forward to fill the vacuum, and I managed to get to within Daltrey-mic-cable distance of the stage for the rest of the show.

The December 1979 show at Cinncinatti's Riverfront Coliseum is to mark another dark day in Who history.

3 DECEMBER 1979
RIVERFRONT COLISEUM CINCINNATI, OHIO

MICHAEL STEELE

It's what we here call 'The Who tragedy'. It changed concert going forever. Eleven people were crushed when the huge crowd on the plaza rushed the doors. A friend and I were running late because of work. We got there and went in on the other side, not knowing what was happening. We saw a great show and left the way we came in. We got to the car, turned on the radio and that's when we heard what had happened. The feeling of shock and disbelief was overwhelming. There's a memorial there now and survivors from the night hold a service there every year on the anniversary.

11 DECEMBER 1979
THE SPECTRUM, PHILADELPHIA PENNSYLVANIA

SHEVA GOWKOW

It wasn't instant love. Aged nine, I liked 'I Can't Explain, 'Substitute' and 'I Can See For Miles' a lot, but the band looked as intimidating as hell and way too cool. But *Tommy* loomed large at school and camp for a couple of years, and when I finally got a copy (two of my first ever record purchases were the 'Pinball Wizard' and 'See Me, Feel Me' singles), it stayed on my little record player's turntable for a while. In high school I started listening to FM radio, where I heard more and loved more of the band; I guess I'd become old enough to get it. My older brother came home with Live at Leeds having found it, complete with all the inserts, in our neighbours' trash. Apparently, their son had gotten it, but as soon as his parents heard it, they grabbed it and tossed it out. His loss was our gain, and my brother immediately blasted it through our little row house, more than loud enough to penetrate the thin wall between us and the neighbours; turns out they hadn't quite gotten rid of it after all…

When a friend introduced me to Pete's solo album, *Who Came First*, I spent hours marveling at that voice while staring at that equally beautiful album cover. All the pieces fell into place, and I now loved The Who with all my heart. In late fall of 1978, I was at Rockages in NYC, spending most of my time in the video room, watching amazing old clips of The Kinks, the Small Faces, Badfinger, Jeff Beck, and of course The Who. In the pre-internet, pre-MTV days, there was no other way to see this stuff. Jeff Stein came in and talked about the movie he'd been working on, then proceeded to show us about 20 minutes or so from the rough cut of *The Kids are Alright*. It was breathtaking – here was this incredible band I'd yet to see live, in all their young glory. When it ended, he looked around the crowded room and said, 'Well?' There was complete silence for about 30 seconds, then a guy sitting in the back yelled out 'PLAY IT AGAIN!' and the place erupted in wild cheers. By the time the film had its Philly debut in 1979, I was more than ready to see this band – my band – on the big screen. It was even better than I'd expected. I could see why ten years before I'd thought they were tough and a little scary, but now I got to see they could be goofy too, and very funny, and altogether magnificent, and absolutely brilliant.

I spent the rest of the summer seeing it over and over again, to the point where I knew every word, every moment by heart. I never tired of it; how do you tire of such joy? Each time, I hated to see it end, and would already be looking forward to the next showing. It became the summer of The Who for me.

Then came December, bringing The Who to Philadelphia for two nights, and I had a ticket for both shows. That first night I had a general admission floor ticket so made sure to get there early. The tragic deaths of Cincinnati were just one week behind us; the Philly shows were being handled by the same promoter, with a similar set up. It was on the minds of everyone in the crowd waiting for the doors to open. It was in the air. Thankfully, there were enough doors, opened simultaneously, and the mad rush to get inside commenced. I found a spot on the floor as close to the stage as I could manage, wearing my heavy winter coat.

The show? Well, it was incredible, absolutely glorious. I couldn't believe I was finally, finally seeing Pete, John, and Roger, big as life and twice as loud. I was ecstatic. I was breathless. It was everything I wanted. I didn't take my eyes off Pete for a second. I can still replay in my head his razor-sharp chords on 'Substitute' opening the show and his backing vocals on 'I Can See for Miles' (including the second chorus when he was flat). I can still see him in that lovely blue sweater and red neckerchief, and I still remember those piercing blue eyes staring out at us.

Meanwhile, the floor got hotter and hotter, all those bodies pressed together. I hadn't taken off that heavy coat, and realised it was now too late. There was no way to remove it in that packed crowd without losing it. So, I stayed bundled up in the hot, hot Spectrum. I barely felt it in that packed crowd until the lights came up and I found I was having trouble breathing. I started walking towards the steps and fell down. Someone helped me up, took one look at me and carried me over to the nearest seat, pulling my coat off in the process and saying 'hey, your face is awfully red'. People wanted to get me to the first aid station to be looked at but I just wanted to get out of there. After a few minutes, I was breathing normally and didn't feel so flushed, so

I went out into the chilly December night. I don't think I put my coat back on, but just walked in a daze to the subway. I wasn't worried about the cold, or how I felt, or anything else. I'd seen The Who. Nothing else mattered.

1980 sees a short European tour followed by a two-legged tour comprising 37 North American shows.

18 APRIL 1980
OAKLAND COLISEUM ARENA OAKLAND, CALIFORNIA

STEVE RUSSEY

How to describe the feeling of seeing one's all-time favourite group in the known universe? Exponential buoyancy! Keith Moon was my main inspiration for taking up the drums… The Who's triumvirate of musical excellence with *Tommy*, *Who's Next* (including the sadly abandoned *Lifehouse* project) and *Quadrophenia* has to be the most powerful combination of musical statements ever conceived.

There I was in the nosebleed seats by way of a reasonably priced $18 ticket. As the house lights went down, Pete, Rog, John and Kenney (who did an excellent job filling some massive shoes) took the stage and lit into 'Substitute'. The din of the crowd burst a hole in the ozone layer and forced a wormhole into a parallel universe. For the next two hours I was in Who heaven. We got a representative sampling of their greatest sonic achievements: 'Baba O'Riley', 'Pinball Wizard', 'Drowned', 'Sparks', 'I Can See For Miles', '5:15' and, of course, 'Won't Get Fooled Again'. I was very pleased they encored with 'The Real Me' and disappointed that, although they had a horn section, they did not do the trumpet blasts during 'My Wife' (why, guys, why?).

The Who were the perfect group for a guy of my age going through adolescence, and especially *Quadrophenia*'s central themes of conformity, alienation, realisation and ultimate individuality. I understood their music and their music understood and spoke to me, basically saying: 'We comprehend what you're going through, we've been there ourselves, and guess what? You will survive, and you'll be successful!' They were very right!

Walking to our cars, we talked about the highlights of the show and which songs we were thankful they performed – 'Young Man Blues', 'I Can't Explain', 'Who Are You', 'See Me, Feel Me', 'My Generation' and 'Sister Disco'. After a long pause one of our party said quietly, 'Personally, I was waiting for 'Boris The Spider'…'.

1981 sees the first major UK tour by The Who since the early 1970s, with 26 dates that mixes arena gigs with theatre shows.

28 FEBRUARY 1981
DEESIDE LEISURE CENTRE, DEESIDE, UK

RICHARD DIXON

I took my girlfriend, now my wife, to Queensferry Ice Rink to see them. I can still remember the long queue snaking around the building and we probably paid on the door. It was standing only, so you can imagine my excitement when we had pushed forward to the stage. There was a great crush but the band was right there. After the first song, my girlfriend felt faint so we had to push out to the back. It has been difficult to forgive her even now! I live in Carlisle so seeing them anywhere apart from Newcastle involves some effort but I have seen them at least 15 times. I may have missed some off! Plenty of people will have seen them far more times, but they have been the background for my life, for which I am eternally grateful.

16 MARCH 1981
ARTS CENTRE, POOLE, UK

PHIL CHAPMAN

It was the last date of their *Face Dances* tour and their first UK tour since the death of Keith Moon. I wondered whether the post-Moon line up, with Kenney Jones on drums and John 'Rabbit' Bundrick on keyboards, would still pack a punch. I needn't have worried; right from the opener, 'Substitute', through new and old material to 'Won't Get Fooled Again', they were an immense unstoppable force and one of the loudest bands I've ever heard. Townshend chucked in a fair few windmills, Daltrey did his full microphone hurling act, Entwistle put all his energy into searing bass lines rather than leaping about the stage and Jones was fully committed behind his kit. The highlight for me was the build up of atmosphere and energy through the last four songs: 'Who Are You', '5:15', 'My Generation' and 'Won't Get Fooled Again'. What a treat! The encore seemed to go on forever, although it was just three songs – 'Summertime Blues', 'Twist and Shout' and 'See Me, Feel Me'. One hell of a concert, and my ears are still ringing decades later.

The Who's dates in 1982 are originally intended to support their album,* It's Hard*, but it is later announced that the tour will be their last. It proves to be their last with Kenney Jones on drums.

22 SEPTEMBER 1982
CAPITAL CENTER, LANDOVER, MARYLAND

KIM COOLEY BARKER, AGE 16

My father started taking me to shows when I was 14 and I felt alive. I remember that feeling from The Who show. I saw them on what they were calling their farewell tour. I must've gotten three of the last tickets for the show because I went with my father and brother and we had nosebleed seats and weren't sat together. The show was great but I always remember my father saying he had someone sitting behind him who chanted 'Who' through the whole thing. He said it was like having a damn owl behind him. I walked away in awe that I'd seen legends play.

25 SEPTEMBER 1982
JFK STADIUM PHILADELPHIA, PENNSYLVANIA

ARUN JOHN GOTT, AGE 16

It was an outdoor concert with about 90,000 people. I actually got to the fence in front of the stage and it felt like there were 90,000 people pushing. I helped save a woman who passed out as a wave of people started to crush us. We picked her up and put her on the stage. Remember, this was after Cincinnati where some people died. I remember The Clash and Santana but little of The Who. I might have had a little heat stroke. I was worried by all the pushing so it was no outdoor general admission concerts for me after that, which meant I missed the Stones.

12 & 13 OCTOBER 1982
SHEA STADIUM, NEW YORK, NEW YORK

TROY MITCHELL OWENS, AGE 20

I saw The Clash open for The Who at Shea Stadium. The place was completely sold out and my friends and I had seats along the first base side and felt like we were a hundred miles from the stage. It was a very cold and wet night and no one had dried off the plastic seats, so everyone was trying to find tissues, napkins or anything to dry them off with.

JOHN MOGAVERO

I guess what stood out for me that night was the rain that was coming down, and Roger singing 'Love Reign O'er Me' – it was just magical! All the songs were great, but when they performed 'Eminence Front', I swear it echoed throughout the whole stadium!

23 & 24 OCTOBER 1982
OAKLAND-ALAMEDA COUNTY COLISEUM OAKLAND, CALIFORNIA

RACHEL NISELY, AGE 19

The Day on the Green concerts, promoted by Bill Graham, were legendary. You could go see bands like The Who and The Clash with T-Bone Burnett opening for less than $15. The day-long shindig culminated in the headliner taking the stage around the time the sun went down. There was this massive party atmosphere and the music was the centerpiece of the vibe. I remember Roger Daltrey's signature vocals, especially as the crowd sang along with 'Baba O'Riley' and 'My Generation'. Pete Townshend's guitar licks ripped through the haze of smoke above the crowd. I have such fond, albeit foggy, memories of those concerts.

STEVE RUSSEY

This was The Who's *Farewell Tour*, or so we thought. The greatest rock group in the known universe was saying goodbye? We couldn't miss it… Opener T Bone Burnett got a lukewarm reception but settled the rowdy crowd down when he said, 'We all know we're here because we love The Who.' They opened with 'My Generation', taking us by surprise as they normally close with it, but it was a show full of surprises, including 'Naked Eye' (an all-time favourite of mine) and 'Tattoo'. A friend and I looked at each other in total disbelief and broke into wide smiles. We were about 40 feet from Pete. He saw us and broke into a very wide grin himself (was he thinking 'those guys are *real* Who fans'?). We got 'Long Live Rock', 'Love Ain't For Keeping' and 'Love, Reign O'er Me'. Mr Entwistle tickled us with 'Boris the Spider' and near the end we got the ultimate thrill when Townshend did the unthinkable, the unbelievable, the unspeakable, the unimaginable… He smashed a guitar. (He probably hadn't done that since about 1969.) We saw Pete raise it high and, almost in slow motion, slam it on the stage multiple times. It didn't shatter quite like the Rickenbackers from days of old, but it brought the whole Who experience full circle. At one point during the evening, some lovely young ladies asked if we had any weed. When we confessed we did not, the girls moved on. This was the fifth or sixth time this had happened over the years. Driving home afterwards I said, 'Maybe we should take up drug use so we can get to know these gorgeous gals better!' We never did take up drug use. Maybe that's why I can recall these events.

31 OCTOBER 1982
SUN DEVIL STADIUM, TEMPE, ARIZONA

ELYSE HENDRICKS

My boyfriend was reluctant to take me to see The Who. I was very into art rock at the time and he thought I would spoil the experience for him. I protested that I had heard The Who and liked them, so he took me, and I was blown completely away. We were close to the stage and I could feel the power of Roger Daltrey's voice pour through me, see the intricacies of Entwistle's playing and marvel at Townshend's riffs and poetic words. An unforgettable experience.

27 NOVEMBER 1982
TANGERINE BOWL, ORLANDO, FLORIDA

CARLA MCLENDON, AGE 26

I have been a Who fan ever since the album *Tommy*. I wore out a couple of copies of *Who's Next* in high school. I loaned that album out to everyone I knew. Unfortunately, some weren't good at taking care of LPs. I purchased all their older material. My first chance to see them live was November 1975 but I was in the army at Fort Campbell, Kentucky and came home to Florida to see my fiancée for Thanksgiving. My next chance was on their 'farewell' tour. Living down the road in Lakeland made it only a 45-minute ride. Along with over 50,000 other fans we eagerly awaited The Who. On the bill were Joan Jett and the Blackhearts and The B52s. Joan Jett was perturbed at the audience chanting 'Who' the whole time. The B52s didn't even make it through their third song before being pelted off the stage by the crowd pelting them with paper cups. The crowd had come to see The Who and they were not disappointed!

MARC STARCKE

I had been a Who fan for seven or eight months when my brother Mike and I found out a new Who record was coming out in early 1982 called *It's Hard* and then that they would be doing a final 'farewell' tour, with one show in Florida, at the Tangerine Bowl in Orlando. So, no South Florida show.

But my brother and I were not complaining. A road trip to see The Who would be like going to Disney World for the first time and then some! We waited on line at a mall in Hollywood, Florida for 24 hours for tickets, complete with house speakers on top of the car. When the main doors to the mall finally opened, Mike and I ran all the way to the record shop inside that had the Ticketron while trying to outrun 200 other teenagers. It was a free-for-all to the record store line. We did alright, ending up fourth in line and with lower bowl seats on Pete's side.

We drove to Orlando from South Florida in a car with five Who freaks in our Gold *Rockford Files* 1979 Firebird. It was the first time I ever heard 'Tattoo', recorded or live. At the time, I thought the song was a bit odd-sounding for The Who but it felt right for the Disney town. But later it ended up being one of my favourite songs of all time.

The concert was a religious experience. It sealed it for us as Who freaks. The B52s and Joan Jett and the Blackhearts were the two opening acts. Why the B52s at a Who concert? What was the promoter smoking? Not the same shit as us, that's for sure! The B52s came on first but they didn't last long. They were bombarded with paper cups and anything the fans could get their hands on. The girl in the band with the beehive hair-do ended up with paper cups stuck in her hair, and the band lasted about one minute before running for cover. It is, to this day, the most unusual thing I have ever seen at a rock concert.

Joan Jett came on next and I liked her music. She was rock 'n' roll all the way, so I didn't expect what was about to happen to her as well. The fans were screaming obscenities at her. When she sang the refrain from the song 'Do You Wanna Touch Me (Oh Yeah)', the 60,000-strong crowd would yell back 'noooooo!'. Next thing we knew, she was screaming back at the crowd, giving it the finger and yelling 'fuck you Orlando' before she slammed her microphone down on the stage and stormed off. She lasted maybe 30 minutes.

The Who came on in the darkness with 'THE WHO' lit up above the stage. They'd recently reinstated 'My Generation' into the setlist a few shows before they reached Orlando. I guess they realised that, despite the perceived negative line in the song, it had to be played – it was the one song that fans complained about that was missing.

The show was simply amazing. Pete's guitar playing was blistering, Roger's voice anthemic, The Ox in his red suit and with his blazingly thunderous playing, and Kenney his usual solid self. The show included a long, jamming version of 'Magic Bus'. At one point, Pete said to the crowd, 'From the Magic Kingdom to the herpes master class.' At another, he stopped playing, hugged his guitar and told a group of chirruping fans up front, 'You can't have my fucking guitar and I'm not going to smash it!'. They went on to play an excellent set that night and confirmed my opinion of them being the greatest rock group in the world!

1 DECEMBER 1982
MISSISSIPPI COAST COLISEUM
BILOXI, MISSISSIPPI

KENT BRUCE, AGE 15

I set out with two friends to see them on what was to be their final tour. I checked out of school because I was 'sick'. We had a three-hour drive to get to the Mississippi Coast Coliseum. The show was sold out and the parking lot full of fans getting ready for the show. News media were there. I don't know why, but the *Clarion-Ledger*, the biggest newspaper in Mississippi, asked me if

I would do an interview. I did the interview and didn't really think about it.

There was no reserved seating and the floor was wide open. I got separated from my friends trying to get a good spot to watch from. I made it to the front barricade right at centre stage. I was playing drums at the time, so really wanted to see Kenney Jones up close. I was waiting for the drums in 'Won't Get Fooled Again'. The floor was packed and it was tough down there. Midway through their set, The Who played 'Baba O'Riley'. After the harmonica part, I felt something hit me. I thought it was just somebody being a jerk, but Daltrey's black harmonica had landed in my arms. People were on the floor scrambling to find it. I just stood there holding it, acting like I didn't know a thing. After the show, I met back up with my friends. They were talking about how good the show was. I pulled the harmonica out and they were stunned. I still have the harmonica to this day.

At some point, I had told my mom I was not coming home that night. The next morning, she called the school and made an excuse as to why I was not there. Unfortunately for me, the *Clarion-Ledger* published the article with my interview in the next morning's paper. It had my name, where I went to school, and what I was doing. My mom was not happy. That's rock and roll....

3 DECEMBER 1982
ASTRODOME, HOUSTON, TEXAS

LEANNE BANKS, AGE 19

I had won an album a week for a year at KLBJ radio in Austin, but couldn't find an album I was interested in. Peggy Simmons, one of the DJs, asked if I would be interested in free tickets to see The Who in Houston. I'd been a fan since seeing *Tommy* when I was in sixth grade. I was going to turn 20 eleven days later. What a great early birthday present! I called my parents to have them pick my son up from daycare. Then I called work and told them I had to take the afternoon off – and I hit the road. I made it from Austin to Houston in record time. It was supposed to be their last tour and I had never seen them live before. I remember crying.

6 DECEMBER 1982
CHECKERDROME, ST LOUIS, MISSOURI

PATRICIA FITZGERALD, AGE 19

For my 19th birthday, I asked for tickets to see The Who and rolls of film. I got both. My sister Wendy, my brother Preston and our best friend Kerrie 'Concert' Hall drove to this show singing 'Happy Birthday' and 'Who the fuck are you?' on the way. Our tickets were far from the stage but halfway through the concert we spotted some empty seats up front and, one by one,

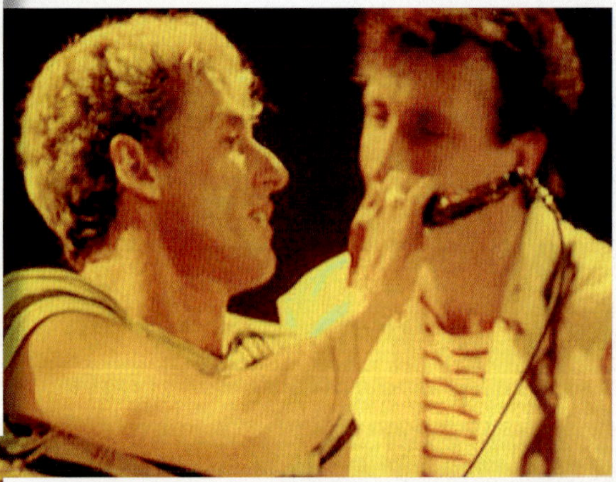

Clockwise from top left: 1979 tour programme owned by Maureen Browning; Alyce Johnson with Roger; St Louis 1982 - photo Patricia Fitzgerald; St Louis 1982 - photo Patricia Fitzgerald; Linda Sweeden at Wembley in 2016 with Roger and Pete

Clockwise from top left: St Louis 1982 - photo Patricia Fitzgerald; St Louis 1982 - photo Patricia Fitzgerald;
St Louis 1982 - photo Patricia Fitzgerald; St Louis 1982 - photo Patricia Fitzgerald; Steve MacLennan with Roger

we made our way towards the stage. I took out my camera and began photographing Roger Daltrey with his signature blond curls, the brilliant Pete Townshend who we had watched for years on VHS tapes smashing his guitar on British TV, and the steady bass of John Entwistle, with his Schlitz-sponsored water bottles visible in every frame. It was a great birthday.

***The Who's only live appearance between 1983 and 1988 is at* Live Aid.**

13TH JULY 1985
WEMBLEY STADIUM, LONDON, UK

PETER SMITH

I was lucky enough to go to *Live Aid* with a couple of friends. The highlights were The Who and David Bowie. The Who performed 'My Generation', 'Pinball Wizard', 'Love Reign O'er Me' and a blistering 'Won't Get Fooled Again' with much mic swinging by Daltrey and lots of arm twirling by Townshend. It was fantastic to see their short set amongst some other stand-out performances. It's a day I will remember forever.

22 DECEMBER 1985, LONDON, UK
DOMINION THEATRE

GRAEME SELKIRK

In the Eighties, I often drove my session guitarist brother-in-law to gigs if I was free, and looked after his guitars. Around 1985, he was booked to do a benefit gig at the Dominion Theatre with Pete Townshend for a women's refuge Pete's wife at the time was involved with. The wonderful Joanna Lumley was also on the bill, doing a 'Widow Twankey' routine with Pete. The nature of the gig meant it was very informal backstage, and I was sitting in the dressing room which was doubling up as a tuning area, and got talking with Pete who was in full costume as Widow Twankey, complete with appropriate headgear. We were having a serious discussion about, as I remember, Who gigs in Scotland, from whence I came. The image of the man looking so ridiculous but talking in such a matter-of-fact way has been lodged in my mind ever since. Alas, no camera phones in those days!

In 1988 The Who perform one show, at London's Royal Albert Hall. But in 1989 they are back on the road in North America, playing a 40-date stadium and concert hall tour, and the UK.

The Who's 25th anniversary tour marks 25 years since Keith had joined the band and is their first full tour since 1982. Kenney Jones is replaced on drums by Simon Phillips. Citing difficulties with his hearing, Pete wanted the band to play at lesser volume than in previous years and to play mainly acoustic guitar, meaning the band had to draft in a second guitarist.

PETE WRIGHT

They started going out again because John Entwistle was broke. I went to see his house and it was like Woburn Abbey. It was unbelievable. It was a massive, massive place. There was Pete Townshend standing in a perspex cage because of his ears, playing an electric acoustic, and he had Boltz Bolton on John's side of the stage also playing guitar.

27 JUNE 1989
RADIO CITY MUSIC HALL
NEW YORK, NEW YORK

HELEN RICHARDSON

I saw The Who performing *Tommy* at Radio City Music Hall. It was overpowering on every level and I was deaf for days afterwards. I also saw them in Chicago in 1974 on the *Quadrophenia* tour, when there was barely concealed anger all around, and Camden, New Jersey at the Tweeter Center in July 2002, after Entwistle's death. Pete and Roger provided a musical eulogy of their own.

27 JULY 1989
CARTER–FINLEY STADIUM
RALEIGH, NORTH CAROLINA

ANDY CLENDENNEN, AGE 19

I was in the Navy, stationed in Norfolk, Virginia. Some fellow shipmates and I saw that The Who would be playing at Carter-Finley Stadium. I was too young to have seen The Who in their heyday but thought that, even without Keith Moon, it would be awesome to see them. The plan was to meet in the stadium parking lot – this was before cell phones – and hang out for a bit and drink a few beers before going in. I was only able to take a half-day off, so I was going to make the three-hour drive separately. I had an 1980 Impala but no clue about oil changes, radiators, air filters or any of that stuff. Get me from Point A to Point B and I'm happy.

I started my trip on a nice sunny afternoon, giving myself plenty of time. Halfway into the drive, I noticed my thermostat start to rise. And rise and rise. There wasn't much in terms of civilization along the way, and I was basically in the middle of nowhere when my radiator blew out on me. Luckily there was a tiny town just up ahead – five or six houses and a couple of businesses on one side of the road, and nothing but farmland and forest on the other side. It was late Thursday afternoon, so most businesses that run on small town time weren't open, but couple of older dudes were hanging out outside of one of the bars. I told them my story and, just as every other small town has an auto repair shop, so did this one. They older dudes knew the owner of the repair shop so gave him a call from the bar and he said he could patch me up, even though he was technically closed. A couple of hours later, I was on my way again with a 'new' radiator. I pulled into the parking lot at the stadium and didn't hear any music. 'Whew,' I thought, 'made it just in time.' And just as I started walking across the lot, they broke into 'Overture' and 'It's a Boy'. I found my seat, and my friends, just as '1921' was starting.

JAMES NIXON

This was one of the first big tours to be sponsored by a corporation. The tour poster was this godawful rendering of them 'in action'. I was in undergraduate school at North Carolina State University. The area was hosting a lot of big outdoor gigs at the time, ranging from Paul McCartney and Wings through to the Rolling Stones and even Pink Floyd. It was the real onslaught of getting everything through Ticketron. But as a student, camping out in line was nothing new.

I had always been a huge fan of The Who and Pete Townshend. They were at one end of the stadium and I was on 'the hill' at the other end, 110 yards away, but they were still fantastic. The highlight of the concert for me was the recently-released 'Eminence Front'. There was a rumour after the show that Pete and Roger had got into a huge fight during the first set break and that Pete had locked his mate in his dressing room. No one really bought it, but it made for a good excuse for a bad drum solo lasting too long! John even moved a few steps, probably for a smoke.

The 1990s sees The Who enter another period of hibernation, with no live shows between 1990 and 1994 and only one show in 1995 before the band are on the road again in 1996 to perform* Quadrophenia *as Pete Townshend originally envisaged it, with horn section, keyboards and backing vocals.

29 JUNE 1996
HYDE PARK, LONDON, UK

PETER SMITH

This was a great gig, with a very strong line-up. The concert was in support of the Prince's Trust and the first time that The Who had played in the UK for some years. I went with my wife Marie, largely to see The Who; however, the presence of Dylan and Clapton on the bill made the event all the more attractive, and the price of £8 seemed a bargain. *Quadrophenia* has grown on me over the years, and I've seen The Who perform it three times; once on the original tour, this show in Hyde Park, and more recently at the Albert Hall Teenage Cancer Trust gig. The Hyde Park show featured a cast of special guests playing the various parts of the rock opera: Phil Daniels (Narration), Trevor McDonald (Newscaster), Ade Edmundson (Bell Boy), Gary Glitter (Rocker), Stephen Fry (Hotel Manager) and Dave Gilmour (guitar on 'Dirty Jobs' and 'Love Reign O'er Me'). The band was introduced by Jools Holland. It was a fun show, although I was a little disappointed that they didn't play any Who classics; I thought we might get one or two as an encore. Instead, we got a reprise of '5:15'.

PAUL BAKEWELL

I've seen many Who gigs, but two memories stand out. I managed to blag my way into the press area at Hyde Park, replete with a nice press pack, whilst Tom Petty was on. It was a cracking line up and *Tommy* was even more surprising, with Gary Glitter as the Godfather. He'd managed to clout Daltrey in the eye with a mic, hence Roger sporting the RAF roundel eyepatch. All good clean fun. I even got to call my mum on one of the many landline phones provided!

By contrast, I got an invite to the filming of Pete Townshend on the VH1 Storytellers series on Sky TV in a plush room in the West End of London in 2000. This proved to be a more relaxed, laidback affair where Pete divulged how he wrote the many Who classics. Interesting stuff. I hung around after the event and surprised Pete with an autograph request as he jumped out of his Roller, which he duly provided. He'd stopped to get a kebab!

19 & 20 OCTOBER 1996
SAN JOSE ARENA, SAN JOSE, CALIFORNIA

SHAWN ROSVOLD

I'm old. Old enough to remember when I first heard 'I Can't Explain' in 1965. My dad was a DJ at a radio station that didn't play that kind of music, so he used to bring home all kinds of 45s for me, and I had 'I Can't Explain'. My first Who LP was *The Who Sell Out*. As a kid living in a small city in Nova Scotia, Canada, I loved hearing the commercials for brands of things I had never heard of. By 1969 I was a failed student, a dropout, trying to figure out my life while working in construction in -40 degree winter weather. I played the hell out of *Tommy* while living in my parents' basement. A friend of my dad's was a radio station programme director and asked if I'd like to get into radio. Who wouldn't want to sit in a nice warm studio, playing records, and getting paid to talk to women on the telephone? Soon after I started in radio, *Live at Leeds* came out and we played the hell of it. I was lucky enough to work at many radio stations, most of which played what is now classic rock, and I got to play a lot of Who and Pete Townshend music. It wasn't until 1996 that I finally got to see The Who live on stage at the San

Jose Arena in California. After working in San Francisco, I moved to New York City. In 1999, Pete Townshend came to town to promote his new album, *A Benefit for Maryville Academy*. He got up at an ungodly early hour and came into our studio to be a guest on our morning show on Q104.3. I cannot express in words how thrilled I was to be able to talk with this wonderful, warm and very funny human being. It was a dream come true.

19 NOVEMBER 1996
CONTINENTAL AIRLINES ARENA EAST RUTHERFORD, NEW JERSEY

EVAN MICHAEL, AGE 21

My friend Jon Blinn and I were in the nosebleeds to see The Who for the first and only time, with a backup band that included Zak Starkey on the drums and Pete's brother Simon on guitar. We were so high up that I thought I was going to fall forward to my death. But those worries all went away when they hit the stage. The power! The volume! They performed all of *Quadrophenia*, with Billy Idol as The Ace Face on 'Bell Boy' and Gary Glitter as The Godfather on 'I've Had Enough'. The encores included an acoustic version of 'Won't Get Fooled Again' performed by just Roger, Pete and John, and 'Behind Blue Eyes', 'Substitute' and 'Who Are You'. An awesome show.

11 DECEMBER 1996
MANCHESTER EVENING NEWS ARENA MANCHESTER, UK

PHIL CHAPMAN

I saw The Who about halfway through their 13-month *Quadrophenia Live* tour. Zak Starkey was already doing a good job in Keith Moon's role. The band of around a dozen musicians included a full brass section and backing vocalists and they sounded great. The line -p was topped out by two special guests, PJ Proby as The Godfather and Billy Idol as The Ace Face. I'd always loved the album and this concert really did it justice. Pete Townshend kept to acoustic guitar for the entire performance but for the encore strapped on the required electric as the band delivered a storming rendition of 'Won't Get Fooled Again'. An unexpected bonus for me was the inclusion of 'Behind Blue Eyes'. I've liked the song ever since I first heard it back in 1971 and never expected to hear it live. The show closed with 'Who Are You', which was given a suitably big finish by the full band.

In 1997, The Who play European, British and North American shows.

6 MAY 1997
FESTHALLE, FRANKFURT, GERMANY

ANSGAR FIRSCHING

They still had three of the original band members and played the whole of *Quadrophenia* and more. I was there with my wife who was pregnant with our oldest daughter. I'm very glad I made it to a Who concert. Pete taught me how to play electric guitar long before Keith Richards taught me the rest.

KAI OLIVER KYPKE, AGE 24

I had moved to the city just a few months earlier, so going to the concert was a 15-minute tram ride. I'd become a fan after seeing The Who's performance of 'A Quick One (While He's Away)' in the Rolling Stones *Rock 'n' Roll Circus* which had just been released. I was worried I'd be disappointed – Pete was just playing acoustic, it was their first tour for eight years and I might be the only one below 40 in the audience. When 'The Real Me' started, I doubted whether it was really live. It was so powerful, flawless and well-timed I thought they had to be miming. I'm so glad I was proven wrong when the odd wrong note was slipped in much later! Roger wore the target eye patch.

My favourites were 'The Real Me', 'I've Had Enough' and '5:15'. The rock opera justified the big band-style the concert presented, although I would have preferred the encores to be played by the four piece and not the entire orchestra. But that's what we call in Germany 'jammern auf hohem niveau' – whining at a high level.

15 AUGUST 1997
ICE PALACE, TAMPA, FLORIDA

FABRIZIO MARCILLO

I live in Ecuador but when a friend told me about this concert, I asked him to get the best seats he could and booked my vacation, bought airline tickets and planned a visit to Disney in Orlando for the family. The Who have been my favourite band since 1970. I would go to the beach in the cold season before sunset with a Parka and two bottles of booze and play *Quadrophenia* on a 90-minute Maxell cassette on my Walkman. I would stay at the deserted beach until sunrise, playing the cassette over and over, singing stuff like 'the beach is a place where a man can feel, he's the only soul in the world that's real'. After one of these beach visits, I wandered sleepily into a cemetery and fell asleep in a grave. I was awoken a few hours later by some people visiting a neighbouring grave. When I came out of the grave I'd been sleeping in they had the fright of their lives!

I was really looking forward to seeing *Quadrophenia* in concert but in July my dad had complications following a routine gall bladder operation. We took him to a hospital in Miami and I said I would skip the concert and the vacation I'd planned. He told me he didn't want to hear any such nonsense and that I should go to the concert.

There is only one way to hear a *Quadrophenia* concert, with Dr Jimmy and Mr Jim, so I bought two bottles of Gilbey's Gin, put them in plastic bags and smuggled them into the concert. When I arrived at the concert, I found out my friend had booked the cheapest seats, even though I'd said I would pay for the seats. I told him to fuck off, bought a soda to mix with my gin and – somehow – ended up in front of the stage when they started playing 'The Real Me'. I'll always remember being just two metres from Pete's boots as he was jumping and soloing away.

After 'The Punk and the Godfather', an usher threw me out from where I was so I went back to my 'friend' and his wife's seats, very far from the stage. We managed to get a little closer for the rest of the concert. I got really wasted on my gin and could almost feel I was Jimmy in the boat and smell the sea and hear the waves as the band played 'Love Reign O'er Me'. After *Quadrophenia*, they played many other classic songs and I really enjoyed every one of them. I really was immersed in the music and the show.

The day after the show, I called back and found out my dad wasn't doing very well, so I returned to Miami. I asked him why had he told me to go to the concert and he said he was OK. He told me he knew that seeing The Who was something I'd always wanted to do and so he wanted me to go. A couple of days later, my dad died. That concert was the last and most interesting gift he could have given me. Now, every time I hear *Quadrophenia*, I remember my dad and his gift to me. I hope I can be like that with my kids when the time comes.

27 FEBRUARY 2000
NEWCASTLE ENTERTAINMENT CENTRE NEWCASTLE, AUSTRALIA

STEVE MCLENNAN

As a die-hard Alice Cooper fan since hearing 'School's Out' in 1972, I was very pleased to receive news that The Coop and a bunch of his legendary rock 'n' roll pals were touring *The Ultimate Rock Symphony* with a full orchestra and band comprising Alice Cooper, Paul Rodgers, Peter Frampton, Gary Brooker, Nikki Lamborn, Billy Thorpe and Roger Daltrey around the time of my birthday. I locked the dates in my calendar for the two Sydney gigs and the one in my hometown, Newcastle.

The Cooper Organisation had always been very kind to me whenever Alice has ventured Down Unda, and for the Newcastle show, I secured passes for myself, my partner Linda and my then five-year-old son, Zac. Zac was very excited to be seeing Alice Cooper perform but somewhat overwhelmed by the prospect of meeting him in person. He had no such qualms about meeting the other rock luminaries, as they hadn't been raised to the same mythical heights in our household as Alice.

The 'meet and greet' process was a little unusual. The performers came out one at a time and were introduced to each of the three small groups of punters separately. There were local radio folk with some competition winners, a group from the local golfing fraternity, and me and my family. Zac, cute as a button, drew people to him like a magnet. The cavalcade of stars all made a beeline to the little kid who had no idea who they were. The conversations went like this:

Me: Zac, this is Peter Frampton, Peter, this is my son, Zac.
Peter: Hi Zac, how ya doing?
Zac (shaking Peter's hand): Hi Peter, I'm good. Are you in Alice Cooper's band?
Peter: Well, I play a couple of songs with Alice tonight.
Zac: What do you play?
Peter: I play guitar.
Zac: Well, my dad plays drums and his friend Trev plays guitar and they're in a band too.

At this point, I got Peter to sign my birthday card. Similar conversations transpired with Paul Rodgers, Gary Brooker and Nikki Lamborn, who all generously shared with Zac their resumes and their joy to be performing as part of 'Alice Cooper's band'. Then Alice Cooper – the man, the myth, the legend – appeared in the doorway. Zac froze and nervously pointed. 'Dad, its Alice... Cooper.' Alice, with managers Shep Gordon and Toby Mamis, made his way over. 'Hey Mac, how's it going? Ah... this must be Zac.'

Zac, almost in a whisper, said, 'Hello, Alice Cooper.' Highly adept at putting starstruck fans at ease, Alice offered Zac a Snickers and engaged in a game of hide-and-seek. As he stalked Zac around the backstage area, Alice reminded me of the Child Catcher from *Chitty Chitty Bang Bang*. Eventually, Alice excused himself to go and chat with the golfers as Roger Daltrey made his way over to say 'hi'. I introduced myself and offered Roger some freshly cooked scones (six plain and six date) I'd had my mum bake that day. Roger seemed genuinely excited. I introduced Roger and Zac to each other.

Roger: 'Ullo Zac. Our drummer's name is Zak as well.
Zac: Well, my dad plays drums and so do I. Are you in Alice Cooper's band?
Roger: Alice Cooper's in my bloody band, mate.
Zac: Are you kidding? Alice Cooper's a star!
Roger: I'm a bloody star too, mate!
Zac: (to me) This guy's a nut!
Me: (to Zac) Roger is a star.
Zac: (to Roger) Not like Alice Cooper.
Roger: You think you're pretty bloody tough, don't ya, mate?
Zac rolled up his sleeve to show Roger his bicep.
Roger: (feeling Zac's five-year-old bicep) Hmmm... not bad. Right. Let's sort this out.

Roger then walked to a table, removed the items that were on it, pulled up two chairs and motioned to Zac. 'Let's arm wrestle'. The room fell silent. All eyes were on the two combatants. Zac and Roger stared intently at each other as they firmly gripped hands together. Paul Rodgers explained the rules of battle.

Peter: You've got this, Zac.
Paul: 1, 2, 3… go!
BAM!

'Not so tough now, are ya mate?' Roger triumphantly exclaimed as he slammed Zac's arm flat on the table. The stunned silence in the room was broken when Toby laughed 'you showed him, Rog'. Zac acknowledged, 'He is pretty strong for an old guy.' More laughter ensued. Zac and Roger shook hands. Alice assured Zac, 'You'll get him next time.'

Zac is now 28, a little over six foot two and a similar build to a Rugby League second-rower. He is the Venom Co-ordinator at Australian Reptile Park which puts him in close physical contact with the most venomous snakes on the planet on a daily basis.

Roger, if you're reading this, I'd like to think that night in Newcastle had a very positive impact on Zac's resilience and his determination. Like Johnny Cash's 'Boy Named Sue', I feel Zac owes you a debt of gratitude for 'the blood in the gut and the spit in the eye' attitude that has held him in such good stead. I hope you enjoyed the scones after the show with a nice hot cuppa.

4 OCTOBER 2000
MADISON SQUARE GARDEN NEW YORK, NEW YORK

TROY MITCHELL OWENS

After seeing them at Shea in 1982 I saw The Who again at Madison Square Garden. Jimmy Page and the Black Crowes were going to open but Page had to back out due to back problems. Jakob Dylan and his band opened instead and while they were good I am a huge Zeppelin fan so not seeing Page was very disappointing. However, The Who were incredible. Daltrey hit all the notes and Pete was on fire on guitar and windmilled his ass off. Everyone clicked that night. 'Won't Get Fooled Again' was the stand out song but there wasn't a dud all night. To see them 18 years after Shea and for them be as great as they were back then blew me and my friends away. The mood of the crowd walking out of MSG that night was pure exhilaration, which is always the sign of an amazing concert.

27 JUNE 2002
HARD ROCK HOTEL, LAS VEGAS, NEVADA

After a handful of UK dates at the start of the year, The Who's 2002 North American dates are thrown into chaos when John Entwistle is found dead at the age of 57. The coroner finds that he died of a heart condition brought on by taking cocaine during a night of debauchery with a Las Vegas stripper after spending the evening in the hotel bar with Roger and Pete.

BARRY BELOTTI

I miss John Entwistle. John was the closest I got to out of the three. He was such a nice person. He loved to hang out after the shows. He founded the band. Without him, that full sound is really missing.

RICHARD DIXON

My parents went on a guided bus tour of the Cotswolds and whilst driving along, the guide pointed out a mansion belonging to John Entwistle. This elicited puzzled looks from all the elderly passengers apart from a smug-looking couple (my parents) and who were able to inform the rest who John was. I am a vet in Carlisle and a late client of ours was a Miss Linton, whose friend was Miss Hartley and a sister of the novelist LP Hartley, who wrote *The Go-Between*. They bred deerhounds and John used to come up here to visit and buy dogs off her. Sadly, I did not know this until after Miss Linton died. How wonderful it would have been if I had got a call to see the dogs on the day of one of his visits!

In Keith's case, and in view of his life style, there was a degree of inevitability although great sorrow when it was actually confirmed that he had died. It didn't come as a great surprise. That was in stark contrast to my feelings when John died. He had reached middle age and as far as I knew was settled in his life in the Cotswolds. I was aware that he had heart problems but I just assumed that they were under control and he wouldn't do anything stupid. My overall feeling when I heard of his death was actually a selfish one. When Keith died, I assumed that the rest of the band would find a replacement drummer but when John went, I thought that would be the end of the band and that I would never see The Who again.

We had a family holiday in Orlando whilst the tour was on. It was unlikely that I would have been able to see them in the States but I do remember the pennants hanging from a row of street lights in Universal Studios with 'RIP John Entwistle'. A nice tribute, but I found it rather depressing as it reminded me that it would be the end of the band. Fortunately, I was wrong as in early 2017 I saw The Who at the Royal Albert Hall performing *Tommy*.

Without John Entwistle, the band draft in Pino Palladino on bass and Pete's brother Simon on rhythm guitar and backing vocals.

1 JULY 2002
HOLLYWOOD BOWL, LOS ANGELES CALIFORNIA

LAUREN J HAMMER

John had died the week before – a devastating loss. In Vegas, whilst mourning, we knew through our information sources what was happening next, even before the band did. They were skipping the first two shows, in Vegas and Irvine, SoCal, but picking up with show number three at the Hollywood Bowl instead of going home to the UK, to lay John to rest.

The new opening night at the Hollywood Bowl was an incredibly painful one. I woke up that day, holding front row centre tickets to see The Who, and/but not wanting to go. Previously unfathomable. But go we did. It was a rough, rough night, but if the show was happening then it was exactly where we needed to be. Pete briefly stopped the show because of me, to make sure that I was okay. At the end of the night, they looked so small and lonely, just the two of them on the stage.

Then it was on to NorCal for Shoreline and the Sacramento Valley Ampitheater. And for the final show of what was supposed to be a six-show opening run, the Gorge, far from civilization, out in the middle of Washington State. In the van, roadtripping from the Seattle-Tacoma area, it was me, my front row travelling Who wife, Stefani, her first Who wife and my dear friend, Deanna, and Stefani's real life (now ex) husband, Gordon. Out of the blue, I had a feeling. A strong feeling. A premonition. 'I think Pete's gonna smash a guitar tonight.' That was a pretty absurd thing to say. He doesn't do that anymore. But I felt it. And what a cathartic release that could be.

Sure enough, late in the show, during 'Won't Get Fooled Again' it happened. Right before my very eyes, as I was front row, right in front of Pete. In over 150 Who shows to date (and still counting), it was my one and only guitar smash. And it wasn't angry Pete smashing. It was just the thing to do. At least from my vantage point, it seemed like it just felt right. I can't think of a better word than cathartic. That captures it. For me. For Pete. And for anyone tuned in enough to get it. And as for me, I felt a little bit like Babe Ruth. It was my shot heard round the world.

30 JULY 2002
SHORELINE AMPHITHEATRE MOUNTAIN VIEW, CALIFORNIA

DAVID HUGHES

We bought tickets to the 2002 tour in March hoping to see a rejuvenated Who as the last time that I had seen them, in 2000, it felt like they were just going through the motions. I won a pair of tickets from the local radio station but they were lawn seats and I'm too old for the lawn! However, I managed to get a pair of seated tickets at the last minute. Then John Entwistle died six days beforehand and I figured that would be the end of the tour. But they came on and played like demons. It was the best Who show I've experienced and we were seated by the soundboard so managed to make off with the set list.

1 AUGUST 2002
MADISON SQUARE GARDEN NEW YORK, NEW YORK

SARA M NOVELLI

At the age of five in 1980, I heard my very first Who song, 'You Better You Bet', on the radio. But it wasn't until they announced their 25th anniversary tour in 1989, when I was aged 13, that I slowly became interested. VH-1 showed a handful of videos from The Who's early career and particularly 'Pinball Wizard', 'I'm Free' and 'See Me, Feel Me' from *Tommy*. Having fallen for Roger Daltrey, I was excited to hear the tour was coming to Rich Stadium but my protective family, assuming I just wanted to fangirl over him and not enjoy the material, forbade me to go. I was finally able to see The Who at Madison Square Garden in 2002! Alas, my excitement turned to grief when the news broke that The Ox had left the building in June. I was a tad bitter, having been deprived of opportunities to see them whilst John was alive. I've seen seven shows since, mainly in the Boston area – eight if you count the MusiCares benefit in New York May 2015. And I've seen four solo Daltrey shows between 2009 and 2011. I hope Pete and Roger keep on keeping on!

14 SEPTEMBER 2002
THE JOINT, PARADISE, NEVADA

JEFFREY EVANS

How absolutely chaotic it was when John Entwistle died. CNN in the lobby of the Hard Rock, interviewing everybody they could. My casino host – because I gamble a lot there – filled me in on the real cause of his death: cocaine and hookers. The show was cancelled and rescheduled to my 30th birthday. I had twelve fourth row tickets in this tiny venue. They played that show for Entwistle and were absolutely fucking amazing. Pete and Roger were inspired; they blew the doors off the building. The fill in on bass, Pino Palladino, was superb. I've never heard Roger's voice sound so good that late into a tour. You could feel Entwistle in that space – it was a celebration of The Ox. I would put this show in my top five of all the shows I've seen, the energy was electric. During 'Love Reign O'er Me', Pete just kept looking up while belting the words from his soul.

2 JULY 2005
LIVE 8, HYDE PARK, LONDON, UK

PETER SMITH

20 years after the original *Live Aid* shows, Geldof and Ure announced another series of benefit concerts, this time as part of the *Make Poverty History* campaign. I managed to get tickets for the Gold Circle so we had an excellent view of the entire day's events. The Who weren't on stage for long, but the intro to 'Won't Get Fooled Again' echoing through the air as the sun began to set was magical. The band were incredibly tight and their performance had a particularly potent energy to it.

The Who Tour 2006-2007 ***is the group's first worldwide tour since 1997 and supports*** **Endless Wire*****, their eleventh studio album, released on 30 October 2006.***

25 & 26 SEPTEMBER 2006
VIRGIN FESTIVAL BALTIMORE, PIMLICO RACETRACK, BALTIMORE, MARYLAND

MEGAN TAYLOR, AGE 22

I went for my birthday. I was drunk by 10am, tailgating in the parking lot, and had a hangover by noon. I was then completely sober for the concert. The Who were amazing live and I had the best time, despite the company I was with. I also got to see my favourite band of all time – the Red Hot Chili Peppers. They took the stage after The Who... I think!

5 NOVEMBER 2006
HOLLYWOOD BOWL
HOLLYWOOD, CALIFORNIA

SHAWN PERRY

I cruised down the 101 on an uncharacteristically warm Sunday night, psyching myself out for my tenth Who show. Arriving promptly at 7pm, I sipped on a $9 cup of Heineken and watched a politely received 45-minute set by a Boulder, Colorado-based power trio called Rose Hill Drive. It's a tough assignment opening for legends. At 8pm the lights came down for the headliner. Kicking into the durable opener 'I Can't Explain', Townshend and Daltrey took command of the stage and never let up. A five-screen backdrop plying old film footage of the original four lifted the performance to new heights of merriment and pageantry. 'The Seeker' and 'Substitute' followed, and it was as if The Who, even without John Entwistle and Keith Moon, had set their sights on becoming the hottest band on the planet. Townshend, sporting dark glasses and a fez to hide his follically-challenged scalp, still swung his arm as wildly as a New York Yankee southpaw warming up for the World Series. Daltrey, even youthful behind the granny shades, had toned down his growl and minimised the microphone lassoing.

The old made way for the new as 'Fragments', its opening sequence borrowing heavily from 'Baba O'Riley', spread its heavy breathing vibe over the 18,000 or so crowded onto the benches and bleachers of the Bowl. But that was just a taste of things to come as we slipped back into the time machine for routine work outs of 'Who Are You', 'Behind Blues Eyes' and the ever predictable but always delectable power chords of 'Baba O'Riley'.

Then it was time for a slew of more new stuff that enigmatically fell out of the sky and massaged the eardrums like a vamp of unexpected houseguests. A slice of *Wire & Glass*, the new mini-opera, implored and sniffed out its admirers, supplemented by a heavy dose of visuals that didn't so much explain the tale as exhort its virtues and timelessness. Other tracks from *Endless Wire* were offered up and copiously consumed by the audience, many of whom could probably care less what they played as long they could say they saw The Who before they died. And while I could argue that no one has actually seen The Who — at least The Who I saw — since 1978, for once I took a beat seat and strapped myself in for the long haul.

Coming down the homestretch, Townshend ditched his fez and Daltrey anxiously paced the stage, possibly in anticipation of screaming his climatic 'yah!' during 'Won't Get Fooled Again'. Although I was mildly thwarted by the absence of Thunderfingers' apocalyptic bass runs on 'My Generation', the ensuing jam section and video clips featuring a variety of dancers were enough to make me forget Entwistle's immortal presence, if only for a moment. Repeated video clips of Entwistle and Moon in their heyday reminded everyone that The Who of yesteryear is the one everyone should remember and respect.

The encore was all *Tommy*, something I never tire of. 'Pinball Wizard' made way for 'Amazing Journey' and the extended 'Sparks' instrumental, where Daltrey voraciously slapped two tambourines together while Townshend, Starkey, Palladino, rhythm guitarist (and Pete's younger brother) Simon Townshend and understudy keyboardist Brain Kehew engaged in a spiral of musical warfare. Then the familiar lexis of 'See Me, Feel Me' fluttered in and gripped the captive witnesses transported through the peaks and valleys that Tommy endured for the sake of sanity. As the crowd chanted, 'Listening to you, I get the music, gazing at you, I get the heat…' from 'We're Not Gonna Take It', I started to exit, not realising that The Who, who used to shun encores entirely, would be back with another 'new' song, 'Tea And Theatre'. The mellow notes flew through the air as I walked out of the Bowl and down the hill. I was glad I had changed my mind. Perhaps another album will get me to an eleventh show and then… who knows?

11 JUNE 2007
ARENA DI VERONA, VERONA, ITALY

CHRISTIAN SUCHATZKI

After a 30-year absence – their last concert there was in 1967 – The Who returned to Italy for a single concert in a location usually reserved for classic operas. This was absolutely fitting for a group like The Who, and what a joy for all the Italian Who fans, young and old, who at last were getting a chance to hear and see their favourite group perform live. Despite an average price of 80 euros, the 12,500 tickets were sold out quickly. As a Who fan for 38 years, I had to be there.

It was a sunny day. In the arena, dealers tried in vain to sell rain capes for two euros. When The Who entered the stage, the Italians received them with overwhelming jubilance. From the first notes of 'I Can't Explain', the crowd was cheering on the group they'd waited 30 years to see. 20 minutes in, a thunderstorm broke over the arena in the middle of 'Who Are You'. The rain was so heavy that they stopped the show and the audience took shelter in the underground arches of the Roman arena for an hour until the storm abated enough for The Who to resume their performance.

It was still raining when fans were allowed to re-enter the arena. The rain capes could now be acquired for ten euros, but sold out as fast as the ticket presale had. The Who proceeded with 'Behind Blue Eyes'. But when Roger Daltrey sang the first verse he suddenly interrupted the song and said 'my voice has gone cold' and, frustrated, left the stage. The others stopped playing and, after a short internal discussion, Pete Townshend told the audience that they were unable to go on with the show because Roger had lost his voice.

The concert teetered on the brink of collapse a second time. What should be done? Disappoint the Italian fans who came here full of expectation? Continue with the show somehow? It was almost 11 pm and The Who had played only five songs. After a short discussion with the local promoter, Pete decided to carry on with the concert and told the audience if they were willing to support him and the band, he could sing most of the songs. Roger was called back on stage and the original setlist was slightly shortened and quickly adjusted so that Pete could do most of the vocals, although Roger tried to sing a couple of songs with a raspy and hoarse voice as well as he could. Even Pete's unloved 'Magic Bus' was included in the rearranged setlist. Against all odds and the continuing rain, the Italian fans accompanied The Who's continued performance with loud cheers and singing refrains.

20 minutes after midnight, the show ended with 'Won't Get Fooled Again' where Roger once again gave his best. When he made his famous scream at the end of the song with evidently damaged vocal cords, I thought it might affect his voice forever. At the end, Roger promised to come back – with his voice! The Who returned in 2016 for concerts in Bologna and Milan.

12 JULY 2008
PAULEY PAVILION
LOS ANGELES, CALIFORNIA

ALYCE JOHNSON

I flew out from Florida to attend this *VH1 Rock Honors* event. I suffer from muscular dystrophy so my friends kept telling me to stay in my room and rest. After a few hours, I was finally told to freshen up and meet my friend in the lobby. I kept on asking why and finally a friend said Roger Daltrey wanted to meet me. I thought it was a bad joke but when I went to the lobby, there was the late Rob Lee with a camera. We drove to the stop we needed to go to. Five males were walking towards me while I sat on the VIP cart. One was Roger and I turned red and could not believe that he was heading my way, shouting out 'where is Alyce? I am looking for Alyce.' I slowly raised my hand.

Roger came right in front in front of me and told me that he could tell just by looking at my eyes that I was lovable, thoughtful, caring and sensitive, and a very sweet and lovely young lady. We talked for a few hours and then I was invited to his sound check. The next night, two guards came up to me and told me that Roger wanted me to go up to the stage and hold on for better balance. Roger came out with Pete and Roger came up to me and told me that I looked beautiful. I truly thought that I was dreaming. They went into 'Baba O'Riley' and after Roger went wild on his harmonica, he gave it to me. When I arrived home, I told my friends that I was treated like a queen by Roger so for ten years now I have been called 'Queen Daltrey'. I have seen him lots since then, with smiles and hugs every time. My flat is called The Who Museum. I have Roger's signed harmonica signed, tambourine and microphone as well as his champagne, a decorated Shure 50th Anniversary Microphone and hundreds of DVDs and CDs and numerous signed VIP concert posters.

14 DECEMBER 2008
O2 INDIGO, LONDON, UK

PETER SMITH

The Who were playing three Christmas shows at this 2,000 capacity venue; the first two for fan club members only, and the third show for the public. I joined the fan club specially to get tickets for the show. Security for getting into the show on the night was quite tight. I had to take along my passport, credit card and booking reference to gain entry and had to wait an hour before getting into the gig. The Indigo wasn't too full so I took a place in the crowd near the front, at the right of the stage where Townshend usually stands. The Who took to the stage without any introduction and launched straight into 'I Can't Explain'. The set was a mixture of old classics and a couple of surprises such as 'Tattoo', which I hadn't seen them play for many years. They were on great form, with lots of windmill arm twirling from Pete and lots of mic swinging from Roger. Roger's voice was very strong and sounding much better than the last couple of times I had seen them. Pete was playing with even more intensity than usual, really bashing at his guitar. He was in a cheeky mood and having lots of chat with the crowd with quite a bit of swearing. A guy in front of me was shouting for 'A Quick One' all night; Pete said he could play that on his own! Someone shouted for 'Bellboy'; Pete replied, 'Keith is fucking dead; we can't play that. Do you want us to bring him back? Wish we could.' They finished with 'Won't Get Fooled Again' and 'My Generation'. The encores were 'Pinball Wizard' and a *Tommy* selection, finishing with 'Tea and Theatre' from the recent album. It was great to see them again.

24 MARCH 2009
ENTERTAINMENT CENTRE BRISBANE, AUSTRALIA

CHRIS HALES

I saw The Who at the Pier Pavilion and Town Hall in Worthing during the 1960s, which cemented my pure appreciation for their energy, their passion for alcohol, music and beating up their instruments – not necessarily in that order! My memories are of spectacular energy from both the band and the fans. Pete smashing his guitar was simply expected and Moonie exploded out of his drums. John just seemed to disappear and Roger was brilliant at banging out the lyrics. When seeing them last in Brisbane, it was like seeing something that had evolved into perfection. Modern technology and sound reproduction has helped groups like The Who become the consummate artists and musicians their passion was pointing them towards.

I had the privilege of being at their last concert in Brisbane where the boys showed that they had reached the top of the mountain. You don't fall to the top of a mountain.

30 MARCH 2010
ROYAL ALBERT HALL, LONDON, UK

PETER SMITH

I'd seen The Who perform *Quadrophenia* on the '73 tour and in Hyde Park in the '90s but had never been a massive fan of the album. And I'd seen The Who a few times in the run up to this gig and Roger had had some problems with his voice. So I was having doubts about this gig. But this was the best Who show I had seen for many, many years. The band played *Quadrophenia* straight through with no other songs and no encore. And it was everything *Quadrophenia* should be: interesting, challenging, sad, rocking and a celebration for all of us of a great band and a great rock opera.

The standard Who line-up (Roger, Pete, Rabbit on keyboards, Zak on drums, Pino on bass, Simon on second guitar) was augmented by a string section, brass section and guests. The sound was big and powerful and did justice to the album tracks. A screen above the stage showed us the story of Jimmy with clips from the film and from the past, Brighton, Mods and Rockers, etc. Eddie Vedder took the part of the Godfather and Tom from Kasabian gave a great performance as the Ace Face (great suit and cute Bellboy uniform!). Roger's voice was pretty strong mostly, but he did seem to be suffering towards the end. Pete played great, and towards the end was really bashing away at his guitar. There was also some excellent acoustic guitar and vocals from Pete on the quieter songs. I was on the floor towards the left of the stage, six rows back. Everyone around me was up on their feet from the start and stayed like that throughout. There were lots of fists in the air and everyone seemed to know every word of every song. There were obviously Who fans from all over the world there. It was an awesome, faultless performance.

11 MARCH 2011
ROYAL ALBERT HALL, LONDON, UK

AJAY MANKOTIA

Pete came up with the concept of *Tommy* after being introduced to the work of Meher Baba, and attempted to translate Baba's teachings into music. *Tommy* was acclaimed upon its release by critics, who hailed it as The Who's breakthrough album. It is an important and influential album in the history of rock music. It pioneered the rock opera format. It was ambitious, inventive, profound. It was banned for its subject matter in some parts of the world. This effort launched the band's career as superstars. The band's instrumental interplay was electrifying and swiftly captured the public's imagination. It broadened rock's scope with an ambitious high concept that brought Sixties pop to adulthood and presaged Seventies progressive rock. In 1972, the band staged a version backed by the London Symphony Orchestra and a film version was released in 1975 featuring Elton John, Tina Turner, Oliver Reed and Jack Nicholson. In 1993, a Broadway stage version opened and ran for two years. The album cover – a stunning gamechanger – was a meshwork of clouds in a void meant to represent 'a kind of breaking out of a certain restricted plane of freedom'. The poetic mysticism of the album cover, its simplicity and bleakness, mirrored the music precisely. It added mystery and coherence.

I had the good fortune of being associated with Barry John's Theatre Action Group's production of *Tommy* in 1978 at Ashoka Hotel, New Delhi. I was also extremely fortunate to see the performance of *Tommy* at Royal Albert Hall, London in 2011. Roger Daltrey was at his classic best – reaching the high scales with consummate melodic ease. The surprise package was Pete Townshend, who was not billed to perform. The crowd leapt to its feet in sheer ecstasy when he walked on to do 'Acid Queen'. The Hall, packed to the rafters, went nuts!

The 2014* The Who Hits 50! *tour marks the 50th anniversary of the band.

2 DECEMBER 2014
FIRST DIRECT ARENA, LEEDS, UK

JASON BARNARD

I went with my wife, who was in her late 30s. She was quite tired by the end; Pete and Roger's show went on so long and they were pushing 70!

30 JUNE 2015
ZENITH, PARIS, FRANCE

OLIVER COIFFARD

My wife and I, along with our three children, attended the Paris concert on the 50th anniversary tour. And to my great surprise, just before The Who arrived on stage, I had the immense pleasure of seeing one of the photos I'd taken back in 1974, was displayed on the stage as part of the retrospective summarising their career in France.

5 JULY 2015
ROYAL ALBERT HALL, LONDON, UK

BARRY JUDD

I was born and bred in Acton. By 1964 we were all aware of The Who, even me as a twelve-year-old, because they were local lads. As the singles came out in early '65, we all bought them and then the first LP. They'd do local gigs like the White Hart in Acton, the Goldhawk, the Railway Tavern and the Oldfield Tavern, but Mum wouldn't let me go because I was too young. My dear late wife's claim to fame is that she was walking through Acton High Street in late '64 and bumped into The Who as they were taking their gear into the White Hart for a gig. She got chatting and managed to steal a kiss off Roger – she was only twelve at the time!

I went to Acton County Grammar School, as did Roger, John and Pete, although they'd left by the time I got there. The headmaster that Roger namechecked in his autobiography, *Thanks a Lot, Mr Kibblewhite*, said to him 'you'll make nothing of your life'. My claim to fame is that Kibblewhite said exactly the same to me.

It was 1968 and I was 16 when Mum finally gave me permission to go and see them at the Lyceum. I can't remember the setlist, just that for the first and only time I witnessed the so-called auto destruction at the end of the gig, where they smashed up all the stuff. It caused massive angst amongst the crowd. People around me just went absolutely frantic. Perhaps that's why they did it. I saw them not long after at an all-night gig at the Roundhouse and then at the Albert Hall, but then I started courting Jackie and my concert days more or less came to an end.

The next time I saw them was in '75, at the Hammersmith Odeon. Me and my friend Bill were promised tickets by another friend's girlfriend but she didn't show. One of the side doors suddenly opened and one of the road crew put his head out and said, 'Look, I've got two tickets here from Keith Moon. Does anybody want 'em?' Well, me and Bill just jumped at them. That was the tour when they first introduced the pencil laser beams, when they flashed the laser beams all over the audience.

I don't think any band has ever matched *Tommy*, *Live at Leeds*, *Who's Next* and *Quadrophenia*, all totally different and yet all completely brilliant. Although The Who were good after that, the subsequent albums didn't seem to have that same sort of power. And, of course, Moon had died. I remember hearing the news and I was as devastated as when I heard that Hendrix had died. Keith Moon was such a powerhouse. Some people call him sloppy. I just think he was brilliant. Townshend said, 'When Kenney Jones came in, at least we had somebody who kept time.' But the only person who was keeping time in that band was John Entwistle. While Moon and Townshend were completely thrashing away and creating a really good sound, you had that thunderous bass going in the background, which kept everything in line.

By the early '80s, they had effectively broken up apart from the *Live Aid* concert in '85 and a couple more. I didn't get to see them until '89 at Wembley Arena, and that was probably the weakest concert I've ever been to by The Who. Townshend had more-or-less given up the lead guitar. He was playing acoustic a lot and playing rhythm and they'd employed another guitarist. You had the horn section plus backing vocalists so there were about 16 people on stage. I christened it 'The Elevator Music Who Concert'. It simply did not have that power. I was hearing a completely different Who.

As the '90s progressed, my son became really interested in The Who and a lot of that's to do with *Quadrophenia*. He's 46 years old now and that generation really picked up on the film, and then the album and, ultimately, The Who. The *Quadrophenia* story and the themes it addresses cut across all generations. It still works. Even my grandson has been to see The Who with me.

The production on the *Quadrophenia* album is full of Townshend with synthesisers and things like that, it's a really full sound. In my opinion, it's one of the best pieces of music ever put together. It really lends itself to an orchestra.

Darren and I have been to every Who concert we could possibly attend in London, right the way through until the O2 in July 2023.

We've attended most of the Teenage Cancer Trust concerts they've played at the Albert Hall. And one of my favourite concerts was the *Quadrophenia and More* tour at the O2 in 2015. When they got to '5:15', the other musicians left Zak Starkey on the stage on his own, playing drums whilst on the big screen behind him, they had John Entwistle playing his famous '5:15' bass solo. That produced a tear, I must admit. And when 'Bell Boy' came along, Daltrey symbolically reached back with his microphone as if he was handing it to Keith, who picked it up on the back screen and went and sang his part of 'Bell Boy'. By this point, I was blubbering.

I've been to see them so many times over the last 20 years. You can't compare The Who from the '60s and '70s to The Who of the 21st century. It just can't be done. But it stands the test of time, and they've accepted their age. They are still the best band around.

8 OCTOBER 2015
MORTLAKE CREMATORIUM, LONDON, UK

JOHN CHARLES MORTON

I met Pete Townshend at Jim Diamond's funeral. Jim had joined my band Happy Ever After in 1966 and he played with us for three years and then went to London and had success with PhD in the Seventies, and on his own. Pete was a friend of Jim's. All the rockers live around the same area and Jim would meet Pete walking along the Thames, or in the local café for lunch. He was a big fan of The Who. I was standing at the buffet after the funeral and Pete was looking at the sausage rolls and the chicken drumsticks, just the two of us. I thought his face looked familiar and I said to him 'are you Tony Hymas?'. Tony was Jim's keyboard player. He said, 'No mate, I'm Pete.' 'Oh sorry. So you are. I'm very sorry.' It was Pete Townshend. How embarrassed was I?

15 DECEMBER 2015
MOTORPOINT ARENA, CARDIFF, UK

PHILIP GOODRIDGE

Zak Starkey was on drums. Roger Daltrey had laryngitis and couldn't sing. They got by on a wing and a prayer. They were still brilliant.

13 FEBRUARY 2016
SSE ARENA, WEMBLEY, LONDON, UK

PETER SMITH

The Who Hits 50! tour was a celebration of the amazing legacy of a legendary band who have given us so much over the years. This was my 21st Who live experience, and the third time I saw them on this particular tour. Roger had been suffering from viral meningitis, which resulted in the postponement of the last leg of their American tour, and this gig was slotted in by way of a warm-up before the band returned to the USA to play the rearranged dates.

It turned out to be another classic Who performance. A sold-out crowd of locals and die-hard Who fans from across Europe gave the band the rousing London welcome they deserved. The evening started with a slide show which took us through the history of the band, and featured many great images of the late Keith Moon and John Entwistle. Indeed, the whole tour served as a celebration of the band's legacy and contribution, as well as a run through of some of The Who's greatest songs. The band walked on stage and launched straight into 'Who Are You' and away we went on another amazing journey through so many classic tunes.

The giant screen behind the stage displayed powerful full-face images of Roger, Pete, Keith and John, along with clips of The Who in the '60s and the '70s and clips from *Quadrophenia*. The sound was crisp; I was sitting halfway back on the terrace to the left of the stage and every note was very clear. When they got to 'Eminence Front', I took the opportunity to have a walk around the arena, finding a spot downstairs on the floor towards the back. I spent the rest of the evening there, enjoying the band and observing the crowd singing along, dancing and generally going wild. The songs from *Tommy* culminated in a powerful crowd singalong to 'Listening to You', which always gets me. I knew we were on the home stretch.

Despite his recent illness, Roger looked and sounded well, although he told us he wasn't 100 per cent and that his 'legs weren't fully there'. It didn't show, and his voice held out fine. As usual, Pete was full of power and angst, twirling and twirling his arm, and squeezing great solos out of his Fender Stratocaster. It was all over too fast and, before too long, the familiar minimalist synthesiser intro signalled 'Baba O'Riley' which then led into the closing song, 'Won't Get Fooled Again', as raw and relevant as ever. Pete said at the end, 'Hope to see you again.' Yes indeed, hope so.

LINDA SWEEDEN

42 years and 41 Who gigs after seeing The Who at Charlton I'm still smitten. My ultimate dream came true at Wembley in 2016 when I finally met Roger and Pete. They didn't want to do the normal 'meet and greet' reserved for those few that can afford it or those part of corporate events. They were looking to meet a real fan. I was totally unaware that my partner was trying everything he could think of to make my wish come true. He contacted anyone that had any connection to The Who via social media, etc. The sponsors of Wembley SSE

Energy picked up on some of his tweets and secretly arranged for me to be a special guest at the Wembley gig. What a surprise! We were greeted by broadcast cameras and a clamour of people interviewing me. We had complimentary food and bubbly and went to the sound check before finally ushered into a small room where Roger and Pete appeared without fanfare. And there I was in the same room as my lifetime heroes!

And what does a woman like me say to her idol after all these years? I said to Roger 'can I have a nose kiss?'. He laughed and said 'why not?' and put his arms around me, gave me a big hug and we rubbed noses! I still ask myself – where did that come from? They were both so warm and friendly. I had my photo taken with them and they signed autographs and chatted about the sound check and stuff. My bucket list is complete and I can die a happy woman.

27 FEBRUARY 2016
JOE LOUIS ARENA, DETROIT, MICHIGAN

BETH BATTJES

I was a late bloomer. I saw *Tommy* on cable in 2012 and have been hooked ever since. I saw them for the first time ever in Detroit. It was special because it was their first stop on the re-scheduled American tour. Roger was sounding wonderful. I took lots of pictures. It was my belated Christmas present from my best friend. I loved every minute of being at a Who concert. We were on the main floor of the arena but several rows back. Before 'My Generation', Pete told a story about the song and how he would riff away until eventually Keith would say 'Pete, for fuck's sake! Stop!'

12 OCTOBER 2016
PALACIO DE LOS DEPORTES MEXICO CITY, MEXICO

BERNARDO RAMÍREZ, AGE 20

Mexicans had to wait a very long time to see The Who. I was part of a large crowd waiting for ten hours in the sun and rain for the doors to open so that I could get a good spot. I got to be in the centre and at the front of the stage. Before the concert began, people went crazy with the photos of the old members of the band and the audience shouted 'Who, Who, Who'.

The lights were turned off and the first chords of 'I Can't Explain' started. It was the end of a very long wait. The crowd responded with a shuddering roar to 'Who Are You'. On 'My Generation', everyone jumped around frantically before singing along to 'Behind Blue Eyes'. During 'Join Together', Pete was dying of laughter listening to people singing. When the song ended, he told the audience that the lyrics of the song were not 'join together *in* the band'.

When they played 'You Better You Bet' the crowd was chanting 'olé, olé, olé – The Who!' Pete's face was full of emotion, not believing what he was seeing.

GUILLERMO VIESCA, AGE 14

The first song I ever heard by The Who was 'Pinball Wizard' and I fell in love with it. I arrived home from school one day and my dad showed me the advertisement; The Who were to Mexico City for the first time ever. The next day I bought tickets, super close to the stage. The wait to see them was the longest four months of my life. I remember being super excited on the day. Suddenly, the lights went out and the first chords to 'I Can't Explain' started. It kept getting better and better after that.

30 MARCH 2017
ROYAL ALBERT HALL, LONDON, UK

JOHN SCHOLLAR

I used to go and watch The Detours because we used to play on the same circuit. There was a pub just up the road from where I used to work in Alperton called the Fox and Goose, and all the bands used to play in there. That's where I first saw The Detours. Commercial Entertainment, who used to manage us, was based at the Oldfield in Greenford. When we weren't playing, if they were on somewhere, we'd go and see them. Loads of bands worked out of there. Even if you weren't playing, you'd go along and have a night out watching the band somewhere, so we all knew The Detours before Keith joined them. And I saw them at the Railway Hotel a few times as well. And when The Detours needed a drummer, because they had a record deal coming up, they grabbed Keith.

He jumped at the chance. Keith's dad got on to Tony, my bass player, and he said, 'What do you think about him joining this lot? I don't like the look of them. I can't see them doing anything.' Of course, after a few months they'd brought out their first record and there was no looking back.

If you went out with him, you never knew if you were going to get home the same day. We were good mates. If he was still alive today, I'd be seeing a lot of him.

The Who were on at the Albert Hall in early 2017 doing *Tommy*, and a friend of my daughter's, who is a really big Who fan, had just had his 50th birthday. He was planning to go to the Albert Hall twice and then Birmingham and I said, 'I'll see if I can fix something up for you.' I rang Roger's secretary and said, 'A mate of mine's had a big birthday and I just want to treat him. Can you get me a VIP pass?' and she said 'yeah'. When I rang up the office there was no 'who are you?'. It was 'hello, John'. That's nice. Well, they did nick our drummer, didn't they?

3 APRIL 2017
ECHO ARENA, LIVERPOOL, UK

LINDA ROGERS

Pete Townshend seemed incredulous that anyone wanted to hear all the old stuff. He said, 'It was all a verrry long time ago!'

7 MAY 2019
VAN ANDEL ARENA GRAND RAPIDS, MICHIGAN

RICHARD E KELLEY

Michigan must hold a special place in Pete Townsend's heart as The Who have appeared there on every tour since 2000. Daltrey had toured solo the year before with a modest, travelling string and horn section, augmented by local players to a create a full symphony orchestra. This tour borrowed the concept and added 40 professional musicians to better present the music of *Tommy* and *Quadrophenia*. The Who rehearsed with their ancillary players in Florida while the local orchestra were learning their parts from charts in the days prior to the opener in Grand Rapids. The two ensembles apparently didn't play together until the day of the show itself.

Fans were greeted with the 'Overture' from *Tommy* followed by 'It's A Boy' and '1921'. Hardly the sonic wallop of 'I Can't Explain' into 'The Seeker' and 'Who Are You' that typified a Who performance. The orchestral portions of *Tommy* were awesome when you could hear them, but the problem was that the volumes of band and orchestra were apparently kept at a minimum so neither drowned the other out. Consequently, both lacked the power and volume to fill the arena. We were witnessing a concert by The Who which was not nearly loud enough! The Who seemingly wasn't playing with the orchestra but both were accompanying the other in a sort of tentative manner. This worked in the heavily orchestrated *Tommy* portion of the show but things got dodgier when the rock was rolled out. By the opening lines of 'Who Are You', it was obvious the band was having difficulty hearing themselves.

A wonderful live debut came next in the form of 'Imagine A Man' from *By Numbers*, with Roger singing the gorgeous ballad while over-privileged drunks bellowed from the front rows. 'Join Together' followed and seemed to fall apart more with every passing second. Daltrey couldn't find the notes while Pete apparently couldn't hear much of anything and proceeded to shoot his singer increasingly dirty looks. When the song ended, Roger remarked to the audience singing raucously along, 'You sound better than we do!' Pete went into a long, technical tirade, explaining the shortcomings of hearing too much in his earpiece. His anger increased and culminated with a very loud, 'I just think this was a SHIT IDEA, Roger!' to his longtime partner. By this point, Daltrey had strapped on an acoustic guitar in anticipation of the next number. Like a schoolboy being chastised by an angry headmaster, he tried to hide behind it, cross-armed and nearly cowering. The orchestra left the stage and Pete took credit for shooing them away.

A lovely 'The Kids Are Alright' followed with just the core band. 'Behind Blue Eyes' came next, with the touring string session returning but the local orchestra still sequestered in the wings. 'Tea and Theatre' returned to the set list for the first time in some years, Pete and Roger duetting beautifully on it.

More relaxed after the small ensemble and duet numbers, Pete asked the crowd, 'Shall we have them back?' as the local orchestra began filing into their seats. Pete began strumming the opening chord sequence for 'I'm The One'. He stopped about 20 seconds in, explaining he was afraid he 'was going to fuck something up'. He played the sequence again and the band and orchestra fell in behind, in a bit of a jumble at first and then they found their footing nicely. At this point, the real magic of the evening revealed itself.

The orchestra had replicated the parts on *Tommy* with every bell and pennywhistle intact. With the five song *Quadrophenia* segment, however, the orchestral parts seemed to have been rewritten with the 40-piece ensemble swooping and soaring and surrounding the band with breathtaking notes and passages, many of them completely unlike the album or previous live presentations of *Quadrophenia*. Though Pete said he couldn't remember her last name during the band introductions, touring violinist Katie Jacoby played the speeding violin crescendo on 'Baba O'Riley'. Her triumphant salute to the rafters with her bow as the music stopped and the lights went down may have been the single greatest visual highlight of the evening.

18 MAY 2022
TD GARDEN, BOSTON, MASSACHUSETTS

SARA NOVELLI

In March 2016 I saw a great show at Boston Garden, complete with sound check, a VIP reception, you name it. At the sound check, the time on the clock was '5:15', which in Whoville they say is happy hour. Everyone was well 'out of their brain on the train'. At the Mohegan Sun Arena in July 2017, the atmosphere was amazing and Roger acknowledged me from the stage, smiling and throwing a kiss. June 2018 saw the best night of the year. Roger and the Boston Symphony Orchestra joined forces to perform *Tommy* at Tanglewood Music Shed in Lenox, Massachusetts. The show was beyond awesome. Roger looked beautiful, as always, and I was surrounded by many friends right in the very front row. Just before the encore, security gave me permission to present a bouquet to Roger. He thanked me with a smooch. In September 2019 I was fortunate to experience one of the best shows in Boston, a show with an orchestra at Fenway Park, home of the Boston Red Sox. As I entered the sound check, I shouted 'happy birthday' to Zak, whose birthday it was that night. The VIP reception was awesome, with Who music blaring and friends schmoozing. The show was nothing short of magical. Fast forward to May 2022 and another phenomenal show at Boston Garden, my first in two and a half years. At the end, we presented Pete with a birthday card as the next day was his 77th birthday. 'Where are my proper presents?' he asked, before Roger led a chorus of 'Happy Birthday'.

Thanks, Pete and Roger, for carrying on even after John and Keith walked through the Mirror Door.

The summer of 2023 sees The Who on their* The Who Hits Back! *tour.

17 JULY 2023
RIVERSIDE CRICKET GROUND, DURHAM, UK

RICHARD DIXON

I first saw the band at the Isle of Wight in 1970 and have lost count how many times I have seen them since. Expecting their *The Who Hits Back!* tour to be the last, I splashed out for 'platinum' tickets for my wife Sue and I. These cost £221 each and turned out to be on the side of the seated area that Ticketmaster said would be reallocated. I had expected to be near the front for that price, but not to worry – the screen was excellent! The Heart of England Orchestra made a great difference to the *Tommy* and *Quadrophenia* tracks – possibly what Pete imagined when he wrote them as operas. Roger's voice is so much better following his Boston operation, and with Zak and the rest of the band on good form it was a memorable night. The usual finale with 'Baba O'Riley' (which must be the most complete rock number) was actually improved by the enthusiastic and charismatic Katie Jacoby on violin. I intend to have 'Baba O'Riley' played as I am carried out of the church in my coffin and I will have to get a recording with her playing!

PETE WRIGHT

In the early days, you'd see anyone else – Gerry and the Pacemakers, Herman's Hermits, The Hollies, The Searchers – they're all standing there in nice suits with amplifiers as big as a small suitcase. And The Who are standing there practically blocking out the sun with their gear. It was so different. From 1969 to 1972 – the tassels, the white boiler suit, the Hiwatt amps – that was obviously the peak. With *Tommy*, and in particular *Quadrophenia*, they were ahead of their audience. *Quadrophenia*'s got a bigger following now than it had in the first place. It was just above the audience at that time.

There's only the Stones and The Who left as I see it. I've taken my wife to see The Who six times and she won't go with me now. She says it's the same old crap every time. I've got a friend who's been 18 times, although two or three times he's gone without me. He says he won't go again because it's the same old thing. But I'd go seven days a week.

CENTRAL PIER
MORECAMBE
IN THE MARINE BALLROOM
Friday, January 6th—
"Happy Jack"
THE WHO
THE DOODLEBUGS HAROLD GRAHAM
TICKETS 10/-
Saturday, January 7th— 7.30 to 11.45
THE HEDGEHOPPERS ANONYMOUS
HAROLD GRAHAM ALAN TAYLOR
with SHARON WINTE
TICKETS 4/6, AFTER 10 p
IN THE LOUNGE
TUESDAY is OLD TYME (Modern Sequ
WEDNESDAY is "DANCE TOGETHER"
HAROLD GRAHAM AND HIS MUSIC
MOTHERS
High St Erdington B'ham.
THE MIDLANDS HOME OF GOOD SOUNDS
Sunday, March 2nd
CHICKEN SHACK
WITH JOHN PEEL
Friday, February 28th
LIVERPOOL SCENE
Saturday, March 1st
THE WHO
Wednesday March 5th
THIRD EAR BAND
AND
EDGAR BROUGHTON
In association with Blackhill Enterprises
RUSS GIBB presents in Detroit
DIRECT FROM ENGLAND
THE WHO
PETER TOWNSEND will perform his new rock opera, "TOMMY," for the first time in the United States!
ALSO
JOE COCKER and his GREASE BAND
FRI.–SAT.–SUN.—MAY 9–10–11
GRANDE BALLROOM
TONIGHT
the who
&
Led Zeppelin
8:00pm may 25
MERRIWEATHER POST PAVILION
Good Seats Still Available Box Office open 6:30
MOTHERS
High St Erdington B'ham.
Phone: 021-373 5514
THE HOME OF GOOD SOUNDS
DEEP PURPLE
+CARA
Friday, July 18th
BLOSSOM TOES
Saturday, July 19th
THE WHO
Wednesday, July 23rd
BLACKHILL ENT
THE DEVIA
The WHO
PLUS
The JAMES GANG
SYRIA MOSQUE
TONIGHT
SUNDAY, OCT. 26th
8:00 P.M.
TICKETS $4-$5-$6
GOOD SEATS STILL AVAILABLE AT BOX OFFICE
TRIANGLE PRODUCTIONS
Presents
The WHO
Featuring their Rock Opera
"TOMMY"
TOMORROW NIGHT 8:30
KIEL OPERA HOUSE
$5.50, $4.50, $3.50
Tickets On Sale at Kiel Box Office
CANADIAN EXCLUSIVE
ONE SHOW ONLY!
CAPITOL THEATRE
WED., 15th OCT. 8.00 P.M.
Tickets available at Both Treble Clef Stores Sparks St. and Rideau St.
$2.50 - 3.50 - 4.50
Performance includes POP OPERA "TOMMY"
THE WHO
PLUS THE FABULOUS
M. R. Q.
TICKETS FREE
WHITE FRONT
Presents...
FREE!
Festival of Music
THE ASSOCIATION
THE ANIMALS
the EVERLY BROS.
THE SUNSHINE COMPANY
FREE!
THE WHO
COW PALACE
SAM RIDDLE
BOROUGH ROAD COLLEGE
Isleworth, Middlesex
NEW YEAR'S BALL
with
THE WHO
AYNSLEY DUNBAR RETALIATION
TERRY LIGHTFOOT'S JAZZ BAND
THE PYRAMIDS
ALMOND MARZIPAN
ABBOTTFIELD DANCE ORCHESTRA
SATURDAY, 25th JANUARY
Double ticket: £2, single £1
N.U.S. Cards 8 p.m.-Late
ON STAGE
CITY HALL HULL
ONE NIGHT ONLY
6.45 & 8.45 p.m.
FRIDAY FEBRUARY 17th 1967
THE WHO
HAPPY JACK, I'M A BOY, LIES, ETC.
THE FABULOUS PINKERTON'S COLOURS
THE MAGIC ROCKING HORSE, ETC.
CRISPIAN ST. PETERS
YOUR EVER CHANGING MIND, ETC.
LOLLIPOP GANG
ROOT & JENNY JACKSON AND THE HIGH TIMERS
T.V. CO-CO DANCERS
THE TROPICAL BOOT COMPANY
Prices: 12/6 · 10/6 · 8/6 · 7/6 · 5/6
TOWN HALL - BIRMINGHAM
Monday, 6th November at 6.30 & 8.45 p.m.
THE WHO
TRAFFIC
THE HERD
Marmalade
RAY CAMERON
THE TREMELOES
TICKETS 12/6 10/6 8/6 7/6 5/-
The PAVILION Bath
BANNISTER PROMOTIONS Present
MON. 25th NOV.
the MUDDY WATERS BLUES BAND
FEATURING OTIS SPAN
ADM. 6/-
MON. 2nd DEC.
THE BAND WAGON
TEARING DOWN THE WALLS OF HEARTBREAK
ADM. 6/-
MON. 9th DEC.
the WHO
ADM. 6/6
MON. 16th DEC.
PLEASE NOTE JEFF BECK WILL NOT NOW APPEAR, INSTEAD WE PRESENT
LED ZEPPELIN
(FORMERLY THE NEW YARDBIRDS)
ADM. 5/6
RUSS GIBB Presents
at
The Grande-Riveria
FRIDAY, OCTOBER 10
SRC
AMBOY DUKES
ALICE COOPER
Admission $3.00
SATURDAY, OCTOBER 11
THE WHO
ALICE COOPER
THE SKY
Admission $4.00
SUNDAY, OCTOBER 12
THE WHO
ALL THE LONELY PEOPLE
AMBOY DUKES
Admission $4.00
ALSO: World's First Sonavision Laser Beam Light Show
TICKETS AVAILABLE AT BOX OFFICE
Grande River at Joy in Detroit
Auchinleck Community Association
Proudly Present for
DANCING
In COMMUNITY CENTRE, AUCHINLECK,
Saturday, 26th April,
BIG BEAT SHOW Featuring International T.V. and Recording Stars
THE WHO
Supported by
THE MERRY MACS & PURE GREED
8.45 p.m. — 12.45 a.m.
Be Early and Don't be Disappointed.
USUAL BUSES.
THE WHO
THE AMEN CORNER
THIS SATURDAY, 23rd AUGUST
at the MARQUEE, BRENTWOOD ROAD, GRAYS, ESSEX
7 Support Groups — AARDVARK • ANDROMEDA CLASSICS • BUM • EVOLUTION • FREEDOM • IPSISSIMUS
Tickets £1 at door • Licensed Bars • 5.30 till 12
Enquiries: Grays Thurrock (0375) 2827
WELW RADIO 1330 PRESENTS
IN PERSON . . .
THE WHO
MUSIC HALL • TONITE • 8:30 P.M.
Tickets at BURROWS • 6.50 • 5.50 • 4.50
AND CONVENTION CENTER
BELAIR PRODUCTIONS
CITY HALL, NEWCASTLE
TONIGHT at 7.30
Following their Gigantic Success at the London Coliseum
THE WHO
to include 'Tommy'
A TWO HOUR NON-STOP CONCERT
21/-, 17/6, 15/-, 12/6, 10/6
City Hall Box Office open till 5.30 and later at 6.45.